The In

—

Volumes III and IV

being

Volume III: Jewish Influence in American Life

and

Volume IV: Aspects of Jewish Power in the United States

By Henry Ford, founder of the Ford Motor Company, and the Editors of *The Dearborn Independent*.

Ostara Publications

The International Jew: Volumes III and IV
being
Volume III: Jewish Influence in American Life
and
Volume IV: Aspects of Jewish Power in the United States

By Henry Ford, founder of the Ford Motor Company, and the Editors of *The Dearborn Independent.*

First published by *The Dearborn Independent*
As
Volume 3: Jewish Influence in American Life (1921)
Volume 4: Aspects of Jewish Power in the United States (1922)

This edition (2016) by Ostara Publications
ostarapublications.com

ISBN 978-1-68418-613-6

CONTENTS

Volume 3: Jewish Influence in American Life

Preface....1
43. The Jews and the "Religious Persecution" Cry....3
44. Are the Jews Victims or Persecutors?....16
45: Jewish Gamblers Corrupt American Baseball....26
46: Jewish Degradation of American Baseball....38
47: Jewish Jazz Becomes Our National Music....49
48: How the Jewish Song Trust Makes You Sing....58
49: Jewish Hot-Beds of Bolshevism in the U.S....68
50: Jew Trades Link with World Revolutionaries....79
51: Will Jewish Zionism Bring Armageddon?....89
52: How the Jews Use Power—By an Eyewitness....100
53: How Jews Ruled and Ruined Tammany Hall....110
54: Jew Wires Direct Tammany's Gentile Puppets....120
55: B'nai B'rith Leader Discusses the Jews....130
56: Dr. Levy, a Jew, Admits His People's Error....140
57: Jewish Idea in American Monetary Affairs....150
58: Jewish Idea Molded Federal Reserve Plan....161
59: Jewish Idea of Central Bank for America....171
60: How Jewish International Finance Functions....181
61: Jewish Power and America's Money Famine....191

Volume 4: Aspects of Jewish Power in the United States

Preface....202
62: How Jews Gained American Liquor Control....203
63: Gigantic Jewish Liquor Trust and its Career....213
64: The Jewish Element in Bootlegging Evil....223
65: Angles of Jewish Influence in American Life....231
66: The Jews' Complaint against "Americanism"....241
67: The Jewish Associates of Benedict Arnold....251
68: Benedict Arnold and Jewish Aid in Shady Deal....262
69: Arnold and His Jewish Aides at West Point....273
70: The Gentle Art of Changing Jewish Names....284

Contents (Continued)

71: Jewish "Kol Nidre" and "Eli, Eli" Explained.....293
72: Jews as New York Magistrates See Them.....302
73: Jews are Silent, the National Voice is Heard.....310
74: What Jews Attempted Where They Had Power.....320
75: The Jewish Question in Current Testimony.....329
76: America's Jewish Enigma—Louis Marshall.....339
77: The Economic Plans of International Jews.....349
78: A Jew Sees His People as Others See Them.....360
79: Candid Address to Jews on the Jewish Problem.....373
80: An Address to "Gentiles" on the Jewish Problem.....382

Volume 3: Jewish Influence in American Life

Preface

The present volume, third in the series, is compiled for the same purpose as its predecessors—to enable new readers of *The Dearborn Independent* to commence their reading with the earlier articles in the series of studies in the Jewish Question.

It was inevitable that the publication first to open the discussion of this Question should be compelled to meet the degrading charge of "anti-Semitism" and kindred falsehoods; but it was also inevitable that if the work of such a publication should prove to be valid, the way would be cleared for discussion by other publications which had not and need not bring upon themselves the charge of racial hatred.

This is precisely what has occurred. An undreamed-of publicity for the essentials of the Jewish Question has been achieved in this country. It is noteworthy that whether the publicity be in agreement with or against *The Dearborn Independent* the essential facts are the same, and these facts were first set forth in this paper.

That, indeed, constitutes the strength of the articles. The facts are provable; they are not disprovable. The reader can confirm the facts from his own observation. With regard to the matters discussed in these volumes, there are too many observers of the Jew to permit misstatements to pass. This also constitutes the dilemma of the self-appointed defenders of the Jews: they may abuse *The Dearborn Independent*, but they cannot disprove the facts. They do not make even an impressive denial of them. The whole situation would be much clarified if Jewish spokesmen would use frankness, instead of a fusillade of cheap and irrelevant abuse.

The year has witnessed much notable discussion of the Jewish Question in magazines of quality. A few have descended to white-washing, fewer still to sheer pro-Jewish propaganda; but such articles as those in the September *Century*; those in the *Atlantic* for February, May and July; The *Nineteenth Century and After* for April; the true and admirable accounts by Lieut. Commander Hugo W. Koehler, of the U. S. Navy, in the World's Work for July, August, September and October—these testify to the reality of the matter. The more serious religious press, as represented by publications like the *Christian Standard,* the *Christian Century,* The *Moody Monthly* which is published by The Moody Bible Institute, Chicago, have also added materially to the literature of the question. In editorial vision and liberty of discussion, the religious press has shown itself to be freer of control than has the secular press.

This volume contains information dealing with the influence of the Jewish idea on American life. The departments of life here studied do not by any means exhaust the list. The studies are more and more centering on the actual operations of the Jewish program upon the American people, and the effect of Jewish conceptions on our common life. These studies are appearing in *The Dearborn Independent* now. They will be gathered into future volumes as may be required.

November, 1921.

The Writer of the Following Letter Is a Jew:
"Gentlemen:
"'Because you believe in a good cause,' said Dr. Johnson, 'is no reason why you should feel called upon to defend it, for by your manner of defense you may do your cause much harm.'
"The above applying to me I will only say that I have received the books you sent me and read both with much interest.
"You are rendering the Jews a very great service, that of saving them from themselves.
"It takes courage, and nerve, and intelligence to do and pursue such a work, and I admire you for it."

43. The Jews and the "Religious Persecution" Cry

We cheerfully give the Jews of the United States credit for knowing when they are getting their money's worth. In the defense that has been set up for them they know that they have not had their money's worth, neither from Jewish money collectors nor from the "Gentile fronts" to whom the money has been paid. The Louis Marshall line of defense has broken down. The boycott has dribbled into nothingness. Speeches in Congress and editorials in newspapers have sounded too hollow to carry conviction. The Question has proved itself far too big for those who have entered the defense for gain, to satisfy personal grudges, or to win what they feel to be the favor of the stronger side. The Jews long ago quit the course which some of the "Gentile fronts" still continue; the Jews recognized the futility of it.

No intelligent Jew in the United States ever was asinine enough to declare that the Jewish Question is a religious question and that *The Dearborn Independent*'s investigation of that question constituted "religious persecution."

No Jew known beyond the next street has ever ventured such a silly charge. But it is apparently all that remains for the "Gentile fronts" to shout about.

From what can be learned from them they are for the most part men of no religion themselves and they use the term "religious persecution" as a red flag which they think will stir people into action. It is rather curious how the cry of "religious persecution" is used to evoke the spirit of persecution against alleged persecutors.

The Dearborn Independent this week goes out of its course to squelch once and for all this cry of religious persecutions. Three statements are sufficient to outline the situation:

First, neither directly nor by implication has *The Dearborn Independent* held that the Jewish Question is a religious question. On the contrary, supported by the highest Jewish authority, this paper has held that the Jewish Question is one of race and nationality. (See Issues of October 9 and 16, 1920).

Second, there is no religious persecution of the Jew in the United States, unless the agitation of various humane societies for the abolition of "kosher killing" may be considered such. The Massachusetts Society for the Prevention of Cruelty to Animals has published a valuable study of the Jewish method of slaughtering animals for food, in which is adduced much scientific evidence to support the conclusion that the Jewish method is "needlessly cruel."

But even this can only with difficulty be stretched into an interference with "the religion of the Jews." The Jewish method of slaughter as now practiced is not commanded in the Old Testament but in the Talmud, and is, therefore, not religious in the authoritative sense, but traditional. Moreover, there is positive evidence that modern methods achieve the Jewish purpose (the disposal of the blood of the carcass) much better than does the Jewish method. This is the only instance where even remotely the religion of the Jews has been touched.

Third, the fact is that while there is no "religious persecution" of the Jews, there is very much real religious persecution by the Jews. That is one of the outstanding characteristics of organized Jewish life in the United States, its active, unceasing, powerful and virulent attacks upon any and all forms of Christianity which may chance to come to public notice.

Now and again we hear of outbreaks of sectarian bigotry between Catholics and Protestants, but these are not to be compared with the steady, relentless, alert, anti-Christian activity of the Jewish organizations. There are doctrinal disputes within the Christian churches, but none that challenge the basis of Christianity itself; organized Judaism, however, is not content with doctrinal disputation, but enlists its vast commercial and political power against everything that it regards as, in its own words, "Christological manifestations."

Now, these are facts, and being facts, they are important, and they ought to be publicly known.

No President of the United States has yet dared to take his inaugural oath on the open pages of the New Testament—the Jews would denounce him. When General Pershing announced that he considered the morale of the American soldier due to the interest of the Christian men and women at home, the Jews had him cut out the word "Christian." Various governors of American states, having used the word "Christian" in their Thanksgiving proclamations, have been obliged to excise it on demand of the Jews.

The word "Christian" was compelled to be cut out of the officers' training manual at the Plattsburg training camp. Everything that would remind the child in school that he is living in the midst of a Christian civilization, in a nation declared by the Supreme Court to be founded on Christian principles, has been ordered out of the public schools on Jewish demand.

People sometimes ask why 3,000,000 Jews can control the affairs of 100,000,000 Americans. In the same way that ten Jewish students can abolish the mention of Christmas and Easter out of schools containing 3,000 Christian pupils.

In a nation and at a time when a minority of Jews can print every year a record of apologies they have extorted from public officials for "having inadvertently used the term 'Christian,'" it is desirable that this charge of "religious persecution" should be placed where it belongs. In the *Daily American Tribune,* a Catholic daily published at Dubuque, Iowa, appeared a recent headline which said a great deal—"Not Persecution of the Jews, But Protection of the Christians."

It is now proposed to let the Jews speak for themselves on this question. The Jewish press has been searched for an authoritative expression charging that the study of the Jewish Question constitutes "religious persecution," and none has been found. That cry has been reserved for "Gentile fronts" for use among Christians. All the attacks from the Jewish camp are against the doctrines and institutions of the Christians. They have carried on an insistent and successful persecution, and the details of it have filled the Jewish press for years past.

Upon reading the following selections, the remark of Dean Swift will probably come to mind: "We are fully convinced that we shall always tolerate them, but not that they will tolerate us."

The Red Cross is objectionable to the Jew. H. Lissauer, in *The Jewish Times,* proposed that the Magen David be substituted for "the red cross" on the Red Cross Society badges worn by Jews.

"We should not let our sensitiveness to charges of intolerance overcome out conscientious religious objections to the cross," says Mr. Lissauer. The editor of *The Jewish Independent* thinks the suggestion "is worthy of serious consideration."

The Gideons are objectionable to the Jew. The Gideons is the name given to the Christian Commercial Travelers' Association of America, whose efforts are responsible for the Bibles which are to be found in most hotel rooms. This is from the *Cleveland Jewish Independent:*

"It is quite evident that the Gideons do not know a typically Jewish name when they see or hear one. The Gideons' object, according to their letterheads, is 'winning commercial traveling men for Christ' and the way this is done is by placing a Christian Bible in each guest room of every hotel.

"The Gideons have been at it a long time, long enough to know better, but the other day they sent a letter to Max Cohen of this city, who is a traveling man but the kind the Gideons have no right to ask for funds, and the person who selected him for an 'easy mark' certainly should have had better sense.

"Mr. Cohen utterly failed to 'fall' for the invitation and instead of sending his little donation he wrote a letter to the secretary, C. A. Johnson, in which he bluntly said: 'Don't you think you ought to use better judgement than to ask me to contribute to a strictly religious work opposite to my own belief?'

"If the Gideons insist upon filling up hotels with Bibles that have no business there they should go to the right persons for contributions."

The Jews do not like the Salvation Army nor the Y.M.C.A. Many thousands of printed lines expressed the fury with which they regarded attempts to "Christianize the Army and Navy" during the war, and the wild arguments with which they sought to make "Y" work and Salvation Army work to appear to be a violation of the principle of no union of Church and State. The same objection was made to religious welfare work during the building of the Panama Canal. If there is any challenge of this on the part of uninformed "Gentile fronts" (the Jews themselves will not challenge it) the evidence can be produced. It is only a matter of space.

The Jews did not like Theodore Roosevelt's choice of a hymn for the Progressive party:

"With Hon. Oscar S. Strauss as the nominee for the governorship of New York on the Progressive ticket, this question rises: Will the voters on the East Side of New York march to the Progressive battle hymn, 'Onward, Christian Soldiers,' or will the song have to be changed to fit the candidate?"—*American Israelite.*

The Jews hate with a malice beyond expression what they call "mission holes," that is, a place of instruction maintained by Christian churches where inquiring Jews may learn what Christianity is and, in many instances, where destitute and neglected Jews may receive assistance and counsel. The boast of how "the Jew cares for his own" is given a jolt by the dire need which has called Christian welfare work into Jewish settlements.

This hatred overrode good judgement so completely that in 1911 Assemblymen Heyman introduced into the New York State legislature a bill making it an offense punishable by fine or imprisonment to entice or tempt a minor under sixteen years of age into a religious mission, Sunday school or church without the written consent of the parents or guardian of the minor!

The language indicates a part of the contempt in which the welfare work undertaken by Christian institutions for the neediest class of children in America is held by the leaders among the Jews; not by the masses of the Jews themselves, however, except when they are terrified by their leaders.

In St. Louis, application for a charter of the Jewish Christian Association was opposed. The converted Jews wanted an association of their own. They represented that they had been ostracized by the Jews and were desirous of organizing and owning their own meeting place. A referee advised against the charter on the ground that "it would be contrary to the broad spirit of religious freedom guaranteed under the constitution of Missouri."

The referee was, of course, coached by Jews. In the name of religious freedom these Jews opposed giving an association freedom enough to preach the gospel.

In Toronto the Jewish leaders issued a proclamation throughout all Toronto Jewry forbidding the use of reading rooms, baths, dispensaries, motion picture shows or anything else which they described as "the petty bribery of conversionist tricksters who seek for their wealthy donators to open the gates of heaven and find salvation for their sins by converting a weak-minded Jew."

By the way, all converted Jews are weak-minded or criminal, if we are to believe the hundreds of statements to that effect in the Jewish papers.

The Jews are, without exception, superior people until they become Christians; then learn what they are from the Jewish leaders!

Among the nice names for this welfare work are "Jesus holes," "mission traps," "Jew-snatchers," "child stealers."

It happened that one of the helpers in the Chicago Gospel Mission was principal of a Chicago public school. The Jews raised a great outcry against him, denounced him as unfit to teach children, and guilty of "the moral turpitude of eating food provided by taxes of which a large share is received from Jews, whose children they seek to entice from their parental religion and whose men and women they are seeking to degrade into liars and hypocrites." All because a competent man was willing to meet Jewish inquirers, or perhaps bring a few of the benefits of civilization into the neglected ghetto. If this school teacher were Christian enough to have a conscience, he would resign, said the Jewish thunderers, and with that never-failing tinge of dark-mindedness they added: "What is done in secret in these haunts can, of course, only be guessed at."

Talk about bigotry! This from a people who encourage the cry that *The Dearborn Independent* is engaged in "religious persecution," though *The Dearborn Independent* has not yet carried even one of the scores of sensational and important stories which show the Federal Government discovering synagogues and rabbis as agents of the illicit liquor traffic. "These haunts" and hints of the things that may go on there, is the only way the *American Israelite* can find to refer to welfare works in which some of the best people, from no motive but the goodness of their hearts, engage.

A book of about 500 pages could be filled with the unreasonable and in many cases, positively vicious statements of leading Jews on any of the subjects touched here.

The Jews do not like the Christian Sabbath. The literature of attack against this institution is voluminous and the arguments extreme. Sunday is Christian, therefore to the Jew it is taboo. Court records in every state bear testimony to the fight of the Jews against Sunday. Few legislatures have escaped being pestered with bills on the subject. The latest fight has been the strongest yet waged, to destroy Sunday by throwing it wide open to Jewish exploitation.

Yet the Jews are most chary of their own Sabbath. When recent college examinations fell on Jewish holy days, the Jews had the examinations changed.

When primary elections last year fell on Jewish days, every power was moved to change them. There are Jewish records of a western governor being remonstrated with because a condemned criminal was sentenced to be hanged on Saturday—did the governor mean to "offend 3,000,000 Jews"?

The St. Louis Charity Fair in 1908 planned to remain open on Friday evening; a great outcry; did the managers of that fair mean to insult the Jews; didn't they know that the Jewish Sabbath began on Friday night?

But when it is a question of maintaining the integrity of Sunday pooh! pooh! "Don't the Christians know that Sunday perpetuates the silliest superstition, that their god Jesus rose from the dead?" When certain people aid the post office employees in an attempt to close the post offices on Sunday, the Jews regard it as a step back toward the dark ages.

Here is a Jewish editorial relating to Governor Cox. It appears that Governor Cox in 1914 stood for a decent Sunday and liquor law enforcement, and this is the threat held out to him:

"At the 59th Jackson Day banquet of the Wayne County (Ohio) Democracy, which was held at Wooster, Governor Cox made the principal address in which he defended laws passed at his instigation. The governor laid particular stress on the fact that for the first time in her history, Ohio now enjoys a 'Christian Sabbath.'

"'I stand or fall by the Christian Sabbath in the next campaign,' the governor is reported to have said.

"There are many who construe the declaration to mean that Governor Cox has bid defiance to the liberal element of the state and will rely upon the religious and class prejudices which he is arousing and keeping alive in the rural districts, to re-elect him to his present office, or, what is clearly plain from his entire attitude, boost him into the nomination for United States Senatorship. The Israelite will take great pleasure about the time the leaves begin to turn in reminding Governor Cox of his statement that he 'will stand or fall by a Christian Sabbath' in the coming campaign."—*American Israelite.*

The literature of Jewish thought toward Sunday presents complete evidence of the leaders' antagonism to this distinctly Christian and Anglo-Saxon institution. Sunday has never been regarded as set apart, in those countries where the Jewish idea has most infiltrated. The decline of Sunday in the United States is directly along the line of those invasions of the Sunday spirit which are mostly aligned with Jewish commercial interests.

In Great Britain and her colonies where the Jew is not permitted to usurp a superior place as chief censor of morals and religion and education, Sunday is decently observed. The situation in this country is that, instead of enjoying its liberty, the Jewish leaders have taken liberties. The student who wishes to know how deep and hard-set is the anti-Sunday program will find all the material he wants in Jewish sources.

The theme of this article is "religious prejudice." You will not find it anywhere within the whole range of the Jewish Question, except on the Jewish side. There is, in the United States, a religious prejudice, but it is strictly Yiddish. If the Christian population bothered one one-hundred-thousandth part as much about Jewish religion as the Jews bother about Christian observances, the whole fabric of Talmudical teaching would be consumed in the bright light to which general attention would bring it, the bright light from which it has always been concealed. Sheer analysis in the interest of mental health, if undertaken by fifty men, would compel the Jewish people by their own decision to abandon the darkness which holds them now.

Jewish Talmudism owes its existence today to the indifference with which it is regarded. This is the far opposite extreme of "religious persecution."

The list of headlines describing the various angles of Jewish anti-Christian religious prejudice is not, however, exhausted. The Jew is prejudiced against the Bible. When he uses that term, he does not mean what the ordinary person means. Therefore, he does what he can to destroy public honor of the Book, unless it be an occasion where a President has been inaugurated, when it will run through the Jewish press like a strong breeze that once more has a Christian statesman ignored the Christian Bible and turned to the Jewish Bible. It is rather a trifling matter to mention; its significance comes solely from the light it throws on the Jewish attitude. It is not a trifling thing in Jewry, as the country will probably be made aware if any future President should be sworn in with, say, the Sermon on the Mount open before him.

And yet, even here, we observe a strange paradox. A Jewish authority says: "The Jew is a paradox. He is at once an idealist and a materialist. He is parsimonious and extravagant. He is courageous and cowardly. He is modest and vulgar. He is persistent and yielding. He is peaceful and warlike"—and so on. And though the Jew opposes the Bible in the schools, he never misses a chance to put it there, with the Jewish trademark. He quotes the Psalms—"We wrote them." He quotes Isaiah— "We Jews did that."

Most people sit open-mouthed at these glorious authors of Scripture and do not know how to answer. It is time the Churches began to learn what to say to the Jewish taunts—"We gave you your god;" "We gave you your bible;" "We gave you your savior." Perhaps it is also time that the Jews themselves considered how long the boast will stand the usage they are giving it.

In any case the literature which the Jews wrongfully claim as their own production, is rather far distant in time to justify its being used as a mantle of glory for the political rabbis, the discredited theatrical and movie magnates, and the violent penmen of the Jewish Press. Rather too distant in time! We, the race that confronts the Jews, have done somewhat more recent work; for example, the Declaration of Independence and the Emancipation Proclamation, not to mention the psalms and pronouncements of great American prophets that have lifted up the world.

So, the Jew is very willing that the Bible should be in the schools, provided it is not what he calls "the Christian Bible." Listen to this:

"Hebrew is to be taught in the Chicago high schools. Students who include this language in their course are to receive the credit now allowed for the study of other classical languages. Of infinite value in the training of the mind are the wonderful narratives of Genesis, and boys and girls will find the history of Israel under the Judges much more appealing than Caesar's bridge over the Rhine."

The people of New Jersey thought so, too; they believed that a reading from this ancient book every day would mean much to the general culture of the pupils. But what did the paper just quoted say about it? It called the cultivated Bible appreciators of New Jersey "soul-snatching enthusiasts" and raised a mighty yell about "the forcible conversion of Jewish children," although it was provided that Jewish or any other children should be excused from the reading if desired. Another mighty yell about excusing the children all on account of the tyranny of reading the Christian Bible in the schools—regardless of the fact, which every school teacher knows, that no class of children is oftener out of school for religious reasons than are the Jews.

Truly, these people are a paradox. They are not fair. They are constituted so that they cannot see the other side of anything. For a time, they actually do convince the secularists that everything public should be secularized down to the last notch of atheistic demand. Non-Jews are fair. They are willing to see the other people's point of view. When it was said to us that the "Merchant of Venice" was a cruelty upon Jewish school pupils, we said, without investigation, "Out goes the Merchant, then!" We discovered later that the Jewish children liked and appreciated the play better than any other group. Brander Matthews helped us discover that.

And so, when they said, "Reading the Bible is sheer proselytizing; it isn't fair," the non-Jew, who wanted to prove that he is fair and unprejudiced above all things else (a weakness the Jews know how to manipulate), said, "Well, then, out goes the Bible!" And it went out. Very well! What next? "You must abolish Christmas, too." "You must not keep Easter—the Jews don't like it." "It is anti-Semitic to observe Good Friday." In other words, to please the sensitive Jewish natures we must eradicate from Christian civilization all that is Christian in it.

In the meantime, what transpires? Having induced "fair-minded" non-Jews to do all these things—and every one above enumerated has been done over and over again at Jewish demand—the Jews then proceeded to sow Judaism on the fields thus denuded of Christianity. "No religion in the institutions of the State"—yet in every state university last year there were, and in every state university this year there probably will be, courses of lectures delivered by Jewish rabbis—the lectures delivered in the colleges themselves—propagandizing the youth of the non-Jews with Judaistic religion, ethics, and economics. That is what the so-called Jewish "Chautauqua" exists for. It is not a Jewish "Chautauqua"; it is Jewish propaganda in public educational institutions.

That is the repayment the Jews have made for our "fair-mindedness." Their demand for complete secularization is merely their preparation of the soil for their carefully organized sowing of the seed of Judaism. And non-Jews permit it to continue, for there is nothing they fear so much as that their opposition will be regarded as "religious prejudice."

The Jew glories in religious prejudice, as the American glories in patriotism. Religious prejudice is the Jews' chief expression of their own true patriotism. It is the only well-organized, active and successful form of religious prejudice in the country because they have succeeded in pulling off the gigantic trick of making not their own attitude, but any opposition to it, bear the stigma of "prejudice" and "persecution." That is why the Jew uses these terms so frequently. He wants to label the other fellow first. That is why any investigation of the Jewish Question is so quickly advertised as anti-Semitism—the Jew knows the advantage of labeling the other man; wrong labels are most useful.

This does not by any means exhaust the list of headlines describing the various avenues in which the expression of virulent Jewish religious prejudice and persecution is found. But it exhausts the space allotted to these articles each week. Therefore, the subject will be concluded next week.

It is not a pleasant subject. Religious prejudice is just as unpleasant to write about as it is to experience in any other way. It is totally contrary to the genius of the American and the Anglo-Saxon. We have always regarded religion as a matter of conscience. To believe as he will is part of every man's fundamental liberty. To interfere with force to change anyone's belief is exceedingly stupid.

Holding these hereditary principles, one chooses to study that active stream of influence in American life which is known as the Jewish stream, and immediately upon doing so, one finds himself classed with the bigots and torturers of other times.

It is now time to show that the cry of "bigot!" is raised mostly by bigots. There is a religious prejudice in this country, there is, indeed, a religious persecution, there is a forcible shoving aside of the religious liberties of a majority of the people, and this prejudice and persecution and use of force is Jewish and nothing but Jewish.

This is the answer to the cry of "religious persecution," and we shall make it so complete and definite that a repetition of the cry against students of the Jewish Question will automatically mark the criers as either too ignorant or too vicious for consideration.

The Dearborn Independent, issue of 4 June 1921

Half of Christendom worships a Jew; the other half worships a Jewess."—Jewish editorial.

"If the gospel story is correct, Judas was a pretty decent sort of fellow. It was only after he had become a convert to Christianity that he became that which has made his memory an accursed thing for nineteen hundred years."—Jewish editorial.

"Our land is frequently called a Christian nation. No doubt the majority of our citizens believe this. No less an authority than Justice Brewer of the Supreme Court so expressed himself in 1892. But the statement is clearly false . . . . This is not a Christian nation. In inspiration, at least, it is a Hebrew nation, for the Constitution which we now enjoy traces back to the Hebrew Commonwealth."—Jewish editorial.

(From the minutes of a meeting of the Committee on Families of the New York Board of Child Welfare.)

Mr. Hebbard: "That is one of the things I have in mind, that a widow brings deliberately into her home a nameless child and the inevitable consequence of that is that her legitimate children are always thereafter pointed out."

Miss Sophie Irene Loeb: "As far as nameless children are concerned, Christ himself was a nameless child. Let us get away from nameless children."

Dr. Dirvoch: "I think where there are three or four children in a home and a little stranger enters that home without a father, you are corrupting the morals of those legitimate children by permitting them to remain in such surroundings."

Miss Loeb: "I say to you that this committee, if it takes such an attitude as that, is one hundred years behind the times."

Mr. Cunnion: "Anything against purity is immoral."

Miss Loeb: "What has that to do with the question of purity? Was the mother of Christ pure?"

Mr. Cunnion: "Certainly."

Miss Loeb: "He had no name!"

Mr. Cunnion: "You can't bring that in here. We believe he was conceived without sin."

Mr. Menehan (to Miss Loeb): "That is very wrong to make that statement."—Cited in a letter of complaint to Mayor Hylan.

“The intimate relation of church and state in the great nonsectarian United States of America received direct demonstration on August 12 (1913), when a deputy sergeant-at-arms of the Senate was hurriedly sent out to get a preacher of any old denomination to open the Senate with prayer. The session opening an hour earlier than usual, the regular chaplain was not at hand, but with still two minutes to spare the deputy returned in an automobile, hurried to the Vice President's office and introduced the Rev. Dr. C. Albert Homas, of Canonsburg, Pennsylvania, to Mr. Marshall just in time for the Vice President to lead the way into the Senate chamber to open the session at 11 o'clock, and once again the Union was saved. We shudder to think what might have happened if no preacher had been captured in time to open the session with prayer!”—Jewish editorial.

“President Wilson in his inaugural address said: ‘The firm basis of the Government is justice, not pity.’ This is sound Jewish doctrine as laid down by Moses and the Prophets in contradistinction to the doctrine of love, as attributed to Jesus. This coming from so good a churchman as President Wilson might be a little surprising were it not that it is a well-known fact that whenever our Christian brethren want to talk to reasoning men they go to the Old Testament for their inspiration.”—Jewish editorial.

“President Wilson at his inaugural gave another instance of the well-known fact that in solemn moments when they need comfort and inspiration, Christians turn to the Old Testament and not to the New. So President Wilson, when he kissed the bible after taking the inaugural oath, selected the passage, Psalm 46.”—Jewish editorial.

“Reference has frequently been made in these columns to a number of addresses made by the late Isaac M. Wise at the celebration in honor of his 80th birthday anniversary in the course of which he predicted that in a quarter of a century from that date (1899) there would be practically nothing left in Protestant Christianity of a belief in the divinity of Jesus Christ or the distinctive dogmas of Christianity, and that all Protestant Christians by whatever name they call themselves, would be substantially Jews in belief. To any one who notes the signs of the times it is apparent that this prophecy is being rapidly fulfilled

. . . . The Jesus superstition and the fantastic dogmas built upon his supposed divine origin, die but slowly, but that they are dying is nevertheless apparent."—Jewish editorial.

44. Are the Jews Victims or Persecutors?

The subject of this article is "Religious Prejudice and Persecution—Are the Jews Victims or Persecutors?" A study of history and of contemporary Jewish journalism shows that Jewish prejudice and persecution is a continuous phenomenon wherever the Jews have attained power, and that in neither action nor word has any disability placed upon the Jew equaled the disabilities he has placed and still contemplates placing upon non-Jews. It is a rather startling reversal of all that we have learned from our Judaized histories, but nevertheless, it seems to be the truth.

Attention is once more called to the fact that the Jews themselves are not raising the cry of "religious persecution" here or elsewhere, but they are allowing their "Gentile fronts" to do it for them—just as they have not denied the statements made in this series (among themselves they freely admit most of them) but let "Gentile fronts" do it for them. The Jews would not be averse to raising the cry of "religious persecution" perhaps, (provided they could make it stand) were they not afraid that it would call attention to their own persecuting activities. But their "Gentile fronts" have brought that upon them.

There is no Christian church that the Jews have not repeatedly attacked.

They have attacked the Catholic Church. This is of special interest just now when Jewish agents are doing their utmost to arouse Catholic sentiment in their favor by circulating charges which these agents personally know to be false. *The Dearborn Independent* has perfect confidence in the information which Catholic leaders may have on the Jewish Question. On this subject the Catholic priesthood is not misled.

Examples of this attack are numerous. "Half of Christendom worships a Jewess," is not a statement but a slur, flung by Jewish men who say in the ritual of morning prayer: "Blessed art thou, O Lord our God, King of the Universe, who hast not made me a woman." The Talmudists' discussions of the Virgin Mother are often vile. The Christian festivals, whose preservation is due to the Catholic custom and conscience, are all attacked by Jews.

The *American Israelite*, whose great prestige in American Jewry is due to its having been founded by Rabbi Isaac M. Wise, opposed the establishment of Columbus Day and berated Governor Hughes for signing the law making it a holiday in New York. The act that established it deserved "the contempt of thinking men." Why? Is not the discovery of America a memorable event? Yes, but Columbus was a Catholic! However, in recent months the Jews are proving him to have been a Jew, so we may expect some day to see Columbus Day insisted upon with Jewish rites.

The Catholic Columbian made editorial reference to the increasing Jewish influence on the American press, in these words: "Jewry is getting its grip on the news of this country as it is on Reuter's and the Havas agency in Europe."—A perfectly polite and true observation.

But the Jewish editorial thunderer came back—"The Columbian, in its sneaking Jesuitical way, does not mention the fact that these (the Jewish) papers are the very cleanest in the country. The Columbian cannot point to a single daily owned by one of its co-religionists that begins to compare with the above papers."

The sweet spirit here evidenced is very significant today when an appeal is being made to create a strong pro-Jewish Catholic sentiment.

If there is in the world any extra-ecclesiastical undertaking by Catholics which has won the undivided approval of the Christian world as the Passion Play of Oberammergau has done, the present writer does not know what it is. Yet in a volume entitled "A Rabbi's Impressions of the Oberammergau Passion Play," Rabbi Joseph Krauskopf, D.D., of Philadelphia, has stigmatized that notable production as reeking with falsehoods and vicious anti-Semitism. In the rabbi's eyes, of course, it is, for to him the entire Christian tradition is a poisonous lie. The whole fabric of Christian truth, specially as it concerns the person of Christ, are "the hallucinations of emotional men and hysterical women."

"Thus," says the rabbi (p. 127) "was invented the cruel story that has caused more misery, more innocent suffering, than any other work of fiction in the range of the whole world's literature." And thus, the simple peasants of Oberammergau, presenting the Catholic faith in reverent pageant, are labeled anti-Semites.

These are not isolated instances. Antagonism to the Catholic Church runs throughout Jewish literature. The Jewish attitude was summed up in an editorial in the *Jewish Sentinel* of November 26, 1920, as follows: "Our only great historical enemy, our most dangerous enemy, is Rome in all its shapes and forms, and in all its ramifications. Whenever the sun of Rome begins to set, that of Jerusalem rises." These, however, are matters well known to Catholic leaders.

In their turn the other Christian denominations have been attacked. When the Methodist Church put on a great pageant entitled "The Wayfarer," Rabbi Stephen S. Wise played critic and made the solemn and silly statement that had he been a South Sea Islander (instead of the itinerant platform performer which he is) his first impulse after seeing "The Wayfarer," would have been to rush out into the street and kill at least three Jews. It says a great deal, perhaps, for the channel in which Rabbi Wise's impulses run, but the tens of thousands of Methodists who saw "The Wayfarer" will not be inclined to attribute such a criticism to the spirit of tolerance which Rabbi Wise so zealously counsels the Christians to observe.

The Episcopal Church also has felt the attack of the Jews. Recently the Jewish press raised a clamor that the Episcopal Church was not competent to teach Americanism in our cities because it held that Christianity and good citizenship were synonymous. And when the Episcopal Church made provision for mission work among the Jews, the torrent of abuse that was poured out gave a very vivid picture of what the Jewish mind naturally turns to when aroused. This abuse is not reproduced here because of its excessive violence and disrespect. It is similar to that which is heaped upon all attempts to explain Christianity to the Jews. "What would the Gentiles do if we sent Jewish missionaries to them?" ask the violent editors. Any Gentile can answer that—nay, even the Jews can answer that.

In the first place, the Jews do not want to teach their religion to Gentiles because there is a Talmudical restriction against it; Talmudically the Gentiles are not good enough to mingle with the religious matters of the Jews. In the second place, the Jews do send missionaries everywhere, not to spread Jewish religious principles, but propaganda favoring the Jews as a race and people, as is done in our colleges through the so-called "Jewish Chautauqua." In the third place, let there be produced one Jewish missionary, who has ever received anything but considerate reception wherever he has appeared.

The Jews are bitter against all Christian denominations because of the conversion of numerous Jews to them. A large number of Jews have become Catholics; one of the Knights of Columbus' most useful lecturers against the menace of radical socialism is a converted Jew. It is so also with the Presbyterian Church which has been the most recent victim of Jewish vituperation. But only upon the Catholic Church has the Jew poured more wrath and malediction than he has poured upon Christian Science. The Christian Science church has attracted large numbers of Jewish converts. Some of them have become very active, devoted members of that form of faith. Scores of columns and pages have been devoted to their denunciation in Jewish newspapers, magazines and books. Christian Science is a peculiar anathema to the Jew.

Where then is the religious prejudice? Search through the publications of all the churches named, and you cannot find in all their history so much of the spirit of prejudice and persecution as you can find expressed in the Jewish press in one single day. Jewry reeks with such prejudice. In politics, education, social functions, public holidays, literature and newspapers, they see everywhere traces of "Christological manifestations" and cry them down.

No public man has ever given public evidence of his Christian faith without rebuke from the Jews. Mr. Bryan, Mr. Marshall, Mr. Taft, Mr. Wilson, two of them Presidents, one of them Vice President, and the other Secretary of State, have all been taken to task from time to time for their sins in this respect. Mr. Marshall is a devout man, whose faith is real to him, and he speaks very naturally about it at times. He has, therefore, been attacked oftener in the Jewish press than has any other public man of recent times.

Nothing is more ludicrous to the Jewish press than a Vice President of the United States openly confessing that he is an "idolator," that is, a worshipper of the dead Jewish imposter whom the Christians ignorantly call "Christ." To Mr. Marshall's honor, be it said, he never apologized, he never begged to withdraw his public statements. Neither did William J. Bryan, whose lecture "The Prince of Peace" contained statements in honor of Christ which brought him into conflict with Jewish spokesmen everywhere, and whose remarks about missions after a trip around the world were savagely attacked by Jews.

Mr. Bryan did not apologize either. Mr. Taft was promptly called down on several occasions for using forms of the word "Christian," which were particularly offensive to the Jewish press because they had advertised far and wide during the Taft campaign that Mr. Taft was practically a Jew in his belief in that he had abandoned all the distinctive Christian doctrines pertaining to Christ. After his lapses in which he used the term "Christian" approvingly, it was explained on his behalf (1) that he was accommodating himself to the audience, and (2) that he used the term as a synonym for civilization! But isn't it significant that the name of Christ should be an integral part of the very name of the highest civilization?

Mr. Taft was a true liberal, liberal enough to tolerate Christian orthodoxy. And that was a rather weak spot, as far as the Jews' estimate of him went.

Mr. Wilson, while President, was very close to the Jews. His administration, as everyone knows, was predominantly Jewish. As a Presbyterian elder, Mr. Wilson had occasional lapses into the Christian mode of thought during his public utterances, and was always checked up tight by his Jewish censors. In 1914, speaking before the American University at Washington, he said:

"That is the reason why scholarship has usually been most fruitful when associated with religion, and scholarship has never been, so far as I can at this moment recall, associated with any religion except the religion of Jesus Christ."

That was terrible. So terrible that Herman Bernstein was chosen to administer the castigation.

And Mr. Wilson made proper reparation:

"My dear Mr. Bernstein: I am sorry that there should have been any unfair implication in what I said at the opening of the American University. You may be sure that there was nothing of the kind in my mind, or very certainly nothing in my thoughts that would discriminate in the important matter you speak of against Judaism. I find that one of the risks and penalties of extemporaneous speaking is that you do not stop to consider the whole field, but address yourself merely to the matter in hand. With sincere respects and appreciation,

Cordially yours, Woodrow Wilson."

The heading given this notice in the Jewish press was, "He Did Not Mean It."

All of the President's offending took place in 1914. The second offense he gave was by taking the position of honorary chairman of the International Lord's Day Congress, which was to be held the next year in connection with the Panama Exposition. It was, however, the Christian Sunday which received the bulk of the abuse on that occasion.

The subject is "religious prejudice." Where does it exist in this country in more continuous and virulent character than among the Jews? Read these items selected at random from Jewish papers:

"District Grand Lodge No. 4, Independent Order B'nai B'rith, voted at the annual election held in San Francisco, March 2 (1911) to exclude from the order Jews who join the Christian Science Church. The body after earnest discussion decided that the portals of the order shall be closed against the Christian Scientist Jews on the grounds that such Jews have abjured Judaism. The vote upon the question was almost unanimous."

"The Jewish Community of Philadelphia has found it necessary to publish a warning to the Jewish people against the Daily Vacation Bible Schools which are being established in various parts of the city, also against certain missions and settlement houses, all of which are traps into which Jewish children are decoyed for the purpose of seducing them from the religion of their parents. These institutions belong to that class of conversionist agencies which wage a campaign for the seeking of converts through workers . . . (who) are a class of criminals that keep just within the law and deserve no better treatment than is usually accorded to people of that kind."

When a bishop of the Episcopal Church said, "We must make the United States indisputably a Christian nation," the Jewish press retorted that such a thing could not be done until the Constitution of the United States had been "abolished." "Christian America" is a persecuting term according to the professional Jewish spokesmen, and the most laborious efforts have been put forth by them to prove on paper that the United States is not and cannot be Christian.

Not only do the Jews disagree with Christian teaching—which is their perfect right, and no one dare question it—but they seek to interfere with it. It is not religious tolerance in the midst of religious difference, but religious attack that they preach and practice. The whole record of the Jewish opposition to Christmas, Easter and certain patriotic songs shows that.

When Cleveland and Lakewood arranged for a community Christmas, the Cleveland Jewish press said: "The writer of this has no idea how many Jews there are in Lakewood, but if there is only one, there should be no community Christmas, no community religion of any kind." That is not a counsel of tolerance, it is a counsel of attack. The Christmas literature of American Judaism is fiercer than the flames of the Inquisition. In the month of January, the Jewish press has urged its readers to begin an early campaign against Christmas celebrations the next Christmas—"Only three hundred and sixty days before Christmas. So let us do our Christmas arguing early and take plenty of time to do it."

If anything, Easter is attacked yet more bitterly. But we refrain, for good reasons, from repeating what Jews commonly say on such occasions. The strange inconsistency of it all is to see the great department stores of the Levys and the Isaacs and the Goldsteins and the Silvermans filled with brilliant Christmas cheer and at Easter with the goods appropriate to the time.

The festivals of the "heathen" are very profitable. Jewish merchants have been chided for this—not over-severely—by certain rabbis. But on the whole, the rabbis had better remain content, for there are no forces more rapidly secularizing the two festival days than are the merchandising and profiteering forces.

Even religious intolerance has its gleesome moments, and the Jews' come whenever the signs appear of the greater secularization of the church. One parallel between the Protocols and the real hopes of the Jews is written in the common Jewish prophecy that Christianity is doomed to perish. It will perish by becoming, to all intents and purposes, Judaism. And it will become Judaism, first, by ousting all the doctrines pertaining to the person of Christ, excising from the Gospels the great "I Ams" which are His distinctive teachings concerning Himself; and, second, by devitalizing Christianity of all the spiritual content which flows from a union by faith with a Person believed to be divine. That is the only way it can be done.

There may be a union of all the churches of the Christian faith because the fundamentals are the same; no union of Christianity and Judaism can occur unless Judaism takes in Jesus as the Messiah, or unless Christianity ejects Him as the Messiah. Judaism sees the union coming by the ejection of the Lord as the Messiah, and rejoices at every sign of it.

Dr. Charles F. Aked, who has since blossomed out as a Jewish spokesman, delivered a sermon in which he cast aside all the "supernatural" elements in the life of Christ, from His birth, to the significance of His death, and was hailed by the Jewish press as "the fulfillment of the prophecy that within fifty years the religion of all the American people, outside the Catholic Church, would be Judaism in principle even though not in name."

"No Jew," says the *American Israelite*, "will conceal his gratification when he finds Christians virtually admitting that liberal Christianity is practically an acceptance of the doctrine of liberal Judaism."

Unfortunately, this is true. Liberal Christianity and Liberal Judaism meet, but only by the surrender of all that is distinctively Christian in doctrine. A liberal Christian is more Jewish than Christian. The statement may sound harsh and arouse resentment, but it is a very simple matter for any liberal Christian to convince himself of this by reading the volume of liberal Jewish doctrine put out by Kaufman Kohler, president of the Hebrew Union College. Liberalism is the funnel by which Christianity is expected to run into Judaism, just as liberalism so-called in other departments of life is expected to bring about certain other Jewish aims.

"Liberalism" in Jewish thought means a wide-open country in every way. Judaism has opposed every significant reform that has come to the country; prohibition, Sunday decency, movie and stage regeneration, and community reverence for sacred things. Judaism has been the prop of the liquor traffic, Sunday desecration, movie and stage excesses, and public contempt for the sacred things of the prevailing religion; and it is all too evident that the Jewish propaganda has made serious inroads everywhere.

A Congregational Church in New Jersey decided to abandon the Bible in some of its classes and substitute sociology, politics, municipal government and kindred subjects for study, and the Jewish press hailed it as another sign that the church was "in a fair way to adopt what is in substance American Judaism." In St. Louis a clergyman, instead of preaching sermons, began to act out moralistic dramas which he himself had written, and the Jewish press again hailed it as a sign of the dissatisfaction of the Christian with his church. Everything done in every branch of the Christian church has been closely watched, and wherever a departure occurred from the distinctly Christian position it was extravagantly applauded; and wherever loyalty to the landmarks appeared, it was just as extravagantly condemned. Judaism does not wish the Christian church to remain Christian. This accounts for destructive Higher Criticism being almost exclusively the work of Jews, although the world has long known them under the guise of "German critics."

Jewish intolerance today, yesterday and in every age of history where Jews were able to exert influence or power, is indisputable except among people who do not know the record. Jewish intolerance in the past is a matter of history; for the future it is a matter of Jewish prophecy. One of the strongest causes militating against the full Americanization of several millions of Jews in this country is their belief—instilled in them by their religious authorities—that they are "chosen," that this land is theirs, that the inhabitants are idolators, that the day is coming when the Jews will be supreme.

How can they otherwise act than in agreement with such declarations? You can see what is meant if you read Jewish articles describing the shoving aside of the New England people by the Jews; the supercilious attitude adopted toward the stock that made America is merely a foreshadowing of what would be the complete attitude if power and influence made it possible. Bolshevism, which began with the destruction of the class that contained all the promise of a better Russia, is an exact parallel for the attitude that is adopted in this country regarding the original stock.

We are not permitted by the Jews to sing "The Battle Hymn of the Republic" in our schools because one of the stanzas has a Christian flavor. The Jews claim that the presence of one Jewish child in any assembly of children ought in "fairness" to prevent the singing of that historic song.

Norman Hapgood, writing in a Jewish publication, said: "I need hardly explain that I do not think Jews ought to insist overmuch on their rights or nationality in a negative sense. They ought to be as much Jews as they can, but ought to be as little as possible of what is merely anti-Christian. For the Jews to try to get a song out of the public schools because it praises Jesus is perhaps natural but hardly wise." Mr. Hapgood received a lot of abuse for his well-conceived counsel.

Again we come to the end of our space with the record hardly scratched. Sufficient has been presented to show the strong, unceasing anti-Christian activity of the Jews in the United States. Had the Jewish press been read extensively by non-Jews during the past 15 years, this present series of articles would have been unnecessary—the people would have known the facts. It is to present some of the facts that are illustrated in the Jewish press along the line of religious intolerance that these two articles have been written.

Jewish spokesmen plead for suppression of facts in the name of "religious tolerance," and they denounce exposure of facts as being "religious persecution." Read the whole non-Jewish religious and secular publications and you will not find one one-hundred-thousandth part of the animosity against the Jewish religion which is found in the Jewish press—continuously found week after week for long years—against the Christian religion. The present writer has never seen nor heard of an article attacking the Jews' religion.

So, once for all, in spiking the cry of "religious persecution," we show that it exists in quantity and strength among the Jews—nowhere else. No one imbued with the American spirit would or could condemn, hinder, or even remonstrate with any person on account of the faith he holds.

As to "religious prejudice" or "persecution" entering into the present series of articles—there they are, reprinted in booklet form for permanent examination: where is the prejudice or persecution? Cite the page!

Jewish spokesmen would use their energy to better advantage, and more to the honor of the Jewish people, if they would address themselves to what is in the articles, rather than to what is not in them. The statements made by *The Dearborn Independent* have been voluminously discussed; but they are still awaiting an answer.

The Dearborn Independent, issue of 11 June 1921

"This clannishness would eventually break down were it not for the deliberate efforts of Jewish leaders who are determined that Israel shall remain an imperium in imperio. If the Jews persist in maintaining a distinct ethnic consciousness and an exclusive community life, anti-Semitism will thrive in America as it has thrived in Europe. The American nation, itself the result of fusion, will not tolerate without protest a foreign element in it."

—Herbert Adams Gibbons in the *Century*, September. Page 789.

45: Jewish Gamblers Corrupt American Baseball

There are men in the United States who say that baseball has received its death wound and is slowly dying out of the list of respectable sports. There are other men who say that American baseball can be saved if a clean sweep is made of the Jewish influence which has just dragged it through a period of bitter shame and demoralization.

Whether baseball as a first-class sport is killed and will survive only as a cheap-jack entertainment; or whether baseball possesses sufficient intrinsic character to rise in righteous wrath and cast out the danger that menaces it, will remain a matter of various opinion. But there is one certainty, namely, that the last and most dangerous blow dealt baseball was curiously notable for its Jewish character.

Yet only lesser Jews were indicted. Inevitably the names of other Jews appeared in the press accounts, and people wondered who they were. A Jewish judge presided. Jewish lawyers were prominent on both sides of the cases. Numerous strange things occurred.

But strangest of all is the fact that although American fans felt that something epochal had happened in baseball, few really know what it is. There has been time enough for others to tell the truth if they were so disposed. Many sport editors have come as near telling it as their newspapers would permit them. But it becomes daily more evident that if the whole matter is to be laid bare, so that Americans may know where to look for danger, *The Dearborn Independent* will have to do it.

And this is not of our own choosing. Baseball is a trivial matter compared to some of the facts that are awaiting publication. Yet it is possible to see the operation of the Jewish Idea in baseball as clearly as in any other field. The process is the same, whether in war or politics, in finance or in sports.

To begin with, Jews are not sportsmen. This is not set down in complaint against them, but merely as analysis. It may be a defect in their character, or it may not; it is nevertheless a fact which discriminating Jews unhesitatingly acknowledge. Whether this is due to their physical lethargy, their dislike of unnecessary physical action, or their serious cast of mind, others may decide; the Jew is not naturally an out-of-door sportsman; if he takes up golf it is because his station in society calls for it, not that he really likes it; and if he goes in for collegiate athletics, as some of the younger Jews are doing, it is because so much attention has been called to their neglect of the sports that the younger generation thinks it necessary to remove that occasion of remark.

And yet, the bane of American sports today is the presence of a certain type of Jew, not as a participant, but as an exploiter and corrupter. If he had been a sportsman for the love of sport he might have been saved from becoming an exploiter and corrupter, for there is no mind to which the corrupting of a sport is more illogical and even unexplainable than the mind of the man who participates in it.

There will be a very full case made out in justification of the use of the above terms "exploiter" and "corrupter" with regard to baseball. But it would be just as easy to make out the same sort of case with regard to wrestling and horse-racing. Wrestling is so completely ruled by Jews as to have become an outlawed sport. The story of wrestling is not only the story of the demoralization of a sport, but also the story of the wholesale bunkoing of the public.

The same is true of horse-racing. The whole atmosphere of this sport has been tinged with dishonesty. The horses remain almost the only well-bred creatures connected with it. Yet why should the art of breeding and training and testing fine horses be debasing? Only because a certain class saw in it a chance to play upon the weaknesses of men for the sake of gain.

That, indeed, explains the presence of the Jew in modern sports and it also explains why the Jewish Idea in sport, instead of being preservative, is corruptive. The Jew saw money where the sportsman saw fun and skill. The Jew set out to capitalize rivalry and to commercialize contestant zeal.

This is not necessarily the only course the Jew could have taken with regard to sports, but it is the course that he most notably has taken, and as scandal follows scandal it would seem to be high time that organized Jewry should undertake to control or repudiate those Jews who have been most instrumental in corrupting and nearly destroying our cleanest, most manly public sports.

It is worth noting that in Chicago, where the Jewish Anti-Defamation League has its headquarters, there was not a word of reproof sent out from Jews to the Jewish culprits, chiding them for their activities. Not a word. But at the same time the pressure of the Anti-Defamation League was heavy on the whole American newspaper press to prevent the public statement that the whole baseball scandal was a Jewish performance from end to end.

Baseball had a close call for its life back in 1875. Rowdyism, gambling, drinking and general disorderliness on the baseball fields brought the sport very low in public estimation, so low that attendance at the games fell heavily.

In this year 1921 there is another public rebuke being administered baseball by the same means—a very heavy reduction of public support in attendance at the games.

The storm began to be heard as far back as 1919. The Cincinnati Nationals had defeated the Chicago Americans in the World Series of that year, and immediately thereafter the country became a whispering gallery wherein were heard mysterious rumors of crooked dealing. The names of Jews were heard then, but it meant nothing to the average man. The rumors dealt with shady financial gains for a number of Jew gamblers of decidedly shady reputation.

But "they got away with it," in the parlance of the field. There was not enough public indignation to force a show-down, and too many interests were involved to prevent baseball being given a black eye in full view of an adoring public.

However, not everyone forgot the incident. Some who had the interest of honest sport at heart, and a regard for facts as well, kept on the trail—long after the trail grew cold, long after the principal wrongdoers forgot their early caution. Where money had once been taken successfully, the gang would be sure to return.

Time went on until the 1920 season began to wane. One day when the Chicago and Philadelphia National League teams were engaged in a series at Chicago, strange messages began to reach the office of the Chicago club. The messages were dated from Detroit and informed the Chicago club and management that several "well-known" Jews were betting heavily on Philadelphia. The bets involved large sums of money, and as the contest was only the ordinary run of daily game, not an important contest at all, the unusual interest of Jewish plungers attracted attention. At the same time it was observed that money began rolling into the pool rooms on Philadelphia.

Chicago club officials called a hasty conference on receipt of the messages. They called in Grover Cleveland Alexander, explained the situation to him, and told him it was up to him to save the game. It was not Alexander's turn to pitch, Claude R. Hendryx having been chosen for that day; neither was Alexander in training to pitch that day. However, he did go to the box, and although he hurled his heart out to beat Philadelphia and thwart the Jew gamblers, he failed.

Then came the big scandal. A Cook County grand jury was called into session at Chicago and asked to investigate. When the grand jury had completed its labors, eight members of the Chicago American League team were under indictment for throwing the World Series of 1919, the previous year, to the Cincinnati Reds. And all along the line of investigation the names of Jews were plentifully sprinkled.

It was discovered that the indictments brought by the first grand jury were faulty; a second one was called and it was under the second group of indictments that the famous trial at Chicago was held.

One difference in the work of the two grand juries was that the second indicted five Jews who had escaped the first one. Two of these men were Carl Zork and Benny Franklin, who were just as much implicated at the time of the first grand jury as the second, but the prosecutor's office did not try to secure their indictment. Why? Because Replogle, the attorney representing the prosecution, said there were enough men indicted without Zork and Franklin. These two St. Louis Jews were represented by Alfred S. Austrian, a Jewish lawyer, of Chicago.

This second grand jury also indicted Ben and Louis Levi and their brother-in-law, D. A. Zelser, gamblers from Des Moines. Their indictment was not secured at the first grand jury investigation directed by Replogle, assistant to Hoyne, who was then acting for the state of Illinois. Between the first and second grand juries a political change had occurred, and the public interests in the second grand jury were in the care of a new prosecuting attorney, Robert Crowe, a former judge.

It becomes necessary at this point in the narrative to give a brief "Who's Who" of the baseball scandal, omitting from the list the names of the baseball players, who are sufficiently known to the public. This list will comprise only those who have been in the background of baseball and whom it is necessary to know in order to understand what has been happening behind the scenes in recent years. For the first name let us take Albert D. Lasker. He is a member of the American Jewish Committee, was recently appointed by President Harding to be chairman of the United States Shipping Board, and is known as the author of the "Lasker Plan," a widely heralded plan for the reorganization of baseball, which practically took the sport out of non-Jewish control. He is reputed to be the second richest Jew in Chicago and was head of the advertising agency which became famous under the Gentile names of Lord & Thomas. Moreover he is a heavy stockholder in the Chicago Cubs—the Chicago Nationals.

The so-called "Lasker Plan" has been attributed to Mr. Lasker, although it is not here intimated that he has specifically claimed to be its originator. The intimation is not made for the reason that to do so might be putting Mr. Lasker in the position of claiming what is not true. Until he makes the claim, the term "Lasker Plan" must remain merely a designation, and not a description of its origin.

This matter brings us to the name of Alfred S. Austrian, a Jewish lawyer of Chicago, who is a warm friend both of Mr. Lasker and of the Replogle aforementioned. It is said that Mr. Austrian was really the originator of the "Lasker Plan" which for certain reasons was handed to Mr. Lasker, who was not averse to publicity and who knew the art of self-advertising. Now, it appears that Austrian was also the legal representative of Charles A. Comiskey, owner of the Chicago Americans, and that he was also, if he is not now, the legal adviser of William Veeck, president of the Chicago National League Club, in which it has just been said that Lasker is a heavy stockholder. It was this club which was touched by the questionable game of August, 1920, and which afterward released Hendryx, the pitcher chosen for and withdrawn from that game. The Chicago National League Club has never explained why it released Hendryx and he has never demanded redress.

Mr. Austrian's further activities will appear when the narrative of the investigation and trial is resumed.

Then there is Arnold Rothstein, a Jew, who describes himself as being in the real estate business, but who is known to be a wealthy gambler, owner of a notorious gambling house at Saratoga, a race track owner, and is reputed to be financially interested in the New York National League Club.

Rothstein was usually referred to during the baseball scandal as "the man higher up." It is stated that in some manner unknown he received the secret testimony given before the grand jury and offered it to a New York newspaper. However, the fact is this: the grand jury testimony disappeared from the prosecuting attorney's safe-keeping. It is stated that, when Rothstein found out it did not incriminate him, he then offered it for publicity purposes.

The price which it is said to have cost is also stated. It is further stated that the New York paper to whom the secret stolen testimony was offered, in turn offered its use for a larger sum to a Chicago newspaper, and that the Chicago newspaper, to protect itself, called up Robert Crowe, the new prosecutor, who advised that, in printing it, the newspaper would incur an unpleasant risk. Other Chicago editors were warned, and the testimony was not printed. Even the New York newspaper thought better of it, and did not print it.

In this connection, Rothstein threatened suit against Ban Johnson. of the National Commission, the big-bodied, big-minded, honest director and protector of straight baseball—but the suit, like others of the kind, has not been brought.

Rothstein is known on Broadway as "a slick Jew." That he is powerful with the authorities has been often demonstrated. His operations on the turf have led to suggestions that he be ruled off.

Alfred S. Austrian, herinbefore mentioned, was the legal adviser of Rothstein during the baseball scandal.

Hugh S. Fullerton, the able sport writer of the *New York Evening Mail,* writing on July 28, 1921, made a plea that "a person guilty of crooked work on a race track should be expelled not only from the race track but from ball parks, tennis courts, football fields and every place where sport is promoted. These sport spoilers must be barred from every sport."

And in the same paper, referring specifically to Rothstein, Mr. Fullerton writes:

"There is in New York a gambler named Rothstein who is much feared and much accused. His name has been used in connection with almost every big thieving, crooked deal on the race track, and he is openly named in this baseball scandal. There has been no legal proof advanced against him beyond the fact that he is the only man in the entire crowd who had money enough to handle such a deal. At least $200,000 was used in actual cash, and no one concerned could command that much money excepting Rothstein, who is either the vilest crook or the most abused man in America.

"Rothstein sits in the box with the owner of the New York Giants. He has the entrée to the exclusive clubhouses on race tracks; he is prominent at fights."

Then, after naming Abe Attell and Bennie Kauff, who also enjoy exceptional privileges around the New York club, Mr. Fullerton makes his plea for the exclusion of "sport spoilers" from every ground where sport is promoted.

Then there is Charles A. Comiskey, who is one of the most impressive examples in the country today of a good Irishman being entirely eclipsed by a Jew. Comiskey was one of the staunchest supporters of honest baseball in this country and he gave great assistance in erecting the major league game to the position it occupied just before the scandal. He used his best endeavors, also, to get the truth about the "throwing" of the World Series by his men. But his efforts were thwarted and even he, perhaps, has not the ghost of a suspicion how it was done.

So that, instead of Mr. Comiskey, we look at the Jew behind him who is Harry Grabiner. With Comiskey in failing health, Grabiner is in charge at Comiskey Park. More than that, he appears to be in charge of Comiskey himself, preventing him from making public statements and otherwise dictating to him—pushing himself forward in a manner that has indelibly and unpleasantly impressed nearly every sport writer in America.

Chicago's support of the White Sox began to slump even before the scandal and it was helped on by the unpopularity of Grabiner's methods which were wholly characteristic of what the Americanized Jew calls the "kikes."

As secretary of the club, Grabiner has grabbed the headship and if Comiskey had power enough to unseat him he would do more than the courts have done to purge the White Sox from its most serious remaining blemish.

There are shady spots at Chicago that neither the grand jury nor the court trial brought out, one of which is now related:

At all ball parks in the American League, and in the National, for that matter, officials of the "home club"—that is, of the club in whose home city the game is being played—"take the gate."

To "take the gate" is to collect the tickets and render a report of the attendance. Tickets are designed and numbered for the different gates—box gate, pass gate, grandstand gate, bleacher gate, and the rest. The accounts are made up showing the number of people who passed through each gate. When all the reports are in, it can be seen at a glance what the paid attendance is, and the shares of the contesting clubs.

In former times it was the custom for the visiting club to assign a secretary to watch the gates and thus insure an honest count, but years ago the "honor system" was adopted, leaving the entire accounting to the "home club," and this "honor system" was strictly observed. No one suspected cheating.

The count was made during the sixth and seventh innings of each day's game, the officials of the home club visiting all the gates, taking the turnstile count, and making the record. Three slips were then prepared showing the home club's share, the visiting club's share, and the grand total.

Under Grabiner's régime the "honor system" as practiced at the Chicago park began to be suspected. It began to be mysteriously suggested that visiting teams were not getting their full share. Through a system of false accounting, it was said, money was being held out. Naturally, with all the other secret investigations that were proceeding in baseball, this clue was not left untouched. Detectives were hired. Watchers were stationed. Secret counts were made. Not only one club nor only two clubs adopted secret methods of finding out what was occurring under Grabiner's secretaryship. They discovered that the "honor system" was not in vogue at that park. Their suspicions were confirmed, the mysterious rumors were verified. It would probably be highly objectionable to pro-Jewish persons to mention the Jewish management with these methods—but there are the facts.

The White Sox of Comiskey's palmy days have certainly ridden to a sorry finish under the Jewish control that has been foisted upon it. And it is typical; for there is no surer clue by which to trace a certain type of Jew than by the near certainty that even with honest money rolling in upon him, he will try to increase the flow by petty dishonesty which, once discovered, declasses him forever. It is typical.

There is a lure in trickery that appeals to some men more than sound and satisfying achievement does. Think of a world-famous baseball club allowing a system that cheated the guest club of a few hundred admission fees!

Then next in this gallery of notables in the background of baseball is the Jew gambler, Abe Attell, whose connection with sports has been of a questionable character ever since his dethronement from his pugilistic pedestal. Attell is known as the "king bee" of the scheme to "throw the games" in the World Series. He knows all about underhanded "throwing" of contests, because he has "thrown" his own fights, now feigning to be beaten when it involved gambling bets and easily winning when the same reasons prompted. Attell is of such a character that he ought to be barred from the grounds of any sport, as Mr. Fullerton suggests. He is the Morris Gest of sport, without Gest's success. All the players named Attell as the "fixer."

Even Rothstein named Attell as the "fixer." It seemed unanimous—with perhaps Attell's own consent—that he should be regarded as the "fixer": it made it so much more comfortable for others. Attell went so far as to say that he approached Rothstein with the proposition to raise a pool to bribe the players to "throw the games," but Rothstein declined. And yet Maharg, another Jew, whose name spelled backward is "Graham," says that a telegram came through signed "A. R." which promised $20,000.

The "A. R." was supposed by some to mean Arnold Rothstein, but others say he is too shrewd even to sign his initials. However, it was asserted that 10 gamblers, all Jews, cleaned up $250,000 on the games and that nearly as much money was used to manage it.

Attell was the "goat," the unanimity being rather startling. It has been known, of course, that men have been so deep in sin that they have been chosen to bear the sins also of their friends on promise that "influence" would be exerted, or on threat that if they didn't stand as "goat" certain past indiscretions would be advertised. Whatever Attell's case might have been, he stood the gaff.

Attell told the ball players that Rothstein was putting up the money.

And Attell was never brought to book. It was even testified that Abe Attell was not Abe Attell at all. Certain moneys lost in a bet had been repaid and the expected testimony in a certain matter turned out to be other than expected. Attell was held in New York for an extradition hearing. Sammy Pass, a Jew, was one of the witnesses. So was Johnny Seys. The hearing resulted in New York refusing the extradition of Abe Attell.

Then came the Dempsey-Carpentier fight, in Jersey, which Abe Attell attended. Chicago officers were in attendance, too, with extradition papers signed by the governor of New Jersey. They intended to take Attell back with them, though without passing through New York. Attell attended the fight, but the underground wires, so active in this entire case, were working, and Attell eluded the western officers.

The next name in the roster will be that of Barney Dreyfuss, a Jew, owner of the Pittsburgh National League Club. Mr. Dreyfuss appeared in the public eye during the conduct of the grand jury inquiry into the shady games, with an insistent demand that the National Commission, the ruling body in baseball, of which Ban B. Johnson is the acknowledged leader, should be abolished, and another plan, the "Lasker Plan," substituted.

It was intended to discredit the National Commission under cover of the rottenness that had been discovered between the Jew gamblers and the venial Chicago players. It was primarily an anti-Johnson move and nothing else, and it was led by a Jew whose principal followers were the rapidly increasing group of Jewish controllers of American baseball. What they have against Ban B. Johnson, impartial investigators have been unable to discover. Mr. Johnson's chief characteristic, with reference to the Jewish side, has been his implacable enmity to crookedness of any kind. That ought not to be a disqualification if baseball is to be saved. Yet the Jew-conceived, Jew-named and Jew-advocated "Lasker Plan" won out.

Carl Zork, the St. Louis Jew who was indicted, is variously described as a shirt-maker and a silk-broker. There are no variations, however, in his description as a gambler. He is part of the Jewish national net of gamblers which acts nationally and makes "killings" on a national scale.

It should be observed that the principal Jewish abuses are nationwide. This was shown in the United States Government's investigation of the white slave traffic; the bootlegging business is nation-wide; so is race-track gambling; baseball pools also are a national network for the catching of "suckers."

There is, therefore, nothing unusual that a shirt-maker from St. Louis and a horse-trader from East St. Louis, and a bootlegger from Albany—together with clever high-ups and hopelessly declassed low-downs—should all be involved in a baseball scandal that breaks in Chicago. They are all really part of a national group.

Carl Zork, for example staged the fight between Attell and a third-class boxer in which Attell welched in the sixth round in order to "throw" the fight, because his friends had all bet on the third-rate man, getting tremendous odds. His friends would never have made the bet, or having made it could never have won it, without Attell's deliberate quitting and feigned whimpering. It was one of the rawest of many raw deals witnessed in Jew-controlled sports, but Attell is that kind of man.

He is a servant for that kind of scheme. It was not by accident that Zork, the silk-broker, and Attell, an ex-prize fighter, should be linked together in the baseball scandal. They had been linked in crooked work before. They are part of the national machinery organized and operated for the purpose of separating "Gentile boobs" from their money.

If there were no "Gentle boobs," or if the "Gentile boob" would only take a square look at the man behind the nation-wide spider web, the gamblers and the Jewish sport purveyors would be in another kind of business, with perhaps less money to flaunt in the faces of honest people.

If fans wish to know the trouble with American baseball, they have it in three words—too much Jew.

Gentiles may rant out their parrotlike pro-Jewish propaganda, the fact is that a sport is clean and helpful until it begins to attract Jewish investors and exploiters and then it goes bad. The two facts have occurred in pairs too frequently and under too many dissimilar circumstances to have their relationship doubted.

When you contrast the grandstands full of Americans supposing they are witnessing "the only clean sport," with the sinister groups playing with the players and the managers to introduce a serpent's trail of unnecessary crookedness, you get a contrast that is rather startling. And the sinister influence is Jewish. So patent was this that even newspapers could not cover the facts this time.

Years before this public scandal broke, involving a whole team, it was noticed that certain Jewish gamblers formed the habit of rooming with certain baseball players. It worried the managers. The fact that the gamblers coddled in among the players was fraught with a suggestion of disturbing unusualness. Managers tried the experiment of trading such players, getting them out of their teams as quickly as possible. However, the snuggling game was continued until it honey-combed the whole of baseball, with the result that it was with no trepidation at all that the Jewish gamblers could walk up and suggest to players that a game be thrown for a price.

The occurrence which formed the basis of the investigation was not the first of the kind—far from it; the approach of the gamblers was too easy, the reception given them by the players was too casual, to warrant that view. Nor were the men whose names were given to the public the only men involved.

The only fact of value brought out of all the trouble is that American baseball has passed into the hands of the Jews. If it is to be saved, it must be taken out of their hands until they have shown themselves capable of promoting sports for sports' sake. If it is not taken out of their hands, let it be widely announced that baseball is another Jewish monopoly, and that its patrons may know what to expect.

The Dearborn Independent, issue of 3 September 1921

46: Jewish Degradation of American Baseball

Every non-Jewish baseball manager in the United States lives between two fears, and they are both describable in the Biblical term "the fear of the Jews." The first fear concerns what the Jews are doing to baseball; the second fear concerns what the Jew would do to the manager if he complained about it. Hence, in spite of the fact that the rowdyism that has afflicted baseball, especially in the East, is all of Jewish origin— the razzing of umpires, hurling of bottles, ceaseless shouting of profane insults; in spite of the fact that the loyalty of players had to be constantly guarded because of the tendency of individual Jewish gamblers to snuggle up to individual players; in spite of the evidence that even the gate receipts have been tampered with—the managers and secretaries of baseball clubs have been obliged to keep their mouths closed. Through fear they have not dared say what they know. As one manager said, "Good God, man, they'd boycott my park if I told you!"

This is in free America, and in the "cleanest game"! It is time for baseball to begin to look round.

Incidentally, the fans have been looking round. The fans know. If managers only knew how much the fans have observed, they might feel more certain of support in the event of a move toward a clean-up.

All that a Jew needs to make him eligible to baseball or any other sport on the same terms with other people, is to develop a sportsman's spirit. The Jew has crowded into all the lucrative sports, but only on the commercial side of them, seldom if ever in sympathy with the sport as a real sportsman. The Jews referred to as gamblers in these articles are not really gamblers: they take no chances; they are not sportsmen enough to gamble; they are "sure thing" men. The "Gentile boobs" who walk into their traps are the people who provide the money. Even in the field of money, the Jew is not a sport—he is a gangster, ringing a gang of his ilk around his victims with as much system as a storekeeper supplies clerks and delivery boys.

Lately the Jews have been endeavoring to prove that they are sports. Venial sport editors are sometimes induced to write certain laudatory articles along that line, and frequently the name of Benny Leonard is used—Benny Leonard, the light-weight fighter. Benny forms an instructive illustration just along this line. Benny declares that he went into the ring without a scar and that he will leave the ring without a scar. Why? Because he will let no one hit him. He will go a long way to avoid pain.

The true wrestler risks and often suffers physical pain. So does the true ring fighter. But it is a Jewish characteristic to avoid, if possible, the pain of contest, just as it is a characteristic to avoid unnecessary effort.

Look at the other light-weight champions and fighters. Kid Lavinge carries scars; his hearing is affected by the blows he took. Battling Nelson was so badly shattered by his fights that operations were necessary. Ad Wolgast, as a result of the honest straight fighting he endured, went into a sanatorium. Imagine Willie Ritchie and Freddie Welsh boasting that they never took a blow! But Benny Leonard is still unscarred. It may be boxing, but it is not fighting.

Wrestling is so tightly controlled by Jewish managers, that a real wrestler is absolutely barred out, for fear he will be able to show that the handful of wrestlers hired by the Jewish trust are not wrestlers at all, but only impositions on the good nature of the public. In order that the statement just made may not be misunderstood, it is repeated: the wrestling game at present is like the chariot race in a circus—the performers are hired men and the race is only a sham.

The Jewish controllers of wrestling will not permit real wrestler to appear—indeed, they go to infinite pains to bar him out—because a real wrestler would immediately show up the game. Wrestling is as much a Jewish business, controlled in its every part, as the manufacture of clothing, and its hirelings are mostly Gentiles.

That is what baseball was coming to. The whole sport was getting down to an "exhibition game" status. The overtone of "money, money, money" grew louder and louder. The sport aspect of the game was beginning to give way to the "show" aspect. There were numerous signs that an attempt was being made to "star" certain persons, to run "headliners," and to pull off a game with a sensational ending—just like a ballet is staged, or a pageant. Thrills were being offered—not as the give and take of the game, the accident of tensest action, but as practiced acting.

That is, baseball was slowly being brought under the level of the box-office idea. There were forces against this metamorphosis of the game. Certain men saw what was coming. There were also forces favoring the change, and wanting it to come. Curiously enough, the forces that favored turning baseball into afternoon vaudeville were Jews, and those who favored keeping the game as part of American outdoor sports were non-Jews.

There were more involved in that Chicago trial—that curious medley of Jewish defendants, witnesses, lawyers and judge—than the mere trial of baseball players accused of unlawfully taking money.

The players were the "Gentile boobs." The players were not a whit different than a candidate for the United States Senate who plays the game according to the Jewish method. Every player on trial was there because he had listened to the suggestions of a Jew. The Jews who made the suggestions were not on trial. Some of them were not even indicted. Some who were called before the grand jury were not required to testify. Others who were indicted were acquitted. The spotlight of the whole scandal was centered on the non-Jewish players who were pushed out in front to do the job and who were known to any number of Jewish witnesses as having been mixed up in whatever shady work there might have been. The "Gentile boobs" had no witnesses; the Jews had all of them.

This is not a whitewash for the players. They deserved all they got for mixing up with the low hangers-on; but they did not deserve it alone. Had they been half men there would have been a few Jewish gamblers cured for life of the little habit of approaching ball players with a shady proposition. The players are Jewish dupes. To be such a dupe is punishment enough.

It would be erroneous, however, to hold the opinion that corruption in baseball began with the matter which was aired in court. Reference was made at the beginning of this article to the fear which the managers feel. This fear is of long standing. The managers had observed certain manifestations of evil years before. They had heard rumors which they did not repeat to their closest friends. They had started quiet investigations, the results of which they did not reveal even to their partners in the clubs. Everybody acquainted with the true situation lived in deathly fear of emitting a whisper that might give a clue to the truth. But the truth is stronger than walls and doors and steel vaults—the truth was known at every stage of the game, by somebody.

Fans may recall that several years ago one of the eastern teams began to get rid of most of its men. It was a strange proceeding and occasioned much discussion. The sport pages speculated about it, and the "wise" ones doped out plausible or fantastic explanations. The true explanation has never yet been given, and it is this: the manager of that club had seen certain things in the World Series of that year which turned him cold. He knew that he saw them; morally he was convinced that something was wrong; he exhausted every available method to get to the truth and failed; so, unable to bring the men to public punishment, he simply got rid of them one by one, and the next season he had practically "rebuilt" his team. That was not more than ten and not less than five years before the 1919 World Series which formed the basis of the Chicago scandal.

It may be stated also that this which follows is the consensus of Jewish opinion as regards baseball: "You can't kill baseball as a business. It will always draw a gang on an afternoon, particularly a Sunday afternoon. It can be 'pepped' up and 'jazzed' up in a way that will make it quite a show."

The Jews are probably right, that baseball cannot be killed as a business. But it can be killed as a sport. And the American baseball fans who value the game as a sport should wish its utter destruction rather than consent that it become a rendezvous for the gangs that now fill the Jew-controlled burlesque houses. Baseball as a business will become a danger in American life, a mob-center, a hang-out of the disorderly and criminal classes.

There is another peculiar Jewish story regarding baseball which has not been told and it necessarily brings in the name of Judge Landis, of Chicago, an upright man with a wise head, whom the Jews would better not try to fool.

When the story is told, however, even the Jews will agree that Judge Landis is too shrewd for them.

Before the baseball scandal the situation was this: Ban Johnson was the head of organized baseball, through the National Commission. He had brought the sport from a minor place to its position as the national game. Ban Johnson was something of an autocrat, as all leaders must be, because as old General Booth of the Salvation Army said: "If the Children of Israel had been managed by a committee, they never could have crossed the Red Sea." Autocracy has its uses, especially in striking out new lines. Ban Johnson used his power for baseball, not for personal aggrandizement. He saw the game grow great, he wanted it kept clean. In his efforts to keep it clean, he made certain enemies. One of those enemies, the Jewish owner of a baseball club, threatened to "get Johnson." As far as the National Commission as the head of organized baseball is concerned, they did "get" him. But so far as his prestige is concerned, so far as his character and reputation are concerned, they did not "get" him.

Judge Landis was a fan. That is, he was a fan, besides being a learned and rather strict judge. Judge Landis was one of the few judges who did not quail before Chicago meat packers and Jewish bootleggers. Judge Landis always went the limit on the numerous cases of Jewish business crookedness that came before him—"blue sky" investment companies, and the like. He was at least one judge who tried Jew and Gentile alike and whose impartiality and fearless righteousness no one doubted.

Judge Landis was a rather uncomfortable man to have on the bench in Chicago. Moreover he was a comparatively poor man. The United States pays its judges only $7,500 a year. That is less than $150 a week, comparatively little on which to live as a Federal judge must live. Yet Judge Landis lived in a modest house and within his income. And no one ever dared tamper with him. An honest judge on the bench, a frugal man outside.

And he was a fan!

Now, while Ban Johnson was doing his best for baseball, and while Judge Landis was seeing a game as often as his duties permitted, certain others were viewing the situation. One of them was Alfred S. Austrian, the Jewish lawyer referred to in the last article, attorney for several ball clubs, friend of Replogle and Lasker, attorney for Rothstein the gambler and several others. Barney Dreyfuss, the Jewish owner of the Pittsburgh Club, was on the trail of Johnson, on persistent enmity. The Jewish coterie in Chicago and the Jewish influence throughout American baseball looked at Johnson and they looked at Judge Landis.

Then the great idea broke! If at one stroke they could rid baseball of Johnson and rid the bench of Landis, what a good job that would be.

Both these men were dangerous to Jews—not that they intended to be, not that they were consciously so—and it would be desirable to remove both from the spheres of their activity.

Then it was that the Jew lawyer, Austrian, came forth with the "Lasker Plan," named for his Jewish friend Lasker, member of the American Jewish Committee, head of Lord & Thomas (Gentile names) and Chairman of the United States Shipping Board.

The "Lasker Plan" proposed that the National Commission with Ban Johnson be superseded by a one-man government, that one man be selected from outside both leagues.

The proposal was not an immediate success. Even the National League was in no hurry to obey this suggestion against Johnson. Indeed, there was so much hesitancy on the part of the Nationals in which the Jewish colleagues expected to find their best support, that the trump card was played.

What was that trump card? It is said to be the secret testimony of the grand jury before which Ban Johnson was glad to appear as a witness to tell the jury everything it would need for a proper prosecution of its inquiry, and before which Alfred S. Austrian also appeared to save some of his clients from the consequences of such testimony. The report is that Austrian was able to reproduce at the National League meeting the secret testimony which Ban Johnson had given before the grand jury, and by that means swing the Nationals against Johnson and in favor of the "Lasker Plan," because in the grand jury room Johnson told the truth about certain elements in baseball, which was held to reflect on National League members. What those elements are may be gathered from a survey of the people who were interested in "getting" Johnson. Johnson is anything but anti-Semitic. He probably has never stopped to think about such a thing. He has never been known to attack Jews as Jews. But he has stood for straight baseball, and for so standing he has won the enmity of the Jews in baseball. These facts are sufficient to justify a conclusion.

So, with Johnson left to head only the American League and not both leagues, the next task was to select the new autocrat of baseball. Not a commission this time, but one man! With all his power, Johnson was never more than one of a commission; but the "Lasker Plan" disposes of such safeguards and leaves the whole authority in one man's hands. It will be interesting to see who becomes the second incumbent of that office, if indeed the "Lasker Plan" lasts long enough to warrant a second autocrat.

Gentle reader, do you suppose for a moment that the Jews who opposed Johnson did not know who the new leader would be? Ah, well they knew! He was to be a man outside both leagues. And he was to be a man whom the Jews would just as soon have off the bench as on it. He was, indeed, none other than Judge Landis, who can be trusted to see through a trick as far as any other living man.

Of course, he would accept a $42,500 job, he who was receiving only $7,500 a year! And, of course, he would resign from the bench! thus the coterie reasoned.

They trooped over to the court to interview the judge. They made so much commotion on their entry that the gavel was banged for order. The interview was held. Judge Landis agreed to accept. This news was widely heralded. The judge tied them down to a seven-year contract. It was assumed in all the interviews in all the newspapers that the judge would resign. It was assumed he would devote the rest of his life to baseball.

The baseball magnates signed up under the "Lasker Plan" put across by Austrian. Judge Landis also signed. And then he remained on the bench!

The reader no doubt remembers how quickly enthusiasm for Judge Landis died down in certain quarters; remembers, too, no doubt, that a fight was started immediately afterward in the United States Congress to force Judge Landis off the bench—not to make him give up the dictatorship of baseball, but to make him quit the bench.

And be this said: in spite of all the collusion and conspiracy and trickery, of which Judge Landis was the unconscious object, baseball fell into the hands of a man who will be just as jealous for its good name as Ban Johnson was. The Austrian-Lasker-Dreyfuss plan has so far failed. And Judge Landis has rendered several decisions which show that on the bench or off the bench he has the same shrewd eye for the detection of a fallacy.

Judge Landis is safeguarded by a seven-year contract. He is free to be absolutely fearless and fair. What his accession means to baseball will be anxiously awaited.

Judge Landis is probably not empowered to stop the steady falling of baseball clubs into Jewish hands, and if this cannot be stopped, his position as supreme dictator becomes little better than that of a police court judge settling disputes relating to the rules and offenses against them. The peril of baseball goes deeper than that.

A few years ago the owners of the American League entered into a gentleman's agreement not to sell their holdings at any time without first consulting all the other owners. The name of a prospective purchaser was to be submitted and considered, and the deal was to wait upon the approval of all the owners in the league. In the face of that fact many people wonder how Harry Frazee became owner of the Boston American club. It is very simply explained: the agreement was not observed in Boston's case, and thus another club was placed under the smothering influences of the "chosen race." The story is worth telling:

Frazee, like so many of his kind, was in the "show business," a manager of burlesque companies. Then he saw a chance in sport. In partnership with Jack Curley, another Jew, he put on the notoriously crooked fight between Jack Johnson and Jess Willard at Havana. Curley has been the principal influence in killing wrestling, by precisely the kind of Jewish policy here described.

Jack Johnson, the Negro, was a fugitive from justice, yet he was champion prize fighter of the world. He was spending money like a wild sailor, and his funds were running low. He was getting into precisely the condition where Jews like to find a man, to use him. Unable to fight in the United States, but still possessing the championship, he was in need of a way out. At this time Frazee and Curley made a proposition to Johnson, said to involve the sum of $35,000, if he would "lay down" before Jess Willard.

And thus Jess Willard, "probably the worst fighter that ever held a title," was made world champion. Frazee and Curley then exhibited Willard on the stage and in circuses, and drew rich dividends. The crooked fight at Havana did not involve Willard, he was too poor a fighter to need "fixing." Only Johnson had to be "fixed" not to knock Willard out, which he could easily have done. But between the time when Curley and Frazee gave Willard the title, and the time when Dempsey took it away from him, the Jewish syndicate made a very rich killing out of the gullible American public.

But Curley is not the subject here, he deserves a separate story. Frazee concerns this article because he became owner of the Boston baseball team. He bought a new show—the Boston club, in the best baseball city of the American League. John J. Lannin, former owner, was a real baseball man, so much so indeed, that the excitement of the games told on his health and it became necessary for him to relieve himself of the strain. Frazee was waiting to cut in, and whether Lannin feared that the proposal of Frazee's name to the American League would result in disapproval, or whether Frazee himself, knowing it, contrived to make it worth while that the agreement between the American League owners should be ignored, remains an open question.

However that may be, the American League woke up one morning to find the little burlesque manager and promoter of a crooked prize fight in their midst. It was a sad shock to the dignity of "the cleanest sport."

What could they do about it? Nothing. Frazee had bought and paid for what he held.

Baseball was about as much of a sport to Frazee as selling tickets to a merry-go-round would be. He wanted to put his team across as if they were May Watson's girly girly burlesquers. Baseball was to be "promoted" as Jewish managers promote Coney Island.

The American League owners rebelled, but let them rebel! What could they do about it?

Frazee began his next inside work almost immediately. Ban Johnson was unalterably opposed to the Frazee idea of sport, and Frazee set out to "get" Johnson. A split occurred in the American League, with Frazee, Til Huston and Jake Ruppert of the New York Club, and Charles A. Comiskey and Grabiner, of the Chicago Club, on one side against Johnson, and the other American owners comprising the other party supporting Johnson.

Frazee got money out of Chicago—the home of Lasker, Austrian, Replogle and Grabiner—to put through his Boston deal. A bank loaned him a quarter of a million dollars—one of Frazee's friends was a director of the bank. Frazee's friend died and Frazee had difficulty with the bank about remaking the notes. He finally was enabled to pay $125,000. Frazee secured this money from the New York American Club by selling "Babe" Ruth. Thus the New York and Boston clubs have become financially interwoven. Boston is referred to as "New York's farm" in baseball circles.

In the meantime, the fans of Boston feel toward Frazee as the fans of Chicago feel toward Grabiner. The "class" of Boston no longer flows through the gates. The attendance at Boston park is smaller than at any other time in the last 15 years.

Now, it is unlikely that Judge Landis could tackle that question. Has he power, or lacking power, has he daring enough to assume power to drive the peril away from the ownership and fringes of baseball? It is probably not his field, but it pertains to the future character of baseball.

The Chicago American League Club is the most recent to attract the desire of Jewish capital.

The Ascher brothers of that city have offered $1,500,000 for the club franchise. The Ascher brothers comprise a Jewish family, Max, Nathan and Harry, who conduct a string of motion picture theaters in Chicago. They have erected their own theatrical circuit. Like Frazee, they wish to add baseball to their string of "show businesses," and are willing to pay the price. At the time of this writing, their offer has not been turned down.

But a significant development—and in Chicago also—is the announcement made by the *Chicago Tribune* that it will curtail the space heretofore devoted to baseball on its sport pages. This, more than anything which has occurred, indicates the new scrutiny with which the game is being viewed.

For a long time many observers have wondered where the "sport" was found in sitting on a bleacher watching a few men earn their salaries. Hours thus spent in a ball park "do not take anything off the waistline of the spectators nor add anything to the chest measurement," says the Tribune; "the majority of spectators get only eye and mouth exercise." "Journalism has overfed it with space," the Tribune rightly says, referring to professional baseball. In ruining baseball and securing control, the Jews may be just in time to take a loss. Better no baseball than every park an afternoon midway filled with the alien and Red elements of the country.

There is, however, a baseball duty devolving upon the police of every city, and that is the abolition of the Jew-controlled baseball pool. Gambling has grown up round the "cleanest game" to the extent of $20,000,000 a year. It flourishes in 150 cities in the country, and in many small towns. The "boobs," of course, are mostly non-Jews, the owners and profit-takers are Jews.

It is as much a part of the national network of the Jewish gambling fraternity as are booze-running and horse-racing. The baseball pool runs more openly than the "books" because the very name "baseball" has seemed to give it the protection of "the cleanest sport." However, it has turned cigar-stores, barber shops, pool rooms, near-beer saloons, and newspaper stands into agencies for the national and international Jewish gambling forces. The bettor is entirely at the mercy of the managers of these pools.

These dishonest money-collecting devices are in violation of the law everywhere. The police could put them out of business easily if they should decide to give their attention to it. And thereby they would be taking the hands of the most undesirable alien class out of the pockets of the American people.

If baseball is to be saved, and there are those who seriously doubt it ever can be restored, the remedy is plain. The disease is caused by the Jewish characteristic which spoils everything by ruthless commercial exploitation. The disease may be too far gone for any cure. There are those who, like the *Chicago Tribune*, deny that professional baseball ever was a sport, and who are glad that Jewish exploiters, like scavengers, have come along to reduce it to garbage. But there is no doubt anywhere, among either friends or critics of baseball, that the root cause of the present condition is due to Jewish influence.

The Dearborn Independent, issue of 10 September 1921

47: Jewish Jazz Becomes Our National Music

About a year ago the following article appeared in the *New York Times*, a newspaper that has never been accused of anti-Semitism, and whose proprietor is one of the best-known Jews in the United States:

"Irving Berlin, Leo Feist and other officers of seven music publishing corporations in this city were charged with violating the Sherman anti-trust law in an equity suit begun yesterday in Federal District Court by the United States Government. The defendants, it was alleged, controlled 80 per cent of the available copyrighted songs used by manufacturers of phonographs, player piano rolls and other musical reproducing instruments, and fixed prices at which the records or rolls were to be sold to the public . . . .

"The corporations involved in the action were the Consolidated Music Corporation, 144 West Thirty-seventh street; Irving Berlin, Inc., 1567 Broadway; Leo Feist, Inc., 231 West Fortieth street; T. B. Harms, Francis, Day and Hunter, Inc., 62 West Forty-fifth street; Shapiro, Bernstein & Company, 218 West Forty-seventh street; Watterson, Berlin & Snyder, Inc., 1571 Broadway, and M. Witmark & Sons, Inc., 144 West Thirty-seventh street.

"The agreement which the government seeks to dissolve is alleged to provide that the defendant would make contracts only through the Consolidated Music Corporation which they had organized. . . ."

Many people have wondered whence come the waves upon waves of musical slush that invade decent parlors and set the young people of this generation imitating the drivel of morons. A clue to the answer is in the above clipping. Popular Music is a Jewish monopoly. Jazz is a Jewish creation. The mush, the slush, the sly suggestion, the abandoned sensuousness of sliding notes, are of Jewish origin.

Monkey talk, jungle squeals, grunts and squeaks and gasps suggestive of cave love are camouflaged by a few feverish notes and admitted to homes where the thing itself, unaided by the piano, would be stamped out in horror. Girls and boys a little while ago were inquiring who paid Mrs. Rip Van Winkle's rent while Mr. Rip Van Winkle was away. In decent parlors the fluttering music sheets disclosed expressions taken directly from the cesspools of modern capitals, to be made the daily slang, the thoughtlessly hummed remarks of high school boys and girls.

The United States Government alleged, in the above complaint, that 80 per cent of these popular songs was under the control of the seven Jewish houses named above; and the other 20 per cent controlled by other Jewish music houses not included in that special group.

It is rather surprising, is it not, that whichever way you turn to trace the harmful streams of influence that flow through society, you come upon a group of Jews? In baseball corruption—a group of Jews. In exploitative finance—a group of Jews. In theatrical degeneracy—a group of Jews. In liquor propaganda—a group of Jews. In control of national war policies—a group of Jews. Absolutely dominating the wireless communications of the world—a group of Jews.

In the menace of the Movies—a group of Jews.

In control of the Press through business and financial pressure—a group of Jews.

War profiteers, 80 per cent of them— Jews.

Organizers of active opposition of Christian laws and customs— Jews.

And now, in this miasma of so-called popular music, which combines weak-mindedness with every suggestion of lewdness—again Jews.

The Jewish influence on American music is, without doubt, regarded as serious by those who know anything about it. Not only is there a growing protest against the Judaization of our few great orchestras, but there is a strong reaction from the racial collusion which fills the concert stage and popular platform with Jewish artists to the exclusion of all others.

The American people have been urged and chided and shamed into the beginning of a rather generous popular support of music in this country, and the first thing they see for their money is that Jewish artists supplant the non-Jewish artists, and use the prestige of their membership in symphony orchestras to work various small business schemes of their own. If they were superior artists, nothing against it could be said, but they are not superior artists; they are only better known and racially favored in Jewish musical circles.

That, however, is a big subject. It will receive attention in its turn. Just now it is the "popular song" that is being considered. However, as something which true lovers and knowers of music may meditate upon in view of future studies of Jewish influence in music, this observation is offered (the italics are ours): "Meanwhile the Oriental, especially the Jewish, infection in our music, seemingly less widespread than the German was or the French is, *may prove even more virulent.* Those not temperamentally immune to it catch it less severely, like Mr. Leo Ornstein; and if they ever throw it off, as he has given some signs of doing, seem to be left devoid of energy and, as it were, permanently anemic.

"*The insidiousness of the Jewish menace to our artistic integrity* is due partly to the speciousness, the superficial charm and persuasiveness of Hebrew art, its brilliance, its violently juxtaposed extremes of passion, its poignant eroticism and pessimism, and partly to the fact that the strain in us that might make head against it, the deepest, most fundamental strain perhaps in our mixed nature, is diluted and confused by a hundred other tendencies.

"The Anglo-Saxon group of qualities, the Anglo-Saxon point of view, even though they are so thoroughly disguised, in a people descended from every race, that we easily forget them, and it is not safe to predicate them of any individual American, are nevertheless the vital nucleus of the American temper. And the Jewish domination of our music, even more than the Teutonic and the Gallic, threatens to submerge and stultify them at every point."

"Let me make a nation's songs and I care not who makes the laws," said one; in this country, the Jews have had a very large hand in making both.

It is the purpose of this and the succeeding article to put Americans in full possession of the truth concerning the moron music which they habitually hum and sing and shout day by day, and if possible to help them to see the invisible Jewish baton which is waved above them for financial and propaganda purposes.

Just as the American stage and the American motion picture have fallen under the influence and control of the Jews and their art-destroying commercialism, so the business of handling "popular songs" has become a Yiddish industry.

Its leaders are for the most part Russian-born Jews, some of whom have personal pasts which are just as unsavory as *The Dearborn Independent* has shown the pasts of certain Jewish theatrical and movie leaders to be.

The country does not sing what it likes, but what the vaudeville "song pluggers" popularize by repeated renditions on the stage, until the flabby mind of the "ten-twent'-thirt'" audiences begin to repeat it on the streets. These "song pluggers" are the paid agents of the Yiddish song agencies. Money, and not merit, dominates the spread of the moron music which is styled "Jewish Jazz." Of the business details, however, more later.

Tin Pan Alley, so-called because it constitutes a group of "song shops," is populated by the "Abies" and "Izzies" and "Moes" who make up the composing staffs of the various institutions.

In this business of making the people's songs, the Jews have shown, as usual, no originality but very much adaptability—which is a charitable term used to cover plagiarism, which in turn politely covers the crime of mental pocket-picking. The Jews do not create; they take what others have done, give it a clever twist, and exploit it. They have bought up all the old hymn books, opera scores and collections of folk songs, and if you stop to analyze some of the biggest "hits" of the Yiddish song manufacturers, you will find they are woven on the motif and the melody of clean songs of the last generation; the music jazzed a little, the sentiment sensualized very much, and set upon their smutty road, across the country.

Because of absolute Jewish control of the song market, both in publishing and in theatrical performance, it is next to impossible for anything but a Jewish song to be published in the United States or, if published, to get a hearing. The proof of this is in the fact that the Yiddish trust owns the business and the so-called "song hits" all bear Jewish names.

A typical incident occurred in New York recently. A non-Jewish song composer had produced work of such commanding merit that musical sentiment demanded its public rendition. Jewish manager after Jewish manager was approached, but the combination was unbreakable. Finally, one New Yorker talked out and said something about "Jewish combine," which had its effect. A Jewish manager protested that he would be glad to give the work to the public. Rehearsals were held and the night of presentation arrived. The first number was a solo and a Jew appeared to sing it. He could not pronounce English words. He sang through his nose. He was most Yiddish in appearance, the long nose, with narrow, sloping forehead, curly hair. The second number was a duet, and behold two Jews appeared, whose pronunciations differed between themselves. The performance was a most hilarious tragedy. The purpose was to kill a non-Jewish product by a poor Jewish rendition. But—the Jewish manager overdid it. It needed just that to bring non-Jewish musical consciousness to the surface and to explode the advertised and money-bought notion that the Jew has predominant artistic genius. Say that he predominates in music—yes; he has paid for and organized that predominance; do not, however, say anything about his predominance in musical genius or art.

Non-Jewish music has been stigmatized as "high brow." It is purveyable only in expensively good society. The people, the masses, are fed from day to day on the moron suggestiveness that flows in a hurtful flood out of Tin Pan Alley.

Tin Pan Alley is the name given to the region in Twenty-eighth street, between Broadway and Sixth avenue, where the first Yiddish song manufacturers began business. Flocks of young girls who thought they could sing, and others who thought they could write song poems, came to the neighborhood allured by dishonest advertisements that promised more than the budding Yiddish exploiters were able to fulfill. Needless to say, scandal became rampant, as it always does where so-called "Gentile" girls are reduced to the necessity of seeking favors from the eastern type of Jew. It was the constant shouting of voices, the hilarity of "parties," the banging of pianos and the blatting of trombones that gave the district the name of Tin Pan Alley.

The first attempt to popularize and commercialize the so-called "popular" type of music was made by Julius Witmark, who had been a ballad singer on the minstrel stage. He ceased performing to become a publisher, and was soon followed by East Side Jews, many of whom have become wealthy through their success in pandering to a public taste which they first debased.

Irving Berlin, whose real name is Ignatz or Isadore Baline, is one of the most successful of these Jewish song controllers. He was born in Russia and early became a singer and entertainer. With the rise of "ragtime," which was the predecessor of "jazz," he found a new field for his nimble talents and his first big success was "Alexander's Rag-Time Band"— a popular piece which by comparison with what has followed it, is a blushing, modest thing.

It was worth noting, in view of the organized eagerness of the Jew to make an alliance with the Negro, that it was Jewish "jazz" that rode in upon the wave of Negro "rag-time" popularity, and eventually displaced the "rag-time."

Berlin has steadily gone the road from mere interestingness to unashamed erotic suggestion. He is the "headliner" in homes as well as in the not-too-particular music halls, but his stuff without its music sometimes savors of vile suggestion.

The motif of this business can be clearly seen in the "Berlin Big Hits." There are the so-called "vamp" songs, such as "Harem Life," and "You Cannot Make Your Shimmy Shake on Tea."

Among the "successes" is the song entitled, "I Like It." It is a "vamp" song which has been sung everywhere, even by myriads of children who could not appreciate the full suggestion of the words, but were hypnotized by the atmosphere which the words created when sung; and by older folks who would not under any circumstances speak the words of the song, but who are victims of the modern delusion that a little flashy music covers a multitude of sins. "I Like It" deals with a girl, "Mary Green, seventeen," whose mother reproves her for flirting with the boys.

(In the writing of this paragraph it was debated whether *The Dearborn Independent* should print what Mary replies to her mother. It was argued that printing the words might give a salutary shock to skeptical readers. It was also argued that the pages of this paper never yet had been defiled by obscenity. Mary's words, sung broadcast through the country, are therefore not given here.)

Readers should reserve comment until they search the piles of moron music rubbish in their own parlors. Readers have listened to much worse stuff than Mary's words, but covered by Yiddish "jazz." It takes cold type to show what a song really is. A good test for a song is to try to read it aloud. Few normal people can.

"O-Hi-O," as sung by Yiddish comedians, has a stench of its own. It may be commented on more extensively later as an example of the Yiddish practice of having three grades of the same song, to suit different degrees of degenerate appetites.

Such songs are not the worst, by any means. Jewish purveyors to degenerate appetites have a peculiarly devilish system of presenting the same song in two or three grades. There will be the song as it is sold at the music store to addle-pated young men and women who fill their leisure with hearing or humming this syncopated senility—young men and women who pitiably imagine they are keeping up with the times. The songs thus sold and sung are rotten enough. But there is the same song, Class 2. The theme and the melody are the same, but it goes "a little further." There is a line or two in each stanza which dips below even the low standard which Jewish "jazz" has permitted in some of our parlors. And there is Class 3—same theme, same melody—but "going the limit."

Young men about town usually know Class 2 and Class 3. The instance has been known that young women have become acquainted with these lower grades also. Forgetfulness by young men while singing at the piano evenings has given hints of the filthier version. And even where version 1 has been strictly adhered to, the mutual knowledge, politely concealed, has created an atmosphere far from wholesome.

The diabolical cunning with which an unclean atmosphere is created and sustained through all classes of society and by the same influence, will not be overlooked by any observer. There is something Satanic about it, something calculated with demonic shrewdness. And the stream flows on and on, growing worse and worse, to the degradation of the non-Jewish public and the increase of Jewish fortunes.

If *the Dearborn Independent* were to print on this page the bare words of the popular songs that are to be found in the parlors of the most respectable section of every city, the reader's sense of decency would cry out against it.

The same words, when drawn out by numerous hyphens and covered up with nervous music, insinuate their way into the hummed tones of age and into the lilts of innocent childhood. Between the movies and the popular songs the Jewish groups dictate the intellectual life of the masses.

Among the latest Jewish "song hits" may be included these titles: "I'll Say She Does"; "You Cannot Shake That Shimmy Here"; "Sugar Baby"; "In Room 202"; "Can You Tame Wild Wimmen?" and an almost endless list of the same nature, some of which titles are too suggestive for print. Yet they have free course everywhere—as everything Jewish does, in this country.

Ministers, educators, reformers, parents, citizens who are amazed at the growth of looseness among the people, rail at the evil results. They see the evil product and they attack the product. They rail at the young people who go in for all this eroticism and suggestiveness.

But all this has a source! Why not attack the source? When a population is bathed in sights, sounds and ideas of a certain character, drenched in them and drowned in them, by systematic, deliberate, organized intent, the point of attack should be the cause, not the effect. Yet, that is precisely where the point of attack has not been made, presumably because of lack of knowledge.

It is of little use blaming the people. The people are what they are made. Give the liquor business full sway and you have a population that drinks and carouses. After preaching abstinence to the victims for a century, the country turned its attention to the victimizers, and the abuse was greatly curtailed. The traffic is still illicitly carried on, but even so, the best way to abolish the illicit traffic is to identify the groups that carry it on.

The entire population of the United States could be turned into narcotic addicts if the same freedom was given the illicit narcotic ring as is now given the Yiddish popular song manufacturers. But in such a condition it would be stupid to attack the addicts; common sense would urge the exposure of the panderers.

A dreadful narcotizing of moral modesty and the application of powerful aphrodisiacs have been involved in the present craze for popular songs—a stimulated craze. The victims are everywhere. But ministers, educators, reformers, parents, and public-spirited citizens are beginning to see the futility of scolding the young people thus diseased. Common sense dictates a cleaning out of the source of the disease. The source is in the Yiddish group of song manufacturers who control the whole output and who are responsible for the whole matter from poetry to profits.

Next to the moral indictment against the so-called "popular" song is the indictment that it is not popular. Everybody hears it, perhaps the majority sing it; it makes its way from coast to coast; it is flung into the people's minds at every movie and from every stage; it is advertised in flaring posters; phonograph records shriek it forth day and night, dance orchestras seem enamored with it, player pianos roll it out by the yard. And by sheer dint of repetition and suggestion the song catches on—as a burr thistle catches on; until it is displaced by another. There is no spontaneous popularity.

It is a mere mechanical drumming on the minds of the public. There is often not a single atom of sentiment or spiritual appeal in the whole loudly trumpeted "success"; men and women, boys and girls have simply taken to humming words and tunes which they cannot escape, night or day.

The deadly anxiety of "keeping up with the times" drives the army of piano-owners to the music stores to see what is "going" now, and of course it is the Yiddish moron music that is going, and so another home and eventually another neighborhood is inoculated.

But there is no popularity. Take any moron music addict you know and ask him what was the "popular" song three weeks ago, and he will not be able to tell. These songs are so lacking in all that the term "popular" means as regards their acceptableness, that they die overnight, unregretted. Directly the Yiddish manufacturers have another "hit" to make (it is always the public that is "hit") a new song is crammed down the public gullet, and because it is the "latest," and because the Yiddish advertisements say that it is a "hit," and because the hired "pluggers" say that everybody is singing it, that song too becomes "popular" for its brief period, and so on through the year. It is the old game of "changing the styles" to speed up business and make the people buy. Nothing lasts in the Yiddish game—styles of clothing, movies nor songs; it is always something new, to stimulate the flow of money from the popular pocket into the moron music makers' coffers.

There hasn't been a real "popular" song of Yiddish origin since the Jewish whistlers and back-alley songsters of New York's East Side undertook to handle musical America—not one, unless we except in genuine gratitude George Cohan's "Over There," a song which came out of a period of strain and went straight to the people's heart.

Two facts about the "popular song" are known to all: first, that for the most part it is indecent and the most active agent of moral miasma in the country, or if not the most active, then neck and neck with the "movies"; second, that the "popular song" industry is an exclusively Jewish industry. But the inside story of the operation of this control of the people's music presents other facts which the people ought to know, and these additional facts will appear in another article.

The Dearborn Independent, issue of 6 August 1921

48: How the Jewish Song Trust Makes You Sing

Jews did not create the popular song; they debased it. The time of the entry of Jews into control of the popular song is the exact time when the morality of popular songs began to decline. It is not a pleasant statement to make, but it is a fact. It would seem to be a fact of which American Jews ought to take solemn cognizance, not to anathematize those who do service by exposing the fact, but to curb that group of Jews who, in this instance, as do other groups of Jews in other instances, bring a stain upon the Jewish name.

The "popular" song, before it became a Jewish industry, was really popular. The people sang it and had no reason to conceal it. The popular song of today is often so questionable a composition that performers with a vestige of delicacy must appraise their audience before they sing. There are songs and choruses that can be purchased in any reputable music store and found in many reputable parlors which cannot be printed in this column of *The Dearborn Independent*. If they were printed here, "Gentile fronts" would be the first to complain that this paper was using obscenity to give interest to these articles. Yet, if those songs were printed, this paper would be doing nothing more than following its policy of going to Jewish sources for its material.

Americans of adult age will remember the stages through which the popular song has passed during the past three or four decades. War songs persisted after the Civil War and were gradually intermingled with songs of a later time, picturesque, romantic, clean.

These latter were not the product of song factories, but the creation of individuals whose gifts were given natural expression. These individuals did not work for publishers but for the satisfaction of their work. There were no great fortunes made out of songs, but there were many satisfactions in having pleased the public taste.

The public taste, like every other taste, craves what is given it most to feed upon. Public taste is public habit. The public is blind to the source of that upon which it lives, and it adjusts itself to the supply. Public taste is raised or lowered as the quality of its pabulum improves or degenerates. In a quarter of a century, given all the avenues of publicity like theater, movie, popular song, saloon and newspaper—in the meantime having thrown the mantle of contempt over all counteractive moral agencies—you can turn out nearly the kind of public you want. It takes just about a quarter of a century to do a good job.

In other days the people sang as they do now, but not in such doped fashion nor with such bewildering continuity. They sang songs nonsensical, sentimental and heroic, but the "shady" songs were outlawed.

If sung at all, the "shady" songs were kept far from the society of decent people. Like the styles of the demimonde that formerly were seen only in the abandoned sections of cities, the songs of smut had their geographical confinement, but like the fashions of the demimonde they broke out of their confines to spread among polite society.

The old songs come readily back to memory. Though years have intervened since they were the fashion, yet their quality was such that they do not die. The popular song of last month—who knows its name? But there are songs of long ago whose titles are familiar even to those who have not sung them.

Recall their names—"Listen to the Mocking Bird"—what song today has been boosted to general acceptance on such a simple theme? The only "birds" the people are encouraged to sing about today are "flappers" and "chickens."

And there were "Ben Bolt"; "Nellie Grey"; "Juanita"; "The Old Folks at Home"; "The Hazel Dell"; "When You and I Were Young, Maggie"; "Silver Threads Among the Gold." What margin did these songs leave for the suggestive, for the unwholesomly emotional?

In those days the people sang; they sang together; they sang wherever they met; it was the days of that now extinct institution known as "the singing school." People could sing together. The songs were common property, known to everybody, proper to everybody.

Is there such singing today? Hardly. At a recent meeting of young men in a church the chorus, "Hail, Hail, the Gang's All Here" was called for, and the chairman in agreeing called out "Mustn't say the naughty word!" With that warning the chorus was given.

In calling for public singing there is an immediate uneasiness about possible indecency. There was not this uneasiness before the days of Jewish jazz. In course of time the fashion of public song underwent a change. An entirely new crop of titles appeared, dealing with an entirely different series of subjects than the songs they displaced.

It was the period of "Annie Rooney"; "Down Went McGinty to the Bottom of the Sea"; "She's Only a Bird in a Gilded Cage"; "After the Ball is Over"—all of them clean, lighter than the preceding fashion in songs, but just as clean, and also giving a true touch to life.

Sentiment was not lacking, but it was the unobjectionable sentiment of "My Wild Irish Rose" or "In the Baggage Coach Ahead."

The non-Jewish period was marked by songs like these: "On the Banks of the Wabash," by Paul Dresser; "In the Shade of the Old Apple Tree"; "When the Sunset Turns the Ocean's Blue to Gold"; "Down by the Old Mill Stream"; "My Sweetheart's the Man in the Moon," by Jim Thornton; "The Sidewalks of New York," by Charles Lawlor.

There was also the "western" and "Indian" strain of songs, represented by "Cheyenne, Cheyenne, Hop on My Pony"; "Arawanna"; "Trail of the Lonesome Pine."

Then came the African period, being the entrance of the jungle motif, the so-called "Congo" stuff into popular pieces. "High Up in the Coconut Tree," "Under the Bamboo Tree," and other compositions which swiftly degenerated into a rather more bestial type than the beasts themselves arrive at.

Running alongside all this was the "ragtime" style of music which was a legitimate development of Negro mistrelsy. Lyrics practically disappeared before the numerous "cake walk" songs that deluged the public ear. "There'll Be a Hot Time in the Old Town Tonight"—the marching song of the Spanish-American War, belongs to that period. The "black and tan" resorts of the South began to reign over the nation's music both North and South. Seductive syncopation captured the public ear. The term, "ma baby," brought in on the flood of Negro melody has remained in uncultivated musical speech ever since. Minstrelsy took on new life. "Piano acts" made their appearance. "Jazz bands" were the rage.

By insensible gradations, now easily traceable through the litter of songs with which recent decades are strewn, we have been able to see the gradual decline in the popular song supply. Sentiment has been turned into sensuous suggestion. Romance has been turned into eroticism. The popular lilt slid into ragtime, and ragtime has been superseded by jazz. Song topics became lower and lower until at last they were dredges of the slimy bottom of the underworld.

The first self-styled "King of Jazz" was a Jew named "Frisco." The general directors of the whole downward trend have been Jews. It needed just their touch of cleverness to camouflage the moral filth and raise it half a degree above the natural stage where it begets nothing but disgust. They cannot gild the lily, but they can veil the skunk-cabbage, and that is exactly what has been done. The modern popular song is a whited sepulcher, sparkling without, but within full of the dead bones of all the old disgusting indecencies. Plain print returns them to their rightful status of disgust.

We are now in the period of "The Vamp"—that great modern goddess upon whom tens of thousands of silly girls are modeling themselves—"The Vamp." The original "vamp" is to be found in a forbidden French novel upon which Morris Gest founded his grossly immoral spectacle called "Aphrodite." In the Jewish popular song and the Jewish motion picture film a unity has at last been reached in "The Vamp." The vamp heroine and the harem scene—a fitting climax!

There is work here for the Anti-Defamation League. That league knows how to put the screws on anyone who disparages the Jews. From important New York publishers, down to inconsequential country newspapers, the Anti-Defamation League makes its power felt. There is work for it in the movies and the popular song industry. Why does not the league put the screws on those Jews who have degenerated the movies and debauched the popular song movement and thus brought shame upon the racial name? Why not? Is it possible that only the non-Jews are to be controlled, and Jews let to run loose? Is it possible that "Gentiles" can be curbed as by bridle and bit and that Jews cannot?

It is repeated: there is work for the Anti-Defamation League among the Jews.

More than that: there are Jews who have begged the Anti-Defamation League to purge the name of Jewry of the shame the liquor Jews, the movie Jews, the popular song Jews, the theatrical Jews, and the others are bringing on that name, and the Anti-Defamation League has not done so. It dare not.

American Jewry is desperately afraid of opening a single seam in its armor by means of a single investigation or reform. They are afraid of how far the fire of self-correction may spread.

It was the intention of *The Dearborn Independent* to give in this article a sample of the manner in which Jewish jazz is written in three classes—No. 1 for general consumption; No. 2 for stage consumption; No. 3 for the lowest resorts. On searching through the songs for the least offensive example it is found that even the least offensive cannot be printed here. The fact is greatly regretted, for certainly some method must be found by which the public can be put into possession of full information as to what is transpiring in this hideous traffic.

The Jewish art of "camouflage" (the reader may not be aware that wartime camouflage was a Jewish invention) has always been operative. "Cover names," "cover nationalities" (these are Jewish terms) have long been known. It is quite common for Jews of the higher type to band themselves together into societies for political and racial purposes, the purposes being camouflaged by a name, such as Geological Society, or Scientific Society, or something of the sort. And thus in the vilest versification, which only a few years ago would have been refused the mails, they have flung broadcast among the youth of the world dangerous ideas under the camouflage of catchy tunes.

The tunes themselves carry a tale with them. There have been cases in the courts dealing with the "adaptation," or stealing, of tunes for "popular song" purposes. If you observe carefully you will catch reminiscent strains in many of the popular songs which you sing. If you sing, "Rocked in the Cradle of the Deep," and then sing, "I'm Always Chasing Rainbows," you will notice a basic resemblance; but that does not prove that "Rocked in the Cradle of the Deep" is itself original, its melody was originally taken from an Opus of Chopin. This is a practice which has been greatly extended of recent years.

The reason for the spread of this particular kind of dishonesty is to be found in the Jewish policy of "speeding up business." Ordinarily one play a week, and one or two new songs a season, was the limit of indulgence. But with the coming of the movies the "one play a week" plan has been smashed to smithereens. To get the people to pay their money every day, the programs are changed every day; and to get new plays every day, something must be cheapened. So with songs. The output is rushed to increase the income of money, and quality is sacrificed all round. There are not enough good songs in the world to supply a new one very week; not enough good plays in the world to supply a new movie every day; and so, what the songs and plays lack in worth, they make up in nastiness. In brief, nastiness is the constant quality on which producers depend to "put across" mediocre songs and otherwise pointless plays. Nastiness is the condiment that goes with cheapness in songs and movies.

Plagiarism is the result of mediocre artists being spurred on by non-artistic promoters to produce something that can be dressed up with sufficient attractiveness to draw the public's money. But even plagiarism requires a little brains mixed with it, and when the rush of demand overwhelms the available brains, the lack is covered up by an elaborate covering of sensualism.

Men who are on the inside of the popular song business, and certain court records, all testify to the exact truth of these statements.

"But how do the Jews do it?" is a question often asked. The answer is, not public demand, nor artistic merit, nor musical ingenuity, nor poetic worth—no; the answer is simple salesmanship. The public doesn't choose, the public simply takes what is persistently thrust upon it. It is a system impossible to any other race but the Jews, for there is no other race that centers its whole interest on the sale. There is no other race that makes so startling a choice in favor of "getting" money to the exclusion of "making" money. Who for a moment would think seriously of using the terms "production" and "service" with reference to popular songs or motion pictures? Motion pictures in their higher reaches might have some claim on those terms—not the typical Jewish pictures, however; but the modern crop of popular songs, never! The terms "production" and "service" do not belong to the popular song industry at all, but the term "salesmanship" does, as the reader will presently see. It is well to remember that where there is only "salesmanship" without the other two qualities, the public is always the sufferer.

"Popularity," when interpreted by the Jews who manufacture jazz for the United States, means "familiarity," that's all. The theory is that a song need not possess merit as regards words or music to be successful. It can be "popularized" artificially by constant repetition, until it becomes familiarized to the public ear, and thus familiarized it becomes "successful."

The principle is expressed in the words of the song, "Everybody's Doin' It." You go to the theater and hear a song. Next day at lunch the café singer is singing the same song. Blaring phonographs used for advertising purposes blat out the same song at you as you pass on the street. You walk past an afternoon band concert in the park—the band is playing the same song. If you are a normal person you have a feeling that perhaps something has been going on in the world while you were engaged with your own affairs. The song—you say to yourself frankly—is silly and the music trivial; but you keep your opinion a secret, because, after all, "everybody's singin' it." Not long after you find yourself humming it. You go home, and your daughter is "practicing up" on the piece. It yells its way through your home and through your neighborhood and through your city and through your state until in sheer disgust, and in one day, the people pitch it bodily out-of-doors. But, behold, another song is waiting to take its place—a song fresh from Yiddish Tin Pan Alley. And the agony is repeated. This occurs from 30 to 50 times a year.

That is the principle—repeat it until it becomes familiar; that gives it the veneer of popularity.

Now, there is a method by which all this is done. Nothing "happens." It is like the "mob risings" which have been practiced in some of our cities—there is always a well-organized center that knows the technology of riot and knows exactly what it is doing. There is a way of making "revolution" as common and as familiar a thought as the movies and popular songs have made "vamps" and "harems" and "hooch" and "Hula Hula." The principle is the same—constant repetition for the purpose of familiarization.

More than one tune has been deliberately rejected by the public, has not been "liked," but the song-tinkers did not allow that little fact to intimidate them; they simply hammered it into the ears and memories of the public, knowing that "familiarization" was obtainable some time. "Whispering," for example, did not catch on for a long time. Long ago it used to be known as "Johnnie's Melody" because John Schoenberger wrote it—but finally it was driven home to its present popularity. There is this to say about it: it is far more deserving of its popularity than is 98 per cent of the so-called "popular" music.

Having the principle, then, that any song can be popularized by constant repetition, the Yiddish music purveyors go about their business very systematically.

The song is procured—by what means, it is not always possible to say. Perhaps one of the "staff" originates a catchy tune, or a girl who plays the church organ in a distant village sends in a pretty little melody. The girl's melody is, of course, sent back as unsuitable, but if it really had a heart of melody in it, a copy is kept and "adapted." In such ways are "ideas" procured.

Then there are plenty of Jewish musical comedies and vaudeville teams. A study of the vaudeville and musical comedy business will show it to be as distinctively Yiddish as are the movies and the popular song industry. So, the Jewish song publisher makes an arrangement with the Jewish manager of the musical comedy show. This arrangement provides that one or more of the song publisher's songs should be sung several times at every performance, in response to the applause and encores of a professional song boosters' claque which is always on hand for such purposes. This claque is paid for just as any other service might be paid for.

The night comes. The song is sung. Persistent applause. Sung again. More applause. Apparently the song is a "hit." As the audience files out the lobby is echoing with the cries of Yiddish song vendors proclaiming the song of the evening to be "the big hit of the season," hundreds of copies being sold in the meanwhile.

That is the usual Broadway introduction.

The next step is to capture the "provinces"—the musical comedies and vaudeville acts playing within 100 miles of the metropolitan centers. Actors called "song pluggers" are engaged. The arrangement with them is that they will sing a particular song exclusively—give no other song a chance. The public pays to hear the actor sing; the manager pays to have him sing; the song publisher pays him to sing a certain song.

From theater to theater, from company to company, from artist to artist, the publishers' agents wend their way, making what terms they can to single artists, vaudeville teams or comedy companies for boosting a new song by giving it prominent place in the program.

There are also the "stag entertainers," the young men who go about to "parties" of one kind another, offering amusement to the guests. This is a class of entertainers known only to the rich, but numerous enough. For instance, when the Prince of Wales toured America he was accompanied by a young man nicknamed "Rosie," of whose racial origin there need be no doubt. "Rosie" played the piano and by songs and antics beguiled the tedium of the royal journey. Well, young men of "Rosie's" sort are quite useful in advertising to select circles the latest product of the Yiddish song factories and they are, of course, regularly utilized for that purpose.

Orchestras, especially those of restaurants and dance halls, are worked in the same way. Get as many people singing and playing introductory renditions as you can: that is the method of gaining an artificial popularity by constant repetition.

The chances are that the song you are humming today is being hummed by you simply because you have perforce heard it so often that it beats unconsciously within your brain. These methods are subject to variation, of course.

There was a great deal of "cutting" until the right Hebrew group survived, and then there was a great deal of "trust" method adopted. The Music Publishers' Association was organized by "Sime" Silberman and Maurice Goodman, and now all the Jewish song manufacturers are included in it. The organization has not changed any of the methods before used but has curtailed the expense. Moreover, it has served to relieve the public to this extent, that, instead of clinging to the one song paid for until the public positively gags on it, the vaudeville or movie performers now sing impartially the various songs of the various publishers forming the trust. More variety has been introduced, that is all. The same old commercialization continues.

As readers of the studies of Jewish theatrical control, which appeared in this paper, will readily understand, the Jewish control of the popular song field means that all non-Jews are barred out. It would be next to impossible for the song of a non-Jew, however meritorious, to reach the public by the usual channels. The musical magazines, the musical critics, the musical managers, the music publishers, the music-hall owners, the majority of the performers are not only all Jews, but are Jews consciously banded together to keep out all others.

The dishonest methods practiced by the Yiddish controllers of this field have been such as to move the Billboard, the leading vaudeville publication, to refuse to print advertisements calling for song poems. Perhaps the reader has seen such advertisements, suggesting that someone has a tune or a song-poem that will probably make a fortune if only sent to an address on Broadway or in the region of Tin Pan Alley. The Billboard says:

"No More Song Poem Ads Accepted

"After investigating the business methods practiced by some Song Poem advertisers, the Billboard believes it to be to the best interest of its readers to eliminate the heading, 'Music and Words' under which Song Poem advertisements appeared, and hereafter, or until existing conditions are changed, the Billboard will not accept any more Song Poem advertising from any concern or person . . . ."

Everywhere the "popular song" has been attacked by keen observers of social tendencies—but the attack has not been made intelligently. No public menace like this can be abolished without showing the public the source of it. Newspapers are now beginning to attack "jazz," "the vicious movies," "the disgraceful dance." Others attack the young folk who sing jazz, the people who patronize the objectionable movies, the throngs who indulge in indecent dancing. But all the time a small group of men are deliberately and systematically forcing jazz and movies and dances upon the country, spending hundreds of thousands in the effort and reaping millions in profits.

If these men were non-Jews, a multitude of fingers would be pointed toward them in identification and denunciation.

Because these men are Jews, they are allowed to go free.

You will stop these abuses when you point out the Jewish group behind them!

People sometimes say, "Well, if you went after any other nationality, you could find just as much fault as with the Jews." Is there any other nationality on which you can fasten the responsibility for vile movies? Is there any other on which you can fasten the responsibility for the illicit liquor traffic? Has any other nationality control of the theater? In the beginning action against the popular song trust, could the United States find anyone to indict besides Jewish song publishers, and could the United States Government lay less than 80 per cent of song control to one New York group alone?

If these things were not strictly Jewish in their origin, method and purpose, how could such statements be made?

Jews say, "Clean up among the Gentiles first, and then turn attention to us." Will the Jews charge Gentile control of movies, popular songs, horse racing, baseball gambling, theaters, the illicit liquor traffic will the Jews charge Gentile predominance in any line recognized by moralists today as dangerously menacing the public welfare?

The question is too big to be explained by prejudice. The facts are too challenging to be thrust aside as universal. It is a Jewish question, made such by a series of Jewish facts.

Not content with hedging life about on every side, from the gold that is used in business to the grain that is used in bread, Jewish influence enters your parlor and determines what you shall sing at your piano or hear upon your music reproducing machine. If you could put a tag marked "Jewish" on every part of your life that is Jew-controlled, you would be astonished at the showing.

The Dearborn Independent, issue of 13 August 1921

49: Jewish Hot-Beds of Bolshevism in the U.S.

Bolshevism is working in the United States through precisely the same channels it used in Russia and through the same agents Revolutionary and Predatory Unionism, as distinct from Business and Uplift Unionism, and Jewish agitators. When Martens, the so-called Soviet ambassador, "left" the United States after being deported, he appointed as the representative of Bolshevik sovietism in the United States one Charles Recht, a Jew, a lawyer by profession, who maintained an office in New York. This office is the rendezvous of all the Jewish union leaders in New York, some of the labor leaders throughout the country, and occasionally of one or two American government officials known to be henchmen of Jewish aspirations in the United States and sympathizers with predatory radicalism.

The situation in New York is important because from that center lines of authority and action radiate to all the cities of the United States. New York is the laboratory in which the emissaries of the revolution learn their lesson, and their knowledge is being daily increased by the counsel and experience of traveling delegates straight out of Russia.

The American does not realize that all the public disturbances of which he reads are not mere sudden outbreaks, but the deliberately planned movements of leaders who know exactly what they are doing. Mobs are methodical; there is always an intelligent core which gets done under the appearance of excitement what had been planned beforehand. Up through the German revolution, up through the French revolution, up through the Russian revolution came the previously chosen men, and to this day in all three countries the groups thus raised to power have not lessened their hold—and they are Jewish groups.

Russia is not more Jew controlled than is France; and Germany, with all her so-called anti-Semitism, tries in vain to loosen the grip of Judah from her throat.

It is this fact of prepared disorder which makes the New York situation of interest today, because its lines of influence and authority reach everywhere throughout the country.

For that reason, and before showing how the Jewish organizations advance Bolshevism and revolution in the United States, the first step will be to describe the condition and extent of the Hebrew labor movement.

Most New Yorkers remember the "Save Fifth Avenue" movement. That avenue, from Fourteenth to Thirty-fourth street, with sections of Broadway, is historic ground. It is wrought into the history of America in a peculiarly intimate way. A little more than 15 years ago it contained the homes of the older families, the establishments of famous publishers, the stores of art dealers, and the famous shopping center. It was a district known throughout the United States as typifying American substance and good taste.

But presently, Americans who thought they were secure in their own city, were aware of an advancing shadow. A subtle atmosphere of deterioration became evident. In the top lofts of buildings, sweatshops had been installed, which noon and night poured into the streets an alien stream—not a glad, hopeful-eyed immigrant rejoicing to be in America and at work, but something darker.

It was the Russian and Polish Jew. He swarmed into this district, the most typically American of any outside of Boston and Philadelphia, from the first. Nowhere else would the sweatshops go except in the very heart of Goy respectability. There were protests and organizations; Jews were appealed to in the name of the city; they smiled and promised, but like a tide coming in, the invasion swept farther and stronger every week. New Yorkers hesitated to go down into the district to trade, and merchants lost their business. Real estate values dropped in consequence, the Jews bought valuable properties at low figures.

Today, at noontime, Fifth Avenue is packed from wall to curb with dark, squat figures in masses of thousands. They parade in dense throngs and make the street impassable. They make a strange, un-American atmosphere, Slavonic with some Oriental admixture. Their tongue is alien, their attitude is one of sullenness mingled with a sense of power. You leave the New York of American meaning whenever you approach that alien throng. They have taken over the district as completely as if they had invaded it with the bayonet.

All this would be very hopeful, of course, if we could take and sustain the attitude of the unsophisticated young reader of fiction, and regard these people as "new Americans." There is a mass of moving stories (mostly written by Jews, by the way) pretending to describe the glowing hearts with which these throngs look out upon America, their intense longing to be American, their love of our people and our institutions. Most unfortunately, the actions of these people and the utterances of their leaders give the lie to this fair picture which, as Americans, we would fain believe. The resistance offered to Americanization, consisting in the limitations put upon the Americanization program, has been sufficient to convince all observers that, so far as the Jewish invasion is concerned, it is not their desire to go the way America is going, but to influence America to go the way they are going. They talk a great deal of what they bring to America, hardly anything at all of what they found here. America is presented to them as a big piece of putty to be molded as they desire, not as a benign mother who is able and willing to make these aliens to be like her own children. The doctrine that the United States is nothing definite as yet, that it is only a free-for-all opportunity to make it what you will, is one of the most distinctive of Jewish political teachings. If it be provincialism to insist that our alien guests become American and cease their endeavors to make America something alien, then there are hundreds of thousands of Americans to plead guilty to provincialism.

"The Melting Pot," a term to which Mr. Zangwill gave currency, is not a very dignified name for our Republic, but aside from that, it is being more and more challenged as descriptive of the process that goes on here. There are some substances in the pot that will not melt. But more significant still, there are rapidly increasing interests who want to melt the pot.

So far as Fifth Avenue was concerned, it was the pot that melted. At least, not the most intrepid Jewish leader will shout much about the American characteristics of the most conspicuous Jewish colony in the world, that of New York.

The lofty buildings in this district are filled with clothing workshops, of which the Jew has a monopoly in the United States. Coatmakers, pantmakers, buttonhole workers, ladies' garment workers, these men are engaged in the "needle trades" in which adult men of no other race participate.

Why the tendency of the Jew to the "needle trades"? It is explained by his aversion to manual labor, his abhorrence of agricultural life, and his desire to arrange his own affairs. Arriving in the city of his destination, the Jew would rather not leave it except for other cities. There is one Hebrew society whose charter would indicate that its work is the placing of Jews in the rural districts, but it does next to nothing in this respect. On the other hand, there is testimony that city colonization goes on apace. Widespread Jewish associations are on the lookout for likely towns in which to settle a few Jews, who in time become a larger colony, and in a little longer time run the place. There is nothing haphazard about it. The Jew is not an adventurer, he does not cut himself off from his base, but all his movements are made under consultation and direction. New York is the great training school in which the newly arrived immigrant receives his instructions as to the method of handling the American goyim.

Thus, preferring any kind of a life in the city, and not taking to the trades which involve much bodily effort, the Jew gravitates to the needle, not in the capacity of a creative artist, as is the commercial tailor, but in the production of quantities of ready-to-wear goods.

Aside from the "white collar quality of the job," the "needle trades" appeal to the Jew because at such work he can practically arrange his own hours. For this reason, the Jew generally prefers piece work to day work, domestic industries to factories—he can arrange his own time. Many people wonder how the Jews of New York have so much time for revolutionary consultation, parades, meetings, demonstrations, restaurant debates and radical authorship. No other class of working people can get the time; other people work pretty steadily. The explanation is at hand: extreme Socialism and Bolshevism have a great deal of "time off."

Trotsky, the present head of Russia, lived that way in New York. His main arrangement was for leisure to work up his scheme. All the East Side leaders knew that Trotsky was to "take the Czar's job," even though he never had an extra dollar to spend. There was nothing haphazard about it. It was prearranged, and the appointed men went directly to their preappointed places. The East Side has other rulers ready now, and they live in the midst of the revolutionary "needle trades."

One point that should not be overlooked in all this, of course, is that the "needle trades" being exclusively Jewish, all their abuses are Jewish too. This is said for the benefit of those apologists for Russian Bolshevism who explain that the reason for it all is the way the poor "Russian" was treated in America. If Americans will ever learn to remember that the Russian is not a Jew, and that Bolshevism is not Russian but Jewish, and if in addition to that the American will ever learn to remember that every Russian-Jewish laborer in New York comes into contact with a Russian-Jewish employer, and every Russian Jew tenant pays his exorbitant rent to a Russian Jew landlord, it will then be clear that once more has the United States been made to bear a slander that does not belong to it.

It may be well to remember also that it was on account of these Russian and Polish Jews, while they yet resided in Russia, that the United States broke off her trade treaty with that country—broke off with the Russia that was a country and a government before America was discovered; and, having by that act contributed to the Jewish throttle on Russia through Germany, it is now proposed that the United States, on account of these same Jews, enter into trade agreements with the present Russian tyranny. Verily, the diplomacy of Judah has come very near determining our foreign policy. If they were strong enough, in spite of President Taft's refusal, to make us break with Russia, they may also be strong enough to make us shake hands with Bolshevism.

The Jewish trade union is exclusively Jewish for the reason that the trades affected are exclusively Jewish. That is, the Jewish trade union is not an American trade union, it is not a mixed trade union, it is Jewish. Like all other Jewish activities the purpose of the trade union is to advance Jewish interests alone. These unions are one aspect of United Israel.

This should be borne in mind with reference to the widespread strikes in the clothing trade and the rapid increase in the price of clothing to the 99,000,000 non-Jews in the United States. In spite of all the strikes, the profits advanced enormously; it may be said that the strikes were essential to the advance of profits; and the country as a whole paid.

Look at some of the figures of the "needle trades" before the war. In the entire United States, the men's and women's clothing manufactured in 1914 had a value of $932,099,000. In New York alone, $542,685,000 was produced. The rest was produced by the Jewish clothing centers in Chicago, Cleveland, New Jersey and Philadelphia.

The figures for the period of the war and since will be staggering. Clothing in the regular trade began to mount in price, until at the end of the war in 1918, it had attained an increase of 200 per cent and 300 per cent. Until well into 1920 the monopoly held up the price. This was done in face of the declaration by the manufacturers of cloth that the whole profiteering persistence was due to the manufacturers of clothing. Russian-Polish Jews, in this country only a few months, drew $50 to $80 a week. Threats of strike were used to get a five per cent increase in wages, which was met by a 20 per cent increase in the cost of clothing. The American public paid.

If, however, these statements were merely an attempt to arouse indignation that for once the workers got more than they earned, the attempt would be a failure. It is pretty hard to find anyone to regret the workers getting hold of a bonanza. The high wages weren't of much use, as it proved, but people at least had the satisfaction of handling them.

These statements are made to show that during the war the Jewish unions waxed fat, a fact which has a bearing on their Bolshevik attitude today. Not all the wage was the gain of the man who earned it—there was the union to pay. Girls in the fur trade in New York earned $55 a week, of which they paid in $27.50 a week to the unions. Other workers paid in like proportion. There was great talk of what would be done. In Russia, of course, they had the government's gold vaults immediately upon the success of the revolution, but in the United States the preliminary funds would have to be supplied by themselves. A great revolutionary stroke was planned of which the written evidence still remains.

There are two divisions of Jewish wealth and power centering in New York. The first is German-Jewish, represented by the Schiffs, the Speyers, the Warburgs, the Kahns, the Lewisohns and the Guggenheims. These play the game with the aid of the financial resources of the non-Jews. The other division is composed of the Russian and Polish Jews who monopolize the hat, cap, fur, garment and toy trades. (By the way it is the Russian and Polish Jew who controls the American stage and movies also.) Between them their grip and influence is far from negligible. They may sometimes have internecine quarrels regarding the division of profits and eager publicists may zealously call attention to these quarrels as evidence of the lack of unity among the Jews, but in the Kehillah and elsewhere they understand each other pretty well, and on the question of Jew vs. "goy" they are indivisibly one.

Between these two forces the attempt to hold up prices was continued until late in 1920. The heads of the Jewish clothing associations announced that the price of clothing would not be lowered. Solidly behind them were the associated Hebrew labor unions, so-called, which threatened dire things if the prices came down. The first great store to reduce prices in New York was Wanamaker's, a non-Jewish house. In fact, there was no reduction of prices among Jewish manufacturers and merchants generally, until in the month of November less than a dozen Jews were called into the presence of a non-Jewish financier, after which a belated effort was made to save the buying market by sensational reductions. The Jewish controllers of the clothing business had just previously stated that not only would prices not go down, but the 1921 prices would go still higher.

There is a distinction between what the Jewish coalition would do and what it could do, but its will and its power never so closely correspond as when the non-Jewish element is asleep, and never are Jewish will and power so widely divorced as when the non-Jewish mind is alert. When the non-Jewish financial mind made itself felt in November, 1920, the bottom dropped out of the Jewish trade prophecies and policies. The only thing to fear is not the alert Jew, but the consequences of sleepiness among the Christians. The Jewish Program is checked the moment it is perceived and identified.

Ordinary people who for five years have been paying high tribute to the clothing trust are entitled to know who comprise that trust. But that is a trifling affair compared with the political uses to which the clothing trust has been put in this country. The clothing trust, being composed exclusively of Jews, most of whom have formed the ax-head of Jewry in the fight against certain Old World governments, is today the heart and center of a movement which, if successful, would leave not a shred of the Republic, its institutions, nor even the liberty, which is every American's by inheritance.

What is the strength of these people? How are they banded together? What are the facts concerning them?

In New York City alone there are 2,760 Jewish cloak and suit manufacturing concerns; 1,200 Jewish clothing manufacturers; 2,880 Jewish fur manufacturers; 600 Jewish skirt manufacturers; 600 manufacturing tailoring establishments; 800 Jewish merchant tailoring concerns.

These employers have organized themselves into associations such as the following:

Associated Boys' Clothing Manufacturers of Greater New York.
Associated Fur Manufacturers.
Associated Shirt Manufacturers.
Association of Embroidery and Lace Manufacturers.
Children's Dress Manufacturers' Association.
Cloak, Suit and Skirt Manufacturers' Protective Association.
Cotton Garment Manufacturers of New York.
Dress and Waist Manufacturers' Association.

East Side Retail Clothing Manufacturers' Association.
Ladies' Hat Manufacturers' Protective Association.
Mineral Water Dealers' Protective Association.
National Association of Separate Skirt Manufacturers.
National Society of Men's Neckwear Manufacturers.
New York Association of House Dress & Kimono Manufacturers.
New York Tailors' Verein.
Shirt Manufacturers' Protective Association.

Among the employed Jews, the unions are numerous but all gathered up into one central organization. For example, the International Fur Workers' Union of the United States and Canada, is made up of the following:

Feather Boa Makers' Union.
Fur Cap Makers' Union.
Fur Cutters' Union.
Fur Dressers' Union.
Fur Dyers' Union.
Fur Floor Walkers' Union.
Fur Hatters' Union.
Fur Head and Tail Makers' Union.
Fur Lined Coat Finishers' Union.
Fur Nailers' Union.
Fur Operators' Union.
Fur Pluckers' Union.
Muff Bed Workers' Union.

In the garment industry, the organizations include every operation in the process of making clothes. There are separate unions for buttonhole makers, vest makers, pants makers, coat cutters, coat operators, coat pressers, coat tailors, coat basters, lapel makers, knee pants makers, clothing turners, overall workers, palm beach workers, shirt makers, vest pressers, and even a washable sailor suit union. These together comprise the Amalgamated Clothing Workers of America.

In children's clothing we have another complete organization:

Children's Jacket Makers (three unions).
Children's Jacket Pressers.
Children's Sailor Jacket Makers' Union.
Children's Cloak and Reefer Workers' Union.
Children's Dressmakers' Union.

In women's wear, there are unions organized around every garment known to the wardrobe, some of which are:

Amalgamated Ladies' Garment Cutters' Union.
Bonnaz, Singer and Hand Embroiderers' Union.
Buttonhole Makers and Button Sewers' Union.
Children's Cloak and Reefer Workers' Union.
Cloak and Suit Tailors' Union.
Cloak and Suit Piece Tailors and Sample Makers' Union.
Cloak Examiners, Squarers and Bushelers' Union.
Cloak Makers' Union.
Cloak Operators' Union.
Cloak, Skirt and Dress Pressers' Union.
Ladies' and Misses' Cloak Operators' Union.
Ladies' Tailors Alteration & Special Order Union.
Ladies' Waist and Dressmakers' Union.
Skirt and Cloth Dressmakers' Union.
Waterproof Garment Workers' Union.
White Goods Workers' Union.
Wrapper, Kimono, House Dress and Bath Robe Makers' Union.

These unions comprise the International Ladies' Garment Workers' Union.

The reader will have an idea, after reading these lists, that the employees represented in these unions are women. The majority are men. It may require something of an effort to remember that, but it is essential. These organizations control an essential business which before the war produced over One Billion Dollars' worth of goods a year, and since the war has probably received for its products each year the amount of a big fat Liberty Loan; and these unions have received 30 to 40 per cent of that for wages and propaganda funds.

Now, let it be said at once that these Jewish unions are not to be confused with the regular Labor Union Movement, as we know it in the United States.

They are not Jews who have gone into the American trades unions. They have started unions of their own which are Jewish in membership, control and purpose. It is true, of course, that the regular trades union movement which heads up in the American Federation of Labor is under the presidency of a Jew, Samuel Gompers, but the membership is mixed, the large majority being non-Jews, and the purpose is not racial.

These Jewish unions comprise a body by themselves and are to be reckoned with, not only as labor union groups, but as racial and political groups whose purposes can be determined by the character and utterances of their leaders, as well as by the actions authorized and approved by the unions themselves.

Now, this Hebrew union movement is a part of the New York Kehillah. Jewish leaders have sought to counteract *The Dearborn Independent*'s account of Kehillah activities by saying that the Kehillah is such a little weak thing. Admittedly, however, the Jewish clothing trust and the Jewish garment workers' unions are among the biggest and most powerful aggregations in the country. Not even a Jewish leader would have the temerity to deny that.

Well, the Amalgamated Clothing Workers of America and the International Ladies' Garment Workers' Union are affiliated with the Kehillah.

More than that: this Kehillah, which Jewish spokesmen with cool contempt for truth would have the public believe was weak and unimportant—this same Kehillah, in its Executive Committee, constitutes The American Jewish Committee.

Is the American Jewish Committee a nonentity? Ask any President of the United States, any Senator or Governor.

The American Jewish Committee heads up in District No. 12 New York City—and the Committee for District No. 12 is also the Executive Committee of the Kehillah.

The men who represent before the world the combined organizations mentioned in this article are the Kehillah, and they are the American Jewish Committee, and besides, they are the men whose failure in candor has left such an impression of dissatisfaction throughout the masses of the Jewish people.

Who are they? Who are these men with whom the Kehillah is said to be such a puling thing?

Louis Marshall, of the law firm of Guggenheimer, Untermeyer and Marshall. Mr. Marshall is not only head of District No. 12, but he is also head of the American Jewish Committee. His headship of the A.J.C. makes him Jewish leader of the United States. His headship of District No. 12 makes him head of the New York Kehillah. Quite an important man? Yes; and an important place, in spite of lying Jewish spokesmen.

Who are the others? Eugene Meyer, Jr., formerly of the Capital Issues Committee of the United States war government.

Who else? Judah L. Magnes. Judah L. Magnes is the organizer and active leader of the New York Kehillah. The two bodies are linked up again. They are linked up by the Kehillah's constitution which is able to decree that its executive committee shall be the American Jewish Committee as far as District No. 12 (New York City) is concerned.

There are other names on the American Jewish Committee which also constitutes the executive committee as the Kehillah—Adolph Lewisohn, Cyrus L. Sulzberger, Felix Warburg, and so on, 36 in all.

In the current annual report of the American Jewish Committee this relation with the Kehillah is acknowledged in a note at the foot of page 123, just as in the constitution of the Kehillah its relation with the A.J.C. is acknowledged and explained.

Now to recapitulate.

The Hebrew labor unions, both of employes and employers, which are in complete control of the garment industry of the United States, represent one wing of Jewish aggression in the realm of political revolutionism. It is not a small wing in itself. Certainly it does not become smaller by its connection with the Kehillah nor the Kehillah by its gain of these workers. The two unions mentioned above number over 337,000 members. That figure is conservative. Besides these there are associated with the Kehillah the members of 1,000 other Jewish organizations, such as synagogues, charitable societies and educational bodies, and 100,000 individual members who belong on their own account.

Link this organization with the powerful American Jewish Committee, and at once the protest of the editors and the spokesmen that the Kehillah is a weak, unimportant body becomes a deliberate falsehood.

And as for those "Gentile fronts" who are ready victims of Jewish propaganda, and who, without personal knowledge, are describing the Kehillah as a large and flourishing charitable society (bad teamwork there!) let them read in the next article what some of the Kehillah leaders are trying to do to the United States.

The Dearborn Independent, issue of 16 April 1921

50: Jew Trades Link with World Revolutionaries

There are more Bolsheviks in the United States than there are in Soviet Russia. Their aim is the same and their racial character is the same. If they are not able to do here what they have done there, it is because of the greater dissemination of information, the higher degree of intelligence and the wider diffusion of the agencies of governmental authority, than obtains in unhappy Russia.

The power house of Bolshevik influence and propaganda in the United States is in the Jewish trade unions which, almost without exception, adhere to a Bolshevik program for their respective industries and for the country as a whole.

This fact is proving most embarrassing to the Jewish leaders at the present moment. It is bad enough that Russian Bolshevism should be so predominantly Jewish, but to confront the same situation in the United States, is a double burden of which Jewish leaders do not know how to dispose.

Yet it is difficult to see how the International Jew can be absolved either from the necessity of being confronted with it, or from the necessity of bearing sole responsibility for it. Russian Bolshevism came out of the East Side of New York where it was fostered by the encouragement the religious, moral and financial encouragement—of Jewish leaders. Leon Trotsky (Braunstein) was an East Sider. Whether he was a member of the New York Kehillah is not known. But the forces which fostered what he stood for centered in the Kehillah, and both the Kehillah and its associated American Jewish Committee were interested in the work he set out to do, namely, the overthrow of an established government, one of the allies of the United States in the recent war. Russian Bolshevism was helped to its objective by Jewish gold from the United States. And now that it is found to be numerically much stronger in the United States than it is in Russia, the fact causes no little embarrassment.

Denial is useless, for the thing is too blatant and has advertised itself too long. What amazes the student of the Jewish Question in the United States is the stupidity which permitted Jewish Bolshevism to flaunt itself so openly during the past few years. The only explanation that seems at all adequate is that the Jews never dreamed that the American people would become sufficiently awake to challenge them. The present widespread exposure of Jewish tactics in the United States has doubtless come as a surprise to the Jewish leaders, and this cannot be accounted for otherwise than that they thought they had gained too strong a grip on the American mind to make a challenge possible.

It remains to be seen whether the Jewish leaders shall be able to control the Frankenstein that their false policies have created.

Following exactly the program which the Jewish leaders approved for Russia, the organized Jews of New York are exhibiting a zeal and a directness which Jewish leaders would like to curb for the present, if we are to judge from some of the complaints that the Bolshevik Jews are making.

Benjamin Schlessinger, president of the International Garment Workers' Union, whose membership numbers 150,000, and which is a part of the New York Kehillah, is one of the complainants. His union, of course, is not the regular American labor union formed for the betterment of working conditions and wages; it is a revolutionary union for the complete change of the social system, involving also a change of government. In an interview printed in the Jewish Forward of April 8, Schlessinger complains against the manner in which Jewish judges have recently come to interfere with Jewish strikes:

"'And Jewish judges come to their assistance. They issue injunctions; and it is said that they do it to save the Jewish name, so that it shall not be said that "all Jews are Bolshevists." So the injunctions become a Jewish affair. . . .

"'We have a gigantic wide-branched Kehillah in New York. In all corners, Jews! All over, what you see and what you hear—Jews. And, of course, also dress; politicians and greater ones.'

"But only we may say this. And I understand Schlessinger . . . . Schlessinger explains it this way: Several reasons are given why judges like (here a Jewish judge is named) twist the law . . . . The real purpose is to break our strike . . . . But, then, after all, there is a reason, a Jewish reason. He wants to demonstrate to the American community, he claims, that not all Jews are Bolshevists."

This excerpt shows several things: that only "we" may say certain things; that Jewish authority is trying to cover the blemish of Bolshevism; and that this is done in order to demonstrate to "the American community" a certain desirable thing. The Jewish community, it is presumed, is not so easily impressed. The Kehillah is apparently trying to call in its kites but they have apparently flown too high in the rarefied atmosphere of revolutionism.

Another big union which makes part of the New York Kehillah is the Amalgamated Clothing Workers of America, whose membership is about 200,000. It is officered by Russian Jews whose pronounced Bolshevik utterances have been widely reported in the Jewish press of New York, until plain and unprivileged Americans have wondered how far treason to the United States Government could go on our own soil.

Sidney Hillman, the president, is one of the most radical Socialists in the United States—so radical that he would probably spurn the name of Socialist as ordinarily used. He is a Sovietist. He is so far "advanced" that to him the regular type of American labor union is "a scab union." The purpose of the American labor union is stated to be the improvement of the workers' condition in industry and the establishment of their industrial rights, whereas the object of Hillman's union is the overthrow of industry and its communization in the hands of the radical element. That is to say, Russia over again. Hillman was born in Russia. He personally knows most of the Bolshevik Jews now ruining that great land.

The secretary of the Amalgamated is Joseph Schlossberg, also born in Russia. Schlossberg has a very free gift of words. One of his promises to his Jewish followers, publicly made at Madison Square Garden, is this:

"The clothing industry is ours. We are not going to permit the employer to determine where his factory shall be, or how many hours we shall work."

Abraham Shiplacoff, a Socialist member of the New York board of aldermen, and next to Sidney Hillman in command of the Amalgamated, is also a free speaker, as the following excerpt will show:

"We are going to move heaven and earth to educate our people that they and they alone are the owners of industry. The workers of Russia have found it out, God bless them!

"If I knew old Sammy Gompers knew as much as that, I would tell you to go and do what the workers did in Turine. Ten thousand of them marched to the factory with music and a flag, and they opened the doors and went to work and said, 'To hell with the owners of the factory.'

"Everybody knows it is war. We are going to control the industry." Always the omission, of course, that the factories so spectacularly captured, cease to run soon after. The Hillmans and the Schlossbergs and the Shiplacoffs are heroic figures on the platform, but in manufacturing the common commodities of life and making both ends meet so that the consumer may be served and the producer rewarded, they have been the most tragic failures. "The workers of Russia have found it out, God help them!"

As a matter of fact, besides the I. W. W., the Amalgamated is the only organization which not only preaches Bolshevism but actually practices it—all in the United States, and all apparently in perfect consistency with its membership in the Kehillah and under the officership of the high gentlemen of the American Jewish Committee. The Amalgamated actually does run the industry which has mulcted such a heavy tax from the American public since 1914.

They tell the factory manager where the factory is to be located. They have a minimum wage of $12 a day, independent of skill or production.

They enforce that rule, that an employee who has worked for two weeks has thereafter a job for life.

No improved machinery can be introduced without the union's permission.

The employer cannot hire even a cartage firm that the union has not first approved.

The employer cannot withdraw from business unless he goes into bankruptcy, else the whole force of the union and its allies will be marshaled against him and his. He must inform the union of all his plans in advance.

This, of course, is part of the endowment of Trotsky to the East Side. He did great missionary work there while waiting to go across and take the Czar's place. Even to this day in the Jew-controlled theaters that crowd Broadway, the picture of Trotsky brings wild delirious cheering, while the portrait of the President of the United States is hissed. A favorite state scene is the Star of David high over all flags. The recent debate between Senators King and France, said to have been organized with the assistance of two rabbis, developed into such an outrageously anti-American pro-Soviet demonstration, that prudence intervened to prevent a vote. Recently when pro-Jewish Germans endeavored to stir up trouble by holding a great mass meeting to protest the alleged "Black horror on the Rhine," the audience was packed with Jews. Not that they love Germany more, but they love any regular government less. While a few days later, at a great American meeting, the Jews of

New York, according to the testimony of incredulous observers, were most conspicuous by their absence.

Now, the Jewish leaders must admit that the Jewish Question does not consist in American citizens uncovering these facts and helping other American citizens to become aware of them; the Jewish Question inheres in the facts themselves and in Jewish responsibility for the facts. If it is "anti-Semitism" to say that Bolshevism in the United States is Jewish, so be it; but to unprejudiced minds it will look very like Americanism.

There is not a single, solitary American-born citizen serving as officer or director of those great unions which form part of the New York Kehillah. These men have not the faintest idea of what America stands for. They are not here to become Americanized, but to change America to their own model. In this they have the articulated support of most of the Jewish rabbis who have been very keen to explain that Americanization does not at all mean what the American means by it.

America will have become what these people want it to be when America is sovietized with Jewish radicals in control, and that is the objective toward which they are working now.

The other officers of the Amalgamated are Jacob Petowsky, secretary, who is a Russian Jew, and J. B. Salutsky, who is also a Russian Jew and "National Director of the Educational Department," which means that he is the propagandist of the union in the United States.

Regarding the assertion that the great radical unions are not officered by native-born citizens (the statement has been made that Russian Jews do not usually complete their citizenship but stop short at the "declaration of intention"), there is some interesting material in a study of 2,000 presidents of Jewish organizations in New York City.

Of this number, 1,054 were born in Russia, 536 in Austro-Hungary, 90 in Rumania, 64 in Germany and four in Palestine. These countries produced 89.1 per cent of Jewish leaders in New York.

Of this number, 531 entered the country between the ages of 14 and 21, and 977 entered over the age of 21.

Of this number, 1,270 are still under 50 years of age.

These figures include all organizations from synagogues to trade unions.

How far they have been Americanized, or wish to be, can only be judged by the policies and activities of the organizations which they direct. The big Jewish labor organizations are the direct offspring of the Jewish Socialist Bund of Russia. It is due to the propaganda of the Bund in the United States that the united Hebrew trades have gone over to the ranks of radicalism. Bundists swarmed to the United States after the abortive revolution of 1905 at which time they failed to put Bolshevism over in Russia, and these Bundists gave their time to the Bolshevizing of the Hebrew Trade Unions in this country. An Agitation Bureau was formed which propagated radical Socialism through the medium of the Yiddish language, which is one of the official languages of the New York Kehillah, made so by the demands of the Kehillah's overwhelming radical constituency.

The Bundists incorporated in 1905 in New York an organization known as "The Workmen's Circle" and "swelled the ranks of the Jewish trade unions," to quote the Kehillah's Register. After a brief attempt to propagate Socialism without reference to the Jewish Question, it was given up, and in 1913 a resolution was adopted declaring that the whole purpose of the work was Jewish. This is attributed, in the Kehillah record, to the spread of "the idea of Jewish nationalism."

Now, care would have to be exercised to avoid confusion between the Hebrew labor unions, radical as they are, and the avowed communistic bodies, if it were not the fact that the unions and the Communists are so inextricably interlocked as to make distinctions unnecessary.

That this is not a judgement dictated by mere adverse attitude may be seen from the following facts:

The Workmen's Circle has 800 branches throughout the United States and is officered by Jews throughout. The membership is 98 per cent foreign-born and is Jewish in like portion.

Among the higher officers of this organization are Joseph Schlessinger, Sydney Hillman, Benjamin Schlossberg, Sam Feinstein and J. B. Salutsky. The names will probably have become familiar to the reader by this time. They form part of the interlocking directorate so commonly found among Jewish organizations, a system which finally heads up in the executive committee of the Kehillah which also composes the leaders of the American Jewish Committee, of which the great public lights of Jewry are members.

Schlessinger is president of the Union of Ladies' Garment Workers, and made a trip to Russia in behalf of communism in the United States, to finance which the members of the Communist party were assessed $1.50 each.

Hillman is president of the Amalgamated Clothing Workers of America.

Schlossberg is secretary of the Amalgamated Clothing Workers of America.

Feinstein is secretary of the United Hebrew Trades.

Salutsky is food commissar to the striking Amalgamated, and is national director of Bolshevik propaganda carried on by his crowd. They are, of course, all Jews.

The line-up is this: Hebrew trade union leaders are also members of the Workmen's Circle and of the Communist party, and the majority of their trade union followers go with them into the other associations. The reverse process is this: Communism and radical Bolshevism then find their way to the consciousness of the American public by the Bolshevik demands of the so-called trade unions of Jewry.

An extreme defense of all this activity might be that these Jewish leaders and workers are only enamored of the idea of Bolshevism, are playing with it academically, and are not to be considered as actively the proponents of a form of government contrary to the Constitution of the United States and to be established by "direct action."

This defense, however, appears insufficient when confronted by another set of facts in which these same union leaders and Communists are shown to be in communication with the Soviet government in the United States—and the Soviet government in the United States is not a mere idea, it is a program. Moscow has repeatedly stated that the purpose of the Lenin-Trotsky government has been World Revolution. And one reason for the colossal economic failure of the Soviet governmental experiment has been the Jewish Soviet leaders' neglect of their proper work to follow this fetish of World Revolution. If one-tenth the effort had been made to govern and feed Russia that has been made to sow Bolshevik ideas in other countries, Russia might today have been in a less unhappy plight. Propaganda is the sole art which the Bolsheviks have mastered.

This Soviet government in the United States, therefore, must be regarded as an advance post of World Revolution. It is so regarded by those who know anything about it. It is so regarded by those who ordered the deportation of L. C. A. K. Martens, the "Soviet Ambassador." Martens was announced to be here for the purpose of opening up trade relations with the United States. He had a vast fund of gold—indeed, it was to explain his gold hoard that he used the story about trade relations. The Government of the United States judged, however, that his purpose here was World Revolution—and the government was right.

Martens has departed but the Soviet Embassy remains. As stated in a former article, Martens' successor is Charles Recht, who is a Russian Jew about 36 years of age. In the same building with Recht is Isaac A. Hourwich, another Russian Jew and attorney, whose office is supposed to be the headquarters whence proceeds much of the Russian Bolshevik propaganda.

Now, the people who go to the offices of Recht and Hourwich are the same people whose names we have been tracing all through this interlocker, with some notable additions. Into the sanctum of ambassadorial Bolshevism in the United States, come, of course, Recht the representative and Hourwich the attorney for Lenin and Trotsky in this country.

Another caller is Judah L. Magnes, head of the New York Kehillah. He is a rabbi without a synagogue, an extreme extremist, a master of the language of agitation, and pro-Bolshevist in his influence and associations. He is credited with being the mediator between rich Jews and radicals when the latter are in need of funds. This is the Judah L. Magnes, head of the Kehillah, who tried to tell New York newspaper reporters what a weak and innocent foundling the New York Kehillah is; the same Judah L. Magnes whom the American Hebrew tried to picture as a diaphanous idealist broken-hearted because the ghetto doesn't fall in with his educational schemes. The Kehillah is not an educational institution; it is not a welfare institution in the charitable sense; it is a nerve-center of Jewish power; in Rabbi Magnes' own words, "a clearing house"; and if it amounted to nothing politically and nationally, the men who are now prominent in it would soon desert it. Kehillah is just what the word signifies—the whole Jewish Community.

Then, of course, there are Benjamin Schlessinger again, president of the Ladies' Garment Workers, and Sydney Hillman, president of the Amalgamated Clothing Workers, and Joseph Schlossberg, another Amalgamated official whose Bolshevik utterances were quoted earlier in this article, and others of the Hebrew trades crowd whose radical relationships have been shown.

In addition, there are certain immigration inspectors from Ellis Island—all Jews, of course; occasionally a courier from Russia who has slipped into the country for a secret purpose; occasionally also a courier to Russia bearing messages from Recht and Hourwich.

Then I.W.W. leaders—Jews. Among them Baletin, secretary of the I.W.W. Metal Machinery Workers' Branch, and Peltner, joint secretary of the I.W.W. branches in New York. In close touch with these Jewish radicals are a number of revolutionists of other countries, representing various violent programs against the established order.

It is through the office of Charles Recht that passports, issued by the State Department of the government of the United States, are being viséed. This statement refers to a regular practice known to have been followed until a few days preceding this writing, and there is no reason to believe it has since been altered. Ambassador Recht, or Acting Ambassador Recht, or whatever he may be called, is in close touch with Soviet authorities and has full notice of all their intentions regarding American affairs.

A frequent subject of conferences in Recht's office is the Soviet propaganda in America. Men like Hillman and Schlossberg and Schlessinger are merely liaison officers between the Soviets and the Hebrew trades unions. The orders received from Moscow are thus transmitted to the Jews in America, and are obeyed along perfectly defined lines.

Of course, Rabbi Magnes, head of the New York Kehillah, could hardly be expected to remain in ignorance of what the whole Kehillah knows. And that Magnes is temperamentally a radical, any two-minute perusal of his speeches will show. He is head of what Schlessinger calls the "gigantic, wide-branched Kehillah," the foremost political racial organization in this country, a close community of a single racial type which has its own code and its own customs and its own method of gaining its ends.

This is not the whole story by any means. Schlessinger and Schlossberg and Hillman and the rest are leaders, but they are not the higher-ups. The connections run straight up to the lofty heights of those who dwell in palaces and sway the finances of the nation, and to those who play large parts in the government of the United States. The Jews who finance radical publications—good conservative Jews who form the standing illustration in the argumentative question, "What possible gain can they hope from Bolshevism?" Jews who pull official wires to gain immunity and privilege for known traitors and revolutionists. Jews who replenish the coffers of dangerous elements. It is a long story, and all of it does not require telling, for the point to be gained is not that everyone should be told, but that the involved persons should be aware that it is known, proved, safely put away, in hope that the occasion to use it may never come. However, it is due the public to tell at least a part of it.

The Jewish leaders never played so stupid a card as when they endeavored to minimize the Kehillah and the place it fills. Nor did their Gentile echoes ever fall for so miserable an imposition.

The Dearborn Independent, issue of 23 April 1921

51: Will Jewish Zionism Bring Armageddon?

When the British Army passed into Jerusalem in the memorable capture of the city in 1917, the Protocols went in with it. A symbolic circle was thus closed, though not in the way the Protocolists had hoped. The man who carried the Protocols knew what they signified, and they were carried not in triumph but as the plans of the enemies of world liberty.

Zionism is the best advertised of all present Jewish activities and has exerted a greater influence upon world events than the average man realizes. In its more romantic aspects it makes an appeal to Christian as well as to Jew, because there are certain prophecies which are held to concern the return of the Jews to Jerusalem. When this return takes place, certain great events are scheduled to ensue.

Because of this admixture of the religious sentiment, it will be rather difficult for a certain class of people to scrutinize modern Political Zionism; they have been too well propagandized into believing that political Zionism and the "return" promised by the prophets are the same thing. Having succumbed to the initial confusion of mistaking Judah for Israel they have entirely mistaken the ancient writings that relate to these two, and have made the single tribe of Judah (whence comes the name Jew) the hub around which all history and humanity swing. Judah was the tribe with which Israel could not live in peace over two thousand years ago, and which has the fateful gift of stirring up the same kind of dissension today. And yet no one ever thought of charging the Ten Tribes of Israel with "anti-Semitism."

Zionism is challenging the attention of the world today because it is creating a situation out of which many believe the next war will come. To adopt a phraseology familiar to students of prophecy, it is believed by many students of world affairs that Armageddon will be the direct result of what is now beginning to be manifested in Palestine.

For these, if for no other reasons, the subject becomes important.

With Zionism as a dream of pious Jews this article has nothing to do. With Zionism as a political fact, every first class government is now compelled to have something to do. It is a bigger question than the German indemnities or American immigration, because it lies back of both, and is rapidly proceeding under cover of both.

It is worthy of note, if only in passing, that Zionism in the active modern political sense took its rise racially and geographically where Bolshevism arose, namely, in Russia, and that its center, the seat of its Inner Actions Committee, was at Berlin. There was always a close relationship between the Zionists of Russia and the New York Kehillah, as is evidenced by public utterances made in Russia after the Revolution in which the Kehillah is extolled.

At the time the war was declared in 1914, the Inner Actions Committee was spread about in various countries. For example: Dr. Schmarya Levin, of Berlin, was in the United States and remained here. He was Russian rabbi, German scholar, and cosmopolitan. Although his headquarters were Berlin, he remained in the United States and became recognized as the leader of the leaders of Zionism, until the great Jewish shift to Versailles. Another member of the Inner Actions Committee was one Jacobson, who was in Constantinople. "When he saw that Constantinople could no longer be the center of Zionist politics, he left and went to Copenhagen, Denmark, where in a neutral country he could be of practical usefulness to the Zionists by transmitting information and funds." (Guide to Zionism, page 80.) In fact, the entire Inner Actions Committee, with headquarters at Berlin, moved freely through a war-locked world, the only exceptions being Warburg and Hantke—and there was no need for the Berlin Warburg to move about, for there were others who represented him.

Dr. Levin gave his sanction for the shifting of the center of Jewish gravity from Berlin to America, and "as early as August 30, 1914, a month after the outbreak of war, an extraordinary conference of American Zionists was called in New York."

What this change of seat meant, has formed the subject of much discussion. In 1914 the Jews apparently knew more about the probable duration of the war than did the principals. It was not to be a mere excursion through Belgium, as some fancied. There was time to dicker, time to show the value of certain Jewish support to the governments. Germany gladly pledged the land of Palestine to the Jews, but the Jews had already seen what Wilhelm had done in that ancient state when he enthroned himself on the Mount of Olives. Evidently the Allies won in the contest of making promises, for on November 2, 1917, when

General Allenby was pushing up through Palestine with his British Army, Arthur James Balfour, the British secretary of state for foreign affairs, issued the famous declaration approving Palestine as a national home for the Jewish people.

"The wording of it came from the British foreign office, but the text had been revised in the Zionist offices in America as well as in England. The British declaration was made in the form in which the Zionists desired it, and the last clauses were added in order to appease a certain section of timid anti-Zionist opinion." (Guide to Zionism, pages 85–86.)

Now please read the declaration and note the italicized clauses just referred to:

"His Majesty's Government view with favor the establishment in Palestine of a national home for the Jewish people and will use their best endeavors to facilitate the achievement of this object, it being clearly understood that nothing shall be done which may prejudice the civil and religious rights of non-Jewish communities in Palestine, or the rights and political status enjoyed by Jews in any other country."

Zionism is of particular interest, not merely because of the quarrels which have arisen among the leaders over money—it is the war of "interest" against "capital"—but also because of the light it throws on the two great armies of Jews in the world, the way in which they use their power where they can, and the trouble that always embroils the nations which become Jewish tools.

People sometimes ask why Jewry, which is capitalistic, should favor Bolshevism, which is the announced enemy of capital. It is an interesting question. Why should a New York Jewish financier, an officer of the government of the United States, help finance a "Red" publication which even our tolerant government cannot stomach? In addition to the fact that it is only "Gentile capital" that is attacked, the answer is that the Jew who has fallen for the worship of the Golden Calf is anxious to keep in the good graces of the Jew of the East—the Mongolian Jews—who are rampaging against orderly systems of society.

It is quite useful when there is a revolution in Paris to have the 600 houses which you may own spared by the incendiary mobs—as were Rothschild's houses. Zionism has been one of the subjects upon which Western and Eastern Jew can unite. Indeed, it was the Eastern Jew that compelled the Western Jew to take a favorable stand on this matter. The Jewish gentlemen who are receiving the freedom of our cities today in their various aspects as "German" and "British" scientists are Eastern

Jews. They have come to a contest with the Jews of America on the question of Money. The Jews of America have smothered some very ugly charges. The Jews of the East, more recently of Germany or England, are not likely to be browbeaten by the moneybags of Jewish New York, for the Eastern type of Jew knows of a situation in which money is the most useless thing in the world—and that is why he is feared and favored by Western Jewry of the Golden Calf.

The Jewish defenders are just now capitalizing the "split" in Jewry. The real split in Jewry will come when Jews of vision begin to support the attempts which have been made to liberate the Jews from their leaders. This internal squabble means nothing but a squabble of leaders; but when the Jews themselves divide, one side for twentieth century light and the destruction of the class power of selfish leaders, then may we look up hopefully.

When the Jew recognizes the honesty of his critics and the righteousness of what they charge, then will there be a "split," but not before. The division in Jewry as evidenced by the contempt of the revolutionary party for the financial party, and as even more strongly evidenced by the fear of the revolutionary party by the financial party, is being brought about by the insincerity of the Western Jew's Zionism. The Western Jew says that the United States is the Promised Land, profits and interest are the "milk and honey" and New York is Jerusalem; the Jew of Russia has another view.

A knowledge of Political Zionism is worth while also as an authoritative illustration of what the Jew does when he is in power. Heretofore there has been Russia to illustrate this, but now there is Palestine. With every fact against them, with every traveler and observer giving them the lie direct, there are still Jewish spokesmen and poor befuddled "Gentile fronts" who insist that Bolshevism is not Jewish and that Russia is not now governed by Jews. It is just this constant denial of facts, this failure to use their opportunity to be honest, that is going to be the judgement of Jewish leaders. Bolshevism all over the world, not in Russia only, but in New York, in Chicago, in New Orleans, in San Francisco, is Jewish.

However, there is no need further to insist upon that, except occasionally to add confirmatory illustrations of it. More to the present point is Palestine. It will be very difficult for the most irresponsible Jewish spokesman to deny that Palestine is Jewish. The government is Jewish, the plan of procedure is Jewish, the methods used are Jewish. Does anyone rise to deny that? Scarcely.

Very well, Palestine will do to illustrate the genius of the Jew when he comes to power.

Professor Albert T. Clay, in the *Atlantic Monthly* (will anyone declare that this long-established and thoroughly respectable Boston publication is "anti-Semitic"?) warns us that the information about Palestine which we receive in America comes to us through the Jewish Telegraph Service (which is the Associated Press of world-wide Jewry) and the Zionist propaganda. "The latter," he says, "with its harrowing stories of pogroms in Europe, and its misrepresentations of the situation in the Near East, has been able to awaken not a little sympathy for the Zionist propaganda."

This propaganda of pogroms—"thousands upon thousands of Jews killed"—amounts to nothing except as it illustrates the gullibility of the press. No one believes this propaganda, and governments regularly disprove it. But the fact that it continues indicates that something besides facts is necessary to keep the scheme going.

In Jerusalem, as this is being written, martial law is proclaimed. There has been a struggle between the native inhabitants, whom the Balfour declaration sought to protect, and the new-come Jews. As in the famous Easter disorders of last year, the wounded in the hospitals show that the Jews were armed and the natives fought with whatever weapons they could find on the spot; the conclusion of all impartial observers under the circumstances being that the Jews prepared for and sought the fight with unprepared natives.

The mark of disorder perpetrated by the Jews is all over the place, the "persecuted" turned persecutor, and lest this should be charged to the general wildness of the people in Palestine let it be said that the rioters were only expressing in deeds what cultivated American and English Jews have expressed in words—namely, that the lawful inhabitants of the land ought to be driven out, in spite of governmental promises to the contrary. One of the first Easter rioters, Jabotinsky, whom the British authorities sentenced to 15 years in prison, was released immediately upon the arrival of Sir Herbert Samuel, and is now traveling in state, and is talked of as a possible successor to Sir Herbert, although he is originally one of the Russian Bolsheviki come down to practice the gentle arts of that tribe in Palestine.

The government is Jewish. Sir Herbert Samuel is High Commissioner, representing the power of the British Government, which holds the mandate over Palestine. The head of the judicial department, who appoints the judges of Palestine, is a Jew. Christian or Moslem judges who do not give the Jews a shade the better of the proceedings are ousted—a condition not unknown in New York. Chaim Weizman is head of the department of works—he is a Jew, now traveling in this country and having the polite lie passed to him occasionally by Judge Julian W. Mack. In fact, at the heads of all departments are Jews, a former New York Jew being head of the department of immigration, who has made splendid rules for the protection of Palestine from an undesirable class of Jews, rules so well adapted for the purpose that if the Congress of the United States should adopt them the cry of "persecution" would girdle the world.

It is to be noted that the Jewish government of Palestine is very much like that of Russia—mostly foreign. Trotsky came from the East Side of New York. A gentleman recently released from Bolshevik custody told the writer that the governor of his prison was an ordinary Jew who formerly lived on Fourteenth street, Detroit. Practically every big American city is represented in the Bolshevik government of Russia. There is another full-fledged government waiting in this country for service wherever necessary.

The methods being adopted to get the land are such as will fill the world with indignation once the world fully understands what is being done. And that it is done with the knowledge and approval of the Zionist Commissioner is indicated by the fact that he suspended the activities of the British officer who endeavored to stop the abuse. It was the old game of lending money at an exorbitant rate of interest to people hard pressed by war and crop failure, and then seizing their land when they could not pay. The bank that did this was the Anglo-Palestine Bank, a Zionist concern. This British officer, to save the people and the land, made arrangements with a British bank to lend them money at 6 1/2 per cent, with five years to pay. If payment failed, the land was to go to the government for redistribution, not to the Zionist bank. This was the humane plan which the Zionist Commissioner forbade, whereupon the British officer resigned. Some effort was afterward made to redress the terrible act, but there it stands as the well-considered action of Jewry in power.

Then follows what is described by every impartial observer as an "arrogant" attempt to expropriate everything in sight. In Russia it could have been done very easily under the plea of "nationalization," but there was Great Britain whose laws do not condone theft. The only schools that have been established in Jerusalem have been built and manned by the so-called "Gentiles," although the Jews of Jerusalem have been the pensioners of world-wide Jewry for centuries. As long ago as 1842 Dr. Murray M'Cheyne noted that the Jerusalem Jews cared nothing for schools because their children were only growing up into pensioners too. But Christians, with a warm regard for the Holy City, set about to improve the miserable condition of the Jewish inhabitants, and thus it came that at the time of the Zionist invasion a considerable number of Jewish children were in attendance at the schools. The new-come Zionist leaders demanded that the best of the schools be given up to them. Of course, this was refused.

"The Council of Jerusalem Jews" then caused it to be published in the Hebrew daily that parents who did not withdraw their children from the schools would be punished. And now look at the typical punishments threatened: If any parent refused whose name was on the list of the American Relief Fund, the relief would be withdrawn. An interesting bit of news to subscribers to that fund.

Doctors would be forbidden to visit the families that had children attending the enlightened schools.

Their names would be sent to the blacklist at the places where circumcision was performed, so that new-born descendants of the recalcitrants might be refused the rite of Moses.

They would be denied all share in Zionist benefits or funds.

If they were in business, they would be boycotted.

If they were workmen, they could get no work.

"Anyone who refused, let him know that it was forbidden for him to be called by the name of Jew. They will be fought by all lawful means. Their names will be put upon a monument of shame and their deeds made to reproach them to the last generation. If they are supported, their support will cease. If they are rabbis, they will be moved far from their office. They shall be put under the ban and persecuted, and all the world will know that in this justice there has been no mercy."

It is the Jewish Bolshevist spirit all over again, that spirit which so many people have been vainly endeavoring to reconcile with the Russian temperament—because it is so un-Russian.

It is tyranny, and not the tyranny of strength, but of meanness and darkness. It is now perfectly clear what was meant by Dr. McInnis, who is Anglican Bishop of Jerusalem, when he said: "The emigrants so far brought in (to Palestine, under the Commission) did not include many respectable English Jews; but they did include a great number of Russians, Poles and Rumanians, many of them thoroughly Bolshevik in their attitude to the government."

If this spirit obtains at the beginning of a movement which the Christian world has been taught by propaganda to regard as a profoundly religious and respectable exodus, it burdens the imagination to forecast what will be done in a period of full and unquestioned rule.

Observing and weighing the events and tendencies of Jewish rule thus far in Palestine, it is not difficult to see the purpose in it all. The Jews still distrust their ability to make a State. They do not distrust the world's willingness to let them have a State; indeed, it is amazing how naturally the Jews place confidence in that portion of the world they have always affected to despise. But deep-seated in the Jew is a distrust of himself. He doesn't know how his people will contrive to live together. He doesn't know how they will contrive to drop the principles and practices which are so destructive of social comity elsewhere. And he feels that, patient as the mandatory power may be now, it is doubtful how long that patience will hold out under the blunders and brutalities that will be inseparable from Zionist rule, if any deductions can be drawn from the facts at hand. Therefore, feeling that the time may be short, he is endeavoring by such actions as interference with the cultural question, with the racial rights if the natives, and by such schemes as the land-grabbing device described above, to get so strong a hold on the situation as will seriously complicate it whenever Great Britain shall feel it to be her duty to the world to step in and attempt to bring some kind of order out of the chaos.

It begins to be very clear that Jewish nationalism will develop along the line of enmity to the rest of the world. Already the dangerous proposal has been made to organize a Jewish army for the protection of the Suez Canal. Instead of thinking of roads and farmsteads, of vineyards and oil presses, of schools and sanitary villages, the Jews are thinking of elevating themselves into the military power that shall stand between East and West on that most strategic strip of ground in the world. The whole situation is fraught with danger, and men who wish well to the Jews are alarmed and saddened by the prospect.

There are three elements of danger in the situation as it exists today: the overwhelmingly predominant Bolshevik element that is being poured into Palestine; the intense, egotistic and challenging nationalism that Zionists exhibit even before they get a potato patch—the taste for world politics and world power; and the racial confusion which now exists in Palestine.

These combined are dynamite. The first is more vital than many realize. Already the Jews who have gone to Palestine at great sacrifice and for pious reasons are complaining that instead of the Psalms of David the people are singing songs of the Red Revolution, and instead of meeting for instruction and prayer there are riotous gatherings extolling Trotsky as Messiah and the Soviet as the kingdom of heaven. On the third anniversary of the Jewish Revolution in Russia, the streets of Jerusalem were placarded with sentiments of blasphemy and treason, and May Day this year was devoted to the exaltation of anarchy.

This fact will be of interest to students of prophecy. It is as certain as any human forecast can be that this sort of thing will not be permitted to go forward in the face of the world. It is unimaginable that the nations responsible to humanity for the conduct of that important strip of territory will remain supine while Bolshevism spreads under the false pretense of a religious movement favored by Christendom. An attempt will be made to stop it. The Jews of Palestine will turn on their sponsor nation. The Jews of Russia will come down to help. Great Britain and perhaps the United States will defend the old pure vision of a Jerusalem redeemed. Then will come to pass the prophecy of Zachariah: "And Judah also shall fight against Jerusalem."

Judah also! It is a thought to make a Jew bethink himself where the lawlessness of the East and the materialism of the West will lead him. Against Jerusalem! What a terrible ending of Judah's present mad delusion.

Palestine has been called the center of the earth. It is. The power that controls Palestine controls the world. Although exercising no sovereignty over the land itself, Great Britain's control of adjacent waters and of Egypt and Persia and India, forms the key of her power. The white race has thus far been the Chosen People to whom the dominion of the earth has been given. Palestine is the key to world military strategy and trade. In question 12 of the *Questions and Answers* published by the department of education, Zionist Organization of America, this occurs:

> 12. What are the commercial possibilities of Palestine?
>
> The location of Palestine between the three continents favors foreign trade.

All this lends itself to dreams of future glory, and many Christian friends of the Jew have pleased themselves by conceiving an universal

Hague at Jerusalem and a new social order going out to bless the nations from Zion. It is the idea conveyed by men like A. A. Berle in books like "The World Significance of a Jewish State." All this might be expected if the Jews of today were Old Testament people, anxious to re-establish the social laws of Moses, which are conceded to be the best safeguards ever devised against pauperism on the one hand and plutocracy on the other. But Palestine has not fallen into the hands of that sort of Jews. Before the dream can be fulfilled Judah must come to himself, as he has not yet, for from of old the Word is—"And Judah also shall fight against Jerusalem."

The racial situation in Palestine just now is very delicate. Americans do not understand it. The Zionist propaganda has always been accepted on the assumption that Palestine is the Jews' land and that they only need help to go back. It is an historical and political fact that Palestine has not been the Jews' land for more than 2,000 years. There are in Palestine 500,000 Moslems, 105,000 Christians and 65,000 Jews. The industry of the land is agriculture. Engaged in this are 69 per cent of the Moslems, 46 per cent of the Christians and 19 per cent of the Jews. Neither numerically nor industrially have they held the land. Yet, as the result of a war bargain, it is handed over to them as regardless of the native inhabitants as if Belgium had been handed over to Mexico. Many of the natives are Semites, like the Jews, but they do not want the Jews among them.

That is a strange fact for those who use the term "anti-Semitism"; why do real Semites also dislike the Jews? Surely Semites are not victims of "anti-Semitism."

The Balfour Declaration, as well as the terms of the Mandate adopted at San Remo, recognized the rights of the native races. Indeed, everyone who knows about the people who have been native to Palestine for 2,000 years recognizes their rights, everybody except the Jews. Bethlehem was a Christian town, as befits the birthplace of Christ. Yet the Jews have contrived that 2,000 Bethlehemites leave Palestine rather than submit to what they see coming. The other races are not so placid about it, hence the trouble. It is now that the last clauses, added as the Zionist historian declares, "in order to appease a certain section of anti-Zionist opinion," begin to get a meaning for the reader. Was the purpose only to quiet disturbing questions until all the arrangements were made? Evidently. It was then a dishonest appeasement! Such may have been the Zionists' intention, but no one need expect perjury on the part of the responsible nations. The end of the matter will see those last clauses redeemed by honest application of their terms to the people involved.

General Allenby promised those native races of Palestine that their rights would be respected. So did the Balfour Declaration. So did the San Remo Conference. So also did President Wilson in the twelfth of his Fourteen Points.

But Judah says, "Let them get out!" "The last clauses were added in order to appease a certain section of timid anti-Zionist opinion."

"Let them get out!" says Israel Zangwill. "We must gently persuade them to 'trek.' After all, they have all Arabia with its million square miles, and Israel has not a square inch. There is no particular reason for the Arabs to cling to those few kilometers. To fold their tents and silently to steal away is their proverbial habit; let them exemplify it now." Aside from the falsity of using the term "Arab," there is the delightful Jewishness of it—let them give it up to us, we want it! Americans have been in their land less than 150 years as a nation, and there is China and Arabia or Siberia for us to go to if we should want to, but we prefer our own country, and so do the native races of Palestine, who have dwelt there for 2,000 years.

The watchmen on the towers of the world are alarmed at what seems brewing in Judah's geographical caldron.

The Dearborn Independent, issue of 28 May 1921

52: How the Jews Use Power—By an Eyewitness

The Jewish Question continues to mount the scale of public attention, attracting ever a higher type of mind to the discussion of its significance. When *The Dearborn Independent* first began to print some of the results of its research into the Question, the initial response was largely from those who disliked the Jew because he was a Jew. This class expected to find in *The Dearborn Independent* a spokesman for all their coarse humor and abuse.

The method that was followed by this paper, however, was not abusive enough, nor bitter enough to satisfy Jew-baiters and Jew-haters, and gradually a new response from another class began to be heard, which by this time has attained massive proportions. The better class of people, seeing that racial and religious prejudice had no part in the work, began to consider the Question with relation to our American life and the future of this nation as a Christian people.

Upon this ascent of the discussion to its proper plane, the better periodicals began to give thoughtful attention to the matter. These publications have been referred to in previous articles. There is to be added to the list the *Century Magazine* for September, which contains an article by Herbert Adams Gibbons which clearly intends to be fair and is certainly able, in spite of a difference of opinion that might exist with regard to some of the author's conclusions.

Mr. Gibbons states some matters more plainly than they have been stated outside the pages of *The Dearborn Independent*, and some matters he states just as plainly; and he will be justified by the unprejudiced reader.

One of the most notable studies of the Jewish Question has come out of the University of the South, at Sewanee, Tennessee. It is entitled "Zionism and the Jewish Problem," the author being the Rev. Dr. John P. Peters, formerly canon residentiary of the Cathedral of St. John the Divine, Morningside Heights, New York, also rector emeritus of St. Michael's Church, New York, and professor of New Testament Languages and Literature in the University of the South. The article has been reprinted from the *Sewanee Review* and makes a brochure of 29 pages.

Dr. Peters begins with an historical sketch of the development of the two lines of thought among the Jews: the nationalistic which made for exclusiveness, and the religious which made for inclusiveness, and he describes the domination of the latter by the former with the coming of modern Zionism, which hc finds to be racial and not religious. He says "the dominant control of the Zionist party is at present in the hands of those who are not religious but merely racial Jews." He believes that the development of race-consciousness along these lines "must be inevitably in the end to make the Jews bad citizens of the United States or of any other country and to keep alive and increase the hostility to the Jews . . ."

This monograph by Dr. Peters will repay study. By permission, *The Dearborn Independent* reprints the article from page 20 to the end, this portion being selected because it deals with Dr. Peters' testimony as an eyewitness of certain conditions in Palestine: (The italics are ours, there being none in the university reprint.)

The experiment of the Zionist homeland is now being tried. It is too early to determine fully how it will work, but it is at least of interest to consider its manifestations so far. My earliest contact with Zionism and Zionistic influences in Palestine dates from 1902. When I first visited Palestine, in 1890, the Jews in Jerusalem were almost exclusively of old oriental Sephardic families. Jerusalem was then still the old Jerusalem within the walls.

There were no houses without. Jewish colonization, economic and philanthropic in character, had just then begun on the Sharon plain, but what little there was in the way of colonization was a feeble, unsuccessful exotic—an attempt to replace the persecuted Jews of Russia on the land, where, however, the Jew, unused to manual and especially farm labor, sat under an umbrella to protect himself from the sun and engaged native Syrians to do the work.

On my next visit, in 1902, more colonies had been planted, and a serious effort was being made to turn the Jewish colonists into farmers. The majority of Jews who had come to Palestine, however, were settled about Jerusalem, and the new Jerusalem without the walls was larger, in space at least, than the old Jerusalem within. The Alliance Israelite had developed there splendid schools to teach agriculture, and manual and industrial arts. I was urgently solicited by the management to visit and inspect these schools. Here I found Jew, Moslem and Christian working side by side without prejudice. This was, in my judgement, the best work of any sort being done in Palestine, for two reasons: first, these schools were teaching the dignity and the worth of manual labor, which the oriental of all sorts had theretofore despised, regarding it as unworthy of any man of intelligence or capacity; secondly, because they brought Moslem, Christian and Jew together on a plane of common work and common worth, the most valuable agent for the breaking down of those ancient prejudices, religious, racial and social, which have been the curse and bane of the land.

I was asked to put this down in writing because, I was told, great pressure was being exerted—I regret to say, especially from America—to prevent the management from continuing this particular work of teaching the Jew, Christian and Moslem on the same plane, the demand being that the Jew should not be brought into such contact with the Moslem and the Christian, and that he alone should be trained, that he might not be infected, as it were, by the others, and that they might not be prepared to compete with him for possession of the land. This spirit I met in a more thoroughly organized and offensive form on my latest visit in 1919 and 1920.

I found immense progress in the development of agricultural colonies. There was still difficulty in persuading the Jew, except only the African or Arabian Jew, to do the actual work of the colony, but colonies were prospering, and fruit-culture, vine-culture and especially the manufacture of wine and liquors on a grand and most scientific scale, had progressed wonderfully. In general, the land occupied by those colonies was not in a proper sense ancient Jewish land. They were on the Sharon and Esdraelon plains and in the extreme upper end of the Jordan Valley; but those regions were being enriched, and the country at large benefited by the colonists.

The great bulk of the Jews were still gathered in Jerusalem as heretofore, and there were on one hand the intellectuals and on the other the parasitic or pauperized Jew, what would ordinarily be regarded as the very best and the very worst. Life in the colonies was often very sweet and very lovely, a wholesome, normal family life, and an exhibition in peace and prosperity of what religious Judaism at its best may be.

In Jerusalem one found the extremes of intensely narrow and bitter orthodoxy, and unbelief with extreme Bolshevik radicalism. Here, too, aggressive Zionism manifested itself in an attitude of bumptiousness and aggressiveness. The country was for the Jew. It belonged to him and he would shortly take possession. One was made to feel that one's presence in the land was objected to. The Hebrew press contained angry diatribes against the existence of Christian schools and missions. The attitude taken by these Zionists at first alarmed, then aroused and irritated enormously, the native population, both Christian and Moslem, making the Jew an object of dread and hatred as he had never been before.

I had opportunities to talk on intimate and friendly terms with leaders in all camps, albeit I was unable, through language difficulties, to communicate with the rank and file as freely as I should like to have done. I myself felt the annoyance and in some places the danger of the animosity aroused. Under government order I was not permitted to visit certain sections of the country on account of the raids or uprisings of the Arabs, partly due to animosity roused by their apprehension of the Jewish invasion, and partly due to banditry, which took advantage of that as an occasion.

In other parts it was difficult to travel, because any stranger, unless he could prove the contrary, was suspected of being an agent of the Zionists, spying out the land for possession by the Jews. It was difficult to obtain lodgings or food, and there were sometimes unpleasantly hostile demonstrations on account of these suspicions. Everywhere it was believed that the Jew by unfair means was seeking to oust the true owners and to take possession of their land.

In Jerusalem it was asserted that the Zionist funds, or the Jewish funds which the Zionists could influence or control, were used to subsidize Jewish artisans or merchants to underbid Christians and Moslems and thus oust them by unfair competition, and that similar means were being used to acquire lands or titles to lands. It was even believed by many that the English authorities were unduly favoring and helping the Jews in these endeavors, as is shown by a letter from a Christian in Jaffa published in the *Atlantic Monthly*:—

"We are already feeling that we have a government within a government. British officers cannot stand on the right side because they are afraid of being removed from their posts or ticked off."

From time immemorial the Jews the world over have contributed for the help of pious Jews in Jerusalem and the other sacred cities, Hebron, Tiberias and Safed, the so-called halukha, or dole, in return for which the Jews in those cities were to win merit for themselves and those who contributed to their support by study of the law, prayer and pious observances. St. Paul carried over the same practice into the Christian Church, causing alms to be collected in the different congregations to be transferred to Jerusalem for the benefit and support of the Christians living there. To this day annual collections are taken in the Roman Catholic churches throughout the world which go to the Franciscans for the same use in Jerusalem. The Greeks and Armenians have like customs. In the past there had been no prejudice with regard to these doles, but now, it was claimed, the Zionist committees were using the moneys thus collected or contributed to organize and help their people in a systematized attempt to gain the upper hand in the land.

Perhaps the attitude of the extremists who possessed the dominating power in the community can best be shown by the utterances of one of their own organs, written in Hebrew. (It should be stated that the English edition of this journal was, as a rule, quite different in its contents from the Hebrew edition.

One article, entitled, 'Malignant Leprosy,' is a denunciation of parents who allow their children to go to any school except those under the control of Jews and conforming to the demands of the local Zionist Committee. Parents are notified that a list has been made by the Zionist Committee of all children who are attending foreign schools, even though they are not subjected to any religious teaching, and it is demanded that they shall be withdrawn from those schools and placed in schools where they shall be taught the Hebrew language, customs and traditions, and kept separate from contamination by the Gentile, with his different ways and customs. Those teaching in foreign schools, or schools not complying with the conditions laid down by this committee, are ordered to withdraw from their positions.

The 'malignant leprosy' is the contamination by the outside world which results from education with the Gentiles. It is admitted in this article, in answer to protests, that the opportunities in some non-Jewish schools are better than in the Jewish schools—for example, in the teaching of foreign languages, so important for conducting business or securing employment; that there is greater diligence in instructing; and better hours and better care of pupils.

Nevertheless, parents are informed that they must sacrifice for the sake of their race those chances for their children, doing their best meanwhile to raise their own schools to the higher level. Those who are failing to live up to these ideals are designated as 'traitors' and by other opprobrious names, and the article ends with this threat of persecution to any who do not obey the orders of the Zionist Committee thus conveyed:

"Let him know at least that it is forbidden him to be called by the name of Jew and there is to him no portion or inheritance with his brethren, and if after a time they will not try to reform, let them know that we will fight against them by all lawful means at our disposal. Upon a monument of shame we will put their names for a reproach and blaming forever, and until the last generation shall their deeds be written. If they are supported, their support will cease, and if they are merchants, with a finger men will shoot at them, and if they are Rabbis, they will be moved far from their office, and with the ban shall they be persecuted, and all the people of the world shall know that there is no mercy in judgement."

This was followed about a month later by a second article, also in Hebrew, entitled 'Fight and Win,' which announced that the threatened persecution would now be carried out:

"The names of the traitorous parents and of the boys and girls who have not taken notice of the warnings ought to be published at once and without delay, in the papers and on public notices, placarded at the entrance of every street. The list of these names should be sent to the heads of every institution and to the rulers of the synagogues, to hospitals, to those who arrange and solemnize marriages, and to the directors of the American Jewish Relief Fund, and so on. It should be the title of 'Black List' and 'Traitors of Their People.'

An order should go forth to all, and if one of these men has a son, he shall not be circumcised; in case of death the body is not to be buried among Israelites; religious marriages will not be sanctioned; Jewish doctors will not visit their sick; relief will not be given to them when they are in need, if they are on the list of the American relief fund—in short, we must hunt them down until they are annihilated. Men will cry to them: "Out of the way, unclean, unclean!"

Because these people will be considered as malicious renegades, there can be no connecting link between them and us. Again, the society of young men and girls of Jerusalem must accept it as a principle to expel from their societies all those who visit these schools; to point the finger of scorn at them; and to make them see that they are put out of the camp. These traitor scholars, boys and girls, must understand themselves that they are sinners and transgressors, who are isolated, driven from all society, separated from the Jewish community, after they have once despised Israel and its holiness, and it will be interdicted to all sons of Israel to come near them . . . . War against the traitors among our people. War by all means legal. War without pity or mercy; that the traitors may know that they must not trifle with the sentiment of a people. Fight and win.

The Zionist Committee, of whom one was an American, followed this by a printed announcement that the time of grace had passed and that forthwith the names of those who were still refractory would be posted publicly on street-corners, and the boycott begin. Miss Landau, a devout Jewess, the head of the best and highest Jewish school for girls in the city, the Eva Rothschild School, one of those, however, whose pupils and teachers were threatened under these rulings because they would not follow the dictates of the Zionist Committee, appealed to the civil authorities. The committee was haled into court and the threatened boycott enjoined.

"With such an attitude on the part of Zionist leaders in Jerusalem it might be expected that violence would ensue. Easter is a time of great excitement and unrest in Jerusalem for Christians, Jews and Moslems alike, for with Easter coincide the Jewish Passover and the Moslem pilgrim feast of Nebi Musa, when Moslems gather from all over Palestine to hear sermons in the Haram Esh-Sherif, and then march to the so-called tomb of Moses near the Dead Sea. The religious excitement of that season which vents itself in curses of each against the others, is always likely to produce physical outbursts if the cursers come into contact with one another.

"The Turks wisely segregated at that time each religion in its own quarter. This, in spite of warnings and requests from the Moslem religious leaders, the English failed to do, either through ultra-confidence in the pax angelicana, or because of objections from Jewish representatives against such segregation as applied to them. For days beforehand hotheads among the Jews and Moslems were inciting to riot, and in their quarter Jewish trained bands were preparing for the conflict, a preparation of which Moslems from long wont probably had no need.

"On Easter morning, 1920, the fanatical Moslems of Hebron arrived at the Jaffa gate with their sacred banner, singing their songs of religious intolerance. There numerous Jews were waiting to greet them. The English Tommies with their officers were all in church. Whose insults were the worst and who struck the first blow is not clear. Battle was speedily joined. The Jews were better armed, with guns against the Moslem knives; but the Moslems were the better fighters. The city within the walls was speedily in their hands. The Jews living there were the old-time Sephardic families, dwelling close packed in miserable slums, with no sympathy with Zionism, peaceful and quite unprepared. Moslem fury vented itself on these poor wretches. Without the walls the Jews were in the vast majority.

"All told, by official count there were at that time 28,000 Jews, 16,000 Christians and 14,500 Moslems in Jerusalem. What the Moslem did within the walls the Jew endeavored to do without the walls. Before my eyes an Arab camp just below the great Jewish quarters was set upon, burned and plundered, the poor inhabitants fleeing for their lives while guns popped from the Jewish quarter. Two men were killed there. When the troops reached the scene the great bulk of rioters whom they rounded up were Jews.

"The subsequent court proceedings also seemed to place the chief responsibility for the outbreak on them. The major sentences were equally divided between Jews and Moslems, but of the criminals who received lighter sentences the majority were Jews. For a week we lived in a state of siege, not allowed to pass in or out of the city gates, or to show ourselves on roof or balcony after sundown, and for months there were guards at every turn, assemblies were prohibited and there was continual danger of a new outbreak.

"The appointment of Sir Herbert Samuel, a Jew, as governor of the new protectorate under the Zionist Mandate, greatly increased the excitement. In Moslem towns like Nablus it was openly said in my presence that no Jew might enter the place and live. The Christians, who had taken no part in the riots, were nevertheless to a man in sympathy with the Moslems, and one saw the curious spectacle of Cross and Crescent making common cause.

"It was prophesied that should Sir Herbert come as governor, he would never enter Jerusalem alive. In point of fact, he landed at Jaffa and came up to Jerusalem under strong guard, with machine-guns before and behind, and the following week made a visit to Nablus and Haifa in the same manner. That was the situation when I left Palestine. Sir Herbert had at that time just issued his declaration and his interpretation of the mandate. English officers and officials almost to a man were against the Zionist Mandate, and their utterances in many cases were extraordinarily frank. Some of the most prominent and best-trained sought transfers to other posts because of their feelings on the matter, and some resigned.

"It has since that time been extremely difficult to obtain reliable information of prevailing conditions. It would seem, however, from all the information I have been able to gather, that Sir Herbert, who is, I believe, not himself a Zionist, has acted with singular tact and discretion. He has shown great fairness and indicated his intention to govern with impartiality, granting no special favors to any, nor allowing outside committees or local organizations to dictate or assume to dictate unfair policies.

"When I left Palestine, Jews were leaving in considerable numbers, especially those claiming American citizenship, so that the outgo was larger than the income. Since then, if I may judge by reports, Jews have been coming in, chiefly from eastern European countries, some parasitic and objectionable, others of a higher type. Some of the latter, graduates of universities, both men and women, may be seen engaged in hard manual labor, I am told, building roads and the like, not despising to do such work in order to secure their Palestinian home and fulfill their aspirations.

"It is too soon to judge the future of the Zionist experiment in Palestine. If the English authorities will give fair play to all, and if the Jews will pursue the old policy of the Alliance Israelite and its schools of seeking to benefit all dwellers of the land alike, to break down, not to build up, religious, racial and social prejudices, then the Jew may perhaps overcome the present prejudice against him, and his invasion of Palestine may prove to be a blessing both to himself and to the land. The methods of those in control of the Zionist movement in Palestine while I was there were, however, aimed in the opposite direction and tended to make the Jew an object of hatred and violence wherever the opportunity for violence offered.

"This has been illustrated again by the recent bloody riot in Jaffa which compelled the expedition of a British warship to that port; and the order issued holding up all immigration shows that not Jaffa only but the whole country is unsafe. The Jews in Palestine are now protected only by force of British arms. Were the British troops withdrawn, the Jews would be exterminated by the angry natives, of whom the Moslems alone outnumber them in the ratio of more than ten to one; and with such action the neighboring countries would sympathize, yielding ready assistance if any were required. Mesopotamia and Egypt are seething with disaffection against British rule, and racial-religious ferment, and Palestine is to them and to the Arabs of Arabia a holy land included in the heritage of Islam. Moslem India also feels this keenly, and the British have been obliged to withdraw Moslem Indian troops from Palestine, because they will not fight fellow-Moslems.

"In this country the Jewish problem which we have hitherto had to face is not a result of religious antipathy. Religiously, politically, and economically, the Jew has the same opportunity as everyone else. The Jewish problem here has been merely a matter of social prejudice, resulting from the extremely difficult task of amalgamating with great rapidity an enormous population, alien in race, culture, custom and habit. In 1880 there were, according to Jewish statistics, 250,000 Jews in this country.

"The Jews now claim 3,500,000, for the most part an undistributed mass huddled together in a few of the great cities—one-third of them in New York. Coming in such great numbers in so short a time and herding together thus, intentionally or unintentionally they help one another to resist the process of Americanization. This enormously increases the incidence of social prejudice. Those who have no conscious prejudice either of religion or of race, are in danger of imbibing or developing such prejudice as a method of protection of their institutions, their traditions and their habits. The Zionist movement, with its intentional development of race consciousness and race peculiarity on the part of the Jew, is an additional obstacle against the efforts of those Jews and those Christians who are seeking to break down prejudice and to bring Jew and Christian together within a common recognition of the Golden Rule: that each should treat the other as he, in like instance, would wish to be treated by him. One of the greatest of English Jews, honored and respected by Jew and Christian alike for his learning, his philanthropy and his godly piety, says of this racial-political Zionism that it has broken his heart, and set the clock backward for his people a hundred years. The Christian lover of his country and his fellow-men may well express a similar feeling on his side."

The Dearborn Independent, issue of 17 September 1921

53: How Jews Ruled and Ruined Tammany Hall

Within the memory even of young men, Tammany Hall has been the synonym of all political trickery, in the vocabulary of popular criticism. Tammany Hall was held up as the worst example of boss rule and political corruption that it was possible to find in either of the parties. Its very name became a stigma.

But even the most unobservant newspaper reader must have observed the gradual fading out of Tammany Hall from public comment, the cessation of the bitter criticism, the entire absence of headlines bristling with ugly charges, and the calling of the hosts of good citizenship to do battle against the grim bossism that maintained its headquarters at the Wigwam.

Why this change? Is it due to the dying out of Tammany Hall as a political force? No, Tammany is still there, as any New York politician will tell you. Is it due, then, to a reform of that organization? No, the Tammany tiger has not changed its stripes. Then, perhaps, this change is due to public sentiment? Not at all. The explanation is to be found along other lines.

There was a time when fearless publications told the truth about Tammany, but *Harper's Weekly* and others which waged fierce war against the Tiger, have either gone out of existence or have fallen under control of the Jews. The silence which has shrouded certain matters must not be noted and set aside without reference to the changed control of the press. There was a time when public bodies like the Citizens' Union organized to oppose Tammany and to keep a volunteer vigil on its activities; these groups have succumbed to Jewish contributions and officership and no longer stand guard.

The outcry against Tammany seemed to be hushed the moment that Tammany patronage fell into the hands of New York Jews, where it now reposes, the Kehillah being the real political center, and Tammany but a distributing station—a sort of organizational "Gentile front" for the more powerful Kehillah. A few Tammany leaders are permitted to strut out in front, but everyone knows that from the Wigwam chiefs the power has departed, it is now to be found in Jewish conferences. Murphy is still the titular head of Tammany, but like a Samson shorn, he is not feared and obeyed as of yore. In fact, the Judaization of Tammany Hall is now complete. Once in a while the Irish—always a match for the Jews rear their heads and show battle, but for the most part Jewish money rules and the Tiger lies down.

Tammany Hall was one of the strongest political organizations ever seen in the United States, potent not only in municipal and state politics, but often exercising a decisive influence on national affairs. It was, without exaggeration, powerful.

If there is one quality that attracts Jews, it is power. Wherever the seat of power may be, thither they swarm obsequiously. As Tammany was power and the gate of power, it was natural that the Jews of the biggest Jewish city in the world should court it. Doubtless, they were also affected by the incongruity of the fact that in the biggest Jewish city, the most solid political power was non-Jewish. That was a condition which called for correction.

When the German Jewish banker, Schoenberg, came to this country under the name of August Belmont to represent the interests of the Rothschilds, his keen eye at once took in the situation and at once he began to court the favor of Tammany. He became a member and a supporter. It was good business for this Jewish banker, because the funds of the Rothschilds were heavily invested in New York tractions. The properties of city tractions were and to a great extent still are, as in all American cities, at the mercy of the local Tammany power, by whatever name it may be known. Belmont was insinuating himself under the wing of power to protect the investments for which he was responsible. August Belmont eventually attained the coveted eminence of Grand Sachem of the Tammany Society. The Belmont family for a time represented the sole Jewish banking support of Tammany Hall, but that honor is now divided among many.

In Richard Croker's day, when corruption went hand in hand with power, and power apparently was none the weaker for it, we find that this notorious leader's intimate friend, business partner and political associate was a Jew—Andrew Freedman. Freedman and Croker lived together at the Democratic Club in Fifth Avenue, Tammany politicians even then having become rich enough to despise Fourteenth Avenue. Freedman held the purse strings of the organization, as head of the Committee on Finance, and he was Croker's representative and mouthpiece when the chief went into exile on an over-sea estate.

The most recent Jewish power in Tammany Hall, and one of the most liberal contributors to Tammany campaign funds, is the lawyer, Samuel Untermeyer, whose specialty of recent years seems to be to serve as the battering ram of the Jewish power against interests which it wants destroyed, and whose efforts are usually camouflaged under exaggerated journalistic advertisements as being wholly in the public interest. Mr. Untermeyer is not in particularly good humor with Tammany these days, because of the recent defeat of his son, Irving Untermeyer, for a judgeship. There was somewhere a slip. The Jews deserted the Wilson ship anyway, apparently seeing what was coming in the way of retribution for the colossal and amazing mismanagement of war business which was principally in their hands; and in the ensuing mix-up, a scion of the house of Untermeyer tasted defeat.

Tammany numbers other Jews among its supporters. Nathan Straus, one of the owners of R. H. Macy & Company, has been for years an active member of the organization and one of the rulers of its inner councils. A Jewish ghetto politician, Henry M. Goldfogle, has represented the Jewish interests in Congress for a number of years, and expected to continue, but he slipped in the election and has recently been "taken care of" by a city appointment.

There is also Judge Rosalsky who has been implicated in a number of interesting matters which illustrate the completeness of the Jewish network of control in New York City. One might mention also M. L. Erlanger and Warley Platzek, justices of the supreme court of the state of New York, but if one began a list of the Jewish judiciary of that city, where would one end?

Another Tammanyite is Randolph Guggenheimer, founder of the corporation law firm of Guggenheimer, Untermeyer and Marshall—Untermeyer being the aforesaid grand inquisitor of Gentile activities generally and Marshall being head of the American Jewish Committee and the Kehillah.

It was doubtless necessary for a Jewry that contemplated control of the judiciary as well as special protection for certain powerful Jewish enterprises that are near enough to the borderline of the law to merit question—it was necessary to obtain control of the supreme political engine through which favors were disbursed in local politics. And control of such organizations can always be had by money. Not that the Jews threw themselves entirely into Tammany. The Jew's natural political home seems to be in the Republican party, for thither he returns after venture elsewhere. But his predilection for the Republican party does not move the Jew to make the mistake of being exclusively the partisan of one group. It is better, as he knows, to control both groups.

As a matter of political fact, strong as is the Jewish element in Tammany, it is still stronger in the ranks of the Republican party, while New York Socialism is completely headed and manned by Jews. This renders it extremely easy for the Jews to swing support in whichever direction they choose, and for Kehillah to fulfill any threat it may make. It also insures that any Jewish candidate on any ticket will be elected. The fluke in the case of young Untermeyer is perhaps not to be entirely explained politically; other causes were doubtless working in that matter.

It is a long time since Ferdinand Levy bore the distinction of being the first Jew in New York to hold a political job. He was only a coroner, and the man who appointed him was only a fire commissioner, but the fire commissioner was Richard Croker. And Levy was solidly backed by the Independent Order of B'nai B'rith, whose success in this matter laid the foundation for more ambitious demands later. But at the beginning, the Kehillah Jews adopted the ancient policy, not of putting forward their own people, but non-Jews who could be useful to Judah. The difference between pro-Jewish politicians who are not themselves Jews, and politicians of the Jewish race, is that the former in office can sometimes go further than the Jew in office can, without detection. This has been true at least up to this time, but it will probably not be true very long, now that the people's eyes are being opened. The Jewish officeholder is only standing for his race, but the "Gentile front" has betrayed the people for the pottage of Jewish favor.

Thus, in the early days of Tammany, indeed until comparatively recent years, we see the "Gentile front" in Tammany offices and basking in the glory of Tammany publicity, but in the background there is always his "Jewish control." This also is a formula for citizens who wish to know the meaning of things otherwise unexplainable—"look for the 'Jewish control.'" To this end, therefore, the Jews have been strong in all parties, so that whichever way the election went, the Jews would win. In New York it is always the Jewish party that wins. The campaign is staged as an entertainment, a diversion for the people; they are permitted to think and act as if they were really making their own government, but it is always the Jews that win. And if after having elected their man or a group, obedience is not rendered to the Jewish control, then you speedily hear of "scandals" and "investigations" and "impeachments," for the removal of the disobedient official. Usually a man with a "past" proves the most obedient instrument but even a good man can often be tangled up in campaign practices that compromise him.

It has been commonly known that Jewish manipulation of campaign matters has been so skillfully handled, that no matter which candidate was elected, there was ready made a sufficient amount of evidence to discredit him in case his Jewish masters needed to discredit him. To arrange this is part of the thoroughness of Jewish control. And, of course, the American people have been sufficiently trained to roar against the public official immediately the first Jewish political hound emits its warning bay.

Amazing as is the technique of the Jewish political process, the readiness with which the American people can be counted on to do their part in forwarding the game is still more amazing.

What Mr. Hylan, the present mayor of New York has done to merit chastisement, is scarcely clear to a non-partisan investigator. But the fact that the Jews have set out to "get" him for something is evident on every side. In the Untermeyer so-called "housing investigation," the people hauled up were non-Jews and the result of the whole business has been a stronger Jewish hold than ever on the housing affairs of New York. Jews are exempt from such inquisitions. The choice prey are non-Jewish business houses whose secrets may be forced and whose good name may be stained under cover of a legal procedure. There is such a thing as blackmail so entirely respectable as to be unsuspected.

Governor Sulzer, of New York, was the choice of the Jews. They subscribed money for his campaign, forced it on him, and kept careful account of it. Finally, under pressure of a compelling sense of justice, Sulzer pardoned a non-Jewish valet of an important Jewish New York family, a young man, whom a coterie of Jews very prominent in the political, financial and social worlds had contrived to "put away" for a period of 30 years. Sulzer had no option but to pardon young Brandt. But he paid the penalty. He was impeached. The Jews who supported him testified against him and their checks were used to assist his dismissal.

The story of young Brandt hangs heavily over the heads of some of the proudest Jewish names in New York.

Playing on both sides of the political fence, and always retaining a string on the men they elect to office, are two Jewish characteristics which should not fail to be reckoned with. *The Dearborn Independent*, in its recent articles showing the hand of Paul Warburg in the Federal Reserve System, was able to prove by Mr. Warburg's own words that his firm, Kuhn, Loeb & Company, during the three-cornered fight between Roosevelt, Taft and Wilson, supported all three. The Jewish owners of R. H. Macy & Company, New York, illustrate the same principle; while Nathan Straus looked after affairs at Tammany Hall, his brother and partner, Isador Straus, was one of the most active opponents of Tammany. Were the interests of the two men therefore different? Not at all.

Take the firm of Guggenheimer, Untermeyer and Marshall. This is a notable firm for the part it plays in the people's business. Every community in America has been affected by Louis Marshall's decisions as head of the American Jewish Committee. Untermeyer is the arch-inquisitor for Jewry. Randolph Guggenheimer, the founder of the firm, achieved the foremost influence of any except the Chief in the old Wigwam, and was a power to be reckoned with in all matters. But Louis Marshall is a "staunch" Republican and a member of the Republican Club. Here again is the favorite method of including all parties under the capacious wing of the Jewish program.

Hence the popularity of "Fusion" in New York City elections. It has become the fad, but its most notable purpose is to insure the election of a Jew whatever his politics may be. In some Assembly Districts it is impossible to find anyone but a Jew to vote for. When Otto A. Rosalsky, a jurist who was implicated in the Brandt scandal, was re-elected Judge of General Sessions in 1920, he was the "Fusion" candidate on both the Democratic and Republican tickets. It was perhaps fortunate for his candidacy that he was. The point just now is that whenever a candidate may be vulnerable, it is very desirable to forestall a fight upon him by eliminating all opposition before the election. "Fusion" is another matter that should be carefully scrutinized in behalf of American rule of American cities.

By the way things are going in New York, these inter-party and "fusion" expedients may soon be unnecessary, because in any event it will be most difficult to avoid electing a Jew. Of the candidates of all parties for the offices of justice of the supreme court of New York, numbering 26, 14 were Jews. Of the Democratic presidential electors, 13 were Jews. Of the Republican presidential electors, 14 were Jews. Of the Socialist presidential electors, 22 were Jews. The strength of Tammany had exactly the same source as the strength of the Kehillah, namely, in the foreign population; the difference being that the Kehillah had a more compact foreign mass to draw upon. But both the Jewish leaders and the Tammany leaders have always been alertly aware of the fact that their power depended upon an uninterrupted flow of immigration, to supply the losses sustained by the Americanization of the people. It is always the un-Americanized foreigner that makes the best material for the Kehillah's and Tammany's purposes. The Kehillah is based upon the principle of recognizing racial minorities, and Tammany has made a specialty of giving representation of racial minorities in its councils.

This was a liberal policy, and was thoroughly American in its original intent (as Tammany was a thoroughly American assemblage at its inception) but it was soon seized upon by the Jews and used to their own ends, and to the eventual ruin of all except Jewish representation. Thus all through the history of immigration activity, Tammany has been on the side of the wide open gate without any restrictions. The lower the type of immigrant, the more easily amenable it is to the ward boss's orders.

Tammany of recent years has been the able seconder of the Kehillah in all efforts to frustrate control of immigration. The third great influx of immigration into the United States occurred in 1884 and was really the cause of the beginning of the degeneration of Tammany Hall. The great wave was composed of Russian, Austrian and Hungarian Jews, whose arrival was followed by a memorable period of crime, the marks of which remain to this day. Indeed, the downfall of Richard Croker was a direct result.

At that time the police department and the police courts before which all criminal cases in the city were first brought, were in the hands of Tammany Hall. The result was a partnership between local government and crime which has not been duplicated outside of Semitic countries.

Immigrant Jews of the shadier type organized an association called The Max Hochstim Association, which was known during the Lexow Investigation as "The Essex Market Court Gang." One of its chief rulers was Martin Engel, Tammany leader of the Eighth Assembly District. The "king" of this Jewish district was a man named Solomon who had changed his name to the less revealing one of "Smith," and who became known as "Silver Dollar Smith" because of the fact that he ruled his little empire from the Silver Dollar Saloon, which gained its name from the silver dollars that were cemented into the floor of his place of business. This saloon was just opposite the Essex Market Court, which was thronged daily by hordes of Yiddish criminals, the bondsmen, false witnesses and lawyers.

Let not the fastidious reader deem it unnecessary to linger longer round the old police court at Essex Market, for out therefrom came a word which has fixed itself in common English speech—the term "shyster," by which a certain type of lawyer is described. A Clinton street lawyer named Scheuster, whose practices were quite characteristic, made himself very obnoxious to Justice Osborne. Whenever another Yiddish lawyer attempted a shady trick, the judge would openly denounce it as "Scheuster practice," and so it came that the first men in the profession to bear the name "shyster" were the Yiddish lawyers of Essex Market Court.

To make a nasty story brief, the Max Hochstim Association became the first organized White Slaver group in America, and the revelations made by the Lexow Committee are shuddering glimpses into that lowest form of depravity—a cooly conducted, commercialized, consolidated traffic in women. The traffic was made to yield dividends to politicians, to Tammany Jews in particular. The Ghetto became the Red Light District of New York. The first man to undertake the export trade in women with foreign countries, especially South America, was a man who later became a Tammany notable.

The surprising fact is that, although these matters are written in official documents, and although the same matters have been written into the record of every similar investigation which has been made, Jewish leaders persist in denying that the leaders in this particular form of depravity are Jews. When the United States Government made a nationwide investigation, it found and recorded the same facts. The New York Kehillah came into existence as a defense organization at a time when the exposure of the Jewish White Slave traffic threatened to overwhelm the New York ghetto.

The Max Hochstim Association was not the only organization of its kind. The other was the New York Independent Benevolent Association, which was organized in 1896 by a party of Jewish white slave dealers as they were returning from the funeral of Sam Engel, brother of Martin Engel, Tammany leader of the red light district.

The gangs that formed the backbone of Tammany power in the slum districts were made up of "cadets." Their principal field of operation was the cheap dance halls. Paul Kelly's gang originated in the halls about lower Broadway.

Monk Eastman's gang grew strong in the Russian Jewish District below Delancey street. And Kid Twist's gang developed close to a dance hall for Galician Jews on the far East Side. All of these three were Jewish gang leaders. They were slavers as their forbears were in the days of Rome's decline; they were bootleggers before the days of prohibition; and they constituted a strong support of the international narcotic ring which to this day has defied the law by corrupting the officers of the law.

It was to associations like these that the lights of Tammany lent their names. Tim Sullivan was a vice president of the Max Hochstim Association. The name of the Honorable Henry M. Goldfogle also appeared on the picnic announcements.

The exposure which resulted when the white people of New York finally succeeded in getting the forces of law to function impartially for a little while, caused many of the implicated Jews to change their names.

These names are now representative of some of the best Jewish families, whose concealed bar sinister is the fact that the foundation of the family fortune was laid in the red light district. Society, sliced down to its seeds, is a queer growth.

It is due in justice to say that men like Tim Sullivan were not the originators of the Jewish abuses referred to, nor willing participants in the gains therefrom. Tammany would do favors for its friends, at the police court or elsewhere; Tammany had its occasional political upheavals; Tammany believed that they who profited by political spoils should divide with the Wigwam's treasury; but with such traffic as seduction and barter in women, Tammany had never been compromised until the Yiddish invasion of New York and the Judaization of the Wigwam. This much must be said for the Irish and American leaders.

The situation is the same in Boston. An Irish city, its chief political control is in the hands of Jews.

The old-time Irish leaders are still permitted to be out in front, but the inner power has departed from them. One Boston ward, where once none but Irish lived, now contains only Jews, but the old-time Irish boss retains his seat. This is by favor of the Jews and nothing else.

The same state of facts accounts in large degree for the connection between a man like Tim Sullivan and the Jews. "Tim," as everyone knew him, was leader of a district inhabited by Irish and Germans. Then the Jews came in. And then began the Jews' practice of profiting by the people's dislike of them.

Foreign Jews well know that they are disliked. It is one of their assets which never fails to produce dividends. They choose the part of the city where they desire to live, and a few move in. Their immediate neighbors move out.

More Jews move in—more of the others move out. The property nearest the Jews always goes down in value. People will sell at a loss rather than live engulfed in a ghetto.

It was so in Tim Sullivan's district. As the Jews swarmed in, the Irish and Germans fled north. Sullivan stood his ground. It was his old territory, he would not leave it, nor remove his family. He cultivated the new arrivals and made a partnership with the ex-kosher chicken butcher, Martin Engel.

The Jews lived under Sullivan's rule for a time, awaiting the moment when they should know what to do for themselves. The Yiddish flood increased until the district was crowded, and then the Jews demanded representation for themselves. With a premonition that a new force had arisen, Tim Sullivan played safe and helped the Jews to get recognition Martin Engel was made leader of the old Eighth. But Sullivan had previously gone to Tammany—or to what remained of the old non-Jewish Tammany—and exacted an understanding that his rule should be left unchanged below Fourteenth street.

From that time forward, in spite of the understanding, Sullivan's power began to wane, principally because he continued to get in deeper and deeper with the Jews. He went into Jewish lines of business. He formed a theatrical partnership with George Kraus, among his enterprises being the Imperial Music Hall, the Dewey Theater, and the traveling Eagle Burlesque Company. Still the old district continued to become crowded and overcrowded and saturated with Yiddish newcomers, for whom neither the name Sullivan nor the traditions of the district had any meaning.

In his closing years, scarcely more than a hanger-on around the former scene of his power, Tim Sullivan bitterly lamented the ease with which he was led into associations that undermined his power. Croker was destroyed in public confidence by the terrific shock of the exposure attending the Jewish "cadet" activities. Sullivan, equally picturesque, was the slowly shoved-out victim of Jewish infiltration. There were other occurrences and other downfalls, all of which are a part of the real story of Tammany.

The Dearborn Independent, issue of 24 September 1921.

"I need hardly explain that I do not think Jews ought to insist overmuch on their rights or nationality in a negative sense. They ought to be as much Jews as they can, but ought to be as little as possible of what is merely anti-Christian. For the Jews to try to get a song out of the public schools because it praises Jesus is natural but perhaps hardly wise. I admit that question, however, is an extremely complex and baffling one. Again, the Jews have naturally taken a great interest in this war, but in that case also they ought to choose as far as possible the more tolerant view. Too much hostility to Russia was shown, it seems to me, when some of their spokesmen were fighting over the wording of the Immigration Act. They seemed to be fighting not for a real gain, but simply to rub their political power in America into the Russian mind." —Norman Hapgood.

54: Jew Wires Direct Tammany's Gentile Puppets

The proposal that non-Jews emigrate from New York City, 500,000 in the first exodus, and 500,000 in the second, to hasten the event which is held to be certain of occurrence, namely, that New York shall become an all-Jewish city, may be a joke; but it is no joke that the Jews themselves discuss and have proposed that the City of New York be separated from the state of New York, and made both a state and city in itself. This would entail three governments—state, county and municipal whose offices the Jews could parcel out as they pleased. Besides, it would rid them of Albany. It is a most amazing fact that the state capital, as bad as it is, has always been able to defeat the New York Jew in his most ardently pursued quests, as notably, his insistent appeal to abrogate the Sunday law.

Of course, if the non-Jews emigrated from New York, the Jews would soon follow. They are not self-sufficient. If New York could be isolated, Jewish initiative would not suffice to provide enough potatoes for the inhabitants.

It is too trite to say that New York is already in the hands of the Jews. But it would be most startling to give a schedule illustrating how completely this is so. The New Yorker himself can scarcely comprehend the extent of his vassalage to the Jew. The average intelligent New Yorker does not know what the Kehillah is, nor yet how it works. Like a child born within the sound of Niagara Falls, the New Yorker takes Jewish supremacy as a matter of course, as the way things should be, and as the way they probably are elsewhere. The New Yorker is thus like a native of the Balkans.

The Hylan administration, ostensibly non-Jewish, is really Jewish, as any New York administration must necessarily be, except there should arise a man whose ambition would be to prove that New York could be better governed if the Jews should be excluded from the government. Well-informed New Yorkers say that the power of Hylan is Hirschfield.

This is a rather peculiar situation to those who do not understand how the Jewish leaders work. Directly you say the Hylan administration is Jewish, it is objected: "But it is the arch-Jewish inquisitor Untermeyer, who is trying to break down the Hylan administration!" Exactly. That is the game. It's inside and outside that does it. There is power gained in making them and there is power gained in breaking them, and often it is profitable to try both ways with the same man. That is the way Russia went: there were Jews plentifully sprinkled throughout the government of Russia (in spite of the "persecution") and there were Jews outside.

Between the two, they got Russia. It is the same in a Texas city today. Four non-Jewish candidates for postmaster were made the center of a political deadlock—up through the deadlock pops a Jew as a compromise candidate for all sections. A sufficient number of Jews were available in that city to keep all the non-Jewish candidates in a deadlock until their own man was trotted out. The "Gentile mind," of course, does not easily realize these turnings and twistings of group conspiracy. And that is why the Jews feel safe, as a rule: they rely on what they call "Gentile stupidity."

The Gentile says, "incredible!" And the traditional Jewish game is incredible, until by mountainous proofs and centuries of illustration the actuality of it is forced home to the mind.

But to return to the New York City government: The police department has its Jewish streak in the higher offices—a Jewish police commissioner who has fortunately escaped thus far the full story of his career. The department of health, where it actually touches the people, is Jewish, although occasionally a distinguished non-Jewish name meets the eye in the roster of the higher officials. The public health is becoming more and more a Jewish monopoly in all our cities. The department of accounts, the board of child welfare, the board of inebriety, the municipal service commission, the board of taxes and assessments, are all under the leadership and domination of Jews.

The judiciary becomes increasingly Jewish, litigation is almost overwhelmingly Jewish, and the consequences to the reputation of the courts of justice and the profession of the law are well understood. Real estate exploitation and speculation is strictly Jewish, the profiteers treating even their own co-nationalists with the utmost cruelty.

In short, New York's most influential press (within New York) is the Yiddish press; New York's real government is the Yiddish Kehillah; New York's real administration of the law is the Yiddish administration; New York's real politics is Jewish. A little more, and New York's official language would be the Yiddish dialect.

In all this Tammany Hall is little more than a name; it is one of the rallying centers which the Jews have left the non-Jew who still interests himself in New York politics. There must be rallying places for the non-Jews, and one or two do not hurt. The Jew has the double advantage in such a matter, for while he claims equality with all, he denies equality with any. That is, any Jew proclaims his right to join any fraternity, or any club, or any society, or any party whose members are chiefly non-Jewish, but where is the Jewish fraternity, or club, or society that admits non-Jewish members?

The newspapers carried the report, after a certain occurrence, that hundreds of Jews had offered to join the Knights of Columbus! It was very typical of Jewish character. But let any non-Jew attempt to join B'nai B'rith or the Hebrew Young Men's Association, or the Menorah Society, or any of the others: he will see how far the principle of equality operates. "We want to be part of yours, but we want our own for ourselves," is the Jewish attitude.

So, politically, the New York Jew has the advantage. He belongs, together with the non-Jew, to organizations like Tammany or the Republican Club—but the non-Jew cannot with him belong to the Kehillah.

It is all so very familiar: the Jew insists on double everywhere. In the Balkans he insists on a double citizenship. He insists on a double protection. He insists on a double standard of education. He insists on all his own religious rights as strenuously as he insists that all Christian majority rights shall be stamped out in this country. He insists that he shall have his Sabbath and that you shall not have yours. He wants his own social rights and yours too—but he wants you to have only your own and not his with it. It casts serious doubts on Jewish intelligence that this course should be so seriously pursued, as if on the one hand the humor of the "nerve," and on the other hand the disgusting impudence of it, had never appeared to his consciousness.

In New York, therefore, the Jew politically belongs twice, while all non-Jews belong but once, and it can easily be perceived that this is an advantage.

In the previous article it was rehearsed how Tammany besmirched its name by association with Jews who used the organization as a protection for their traffic in vice. This was in 1894. The revelations were so terrible that in any other community they would have led to a complete abolition of any possible chance of recovery, but as it was never made plain to the people that the traffic in vice was not a sudden appearance of rottenness among Americans, but was the normal activity of an alien racial strain, the moral power of exposure was dissipated. The people were left staggered by what they were allowed to believe about the origin of the horror.

People said it was Tammany because the press said it was Tammany, and yet people could not understand how it could be Tammany, and so in the midst of hesitancy the fire of reform burned out. It was exactly like these days when we are told that "American business men" abroad are doing terrible things; yet even while the press declares them to be "American" we cannot understand how Americans could do such things and we never get the key to the matter, nor see the solution, until we stumble on to the fact that these so-called "Americans" are not Americans at all, but alien Jews.

Over in Canada the name, "American" is becoming a stigma because it is borne by men who are not Americans. What Canadians point out in the United States as definitely "American" is mostly Jewish, but how are the Canadians to know? The national name suffers. The whole cause of evil is camouflaged and a nation pays the price of a racial group's misdeeds. There should be some method of protecting this forging of national names.

Thus Tammany became a synonym for what was not characteristically Tammany at all, but what was characteristically Jewish.

The exposure of 1894 disclosed that vice was really a thing of cold blood. Evil that springs from passion and impulse really amounts to far less than is commonly supposed. It is when passion is deliberately cultivated and impulse stimulated, that the great bulk of the world's social evil occurs. And this stimulation is undertaken in cold blood by those who make profit out of providing the means of gratification—

like the old-fashioned bar keepers who served very salty free lunches to stimulate the sale of beer.

This kind of vice is not a thing to be shamed by exposure as can be done with involuntary vice, as it might be called. This cold-blooded merchandising of human weakness was merely a matter of profits, and if business had been interfered with by a Lexow Committee it was rather unfortunate, but good business required that operations be resumed at the earliest possible moment. And so, though the investigations of 1894 were successful and the exposure duly made, it was not to be expected that mere oratory and printer's ink would suffice to keep the serpent down.

It was only seven years before scandal flamed again throughout the length and breadth of New York, and strangely enough—strange enough in all conscience for "Gentile fronts" of this day and generation to heed!—it was found again that the traffic in evil and its ramifications all over the land, and even to foreign countries, was in the hands of Jews. There was no doubt about it. There was even no accident about it. The fact was as continuous as it was colossal.

William Travers Jerome, then Justice of the Court of Special Sessions, made in 1901 a ringing indictment of conditions in the city and used the full power of his court to punish wrongdoers; he even went so far as to specify individuals and political connections—but he did not mention the keyword of it all, which was "Jew." It was doubtless wise for him that he did not, else he could not have enjoyed the subsequent political career which came to him.

Tammany was defeated in the election of 1901. The defeat was due to the same cause—the stigma of Jew-controlled vice traffic under political protection. It was at this time that Richard Croker "abdicated." He was a rich man. He sailed for Ireland, where he became a country squire on his Wantage estate.

Public curiosity was fed the statement that Croker had selected Lewis Nixon to be his successor, but this turn in Tammany's career is too important to be thus misstated. The truth is that when Croker left he surrendered Tammany to the Jews.

Croker could confirm this if he would talk, if he should be permitted to talk. It is, however, not well to have garrulous old men spilling the secrets of other days. Croker in his age took a bride who is said to be of "Indian descent," and he has not been much in touch with his family nor the public since.

Lewis Nixon was the convenient and perhaps unconscious "Gentile front." The real ruler of Tammany in Croker's stead was Andrew Freedman, mentioned in the former article as Croker's friend and house mate.

(Judging from the habit of individual Jews to room with baseball players before the baseball scandal, and the result of another Jew's living with Croker, it might be just as well to keep an eye on those other men who are in positions to do favors or influence legislation, whose close cronies happen to be Jews. Some of these friendships may indeed be perfectly conceived; but there are numerous instances where the plans of the "Jewish friend" are very completely matured through the agency of the "Gentile chum.")

So, upon departure of Croker from these shores, we find Tammany under the dictatorship of a Jew who was Croker's chief influence, if not his absolute master.

But by the time this occurred, it was useless for Tammany to rebel. Tammany men who had noticed the infiltration of Jews and were alarmed by it had consoled themselves with the thought that, at least, the higher offices were immune from Jewish occupation. This consolation served only to permit the filling of the lower offices by Jews, with less protest from the membership. By the time the Jews were ready to permit Croker to "abdicate," they had permeated every part of the Wigwam and the assumption of supreme control was thus made a simple matter. Croker stepped aside; instantly into his place stepped the Jew, Freedman, operating through Nixon.

It was too late for Tammany to remonstrate. Tammany could not protest against the Wigwam becoming Jewish, because the Wigwam already was Jewish. To remonstrate then was to ruin Tammany. Becoming reconciled to what seemed to be inevitable, Tammany leaders saw that their only hope of survival came through preserving Jewish support.

Presently even Nixon was relegated to the background and Freedman issued his orders directly. The Jews, however, with great astuteness continued to make much of Nixon, because he was the last thin veil which concealed the change which had come over Tammany, and he was valuable to that extent. He was, unwillingly, perhaps, their puppet, but even puppets must be accorded their proper dignity. Nixon was tendered a great reception in 1902, but the influential men on the reception committee were mostly Jews: Andrew Freedman was chairman; then followed the names of Oliver H. P. Belmont, Max F.

Ihmson, Samuel Untermeyer, Nathan Straus, Randolph Guggenheimer, Henry M. Goldfogle, Herman Joseph, and others.

On the executive committee of Tammany Hall at this time were Randolph Guggenheimer, Isaac Fromme, Nathan Straus, Henry M. Goldfogle, O. H. P. Belmont, and other Jews.

On the committee on law were Samuel Untermeyer, M. Warlet Platzek, Abraham Levy, Henry W. Unger, Morris Cukor and Fred B. House.

Andrew Freedman had complete control of the committee on finance that was nominally headed by Lewis Nixon.

Randolph Guggenheimer was president of the municipal council. Ferdinand Levy was on the committee on resolutions and correspondence.

Jews had so spread themselves as to constitute a controlling group in all the assembly districts that were under tribute to Tammany. In the "Fighting Eighth" district, Martin Engel was leader. His chief aid was "Manny" Eichner, chairman of the Isidor Cohn Association and of the Young Men's Democratic Association. His other assistants, Max J. Porges, Max Levein, and Moe Levy were floor managers of the dances and balls of the Florence Sullivan Association.

In the Tenth district, Simon Steingutt, "Mayor of Second Avenue," was one of the hardest workers in Tammany affairs.

Edward Mandell was the active Jewish Tammany man in the Twelfth district. In the Eighteenth district, Maurice Blumenthal was one of the principal workers. He devoted his career chiefly to the training of Jewish speakers for the Wigwam.

The Eighteenth district was known as "the Gashouse district," notorious for the Gashouse scandals over padded pay rolls, and here Charley Murphy ruled, his aides being Julius Simon, Edward E. Slumasky, Joseph Schlesinger, Leopold Worms, Hugo Siegel, Alfred B. Marx, Nathan Fernbacher, and other Jews.

And so on through the list. Among the Sachems of the Tammany Society there were to be found the wealthier and more socially exalted Jews.

However, the Jews made their cyclically recurrent mistakes: they carried things with too high a hand, and rebellion broke out. It is this Jewish tendency to boast and overdo that has always given the game away. Superficial observers and writers like John Spargo and Norman Hapgood have observed the recurrent periods of protest against Jewish presumption and bumptiousness and have explained them as being recurrent spasms of a vile poison which is supposed to reside in the blood of the Gentiles the vile poison of anti-Semitism. That, of course, is the conventional Jewish propagandist explanation, and Spargo and Hapgood are merely retailing it. They say it always breaks out after wars. Why after wars? Because in wars the world sees more clearly than at other times the real purpose and personality of the Jew. Thus, it is not anti-Semitism that breaks out— it is Semitism, gross and exaggerated Semitism; and the serum that forms in the social body to encist and control the germ of Semitism comes in the form of public exposure and protest. That serum is working now the serum of publicity, and the Jewish program cannot endure it. Study the history of all things whatsoever into which Jews inject themselves, from summer resorts to empires, and you see the same cycle appearing.

Thus it happened in Tammany Hall—"too much Jew" engendered revolt. Lewis Nixon became aware of his position. As a gentlemen of standing and responsibility he could not continue in a position whose falsity had become clear to him. When he accepted the leadership of Tammany Hall, it was not with a purpose to continue the old order. His understanding was that he was to be left free to restore Tammany to the plane of its former serious purpose and respectable character. He discovered he was being used as the "respectable Gentile front" behind whose name the Jews expected to carry on the old game. Therefore, in May, 1902, three months after the great reception above mentioned, Nixon resigned as leader of Tammany Hall. Doubtless the reception that was tendered him was for the purpose of inducing him to love the exaltation of his position so much that he would sacrifice its moral obligations.

Nixon accompanied his resignation with a speech in which he protested that ever since he had accepted the leadership of Tammany he had been hampered in his every action by a group headed by Andrew Freedman; they dictated the names that were to be placed on the list of Sachems: "When I rebelled, I found that at every turn I would be opposed by this coterie of interferers; I found that all my important acts had to be viséed before they could become effective." He said he could no longer retain his position and his self-respect; he had to give up one or the other.

With this Mr. Nixon vanished from the scene of Tammany politics.

The resignation of Mr. Nixon had a bad effect on the reputation of Tammany with the public. The plan had been to allow him to serve as long as ordinarily and then replace him with a Jew by means of the usual process of selection. But the resignation and the explanation that accompanied it, showing as it did the Jewish influence in Tammany, made it seem inadvisable to follow with a Jewish leader. So the district leaders were obliged to find another "Gentile front," only this time one who would prove sufficiently docile. There was enough rankling disfavor against the Jews in the old organization to warrant this observance of appearances, at least.

The dictatorship of Freedman was seen to be a failure, much as the dictatorship of Trotzky is seen to be a failure. A rearrangement of committees automatically eliminated him from control, at the same time the name of Croker was dropped. A triumvirate of leaders was chosen, of whom Charles F. Murphy became and remains the chief. "Boss Murphy" he is called. Mr. Murphy has been an ideal "front," not attempting to do anything, not attempting to interfere with the Jews doing anything, keeping wisely silent and thereby gaining a reputation for silent wisdom. Mr. Murphy is a millionaire. Those who do the higher Jewish leaders' bidding get their reward that way; there is no other reward they can hope for; certainly they never have a reward of public confidence and the people's gratitude.

That is the status of Tammany Hall at the present time. A few of the Old Guard are left at their posts, but they are officers in name only. Tammany is no longer denounced by the public press, but the Jewish leaders of Tammany live daily to a chorus of praise in the Jewish-controlled newspapers of New York. Samuel Untermeyer, for example, receives more publicity in New York than does the President of the United States, but it is not discriminating publicity; it does not penetrate to the inner purposes and consequences of his actions.

Those who were the lesser Jewish lieutenants of Tammany a few years ago have now arrived at posts of influence and affluence. Morris Cukor was made president of the municipal service commission, to be succeeded by former State Senator Abraham Kaplan. Fred B. House rose to be a city magistrate. The city marshals are mostly Jewish. Jews predominate in the College of the City of New York. Jews control the municipal courts, the city magistrates' courts, the city court, the New York state court of appeals, the New York state supreme court. They rule in the departments enumerated in the fore part of this article. The New York judiciary has a distinctly Semitic complexion.

The leadership of the Tammany-controlled districts tells the same story. In the second, the leader is M. S. Levine; in the Sixth, David Lazarus; in the Eighth, S. Goldenkranz, F. Bauman and S. Salinger; in the Ninth, Mrs. P. Lau, in the Seventeenth, Nathan Burkan—and so on.

The Jewish conquest of Tammany, however, is only one phase of the conquest of New York. The Jewish objective is more than political. Merely to strive that the lucrative and powerful offices of the city shall fall to their people, is not the end in view. New York has been turned into the Red Center of America. There most of the alien treason carried on against the government of the United States has its source. The United States Government has been compelled at times to regard New York as almost alien soil, but even that watchfulness on the part of the national government is relaxed as Jewish influence becomes more potent at Washington. Tammany is a convenient cover for ostensible political activity as the Kehillah is for the more radical and anti-American racial activity. The United States Government could not do better than to investigate through a committee of invulnerable Americans—the Jewish activities of that center. And that there is much to investigate is indicated by the rush of Jews to Washington when it was recently proposed in the United States Senate that such a thing be done.

The Dearborn Independent, issue of 1 October 1921

55: B'nai B'rith Leader Discusses the Jews

To the pro-Jewish spokesmen who have filled the air with cries of "lies" and "slander," to those self-appointed guardians of "American ideals" who rule out with rare finality all those who would dare suggest that possibly there is a hidden side of the Jewish Question, it must come as something of a jolt to be reminded that in this series there is scarcely a line that is without high Jewish authority.

The Protocols themselves are written for centuries in Jewish authoritative teachings and records. All the plans that have been described from time to time in these articles are written in the fundamental laws of the Jews. And all that the ancients have taught, the modern Jews have reaffirmed.

The writer of these articles has had to take constant counsel of prudence in his selection of material, for the Jews have always counted confidently on the fact that if the whole truth were told in one comprehensive utterance, no one would believe it. Thus, bigots and minds bursting with the discoveries they have made, have never been feared by the Jews. They counted on the incapacity of the non-Jews to believe or receive certain knowledge. They know that facts are not accepted on proof, but only on understanding. Non-Jews cannot understand why human beings should lend themselves to certain courses. They are, however, beginning to understand, and the proof is therefore becoming more significant.

There are yet more important revelations to be made, always following closely the best Jewish sources, and when these revelations are made, it will be impossible for the Jewish leaders to keep silent or to deny. The time is coming for American Jewry to slough off the leadership which has led it and left in the bog. Leadership knows that. Indeed, it is amazing to discover the number of indications that the attempts made to suppress *The Dearborn Independent* have been made principally to prevent the Jews reading it.

The leaders do not care how many non-Jews read these articles; but they do not desire their own people to read them. The Jewish leaders do not desire their people's eyes to be opened.

Why? Because, just now, only Jews can truly know whether the statements made in these articles are true or not. Non-Jews may know here and there, as their observations may confirm the printed statements. But informed Jews really know. And large numbers of the masses of the Jews really know. When they see the truth in all its relationships in these articles, the hitherto "led" Jew may not be so tractable. Hence the effort to keep the non-Jewish point of view away from him.

In support of the statements that these articles have been based on Jewish authority, we quote today a series of declarations by one of the most able of the presidents of the B'nai B'rith, Leo N. Levi. Mr. Levi was American-born and died in 1904. He was a lawyer of distinction and attained the presidency of the international Jewish order, B'nai B'rith, in 1900. He took part in the international politics of his people and is credited with collaborating with Secretary of State John Hay on several important matters. The utterances here quoted were for the most made while he was president of B'nai B'rith, but all of them were published the year after his death under B'nai B'rith auspices. There is therefore no question of their Jewishness.

Non-Jewish defenders of the Jewish program have pretended to much indignation because of references that have been made to the Oriental character of certain Jewish manifestations. The references in these articles have been two in number, once regarding Oriental sensuality as it has been introduced to the American stage by Jewish theatrical panderers, and again in quoting Disraeli, the Jew who became premier of Britain, to the effect that the Jews—his people—were "Mosaic Arabs."

But it never seemed to have occurred to Leo N. Levi to deny the Oriental character of his race. Instead, he asserted it. On page 104 of the B'nai B'rith memorial, he excuses certain social crudities of the Jew on the ground "that hailing originally from the Orient and having been compelled for twenty centuries to live in a society of his own, he has preserved in his tastes much that is characteristically Oriental."

Again on page 116, he excused the multiplicity of religious rites as being due to the fact that the Jew "drew upon his Oriental imagination for a symbolism that appealed to his ideal emotions." On page 312, he speaks of the Jews' "Oriental devotion to their parents." This easy recognition of the fact is commended to those bootlicking editors who, out of the vastness of their ignorance of the Jewish Question, have seen in the reference to Orientalism an "insult" to the Jews and an unfailing indication of anti-Semitism.

The Jewish Question! Ah, that is another point which pro-Jewish spokesmen hasten to deny, but they will be somewhat disturbed by the candor with which true Jewish spokesmen admit the Question.

In a strong passage on page 101, Mr. Levi says:

"If I have dwelt so long upon this subject, it is because I recognize that if the Jew has been denied so much that is rightfully his, he often claims more than is his due. One of the claims, most persistently urged, is that there is no Jewish Question; that a Jew is a citizen like any other citizen and that as long as he abides by the law and does not subject himself to criminal prosecution or civil action, his doings are beyond legitimate inquiry by the public at large.

"This contention on his part would certainly be well based if he claimed nothing further than the right to live in peace, but when he demands social recognition the whole range of his conduct is a legitimate subject of inquiry against which no technical demurrers can be interposed . . . . nor must the Jew be over-sensitive about the inquiry.

"The inconsistencies and the unwisdom exhibited in the consideration of the Jewish Question are not to be found altogether on the side of those who are hostile to the Jews."

"Since then the refugees from Russia, Galicia and Rumania have raised the Jewish Question to commanding importance. Since then it has dawned on the world that we are witnessing another exodus which promises soon to change the habitat of the Jews to the Western Hemisphere." (Page 59)

"The Jewish Question cannot be solved by tolerance. There are thousands of well-meaning people who take to themselves great credit for exhibiting a spirit of tolerance toward the Jews." (Page 98)

Mr. Levi also lays down rules for "the study of the Jewish Question," and he says that if they were followed the result "would be startling at once to the Jews and the general public." (Page 93) How far present Jewish leadership has departed from that frank and broad view taken by Mr. Levi, is everywhere evident.

Not that Mr. Levi was a critic of his people, but he was a lawyer who was accustomed to weighing facts, and he saw facts that weighed against his people. But he was pro-Jewish even in his most severe observations. He could make an attack on the rabbis, taunting them with the saying that "many of you are 'rabbis for revenue only,'" but he could also insist on Jewish solidarity and exclusiveness. In this connection it may be interesting to see how strongly Mr. Levi supports the contention of

Jewish leaders (as outlined in *The Dearborn Independent* of October 9 and 16, 1920) that the Jews are a race and not merely a religion, a nation and not merely a church, and that the term "Jew" is biological rather than theological.

This is specially commended to the attention of those dim-minded shouters of "religious prejudice," who come into action whenever the Jewish Question is mentioned. (Of "religious prejudice" there are many examples to give in future articles.)

"Certain it is that thus far the race and the religion have been so fused, as it were, that none can say just where the one begins and the other leaves off." (Page 116)

Attacking the contention of the "liberals" or "reformed Jews" to the effect that "Jew" is the name of a member of religious denomination, and not of a member of a certain race, Mr. Levi says:

"Nothing to my mind is more pregnant with error than this postulate of unreason. (Page 185) It is not true that the Jews are only Jews because of their religion." (Page 189)

"The Jews are not simply an indiscriminate lot of people who hold to a common belief." (Page 190)

"A native Eskimo, and American Indian might conscientiously adopt every tenet of the Jewish church, might practice every form and ceremony imposed by the Jewish laws and the Jewish ritual, and as far as the religion is concerned, be a Jew, but yet, no one who will reflect for a moment would class them with the Jews as a people. If the truth were known, a very large percentage of so-called Christians would be found to be believers in the essentials of the Jewish religion, and yet, they are not Jews.

"It requires not only that men should believe in Judaism, but that they should be the descendants in a direct line of that people who enjoyed a temporal government and who owned a country up to the time of the destruction of the second commonwealth.

"That great event took away from the Jews their country and their temporal government; it scattered them over the face of the earth, but it did not destroy the national and race idea which was a part of their nature and of their religion."

"Who shall say, then, that the Jews are no longer a race? . . . . Blood is the basis and sub-stratum of the race idea, and no people on the face of the globe can lay claim with so much right to purity of blood, and unity of blood, as the Jews."

"If I have reasoned to any purpose, the inquiry of rights in the premises is not to be limited to Jews as exponents of a particular creed, but to the Jews as a race." (Pages 190-191)

"The religion alone does not constitute the people. As I have already maintained, a believer in the Jewish faith does not by reason of that fact become a Jew. On the other hand, however, a Jew by birth remains a Jew, even though he abjures his religion." (Page 200)

This is the view of such men as Justice Brandeis, the Jew who sits on the Supreme Court of the United States. Justice Brandeis says, "Let us all recognize that we Jews are a distinct nationality of which every Jew, whatever his country, his station, his shade of belief, is necessarily a member."

Believing all this, Mr. Levi subscribes to the Jewish law and practice of exclusiveness.

Describing the state of the Jews, Mr. Levi says (page 92): "The Jews have not materially increased or diminished in numbers for 2,000 years. They have made no proselytes to their religion . . . . They have imbibed the arts, the literature and the civilization of successive generations, but have abstained very generally from intermixture of blood . . . . They have infused their blood into that of other peoples but have taken little of other peoples into their own."

As to intermarriage between the Jew and non-Jew, Mr. Levi calls it miscegenation. "In remote countries, sparsely populated, the choice may lie between such marriages and a worse relation." Those are his words on page 249. He does not advise the worse relation, but he has said quite enough to indicate the Jewish view of the case. He continues:

"It seems clear to me that Jews should avoid marriages with Gentiles and Gentiles with Jews, upon the same principle that we avoid marrying the insane, the consumptive, the scrofulitic or the Negro." (Page 249)

This exclusiveness goes down through all human relations. The Jew has one counsel for non-Jews and another for himself in these matters. Of the non-Jew he demands as a right what he looks down upon as shady privilege. He uses the Ghetto as a club with which to bludgeon the non-Jew for his "bigotry," when as a fact he chooses the Ghetto for well-defined racial reasons. He condemns the non-Jew for the exclusion of the Jew from certain sections of society, when as a Jew his whole care is to keep himself unspotted from that very society to which he seeks entrance. The Jew insists on breaking down non-Jewish exclusiveness while keeping his own. The non-Jewish world is to be public and common, the Jewish world is to be kept sacrosanct. Read the teachings of this enlightened leader of Jewry as published by the B'nai B'rith.

He favors the public school for non-Jewish children, not for Jewish children; they are to be kept separate; they are the choice stock of the earth:

"Because the government tenders free education, it does not follow that it must be accepted; if education be made compulsory, it does not follow that government schools must be attended . . . . As a citizen, I favor free schools, because the education they afford, imperfect as it is, is better than none, and society is benefited thereby; but as an individual I prefer to pay to support free schools and send my children to more select places." (Page 253) He speaks of the fact that "all classes of children frequent the public schools" as an argument against Jewish children going there.

"In my judgement, Jewish children should be educated in Jewish schools." (Page 254) "Not only is it a positive and direct advantage to educate our children as Jews, but it is absolutely necessary to our preservation. Experience has shown that our young people will be weaned from our people if allowed indiscriminately to associate with the Gentiles." (Page 255)

Discussing the possibility of Jews losing their crudeness, Mr. Levi asks, "How shall we best accomplish that end?" Then he quotes the frequent answer: "Since the exemplars of gentility most abound among the Gentiles, we should associate with them as much as possible, in order to wear our own rudeness away." He meets the suggestion this way:

"If gentlemen were willing to meet all Jews on a parity because they are Jews, we should doubtless derive much benefit from such association. But, while it is true that no gentleman refuses association with another because that other is a Jew, he will not, as a rule, associate with a Jew unless he be a gentleman. As we are far from being all gentlemen, we cannot reasonably expect to be admitted as a class into good society. So, better keep by ourselves," concludes Mr. Levi. (Page 260)

That is, Mr. Levi admits the willingness of society to meet Jews on equal terms, as with all others, but not on unequal terms. And this being so, Mr. Levi holds they had better meet as little as possible, they had better keep apart; in the formative years, certainly, Jewish young people should be kept rigidly apart from non-Jews. The exclusiveness of which the Jews complain is their own. The Ghetto is not a corner into which the non-Jews have herded the Semites; the Ghetto is a spot carved out of the community and consecrated to the Chosen People and is therefore the best section of the city in Jewish eyes, the rest being "the Christian quarter," the area of the heathen. Mr. Levi himself admits on page 220 that there is no prejudice against the Jew in this country.

Certain wild-eyed objectors to the series of studies on the Jewish Question have made the assertion that *The Dearborn Independent* has declared cowardice to be a Jewish trait. That the statement is false as regards this paper does not change the fact that the subject has been generally discussed in and out of army circles. If it ever becomes necessary to discuss it in these studies, the facts will be set forth as far as they are obtainable. But the point just now is that Mr. Levi has had somewhat to say which may repay reading:

"Physical courage has always been an incident, not an element, of Jewish character. It has no independent existence in their make-up, and always depended on something else. With some exceptions this may be said of all Oriental people. The sense and fear of danger is highly developed in them, and there is no cultivation of that indifference to it which has distinguished the great nations of Western Europe." (Page 205)

Were a non-Jew to call attention to this difference between the Jews and others, he would be met with the cry of "anti-Semitism" and he would be twitted with the fact that all his relatives may not have served in the war. Loudest to twit him would be those who served in what our soldiers called "the Jewish infantry," the quartermaster's corps in the late National Army.

It is to this aversion to danger, however, that Mr. Levi attributes the Jews' greatness among the nations. Other nations can fight, the Jews can endure, and that, he says, is greater. Note his words (the italics are his own):

"Other nations may boast conquests and triumphs born of aggression, but though the fruits of victory have been manifold, they have not been enduring; and it may be truly said that the nation whose greatness grows out of valor passes through the stages of discord and degeneracy to decay . . . In the virtue of endurance, I believe the Jews have a safeguard against the decay that has marked the history of all other peoples."

It appears, therefore, that the draft-dodger, if he can endure long enough, may yet come to own the country.

Jewish leaders have lately tried to minimize as "wild words" the disclosures made by Disraeli with reference to the Jews' participation in European revolutions. What Disraeli said can be found in his "Coningsby," or in the quotations made therefrom in *The Dearborn Independent* of December 18, 1920. With reference to the German Revolution of 1848, Disraeli wrote—before it had taken place:

"You never observe a great intellectual movement in Europe in which the Jews do not greatly participate . . . . That mysterious Russian Diplomacy which so alarms Western Europe is organized and principally carried on by Jews. That mighty revolution which is at this moment preparing in Germany, and which will be, in fact, a second and greater Reformation, and of which so little is yet known in England, is entirely developing under the auspices of Jews."

It is interesting, therefore, to hear Mr. Levi confirming from the American side those significant statements made by Disraeli.

"The revolution of 1848 in Germany, however, influenced a great many highly educated Jews to come to America." (Page 181) "It is unnecessary to review the events of 1848; suffice it to say, that not a few among the revolutionists were Jews, and that a considerable number of those who were proscribed by the government at home, fled to the United States for safety." (Page 182) These German Jews are now the arch-financiers of the United States. They found here complete liberty to exploit peoples and nations to the full extent of their powers. They still maintain their connections with Frankfort-on-the-Main, the world capital of International financial Jewry.

With these quotations from the speeches and writings of Leo N. Levi, a famous president of the B'nai B'rith, it would seem to be a fair question as to the reason for the denial and denunciation which have followed the making of these statements in the course of this series of studies. Leo N. Levi studied the Jewish Question because he knew a Jewish Question to exist. He knew that the Jewish Question was not a non-Jewish creation but appeared wherever Jews began to appear in numbers. They brought it with them. He knew the justice of many of the charges laid against the Jews. He knew the impossibility of disproving them, the futility of shrieking "anti-Semitism" at them. He knew, moreover, that for the Jews to solve the Jewish Question by departing from the peculiar racial traditions of superiority, would be to cease to be Jews. Therefore, he threw his whole influence on the side of the Jews remaining separate, maintaining their tradition of The Chosen Race, looking upon themselves as the coming rulers of the nations, and there he left the Question just about where he found it.

But in the course of his studies he gave other investigators the benefit of his frank statements. He did not put lies into the mouths of his people. He was not endeavoring to maintain himself in position by prejudiced racial appeals. He looked certain facts in the face, made his report, and chose his side. Several timers in the course of his argument, his very logic led him up to the point where, logically, he would have to cast aside his Jewish idea of separateness. But with great calmness he discarded the logic and clung to the Jewish tradition. For example:

"The better to facilitate such happiness in every country and in every age, various kinds of organizations have existed as they exist today. The Jews have theirs.

"For many reasons they are exclusive. In theory they should not be so. In our social organizations we should, in deference to the argument which I have already named, admit any congenial and worthy Gentile who honors us with his application. But what may be theoretically correct may be found practically wrong. It certainly is a wrong to exclude a worthy person because he does not happen to be a Jew; but on the other hand, where are you to draw the line?"

This is frankness to a fault. Of course, it is wrong, but the right is impractical! Logic goes by the boards in the face of something stronger. Mr. Levi is not to be blamed for having gone to his tribe. Every man's place is with his tribe. The criticism belongs to the lick-spittle Gentile Fronts who have no tribe and become hangers-on around the outskirts of Judah, racial mongrels who would be better off if they had one-thousandth of the racial sense which the Jew possesses.

This brief survey of the philosophy which Mr. Levi both lived and taught, and which is shared by the leaders of American Jewry, is in strict agreement with Jewish principles all down the centuries. In his published addresses Mr. Levi does not touch upon all the implications of the separateness which he enjoins upon his nation.

Why do they keep by themselves?

What is it that keeps them distinct?

Is it their religion? Very well; let us regard them as a sect of religious recluses and wish them well in their endeavors to keep themselves unspotted of the world.

Is it their race? So their leaders teach. Race and nationality are strictly claimed.

If this is so, there must be a political outlook. What is it? Palestine? Not that any one can notice. A great deal may be read about it in the newspapers, the newspapers in turn being supplied through the Associated Press with the *Jewish Telegraph Agency's* propaganda dispatches; but no one in Palestine notices the Land becoming more Jewish.

Jewry's political outlook is world rule in the material sense. Jewry is an international nation. It is this, and nothing else, which gives significance to its financial, educational, propagandist, revolutionary and immigration programs.

The Dearborn Independent, issue of 14 May 1921

56: Dr. Levy, a Jew, Admits His People's Error

A Jew of standing, Dr. Oscar Levy, well known in English literary circles and a lover of his people, has had the honesty and the wisdom to meet the Jewish Question with truth and candor. His remarks are printed in this article as an example of the methods by which Jewry can be saved in the estimation of Twentieth Century Civilization.

The circumstances were these: George Pitt-Rivers, of Worcester College, Oxford, wrote a most illuminating brochure entitled, "*The World Significance of the Russian Revolution*," which is published and sold for two shillings by Basil Blackwell, Oxford. The book is the result of unprejudiced observation and study and agrees with the statements made in *The Dearborn Independent* about the personnel of Bolshevism. The manuscript was sent to Dr. Oscar Levy, as a representative Jew, and Dr. Levy's letter was subsequently published as a preface to the book.

That the reader may understand the tenor of Mr. Pitt-Rivers's book, section XVI, pp. 39–41, is herewith given in full, and is followed by Dr. Levy's comments. The italics throughout are intended to remind the reader of remarks on similar lines made in this series:

It is not unnaturally claimed by Western Jews that Russian Jewry, as a whole, is most bitterly opposed to Bolshevism. Now although there is a great measure of truth in this claim, since the prominent Bolsheviks, who are preponderantly Jewish, do not belong to the orthodox Jewish Church, it is yet possible, without laying oneself open to the charge of anti-Semitism, to point to the obvious fact that Jewry, as a whole, has, consciously or unconsciously, worked for and promoted an international economic, material despotism which, with Puritanism as an ally, has tended in an ever-increasing degree to crush national and spiritual values out of existence and substitute the ugly and deadening machinery of finance and factory.

It is also a fact that Jewry, as a whole, strove every nerve to secure and heartily approved of the overthrow of the Russian monarchy, which they regarded as their most formidable obstacle in the path of their ambitions and business pursuits. All this may be admitted, as well as the plea that, individually or collectively, most Jews may heartily detest the Bolshevik régime, yet it is still true that the whole weight of Jewry was in the revolutionary scales against the czar's government. It is true their apostate brethren, who are now riding in the seat of power, may have exceeded their orders; that is disconcerting, but it does not alter the fact. It may be that the Jews, often the victims of their own idealism, have always been instrumental in bringing about the events they most heartily disapprove of; that perhaps is the curse of the Wandering Jew.

Certainly, it is from the Jews themselves that we learn most about the Jews. It is possible that only a Jew can understand a Jew. Nay, more, it may be that only a Jew can save us from the Jews, a Jew who is great enough, strong enough—for greater racial purity is a source of strength in the rare and the great—and inspired enough to overcome in himself the life-destructive vices of his own race. It was a Jew who said, "Wars are the Jews' harvest"; but no harvest so rich as civil wars. A Jew reminds us that the French Revolution brought civil emancipation for the Jews in Western Europe.

Was it a Jew who inspired Rousseau with the eighteenth-century idea of the sameness of man according to nature? Dr. Kallen, a Zionist author, writes: "Suffering for 1,000 years from the assertion of their difference from the rest of mankind, they accepted eagerly the escape from suffering which the eighteenth century assertion of the sameness of all men opened to them . . . . They threw themselves with passion into the republican emancipating movements of their fellow subjects of other stocks."

It was a Jew, Ricardo, who gave us the nineteenth century ideal of the sameness of man according to machinery. And without the Ricardian gospel of international capitalism, we could not have had the international gospel of Karl Marx. Moses Hess and Disraeli remind us of the particularly conspicuous part played by Jews in the Polish and Hungarian rebellions, and in the republican uprising in Germany of '48. Even more conspicuous were they in the new internationalism logically deducible from the philosophy of Socialism. This we were taught by the Jew Marx, and the Jew Ferdinand Lasalle, and they but developed the doctrine of the Jew David Ricardo.

It was Weininger, a Jew—and also a Jew hater—who explained why so many Jews are naturally Communists. Communism is not only an international creed, but it implies the abnegation of real property, especially property in land, and Jews, being international, have never acquired a taste for real property; they prefer money. Money is an instrument of power, though eventually, of course, Communists claim that they will do away with money—when their power is sufficiently established to enable them to command goods, and exercise despotic sway without it. Thus the same motives prompt the Jew Communist and his apparent enemy, the financial Jew. When owners of real property in times of economic depression feel the pinch of straightened circumstances, it is the Jewish usurers who become most affluent and who, out of goodness of their hearts, come to their assistance—at a price.

To these and other statements, Dr. Levy, as a Jew, made this reply:

> Dear Mr. Pitt-Rivers:
>
> When you first handed me your MS. on *The World Significance of the Russian Revolution,* you expressed a doubt about the propriety of its title. After a perusal of your work, I can assure you, with the best of consciences, that your misgivings were entirely without foundation.
>
> No better title than *The World Significance of the Russian Revolution* could have been chosen, for no event in any age will finally have more significance for our world than this one. We are still too near to see clearly this Revolution, this portentous event, which was certainly one of the most intimate and therefore least obvious, aims of the world-conflagration, hidden as it was at first by the fire and smoke of national enthusiasms and patriotic antagonisms.
>
> It was certainly very plucky of you to try and throw some light upon an event which necessarily must still be enveloped in mist and mystery, and I was even somewhat anxious, lest your audacity in treating such a dangerous subject would end in failure, or what is nearly the same, in ephemeral success. No age is so voracious of its printed offspring as ours. There was thus some reason to fear lest you had offered to this modern Kronos only another mouthful of his accustomed nourishment for his immediate consumption.
>
> I was, I am glad to report, agreeably surprised—surprised, though not by the many new facts which you give, and which must surprise all those who take an interest in current events—facts, I believe, which you have carefully and personally collected and selected, not only from books, but from the lips and letters

of Russian eye-witnesses and sufferers, from foes as well as from friends of the Great Revolution.

What I appreciate more than this new light thrown on a dark subject, more than the conclusion drawn by you from this wealth of facts, is the psychological insight which you display in detecting the reasons why a movement so extraordinarily bestial and so violently crazy as the Revolution was able to succeed and finally to overcome its adversaries. For we are confronted with two questions which need answering and which, in my opinion, you have answered in your pamphlet. These questions are: (1) How has the Soviet Government, admittedly the government of an insignificant minority, succeeded not only in maintaining but in strengthening its position in Russia after two and a half years of power? and (2) Why has the Soviet Government, in spite of its outward bestiality and brutal tyranny, succeeded in gaining the sympathies of an increasing number of people in this country?

You rightly recognize that there is an ideology behind it and you clearly diagnose it as an ancient ideology. There is nothing new under the Sun, it is even nothing new that this Sun rises in the East. . . .

For Bolshevism is a religion and a faith. How could these half-converted believers ever dream to vanquish the "Truthful" and the "Faithful" of their own creed, these holy crusaders, who had gathered round the Red Standard of the Prophet Karl Marx, and who fought under the daring guidance of these experienced officers of all latter-day revolutions—the Jews?

I am touching here on a subject which, to judge from your own pamphlet, is perhaps more interesting to you than any other. In this you are right. There is no race in the world more enigmatic, more fatal, and therefore more interesting than the Jews.

Every writer, who, like yourself, is oppressed by the aspect of the present and embarrassed by his anxiety for the future, *must* try to elucidate the Jewish Question and its bearing upon our Age.

For the question of the Jews and their influence on the world past and present, cuts to the root of all things, and should be discussed by every honest thinker, however bristling with difficulties it is, however complex the subject as well as the individuals of this Race may be.

For the Jews, as you are aware, are a sensitive Community,

and thus very suspicious of any Gentile who tries to approach them with a critical mind. They are always inclined—and that on account of their terrible experiences—to denounce anyone who is not with them as against them, as tainted with "medieval" prejudice, as an intolerant Antagonist of their Faith and of their Race.

Nor could or would I deny that there is some evidence, some prima facie evidence of this antagonistic attitude in your pamphlet. You point out, and with fine indignation, the great danger that springs from the prevalence of Jews in finance and industry, and from the preponderance of Jews in rebellion and revolution. You reveal, and with great fervor, the connection between the Collectivism of the immensely rich International Finance—the Democracy of cash values, as you call it—and the international Collectivism of Karl Marx and Trotsky—the Democracy of and by decoy-cries . . . . And all this evil and misery, the economic as well as the political, you trace back to one source, to one "fons et origo malorum"—the Jews.

Now other Jews may vilify and crucify you for these outspoken views of yours; I myself shall abstain from joining the chorus of condemnation! I shall try to understand your opinions and your feelings, and having once understood them—as I think I have—I can defend you from the unjust attacks of my often too impetuous Race.

But first of all, I have to say this: There is scarcely an event in modern Europe that cannot be traced back to the Jews. Take the Great War that appears to have come to an end, ask yourself what were its causes and its reasons: you will find them in nationalism. You will at once answer that nationalism has nothing to do with the Jews, who, as you have just proved to us, are the inventors of the international idea. But no less than Bolshevist Ecstasy and Financial Tyranny can National Bigotry (if I may call it so) be finally followed back to a Jewish source—are not they the inventors of the Chosen People Myth, and is not this obsession part and parcel of the political credo of every modern nation, however small and insignificant it may be? And then think of the history of nationalism. It started in our time and as a reaction against Napoleon; Napoleon was the antagonist of the French Revolution; the French Revolution was the consequence of the

German Reformation; the German Reformation was based upon a crude Christianity; this kind of Christianity was invented, preached and propagated by the Jews; *therefore,* the Jews have made this war! . . . . Please do not think this is a joke; it only seems a joke, and behind it there lurks a gigantic truth, and it is this, that all latter-day ideas and movements have originally sprung from a Jewish source, for the simple reason, that the Semitic idea has finally conquered and entirely subdued this only apparently irreligious universe of ours.

. . . . There is no doubt that the Jews regularly go one better or worse than the Gentile in whatever they do, there is no further doubt that their influence today justifies a very careful scrutiny, and cannot possibly be viewed without serious alarm. The great question, however, is whether the Jews are conscious or unconscious malefactors. I myself am firmly convinced that they are unconscious ones, but please do not think that I wish to exonerate them on that account . . . . A conscious evildoer has my respect, for he knows at least what is good; an unconscious one—well, he needs the charity of Christ—a charity which is not mine—to be forgiven for not knowing what he is doing. But there is in my firm conviction not the slightest doubt that these revolutionary Jews do not know what they are doing; that they are more unconscious sinners than voluntary evildoers.

I am glad to see that this is not an original observation of mine, but that you yourself have a very strong foreboding about the Jews being the victims of their own theories and principles. On page 39 of your pamphlet you write: "It may be that the Jews have always been instrumental in bringing about the events that they most heartily disapprove of; that maybe is the curse of the Wandering Jew." If I had not the honor, as well as the pleasure, of knowing you personally, if I were not strongly aware of your passionate desire for light and your intense loathing of unfairness, this sentence, and this sentence alone, which tells the truth, will absolve you in my eyes from the odious charge of being a vulgar anti-Semite.

No, you are not a vulgar, you are a very enlightened, critic of our Race. For there is an anti-Semitism, I hope and trust, which does the Jews more justice than any blind philo-Semitism, than does that merely sentimental "Let-them-all-come Liberalism" which in itself is nothing but the Semitic Ideology over again. And thus you can be just to the Jews without being "romantic" about them.

You have noticed with alarm that the Jewish elements provide the driving forces for both Communism and capitalism, for the material as well as the spiritual ruin of this world. But then you have at the same time the profound suspicion that the reason of all this extraordinary behavior may be the intense Idealism of the Jew. In this you are perfectly right. The Jew, if caught by an idea, never thinks any more in watertight compartments, as do the Teuton and Anglo-Saxon peoples, whose right cerebral hemisphere never seems to know what its left twin brother is doing; he, the Jew, like the Russian, at once begins to practice what he preaches, he draws the logical conclusion from his tenets, he invariably acts upon his accepted principles. It is from this quality, no doubt, that springs his mysterious force—that force which you no doubt condemn, but which you had to admire even in the Bolshevists. And we must admire it, whether we are Jews or whether we are Christians, for have not these modern Jews remained true to type, is there no parallel for them in history, do they not go to the bitter end even in our day? . . . .

Who stirred up the people during the late war in Germany? Who pretended to have again the truth, that truth about which Pontius Pilate once shrugged his shoulders? Who pleaded for honesty and cleanliness in Politics, that honesty which brings a smile to the lips of any experienced Pro-consul of today? Writers, who were mostly Jews: Fried, Fernau, Latzko, Richard Grelling—the author of "J'accuse." Who was killed and allowed himself to be killed for these very ideas and principles? Men and women of the Jewish Race: Haase, Levine, Luxemburg, Landauer, Kurt Eisner, the Prime Minister of Bavaria. From Moses to Marx, from Isaiah to Eisner, in practice and in theory, in idealism and in materialism, in philosophy and in politics, they are today what they have always been: passionately devoted to their aims and to their purposes, and ready, nay, eager, the shed their last drop of blood for the realization of their visions.

"But these visions are all wrong," will you reply. . . . . "Look where they have led the world to. Think, that they have now had a fair trial of 3,000 years' standing. How much longer are you going to recommend them to us and to inflict them upon us? And how do you propose to get us out of the morass into which you have launched us, if you do not change the path upon which you have led the world so disastrously astray?"

To this question I have only one answer to give, and it is this: "You are right." This reproach of yours, which—I feel it for certain—is at the bottom of your anti-Semitism, is only too well justified, and upon this common ground I am quite willing to shake hands with you and defend you against any accusation of promoting Race Hatred: If you are anti-Semite, I, the Semite, am an anti-Semite too, and a much more fervent one than even you are . . . . We (Jews) have erred, my friend, we have most grievously erred. And if there was truth in our error 3,000, 2,000, nay, 100 years ago, there is now nothing but falseness and madness, a madness that will produce an even greater misery and an even wider anarchy. I confess it to you, openly and sincerely, and with a sorrow, whose depth and pain an ancient Psalmist, and only he, could moan into this burning universe of ours . . . . We who have posed as the saviours of the world, we who have even boasted of having given it "the" Saviour, we are today nothing else but the world's seducers, its destroyers, its incendiaries, its executioners . . . . We who have promised to lead you to a new Heaven, we have finally succeeded in landing you in a new Hell . . . . There has been no progress, least of all moral progress . . . . And it is just our Morality, which has prohibited all real progress, and—what is worse—which even stands in the way of every future and natural reconstruction in this ruined world of ours . . . . I look at this world, and I shudder at its ghastliness; I shudder all the more as I know the spiritual authors of all this ghastliness. . . .

But its authors themselves, unconscious in this as in all they are doing, know nothing yet of this startling revelation. While Europe is aflame, while its victims scream, while its dogs howl in the conflagration, and while its very smoke descends in darker and even darker shades upon our Continent, the Jews, or at least a part of them and by no means the most unworthy ones, endeavor to escape from the burning building, and wish to retire from Europe into Asia, from the somber scene of our disaster into the sunny corner of their Palestine. Their eyes are closed to the miseries, their ears are deaf to the moanings, their heart is hardened to the anarchy of Europe: they only feel their own sorrows, they only bewail their own fate, they only sigh under their own burdens . . . . They know nothing of their duty to Europe, which looks around in vain for help and guidance, they know nothing even of their own great ancestor to whose heart the appeal of pity was never made in vain: they have become too poor in love, too sick at heart, too tired of battle, and lo! these sons of those who were once the bravest of soldiers are now trying to retire from the trenches to the rear, are now eager to exchange the grim music of the whistling shells with that of the cowbells and vintage songs in the happy plain of Sharon . . . .

And yet we are not all Financiers, we are not all Bolshevists, we have not all become Zionists. And yet there is hope, great hope, that this same race which has provided the Evil will likewise succeed in supplying its antidote, its remedy—the Good. It has always been so in the past— was not that fatal Liberalism, which has finally led to Bolshevism—in the very midst of that dark nineteenth century, most strenuously opposed by two enlightened Jews—Friedrich Stahl, the founder of the Conservative Party in Germany, and by Benjamin Disraeli, the leader of the Tory Party in England? And if these two eminent men had no suspicion yet that their own race and its holy message were at the bottom of that unfortunate upheaval, with which their age was confronted: how eager, how determined, how passionate will be the opposition of the Disraelis of the future, once they have clearly recognized that they are really fighting the tenets of their own people, and that it was their "Good," their "Love," their "Ideal," that had launched the world into this Hell of Evil and Hatred. A new "Good" as new Love, a true Love, an intelligent Love, a Love that calms and heals and sweetens, will then spring up among the Great in Israel and overcome that sickly Love, that insipid Love, that romantic Love, which has hitherto poisoned all the Strength and all the Nobility of this world. For Hatred is never overcome by Hatred: it is only overcome by Love, and it wants a new and a gigantic Love to subdue that old and devilish Hatred of today. That is our task for the future—a task which will, I am sure, not be shirked by Israel, by that same Israel which has never shirked a task, whether it was for good or whether it was for evil . . .

Yes, there is hope, my friend, for we are still here, our last word is not yet spoken, our last deed is not yet done, our last revolution is not yet made. This last Revolution, the Revolution that will crown our revolutionaries, will be the revolution against the revolutionaries. It is bound to come, and it is perhaps upon us now. The great day of reckoning is near. It will pass a judgement upon our ancient faith, and it will lay the foundation to a new religion. And when that great day has broken, when the values of death and decay are put into the melting pot to be changed into those of power and beauty, then you, my dear Pitt-Rivers, the descendant of an old and distinguished Gentile family, may be assured to find by your side, and as your faithful ally, at least one member of that Jewish Race, which has fought with such fatal success upon all the spiritual battlefields of Europe.

Yours against the Revolution and for Life ever flourishing,
OSCAR LEVY,
ROYAL SOCIETIES CLUB,
ST. JAMES STREET,
LONDON, S. W.,
JULY, 1920.

The Dearborn Independent, issue of 30 April 1921

57: Jewish Idea in American Monetary Affairs

Mr. Brisbane says that Jewish bankers exercise their large measure of control because they are abler than the other bankers. It was very good of Mr. Brisbane to say so, and it adds to the sum of his weekly, almost daily, worship at the Jewish shrine, but it is scarcely true. Jewish bankers do not yet control the United States, and the principal reason they do not is that they are not abler than the other bankers. Doubtless they seek control; doubtless they have almost grasped it on several occasions; but not yet.

Nevertheless they form such a formidable force, and with their international connections constitute such a political problem, that the mere fact of their failing to top the column of control is not so reassuring as it sounds.

The great Jewish banking houses of the United States are foreign importations, as perhaps everyone knows. Most of them are sufficiently recent to be considered in their immigrant status, while the thought of them as aliens is stimulated by their retention of oversea connections. It is this international quality of the Jewish banking group which largely accounts for Jewish financial power: there is team-play, intimate understandings, and while there is a margin of competition among themselves (as at golf) there is also a wiping out of that margin when it comes to a contest between Jewish and "Gentile" capital.

Four conspicuous contemporary names in Jewish-American finance are Belmont, Schiff, Warburg and Kahn. All of them, even the most recent, are of foreign origin.

August Belmont was the earliest and arrived in America in 1837 as the American representative of the Rothschilds in whose offices he had been raised. His birthplace was that great center of Jewish international finance, Frankfort-on-the-Main. He became the founder of the Belmont family in America, which has largely forgotten its Jewish origin. Politics was a part of his concern in this country, and during the critical time from 1860 to 1872 he was chairman of the National Democratic Committee. His management of the Rothschild interests was exceedingly profitable to that house, although the operations in which he engaged were quite simple compared with the operations of the present day.

Jacob Schiff is another Jewish financier who was given to the world by Frankfort-on-the-Main. He entered the United States in 1865, after having passed his apprenticeship in the office of his father, who was also an agent of the Rothschilds. The name Schiff runs a long way back without change, unlike the name of Rothschild. Originally named Bauer, this family of financiers took a new name from the red shield which adorned their house in the Jewish section of Frankfort and thus became "Rot-schild." Commonly the last syllable is pronounced as if it were "child"; it is "schild," shield. An epoch-making family in itself, it has trained hundreds of agents and apprentices, of whom Jacob H. Schiff was one. He became one of the principal channels through which German-Jewish capital flowed into American undertakings, and his agency in these matters gave him a place in many important departments of American business, especially railroads, banks, insurance companies and telegraph companies. He married Theresa Loeb, and in due time came to be head of the firm of Kuhn, Loeb & Company.

Mr. Schiff, too, was interested in politics with a Jewish angle, and was perhaps the moving force in the campaign which forced Congress and the President to break off treaty relations with Russia, then a friendly nation, on a strictly Jewish question which had been skillfully given an American aspect. Mr. Schiff was of inestimable assistance to Japan in the war against Russia, but is understood to have been disappointed by Japan's shrewdness in preventing too high a return being made for that assistance.

Associated with Mr. Schiff in Kuhn, Loeb & Company is Otto Herman Kahn, who is probably more international than were either of the two gentlemen mentioned above and is more constantly engaged in dabbling in mysterious matters of an international nature. This characteristic may be accounted for, however, by his experience of many countries. He was born in Germany and is also a product of the Frankforton-the-Main school of finance, having had connection with the Frankfort Jewish house of Speyer.

Of just how many countries Mr. Kahn has been a citizen is a question not easy to determine here because of the doubt that was recently cast upon his American citizenship by a protest against his being permitted to cast his vote last year and by his failure—the announced cause being physical indisposition—to cast his vote. If Mr. Kahn is a citizen of the

United States (a status that will be readily proclaimed upon proof that he is), that probably increases the number of his citizenships to three. He was a German citizen by birth, and served in the German Army. And in 1914, in August, at the time of the outbreak of the European War, when efforts were being made, which afterwards succeeded, to put Paul M. Warburg, a member of the firm of Kuhn, Loeb & Company, on the Federal Reserve Board, Mr. Warburg testified that at that time Mr. Kahn was not a citizen of the United States.

Senator Bristow—"How many of these partners are American citizens, or are they all American citizens . . . ."

Mr. Warburg—"They are all American citizens except Mr. Kahn."—(p. 7, Senate Hearings, August 1, 1914.)

Senator Bristow—"Now, the members of your firm, are they all American citizens except Mr. Kahn?"

Mr. Warburg—"Except Mr. Kahn, yes."

Senator Bristow—"Was Mr. Kahn ever an American Citizen?"

Mr. Warburg—"No."

Senator Bristow—"He never was?"

Mr. Warburg—"No; he is a British subject."

Senator Bristow—"He is a British subject?"

The Chairman—"He lives in England, does he not?"

Mr. Warburg—"No. At one time he thought he would move to Europe, and that was when the question arose of his standing for Parliament; then he changed his mind and moved back to the United States."

Senator Bristow—"He was at one time a candidate, or a prospective candidate for Parliament, was he not?"

Mr. Warburg—"No; he was not; but there was talk about it; it had been suggested, and he had it in his mind. Something had been written about it in the papers."—(p. 76, Senate Hearings, August 3, 1914.)

So, that if Mr. Kahn is a citizen of the United States now, which as a matter of fact has been disputed, then he has been a citizen of three countries, Germany and Great Britain being the other two.

Mr. Kahn, by the way, is one of those Jews whose adoption of another form of faith brings no denunciation whatever from the Jews themselves. A most peculiar circumstance! But doubtless not inexplicable. Mr. Kahn is not called a "renegade Jew" nor any of the other nasty names heaped upon Jewish converts to Christianity, because he does not deserve them. They would not fit him. He is not renegade. And he never was regarded for a moment by Jacob H. Schiff as anything but a Jew, else that "Prince of Israel" would not have chosen him to remain in America and run the business of Kuhn, Loeb & Company, at a time when it seemed undesirable to put the junior Schiff in full charge of it.

Doubtless it was Mr. Kahn's desire, just at the time Jacob Schiff made his wishes known, to go to England and stand for Parliament.

But from New York he fulfills, probably as well as he could from London, those mysterious missions which frequently take him to the Continent, at which times he makes what are regarded as certain authoritative decisions, though just whose decisions it is not always possible to say.

In Paris particularly, and at points east thereof, Mr. Kahn has been established in the position of spokesman of the American Financial Hierarchy, which, of course, he is not. But he undoubtedly is the spokesmen of some group, possibly the group which so ably put through the Jewish program at the Peace Conference, the group that impressed Eastern Europe with the feeling that the United States of America was a very powerful Semitic empire. Mr. Kahn's trips abroad are usually unheralded, but their results richly repay observation.

A fourth member of the Jewish financial group in America (which is the form of statement which Mr. Chaim Weizmann would sanction, rather than to say "Jewish-American financiers") is Mr. Paul Warburg, to whose testimony we have just alluded.

Mr. Warburg is the most recent of all. He was born in Germany in 1868; he came to the United States in 1902; he became an American citizen in 1911. He came to the United States for the express purpose of reforming our financial system, and it is hardly possible to understand fully the system in operation today without reference to Paul Warburg. He is a man of very fine mind, a money-maker, but something more—a shrewd student of the systems by which money is made.

There are two types engaged in the mere work of money-making which is better described as "money-getting," without reference to production; one type grubs away under whatever system obtains, regarding it as fixed as the solar system; another type is sufficiently detached to see the system as an artifice which may be mended, remodeled or supplanted altogether. Paul Warburg, scion of a long line of German Jewish bankers, is of the latter type.

He is not content with the fact that the cash-register fills itself with money; he wants also to know how the cash-register works, and whether it can be worked. He is thus a student of money and of the number of ways in which it can be manipulated.

Perhaps it will be best to let him tell his own story as far as he goes. When he told it to the Committee on Banking and Currency of the United States Senate in executive session, there was some dispute as to whether the proceedings should be recorded by stenographer. It was finally agreed that notes should be made but should not be divulged. The testimony was printed, "in confidence" on August 5, 1914, and nominally "made public" on August 12.

The Warburgs are one of the international families whose importance was not realized until the war, and would not have been realized then if their internationalism had not been so apparent. It was an interesting spectacle to see brothers occupying important places of counsel on either side of the great struggle.

Paul Warburg learned the rudiments of banking in his father's bank at Hamburg, Germany, studying the over-sea trade which is the foundation of that city's business. The banking house of Warburg in Hamburg dates from 1796.

"After that I went to England, where I stayed for two years, first in the banking and discount firm of Samuel Montague & Company, and after that I took the opportunity of staying two months in the office of a stockbroker in order to learn that part of the business.

"After that I went to France, where I stayed in a French bank, so that-"

The Chairman—"What French bank was that?"

Mr. Warburg—"It is the Russian bank for foreign trade, which has an agency in Paris.

"And after that I went back to Hamburg and worked there again for a year, I think.

"Then I went round to India, China and Japan.

"And then I came to this country for the first time in 1893. I stayed here only a short time then, and went back to Hamburg, and then became a partner of the firm in Hamburg."

The Chairman—"How long were you in Hamburg then in the banking business?"

Mr. Warburg—"Until 1902 . . . . And then I moved over here to this country to become a partner of Kuhn, Loeb & Company."

"I explained in the curriculum which I gave you, Mr. Chairman, that by marriage I am related to members of the firm, the late Mr. Loeb having been my father-in-law, which brought about a desire on the part of the family to bring me over here . . . . I ought to say that I got married in this country in 1895 and that I have been in this country every year since, for several months . . . . That is the history of my banking education."

It will be recalled that Jacob H. Schiff also married a daughter of Mr. Loeb, so that Mr. Warburg married the sister of Mrs. Jacob H. Schiff. Felix Warburg, Paul's brother, who is also in the firm, married Mr. Schiff 's daughter.

Mr. Warburg immediately cast a critical eye upon the state of financial affairs in the United States and it is significant of the grasp he already had on such matters that he found the country rather behind the times.

He conceived the ambition—the very daring ambition—of taking hold of the United States' monetary system and making it what he thought it ought to be.

This alone would make him a remarkable man. It illustrates very well that detached point of view which the Jew is more fitted to take than any other man perhaps. He sees countries and systems with the same freedom from intimate bias with which another man would view assorted fish upon a market stall. Most of the world is engaged in doing its work and indulging its national, racial, domestic and social affections and inclinations; a small minority stands in the background and watches the entire mass at its unconscious maneuvers, and studies it as an observer studies a hive of bees. The man at work has no time except for his job. One man, standing back and studying 1,000 men at work, is able to see how he might utilize their labor or possess himself of a first toll on their production. Doubtless there must be men to stand at a sufficient distance from things to get a correct idea of their interrelationship, and doubtless such an attitude may be made of great service to the race, but doubtless it has also contributed to the selfish manipulation of natural and social processes.

Mr. Warburg testified: "When I came here I was at once impressed by the lack of system, by the old-fashioned nature of the system that prevailed here; and I got immediately into one of those periods of high interest rates, where call money went up to 25 and 100 per cent; and I wrote an article on the subject then and there for my own benefit.

"I was not here three weeks before I was trying to explain to myself the roots of the evil. I showed the article to a few friends but I kept it in my desk, because I did not want to be one of those who try to inform and educate the country after they have been here for a month or so;

and I kept that article until the end of 1906, shortly before the panic, when those conditions arose again, and when one newspaper wanted for an issue at the end of the year an article dealing with the conditions in our country.

"Then I took out that article and touched it up and brought it up to date; and that was the first article of mine that was published. It was called, 'Defects and Needs of Our Banking System.' . . . .

"That was, however, the first time that I know of that the question of the discount system and the concentration of reserves was really brought out; and I got a great many encouraging letters asking me to go on and explain my ideas."

Mr. Warburg was perfectly willing to talk to the committee about himself, but not about Kuhn, Loeb & Company, his firm.

"I cannot discuss the affairs of my firm nor my partners," he said, "nor be asked to criticize acts of my partners, either to approve them or in any other way," but eventually he did tell a number of things which students of American financial affairs have considered interesting. Of which more later.

On page 77 of the testimony, more personal matters appear: Senator Bristow—"When did you become a citizen of the United States, Mr. Warburg?"

Mr. Warburg—"1911. Did I not answer that?"

Senator Bristow—"Perhaps so. Did you intend to become a citizen when you came to the United States in 1902?"

Mr. Warburg—"I had no definite intentions then, because some of the reasons that brought me over here were family reasons; . . . . That had a good deal to do with my first coming here; and I was not sure at all that I would stay here when I came."

Senator Bristow—"When did you decide to become a citizen of the United States?"

Mr. Warburg—"In 1908, when I took out my papers."

Senator Bristow—"When you took out your first papers? You took out your second papers then, in 1911?"

Mr. Warburg—"Yes."

Senator Bristow—"You made your declaration in 1908; that is when you decided to become an American citizen?"

Mr. Warburg—"Yes."

Senator Bristow—"Why did you wait as long as you did after you came to this country, before deciding to become a citizen of this country?"

Mr. Warburg—"I think that a man that does not come here as an immigrant; a man who has had, if you may call it such, a prominent position in his own country, will not give up his nationality so easily as a man who comes over here knowing that he does not care for his own country at all. I had been a very loyal citizen of my own country; and I think that a man who hesitates in giving up his own nationality and taking a new one, is apt to be more loyal to his new country when he does change his nationality than a man who gives up his old country more lightly."

Senator Bristow—"Yes."

Mr. Warburg—"I may add this: That a thing which had a great deal of influence on my making up my mind to remain in this country and work here, and become a part and parcel of this country, was that monetary reform work, for I felt I had a distinct duty to perform here; and I thought I could do that; and in fact I have been working on it since 1906 or 1907. Then I felt that it was the right thing for me to become an American citizen and work here and throw in my lot definitely with this country."

Senator Bristow—"When you became an American citizen; and the motive which induced you to become an American citizen was, then, as I understand it, largely with a view of laboring to bring about a reform of the American monetary system?"

Mr. Warburg—"Well, you put it nearly exclusively on that. I think a man wants to feel that he is going to do some useful work in his country; that he has a mission to perform; and that is what happened to me . . . . Moreover, I had been long enough in this country then to have thoroughly taken root and feel that I was a part and parcel of it."

Senator Bristow—"Yes. When did you first become active in promoting the monetary reforms in the United States?"

Mr. Warburg—"1906."

Senator Bristow—"What was your method of promoting your ideas with regard to monetary reforms?"

Mr. Warburg—"Mainly writing."

Senator Bristow—"Were you connected with the Monetary Commission?"

Mr. Warburg—"No, not directly . . . ."

Senator Bristow—"Were you consulted in regard to the report of the Monetary Commission in any way?"

Mr. Warburg—"Yes, Senator Aldrich consulted with me about details, and I gave him my advice freely."

Senator Bristow—"And in regard to the bill which was prepared by Senator Aldrich in connection with the commission, were you consulted in regard to that?"

Mr. Warburg—"Yes."

Senator Bristow—"What part did you have in the preparation of that bill, directly or indirectly?"

Mr. Warburg—"Well, only that I gave the best advice that I could give."

Most readers will recall that the name of "Aldrich" was, a few years ago, the synonym for the money power in government. Senator Aldrich was an able man and a tireless worker. His character for thoroughness and industry did more than anything else to disabuse the popular mind of the notion that such men were mere "tools of the money interest," or engaged in their work out of lust for gain, or out of sheer pleasure in legislating against the interests of the people.

Senator Aldrich led on tariff and financial matters because he understood them; and he understood them by tireless study of them; and, therefore, he was the master of other men who had not paid the price of knowledge. But, he understood these matters from the standpoint of the business interests only. He was sincerely desirous of the prosperity of the country, but that prosperity was written in banking balances. Fifteen years ago it might not have been possible to judge him thus calmly, because then he represented in the public mind, more than any individual does today, the concentrated power of the financial group. Their prosperity was his first care, possibly because he believed that their prosperity was also the country's.

It was such a man, then, that came to Mr. Warburg for advice. The labors of Senator Aldrich comprise many volumes of difficult material and Senator Aldrich's appeal to Mr. Warburg was a very high compliment to the quality of the latter's mind and financial experience—this, of course, assuming that Mr. Warburg's counsel was not forced upon the Aldrich committee by the New York money interests.

In his testimony, Mr. Warburg did not tell all. The omission, however, was supplied by an article in Leslie's Weekly in 1916, the author being B. C. Forbes.

It is a story of which Current Opinion said: "It reads like the opening in a shilling shocker."

It appears that the conferences between Mr. Warburg and Senator Aldrich took place on an isolated island off the coast of Georgia—Jekyl Island. Included in the party, besides Senator Aldrich and Mr. Warburg, were two New York bankers and the then Assistant Treasurer of the United States. The mysteriousness of it all was well brought out by Mr. Forbes:

"Picture a party of the nation's greatest bankers stealing out of New York on a private railroad car under cover of darkness, stealthily hieing hundreds of miles south, embarking on a mysterious launch, sneaking out to an island deserted by all but a few servants, living there a full week under such rigid secrecy that the name of not one of them was once mentioned lest the servitors learn their identity and disclose to the world this strangest, most secret episode in the history of American finance.

"The utmost secrecy was enjoined upon all. The public must not glean a hint of what was to be done. Senator Aldrich notified each one to go quietly into a private car which the railroad had received orders to draw up at an unfrequented platform. Drawn blinds balked any peering eyes that might be around. Off the party set. New York's ubiquitous reporters had been foiled. So far so good. After bowling along the railroad hour after hour into southern country, the order was given to prepare to disembark.

"Stepping from the car when the station had been well cleared of travelers, the members of the expedition embarked in a small boat. Silence reigned, for the boatmen must not find out how distinguished were their passengers.

"In due time they drew up at another deserted pier. They were at Jekyl Island, off Georgia. The island was entirely unpeopled save for half a dozen servants.

"'The servants must under no circumstances learn who we are,' cautioned Senator Aldrich.

"'What can we do to fool them?' asked another member of the group. The problem was discussed.

"'I have it,' cried one. 'Let's all call each other by our first names. Don't ever let us mention our last names.'

"It was so agreed.

"The dignified veteran Senator Aldrich, king of Rhode Island and a power second to none in the United States Senate, became just 'Nelson'; . . . . and the quiet, scholarly member of the powerful international banking firm of Kuhn, Loeb & Company, became 'Paul.'

"Nelson had meanwhile confided to Harry, Frank, Paul and Piatt that he was to keep them locked up on Jekyl Island, cut off from the rest of the world, until they had evolved and compiled a scientific currency system for the United States, a system that would embody all that was best in Europe, yet so modeled that it could serve a country measuring thousands where European countries measured only hundreds of miles."

Mr. Forbes does not omit to write this further description of Mr. Warburg's condition at the time:

"unable then to speak idiomatic English with perfect freedom and without an accent, an alien not naturalized."

Mr. Forbes also wrote—"Here is a German-American, but the sort of one that makes the hyphen look like a badge of honor."

That was in 1916. Hyphens went out of fashion, though not entirely out of use, soon after.

Thus far the story of Paul Warburg.

The Dearborn Independent, issue of 18 June 1921

58: Jewish Idea Molded Federal Reserve Plan

The last view the reader had of Paul M. Warburg in the preceding article was as "an alien not naturalized" secretly closeted with Senator Nelson W. Aldrich and a party of bankers on an obscure island off the southeastern coast of the United States, all the members of the party concealing their identity even from the servants by calling each other by their first names.

That conference in its ultimate results was of the utmost importance to the United States, for then and there were formulated those fiscal devices, those financial methods, those "monetary reforms" which have exerted an influence on every citizen, rich and poor, of the Republic.

Much history was made in that little trip. It irresistibly calls to memory that other trip made in 1915—almost two years before America's entry into the war—by Bernard M. Baruch. As readers of *The Dearborn Independent* of November 27, 1920, will recall, Mr. Baruch had been financial backer of the Plattsburg camp, and in his testimony he said he thought that General Wood would admit this. Then— "I went off on a long trip, and it was while on this trip that I felt there ought to be some mobilization of the industries, and I was thinking about the scheme that practically was put into effect and was working when I was chairman of the board. When I came back from that trip I asked for an interview with the President . . . . The President listened very attentively and graciously as he always does." Mr. Baruch was an authority on the President's demeanor, for there was a long period in 1917 and 1918 during which he called at the White House every afternoon.

Two momentous trips in our recent history, both of them signalized and given their principal meaning by the presence of Jews. Not that there should not have been Jews in either case; to insist upon their total exclusion would be going too far. The Jew as a citizen, bearing his part, is one matter; the Jew as a master, directing the national show, is quite another thing. It is by no means agreed that Barney Baruch was the only man in the United States who could have run this nation's war business. That is the explanation made of the high place he took—that he was the only man who could do it. Nonsense! If that be so, let us close up the nation and hand the keys over to the New York Kehillah. Mr. Baruch could say—"I probably had more power than any other man did in the war; doubtless that is true," but he had that power because he was for the time the head and front of the Jewish group for war purposes.

If the explanation of Jewish mastery at critical moments were "brains," well and good, but if it were, it would be more evident to the people; brains do not need to be advertised, they advertise themselves. There is another reason.

The British public recently awoke to the fact that not Lloyd George but Mr. Montagu and Sir Alfred Mond were in charge of the recent negotiations over the German indemnities. These gentlemen are both Jews, one of them of German descent. Of all the British Empire are they the only two men to advise the premier in a great crisis? If they are, why is it? The Montagus, we know, control the silver of the world; Sir Alfred Mond, we know, turned a very neat trick of keeping the sign of the Cross off the war memorials raised to the soldiers of the empire; their Jewishness always so apparent. Both financiers; both the close advisers of the premier; as Baruch to Wilson, so they to Lloyd George.

Apparently there are no Anglo-Saxons on either side of the sea capable of managing these deep matters, if we are to judge from the war administrations—those that have passed off the stage and those that still linger. Lloyd George, for once stung to the quick by the criticism of the British public of his tendency to closet himself with Jews when confronted with a crucial question, retorted bitterly—with what? With the old outworn Jewish propagandist boast, that it ill became people who sang Jewish psalms in church to rag the race that wrote them! A most illuminating defense! The world would give a good deal for a true psalm from Sir Alfred Mond, Mr. Montagu, or even Sir Philip Sassoon, who is soon to become the premier's son-in-law.

In our own history, Barney Baruch boldly claims his place, he unhesitatingly asserts that he had more power than any man in the war. If Allenby in Palestine needed a locomotive, if the Americans in Russia needed clothing, if the munition mills needed copper—it was Baruch who gave or withheld the word.

Mr. Warburg, being of somewhat finer grain, probably due to his having less than Mr. Baruch of the rough experience of "the Street," does not make the claim that he is the chief factor in the present monetary system of the United States, nor does *The Dearborn Independent* undertake to make it for him lest the cry of "anti-Semitism" wax wrathful again; but fortunately the fact is amply attested by a Jew whose knowledge of the matter is unquestionable.

Readers have doubtless become aware by this time that for a non-Jew to say that a certain Jew is a most important factor in any field is to be guilty of anti-Semitism, while for a Jew or a "Gentile front" to say it is perfectly proper. It is a rather odd etiquette in which simple minds sometimes become confused.

Professor E. R. A. Seligman, of Columbia University, is the sponsor of this great honor for Mr. Warburg. What Professor Seligman says is of such importance, both as to its source and its subject, that quotation is justified: (the italics in all cases are ours)

"It is in a general way known to the public that Mr. Warburg was in some way connected with the passage of the Federal Reserve Act, and his appointment to his present responsible position on the Federal Reserve Board was acclaimed on all sides with a rare degree of approval and congratulation; but I fancy it is known only to a very few how great is the indebtedness of the United States to Mr. Warburg. For it may be stated without fear of contradiction that in its fundamental features the Federal Reserve Act is the work of Mr. Warburg more than of any other man in the country . . . .

"When the Aldrich commission was appointed it was not long before Senator Aldrich—to his credit be it said—was won over by Mr. Warburg to the adoption of these two fundamental features. The Aldrich Bill differed in some important particulars from the present law . . . . The concession in the shape of the twelve regional banks that had to be made for political reasons is, in the opinion of Mr. Warburg as well as of the writer of this introduction, a mistake; for it will probably, to some extent at least, weaken the good results which would otherwise have followed. On the other hand, the existence of a Federal Reserve Board creates, in everything but in name, a real central bank; and it depends largely upon the wisdom with which the board exercises its great powers as to whether we shall be able to secure most of the advantages of a central bank without any of its dangers . . . .

"In many minor respects also the Federal Reserve Act differs from the Aldrich Bill; but in the two fundamentals of combined reserves and of a discount policy, the Federal Reserve Act has frankly accepted the principles of the Aldrich Bill; and these principles, as has been stated, were the creation of Mr. Warburg and of Mr. Warburg alone.

". . . . It must not be forgotten that Mr. Warburg had a practical object in view. In formulating his plans and in advancing slightly varying suggestions from time to time, it was incumbent on him to remember that the education of the country must be gradual and that a large part of the task was to break down prejudices and remove suspicions. His plans, therefore contain all sorts of elaborate suggestions designed to guard the public against fancied dangers and to persuade the country that the general scheme was at all practicable. It was the hope of Mr. Warburg that with the lapse of time it might be possible to eliminate from the law not a few clauses which were inserted, largely at his suggestion, for educational purposes.

"As it was my privilege to say to President Wilson when originally urging the appointment of Mr. Warburg on the Federal Reserve Board, at a time when the political prejudice against New York bankers ran very high, England also, three-quarters of a century ago, had a practical banker who was virtually responsible for the idea contained in Peel's Bank Act of 1840. Mr. Samuel Jones Lloyd was honored as a consequence by the British Government and was made Lord Overstone. The United States was equally fortunate in having with it a Lord Overstone . . . .

"The Federal Reserve Act will be associated in history with the name of Paul M. Warburg . . . ."—(pp. 387-390, Vol. 4, No. 4, *Proceedings of the Academy of Political Science,* Columbia University).

It surely cannot be considered invidious for *The Dearborn Independent* thus to introduce to the people of the United States a gentleman whose influence upon the country is so vital. Just how vital can be understood only by those who have studied the puzzle of a country filled with the good things of life, and still unable to use them or to share them because of a kink in the pipe line called "money."

But that Mr. Warburg himself is not entirely unaware of his position is indicated on page 56 of his testimony quoted last week. Mr Warburg had just told the Senate Committee that he was making a heavy financial sacrifice to accept the position on the Federal Reserve Board offered him by President Wilson, and into the fitness of which appointment the Senate was carefully inquiring:

Senator Reed—"May I ask what your motive is, or your reason for making that sacrifice?"

Mr. Warburg—"My motive is that I have, as you know, taken a keen interest in this monetary reform since I have been in this country. I have had the success which comes to few people, of starting an idea and starting it so that the whole country has taken it up and it has taken some tangible form."

Professor Seligman advises us of the strategy that was used to get the whole country to take up Mr. Warburg's idea, and of the fact that some of the items inserted to appease the public might easily be removed when the public shall have become accustomed to Mr. Warburg and the Federal Reserve Board; but Mr. Warburg adds another hint, to the effect that you can do some things by administration which you cannot do by organization.

For example: Mr. Warburg wanted only one central bank which should be the sole arbiter of finance in the United States. The United States Government would have almost nothing to do save to make the money and stand back of it; the bankers of the United States, and the people thereof, would have nothing to do except what they were told; the one central bank would be the real financial governing authority.

When asked by Senator Bristow to state the fundamental difference between the Aldrich plan and the present Federal Reserve plan, Mr. Warburg replied:

"Well, the Aldrich Bill brings the whole system into one unit, while this deals with 12 units, and unites them again into the Federal Reserve Board. It is a little bit complicated, which objection, however, can be overcome in an administrative way; and in that respect I freely criticized the bill before it was passed."

There is evidently, then, a method of administration for which severe critics might even use the word "manipulation," by which the plain provisions of a banking law, whatever they may be, may be, if not evaded, then somewhat adapted.

This idea is brought to mind by a more colloquial expression of Mr. Warburg's to be found in his address on "bank acceptances" delivered in 1919:

"In this connection I am reminded of a story I once heard concerning a man belonging to a species now soon to be extinct and to be found by our children in Webster's dictionary only, the 'bartender.' A man of this profession, in pre-historic times, was abandoning his position and was turning over his cash-register to his successor. 'Please show me how it works,' said the newcomer. 'I will show you how it works,' said the other, 'but I won't show you how to work it.'"

The politics of Mr. Warburg and the firm of Kuhn, Loeb & Company formed part of the inquiry, and Mr. Warburg made some interesting revelations which illustrate the oft-repeated statement that it is part of Jewish policy—perhaps of large financial firms generally—to attach themselves to both parties so that certain interests may be the winners regardless of which party is defeated.

Senator Pomerene—"What are your politics?"

Senator Nelson—"No; we have not raised that before this committee."

Senator Reed—"It has not been raised here, but I should like to know."

Senator Pomerene—"It has been raised before the Senate." Senator Reed—"I will say why I should like to know."

Senator Pomerene—"Well, I have no objection to saying what was in my own mind."

The Chairman—"I will say that I do not know what Mr. Warburg's politics are."

Senator Pomerene—"Well, I did not."

Senator Shafroth—"I do not know and I do not care to know."

Senator Pomerene—"I heard the statement made that the entire board was Democratic, and I had understood that Mr. Warburg was a Republican, or had been, in his affiliations."

Mr. Warburg—"Well, so I was; and my sympathies were entirely, in the early campaign, for Mr. Taft against Mr. Roosevelt in the first fight. When later on Mr. Roosevelt became President Wilson's opponent my sympathies went with Mr. Wilson . . . ."

Senator Reed—"Well, you would count yourself a Republican, generally speaking?"

Mr. Warburg—"I would."

Senator Bristow—"It has been variously reported in the newspapers that you and your partners directly and indirectly contributed very largely to Mr. Wilson's campaign funds."

Mr. Warburg—"Well, my partners—there is a very peculiar condition—no; I do not think any one of them contributed largely at all; there may have been moderate contributions. My brother, for instance, contributed to Mr. Taft's campaign."

Senator Bristow—"Just what would you consider a moderate contribution to a presidential campaign?"

Mr. Warburg—"Well, that depends who the man is who contributes; but I think anything below $10,000 or $5,000 would not be an extravagant contribution, so far as that should be—"

(Examination resumed another day)

Senator Bristow—"Now, Mr. Warburg, when we closed Saturday some Senator asked you in regard to political contributions, and I understood you to say that you contributed to Mr. Wilson's campaign."

Mr. Warburg—"No; my letter says that I offered to contribute; but it was too late. I came back to this country only a few days before the campaign closed."

Senator Bristow—"So that you did not make any contribution?" Mr. Warburg—"I did not make any contribution; no."

Senator Bristow—"Did any members of your firm make contributions to Mr. Wilson's campaign?"

Mr. Warburg—"I think that is a matter of record. Mr. Schiff contributed. I would not otherwise discuss the contributions of my partners, if it was not a matter of record. I think Mr. Schiff was the only one who contributed in our firm."

Senator Bristow—"And you stated that your brother had contributed to Mr. Taft's campaign, as I understand it?"

Mr. Warburg—"I did. But again, I do not want to go into a discussion of my partners' affairs, and I shall stick to that pretty strictly, or we will never get through."

Senator Bristow—"I understood you also to say that no members of your firm contributed to Mr. Roosevelt's campaign."

Mr. Warburg—"I did not say that."

Senator Bristow—"Oh! Did any members of the firm do that?"

Mr. Warburg—"My answer would please you probably; but I shall not answer that, but will repeat that I will not discuss my partners' affairs."

Senator Bristow—"Yes. I understood you to say Saturday that you were a Republican, but when Mr. Roosevelt became a candidate, you then became a sympathizer with Mr. Wilson and supported him?"

Mr. Warburg—"Yes."

Senator Bristow—"While your brother was supporting Mr. Taft?" Mr. Warburg—"Yes."

Senator Bristow—"And I was interested to know whether any member of your firm supported Mr. Roosevelt."

Mr. Warburg—"It is a matter of record that there are."

Senator Bristow—"That there are some of them who did?" Mr. Warburg—"Oh, yes."

Senator Bristow—"Will you please indicate—or do you care to indicate—what members of your firm supported Mr. Roosevelt in that campaign?"

Mr. Warburg—"No, sir; I shall have to go on the principle that I cannot disclose the business of a member of my firm."

The result was this: that in a three-cornered fight between three candidates, Roosevelt, Taft and Wilson, the men who constituted the firm of Kuhn, Loeb, & Company, chief Jewish financial institution of the United States, distributed their support among all three. Schiff for Wilson; Felix Warburg for Taft; and an unknown for Roosevelt—was that unknown Mr. Kahn? In any case, Wilson won, and the above examination relates to a member of the firm of Kuhn, Loeb & Company receiving an important appointment which gave him large power over the finances of the United States.

The point of not discussing the affairs of Kuhn, Loeb & Company was frequently made by Mr. Warburg.

"I cannot discuss the affairs of the firm nor my partners, nor be asked to criticize acts of my partners, either to approve them or in any other way. I would like to say that before we come to the point where I would feel that I should not answer any question," said Mr. Warburg.

The principle of this objection was conceded by the Senate Committee, but that it ought to serve as a blanket injunction against a number of pertinent inquiries was doubted.

Senator Bristow—"But you are a partner in this firm, and have you not had something to do with its operations and its management?" Mr. Warburg—"Yes."

Senator Bristow—"Does that not go to show your general views and practices as a financier and as a citizen and as a business man?"

Mr. Warburg—"Yes; but you have got to take them individually. . . . I cannot permit my firm to be drawn into this discussion."

Senator Bristow—"But how can you divest yourself from your firm when you have been one of the managers of the firm?"

Mr. Warburg—"I shall divest myself of the firm."

Senator Bristow—"If the firm has done something that I might think was improper—to illustrate, being called upon to say whether or not I approve your nomination to this responsible position—have I not a right to know what your attitude was in regard to that transaction which your firm performed?"

Mr. Warburg—"Well, inasmuch as my answer there might be a criticism of my firm, I would beg to be excused, and I would leave it to the committee to draw its own conclusions. . . ."

In examining Mr. Warburg about the handling of $100,000,000

Southern Pacific securities, the same difficulty was experienced; Mr. Warburg objected, "but we are getting here again into the transactions of my firm!"

To which Senator Bristow retorted—"Ah! but when you participated in the profits of the transaction, is it not a part of your business life?"

Mr. Warburg—"Certainly it is a part of my business life, and there is no reason why I should not be proud of it. But as a matter of principle I think we should not get into a discussion of the business of my firm."

Senator Bristow—"I am discussing your business."

Mr. Warburg—"No, you are discussing the firm's business."

Senator Bristow—"Did you get any of the profits that came from the handling of this $100,000,000?"

Mr. Warburg—"You may take it that whatever my firm did I got my profits—my share in the profits."

Senator Bristow—"Your share in the profits. Now, without being specific, I take it for granted that this was quite material; that that was quite a material interest in size; that is, that you are one of the important members of the firm."

Mr. Warburg—"I am one of the important members of the firm."

Senator Bristow—"Yes, I think the testimony and the report here show that you are the third important member—or the second, which is it?—of the firm."

Mr. Warburg—"We are not numbered."

Senator Bristow—"You are not; all right."

Mr. Warburg—"There is Mr. Jacob H. Schiff who is the senior."

Senator Bristow—"Yes."

Mr. Warburg—"And the others rank very much alike."

Senator Bristow—"Yes. We may take it for granted, then, that whatever profits accrued to your firm in the handling of this business here since you became a member of it, you participated in the profits as one of the partners."

Mr. Warburg—"Yes, sir."

Senator Bristow—"Yes. So I will assume then, of course, that you participated in the marketing of $113,000,000 of Union Pacific, and so on."

The responsibilities of a member of the Federal Reserve Board, especially such a member as Paul M. Warburg would be (for it was recognized that because of his purpose and connections he would become a dominating factor), were very great, especially at the time when the appointment was being considered. They are as important now, of course, but in a different way; it is not now a question of military safety. This thought was evidently in the mind of the senators, as the following shows:

Senator Hitchcock—"Mr. Warburg, one of the important functions of the board is to guard the gold supply of the country, and it has been thought that it is very important to have men on the board who had at heart only the interests of the United States, and had no foreign interests or alliances.

You have said that you proposed to divest yourself altogether of your banking connections in Germany. Have you any other interests in Europe?"

"No, not to speak of," said Mr. Warburg. "I may have very unimportant things, like everybody has; but I could dispose of those; it would not amount to anything."

Senator Hitchcock—"Nothing in the line of banking?"

Mr. Warburg—"No."

A few moments later the chairman, Senator Owen, said—(the date was August 1, 1914)—"We are on the eve of a great European war, and the organization of this board is of great national importance."

At this time, Mr. Warburg was a member of the Hamburg firm. He testified (p. 7)—"I am going to leave my Hamburg firm, though the law does not require me to do so."

A part of the German firm of his father and brothers, a part of the American firm to which he and his brother were related by marital as well as financial ties, Mr. Warburg repeatedly said he would break off all business relationships so that he, like Caesar's wife (to quote himself), should be above suspicion.

The Dearborn Independent, issue of 25 June 1921

59: Jewish Idea of Central Bank for America

According to his own statements and the facts, Paul M. Warburg set out to reform the monetary system of the United States, and did so. He had the success which comes to few men, of coming an alien to the United States, connecting himself with the principal Jewish financial firm here, and immediately floating certain banking ideas which have been pushed and manipulated and variously adapted until they eventuated in what is known as the Federal Reserve System.

When Professor Seligman wrote in the Proceedings of the Academy of Political Science that "the Federal Reserve Act will be associated in history with the name of Paul M. Warburg," a Jewish banker from Germany, he wrote the truth. But whether that association will be such as to bring the measure of renown which Professor Seligman implies, the future will reveal.

What the people of the United States do not understand and never have understood is that while the Federal Reserve Act was governmental, the whole Federal Reserve System is private. It is an officially created private banking system.

Examine the first thousand persons you meet on the street, and 999 will tell you that the Federal Reserve System is a device whereby the United States Government went into the banking business for the benefit of the people. They have an idea that, like the Post Office and the Custom House, a Federal Reserve Bank is a part of the Government's official machinery.

It is natural to feel that this mistaken view has been encouraged by most of the men who are competent to write for the public on this question. Take up the standard encyclopedias, and while you will find no misstatements of fact in them, you will find no direct statement that the Federal Reserve System is a private banking system; the impression carried away by the lay reader is that it is a part of the Government.

The Federal Reserve System is a system of private banks, the creation of a banking aristocracy within an already existing autocracy, whereby a great proportion of banking independence was lost, and whereby it was made possible for speculative financiers to centralize great sums of money for their own purposes, beneficial or not.

That this System was useful in the artificial conditions created by war—useful, that is, for a Government that cannot manage its own business and finances and, like a prodigal son, is always wanting money, and wanting it when it wants it—it has proved, either by reason of its inherent faults or by mishandling, its inadequacy to the problems of peace. It has sadly failed of its promise, and is now under serious question.

Mr. Warburg's scheme succeeded just in time to take care of war conditions, he was placed on the Federal Reserve Board in order to manage his system in practice, and though he was full of ideas then as to how banking could be assisted, he is disappointingly silent now as to how the people can be relieved.

However, this is not a discussion of the Federal Reserve System. General condemnation of it would be stupid. But it is bound to come up for discussion one day, and the discussion will become much freer when people understand that it is a system of privately owned banks, to which have been delegated certain extraordinary privileges, and that it has created a class system within the banking world which constitutes a new order.

Mr. Warburg, it will be remembered, wanted only one central bank. But, because of political considerations, as Professor Seligman tells us, twelve were decided upon. An examination of Mr. Warburg's printed discussions of the subject shows that he at one time considered four, then eight. Eventually, twelve were established. The reason was that one central bank, which naturally would be set up in New York, would give a suspicious country the impression that it was only a new scheme to keep the nation's money flowing to New York. As shown by Professor Seligman, quoted in the last number, Mr. Warburg was not averse to granting anything that would allay popular suspicion without vitiating the real plan.

So, while admitting to the Senators who examined him as to his fitness for membership on the Federal Reserve Board—the Board which fixed the policies of the banks of the Federal Reserve System and told them what to do—that he did not like the 12 district banks idea, he said that his objections to it could "be overcome in an administrative way." That is, the 12 banks could be so handled that the effect would be the same as if there were only one central bank, presumably in New York.

And that is about the way it has resulted, and that will be found to be one of the reasons for the present situation of the country.

There is no lack of money in New York today. Motion picture ventures are being financed into the millions. A big grain selling pool, nursed into existence and counseled by Bernard M. Baruch, has no hesitancy whatever in planning for a $100,000,000 corporation. Loew, the Jewish theatrical man, had no difficulty in opening 20 new theaters this year

But go into the agricultural states, where the real wealth of the country is in the ground and in the granaries, and you cannot find money for the farmer.

It is a situation which none can deny and which few can explain, because the explanation is not to be found along natural lines. Natural conditions are always easiest to explain. Unnatural conditions wear an air of mystery. Here is the United States, the richest country in the world, containing at the present hour the greatest bulk of wealth to be found anywhere on earth—real, ready, available, usable wealth; and yet it is tied up tight, and cannot move in its legitimate channels, because of manipulation which is going on as regards money.

Money is the last mystery for the popular mind to penetrate, and when it succeeds in getting "on the inside" it will discover that the mystery is not in money at all, but in its manipulation, the things which are done "in an administrative way."

The United States has never had a President who gave evidence of understanding this matter at all. Our Presidents have always had to take their views from financiers. Money is the most public quantity in the country; it is the most federalized and governmentalized thing in the country; and yet, in the present situation, the United States Government has hardly anything to do with it, except to use various means to get it, just as the people have to get it, from those who control it.

The Money Question, properly solved, is the end of the Jewish Question and every other question of a mundane nature.

Mr. Warburg is of the opinion that different rates of interest ought to obtain in different parts of the country. That they have always obtained in different parts of the same state we have always known, but the reason for it has not been discovered. The city grocer can get money from his bank at a lower rate than the farmer in the next county can get it from his bank. Why the agricultural rate of interest has been higher than any other (when money is obtainable; it is not obtainable now) is a question to which no literary nor oratorical financier has ever publicly addressed himself. It is like the fact of the private business nature of the Federal Reserve Sysem—very important, but no authority thinks it worth while to state. The agricultural rate of interest is of great importance, but to discuss it would involve first an admission, and that apparently is not desirable.

In comparing the present Federal Reserve Law with the proposed Aldrich Bill, Mr. Warburg said:

Mr. Warburg—"........ I think that this present law has the advantage of dealing with the entire country and giving them different rates of discount, whereas, as Senator Aldrich's bill was drawn, it would have been very difficult to do that, as it provided for one uniform rate for the whole country, which I thought was rather a mistake."

Senator Bristow—"That is, you can charge a higher rate of interest in one section of the country under the present law, than you charge in another section, while under the Aldrich plan it would have been a uniform rate."

Mr. Warburg—"That is correct."

That is a point worth clearing up. If Mr. Warburg, having educated the bankers, will now turn his attention to the people, and make it clear why one class in the country can get money for business that is not productive of real wealth, while another class engaged in the production of real wealth is treated as outside the interest of banking altogether; if he can make it clear also why money is sold to one class or one section of the country at one price, while to another class and in another section it is sold at a different price, he will be adding to the people's grasp of these matters.

This suggestion is seriously intended. Mr. Warburg has the style, the pedagogical patience, the grasp of the subject which would make him an admirable public teacher of these matters.

What he has already done was planned from the point of view of the interest of the professional financier. It is readily granted that Mr. Warburg desired to organize American finances into a more pliable system. Doubtless in some respects he has wrought important improvements. But he had always the banking house in mind, and he dealt with paper. Now, if taking up a position outside those special interests, he would address himself to the wider interests of the people—not assuming that those interests always run through a banking house—he would do still more than he has yet done to justify his feeling that he really had a mission in coming to this country.

Mr. Warburg is not at all shocked by the idea that the Federal Reserve System is really a new kind of private banking control, because in his European experience he saw that all the central banks were private affairs.

In his essay on "American and European Banking Methods and Bank Legislation Compared," Mr. Warburg says: (the italics are ours)

"It may also be interesting to note that, contrary to a widespread idea, the central banks of Europe are, as a rule, not owned by the governments. As a matter of fact, neither the English, French, nor German Government owns any stock in the central bank of its country. The Bank of England is run entirely as a private corporation, the stockholders electing the board of directors, who rotate in holding the presidency. In France the government appoints the governor and some of the directors.

In Germany the government appoints the president and a supervisory board of five members, while the stockholders elect the board of directors."

And again, in his discussion of the Owen-Glass Bill, Mr. Warburg says:

"The Monetary Commission's plan proceeded on the theory of the Bank of England, which leaves the management entirely in the hands of business men without giving the government any part in the management or control. The strong argument in favor of this theory is that central banking, like any other banking, is based on 'sound credit,' that the judging of credits is a matter of business which should be left in the hands of business men, and that the government should be kept out of business. . . . .

"The Owen-Glass Bill proceeds, in this respect, more on the lines of the Banque de France and the German Reichsbank, the presidents and boards of which are to a certain extent appointed by the government. These central banks, while legally private corporations, are semi-governmental organs inasmuch as they are permitted to issue the notes of the nation—particularly where there are elastic note issues, as in almost all countries except England—and inasmuch as they are the custodians of practically the entire metallic reserves of the country and the keepers of the government funds. Moreover in questions of national policy the government must rely on the willing and loyal co-operation of these central organs."

That is a very illuminating passage. It will be well worth the reader's time, especially the reader who has always been puzzled by financial matters, to turn over in his mind the facts here given by a great Jewish financial expert about the central bank idea. Observe the phrases:

(a) "without giving the government any part in the management or control."

(b) "these central banks, while legally private corporations . . . . are permitted to issue the notes of the nation."

(c) "they are custodians of practically the entire metallic reserves of the nation and the keepers of the government funds."

(d) "in questions of national policy, the government must rely on the willing and loyal co-operation of these central organs."

It is not now a question whether these things are right or wrong; it is merely a question of understanding that they constitute the fact.

It is specially notable that in paragraph (d) it is a fair deduction that in questions of national policy, the government will simply have to depend not only on the patriotism but also to an extent on the permission and counsel of the financial organizations. That is a fair interpretation: questions of national policy are, by this method, rendered dependent upon the financial corporations.

Let that point be clear, quite regardless of the question whether or not this is the way national policies should be determined.

Mr. Warburg said that he believed in a certain amount of government control—but not too much. He said: "In strengthening the government control, the Owen-Glass Bill therefore moved in the right direction; but it went too far and fell into the other and even more dangerous extreme."

The "more dangerous extreme" was, of course, the larger measure of government supervision provided for, and the establishment of a number of Federal Reserve Banks out in the country.

Mr. Warburg had referred to this before; he had agreed to the larger number only because it seemed to be an unavoidable political concession. It has already been shown, by Professor Seligman, that Mr. Warburg was alive to the necessity of veiling a little here and a little there, and "putting on" a little yonder, for the sake of conciliating a suspicious public. There was also the story of the bartender and the cash register.

Mr. Warburg thinks he understands the psychology of America. In this respect he reminds one of the reports of Mr. von Bernstorff and Captain Boy-Ed of what the Americans were likely to do or not to do. In the *Political Science Quarterly* of December, 1920, Mr. Warburg tells how, on a then recent visit to Europe, he was asked by men of all countries what the United States was going to do. He assured them that

America was a little tired just then, but that she would come round all right. And then harking back to his efforts of placing his monetary system on the Americans, he said:

"I asked them to be patient with us until after the election, and I cited to them our experiences with monetary reform. I reminded them how the Aldrich plan had failed because, at that time, a Republican President had lost control of a Congress ruled by a Democratic majority; how the Democrats in their platform damned this plan and any central banking system; and how, once in full power, the National Reserve Association was evolved, not to say camouflaged, by them into the Federal Reserve System."

Remembering this play before the public, and the play behind the scenes, this "camouflaging," as Mr. Warburg says, of one thing into another, he undertook to assure his friends in Europe that regardless of what the political platforms said, the United States would do substantially what Europe hoped it would.

Mr. Warburg's basis for that belief was, as he said, his experience with the way the central bank idea went through in spite of the advertised objection of all parties. He believes that with Americans it is possible to get what you want if you just play the game skillfully. His experience with monetary reform seems to have fathered that belief in him.

Politicians may be necessary pawns to play in the game, but as members of the government Mr. Warburg does not want them in banking. They are not bankers, he says; they don't understand; banking is nothing for a government man to meddle with. He may be good enough for the Government of the United States; he is not good enough for banking.

"In our country," says Mr. Warburg, referring to the United States, "with every untrained amateur a candidate for any office, where friendship or help in a presidential campaign, financial or political, has always given a claim for political preferment, where the bids for votes and public favor are ever present in the politician's mind, ... a direct government management, that is to say, a political management, would prove fatal . . . . There can be no doubt but that, as drawn at present (1913), with two cabinet officers members of the Federal Reserve Board, and with the vast powers vested in the latter, the Owen-Glass Bill would bring about direct government management."

And that, of course, in Mr. Warburg,s mind, is not only "dangerous," but "fatal." Mr. Warburg had almost his whole will in the matter. And what was the result?

Turn to the testimony of Bernard M. Baruch, when he was examined with reference to the charge that certain men close to President Wilson had profited to the extent of $60,000,000 on stock market operations which they entered into on the strength of advance information of what the President was to say in his next war note—the famous "leak" investigation, as it was called; one of the several investigations in which Mr. Baruch was closely questioned.

In that investigation Mr. Baruch was laboring to show that he had not been in telephone communication with Washington, especially with certain men who were supposed to have shared the profits of the deals. The time was December, 1916. Mr. Warburg was then safely settled on the Federal Reserve Board, which he had kept quite safe from Government intrusion.

The Chairman—"Of course the records of the telephone company here, the slips, will show the persons with whom you talked."

Mr. Baruch—"Do you wish me to say, sir? I will state who they are."

The Chairman—"Yes, I think you might."

Mr. Baruch—"I called up two persons; one, Mr. Warburg, whom I did not get, and one, Secretary McAdoo, whom I did get—both in reference to the same matter. Would you like to know the matter?"

The Chairman—"Yes, I think it is fair that you should state it."

Mr. Baruch—"I called up the Secretary, because someone suggested to me—asked me to suggest an officer for the Federal Reserve Bank, and I called him in reference to that, and discussed the matter with him, I think, two or three times, but it was suggested to me that I make the suggestion, and I did so." (pp. 570-571)

Mr. Campbell—"Mr. Baruch, who asked you for a suggestion for an appointee for the Federal Reserve Bank here?"

Mr. Baruch—"Mr. E. M. House."

Mr. Campbell—"Did Mr. House tell you to call Mr. McAdoo up and make the recommendation?"

Mr. Baruch—"I will tell you exactly how it occurred: Mr. House called me up and said that there was a vacancy on the Federal Reserve Board. and he said, 'I don't know anything about those fellows down there, and I would like you to make a suggestion.' And I suggested the name, which he thought was a very good one, and he said to me, 'I wish you would call up the Secretary and tell him.' I said, 'I do not see the necessity; I will tell you.' 'No,' he said, 'I would prefer you to call him up.'" (p. 575)

There we have an example of the Federal Reserve "kept out of politics," kept away from government management which would not only be "dangerous," but "fatal."

Barney Baruch, the New York stock plunger, who never owned a bank in his life, was called up by Colonel E. M. House, the arch-politician of the Wilson Administration, and thus the great Federal Reserve Board was supplied another member.

A telephone call kept within a narrow Jewish circle and settled by a word from one Jewish stock dealer—that, in a practical operation, was Mr. Warburg's great monetary reform. Mr. Baruch calling up Mr. Warburg to give the name of the next appointee of the Federal Reserve Board, and calling up Mr. McAdoo, secretary of the United States Treasury, and set in motion to do it by Colonel E. M. House—is it any wonder the Jewish mystery in the American war government grows more and more amazing?

But, as Mr. Warburg has written—"friendship or help in a presidential campaign, financial or political, has always given a claim to political preferment." And as Mr. Warburg urges, this is a country "with every untrained amateur a candidate for office," and naturally, with such men comprising the government, they must be kept at a safe distance from monetary affairs.

As if to illustrate the ignorance thus charged, along comes Mr. Baruch, who quotes Colonel House as saying, "I don't know anything about those fellows down there and I would like you to make a suggestion." It is permissible to doubt that Mr. Baruch correctly quotes Colonel House. It is permissible to doubt that all that Colonel House confessed was his ignorance about "those fellows." There was a good understanding between these two men, too good an understanding for the alleged telephone conversation to be taken strictly at its face value. It is possibly quite true that Mr. House is not a financier. Certainly, Mr. Wilson was not. In the long roll of Presidents only a handful have been, and those who have been have been regarded as most drastic in their proposals.

But this whole matter of ignorance, as charged by Mr. Warburg, sounds like an echo of the Protocols:

"The administrators chosen by us from the masses will not be persons trained for government, and consequently they will easily become pawns in our game, played by our learned and talented counsellors, specialists educated from early childhood to administer world affairs."

In the Twentieth Protocol, wherein the great financial plan of world subversion and control is disclosed, there is another mention of the rulers' ignorance of financial problems.

It is a coincidence that, while he does not use the term "ignorance," Mr. Warburg is quite outspoken concerning the benighted state in which he found this country, and he is also outspoken about the "untrained amateurs" who are candidates for every office. These, he says, are not fitted to take part in the control of monetary affairs. But Mr. Warburg is. He says so. He admits that it was his ambition from the moment he came here an alien Jewish-German banker, to change our financial affairs more to his liking. More than that, he has succeeded; he has succeeded, he himself says, more than most men do in a lifetime; he has succeeded, Professor Seligman says, to such an extent that throughout history the name of Paul M Warburg and that of the Federal Reserve System shall be united.

The Dearborn Independent, issue of 2 July 1921

60: How Jewish International Finance Functions

Such has been the development of international bankers that they can no longer be regarded in their professional capacity as the nationals of any country, entitled to do business under their own government's supervision exclusively. They are really world citizens, with world-wide interests, and as such ought to be made amenable to some form of supernational control.—George Pattullo, in *Saturday Evening Post.*

Not only did the Jewish financial firm of Kuhn, Loeb & Company use far-sighted prudence in splitting its political support—one Warburg supporting Wilson, another Warburg supporting Taft and an unnamed member of the firm supporting Roosevelt, all at one time, as Paul M. Warburg testified—but it split its activities in several other ways also.

The international interests of the Jews comprising this firm are worthy of note. The influence which forced the United States to repudiate a commercial treaty with Russia while Russia was a friendly country (1911), and thus to compel all business between the United States and Russia to pass through German-Jewish hands, was generated by Jacob H. Schiff. Russia seems to have been the country on which he chose to focus his activities.

The full story is told in *The Dearborn Independent* of January 15, 1921, under the title, "Taft Once Tried to Resist the Jews and Failed," and is reprinted in the first combined volume of this series.

Mr. Schiff's activity consisted in forcing the Congress of the United States to do a thing that was repugnant to the reason and conscience of President Taft, and which he personally refused to do or to recommend. Mr. Schiff left the White House in great anger with the threat, "This means war." It did not mean as much war as it might have, for President Taft acquiesced gracefully in the Jewish victory and has since been extremely laudatory of them on the public platform.

Mr. Schiff's firm also helped finance the Japanese war against Russia, and in return desired Japan as a Jewish ally. The wily Japs, however, saw the game and kept their relations with Mr. Schiff to purely business matters. Which fact is well worth bearing in mind when reading the widespread propaganda for war with Japan. If you will give particular attention, you will observe the same interests which are just now engaged in most loudly "defending" the Jew, are most active in spreading anti-Japanese sentiments in this country.

The Japanese war with Russia, however, enabled Mr. Schiff to advance his plan to undermine the Russian Empire, as it has now been accomplished by Jewish Bolshevism. With funds provided by him, the basic principles of what is now known as Bolshevism, were sown among the Russian prisoners of war in Japan, who were sent back as apostles of destruction. Then followed the horrible murder of Nicholas Romanoff, Czar of Russia, with his wife, his crippled son, and his young daughters, the full tale of which has now been told by the Jew who managed the crime.

For the part he played in destroying Russia, Mr. Schiff was wildly hailed in New York the night the news came that the Emperor had abdicated.

Meanwhile, the Jew who was "to take the Czar's job" (as the common New York ghetto phrase ran, weeks before the event) had left New York to be in waiting.

This Jew was passed out of the United States at the request of a very high American personage whose subservience to the Jews was one of the marvels of the past seven years. Halted by the British, this Jew was released from their toils at the request of a very high American personage. And thus, the Jewish Bolshevik Revolution in Russia, the program of which was made in America, was set in operation without a hitch.

This whole firm is German Jewish, its members having originated in Germany. It had German connections. How far it maintained those connections through all subsequent events is a separate question.

Mr. Otto Kahn's allotted portion of the world seems to be Great Britain and France. Mr. Kahn is of German origin, like the rest of the firm, but he has not publicly shown such concern for Germany as have the other members. Mr. Schiff was once very active for the settlement of a peace on the basis of a victorious Germany.

Mr. Paul M. Warburg also had interests, discussion of which is postponed for the present. But Mr. Kahn succeeded, through the connivance of American authority and the excessive repression of the newspapers, in conveying the impression that by some species of occult separatism he was not "German-minded."

Therefore Mr. Kahn flits lightly everywhere—except Germany. He is sufficiently French to be able to tell in the first column on the first page of Le Matin on what terms America will do business with Europe, and he speaks as one having authority. He is sufficiently British to have thought of standing for the British Parliament, when an unfortunate event made it necessary for him to remain in the United States. Mr. Kahn sometimes flits farther East into the more Jewish portions of Europe, and his comings and goings are marked by certain changes with which his name remains most ostentatiously disconnected.

Mr. Kahn has very recently been telling France on what terms the United States will help her. There apparently being no other spokesman, Mr. Kahn's word is accepted as authority. France is one of the most Judaized countries in the world, the haunt of International Jewish Financiers who exercise their power (thus saving France the trouble of passing laws) to keep the emigrant Jew out of France; so that France presents the spectacle of being Judaized by Jewish finance and not by immigrant Semitic hordes, and is thus a fit platform from which Mr. Otto Herman Kahn may utter his pronouncements.

In his last declaration to France, Mr. Kahn prepares her to expect little by stating that "America is a country of immense resources; but the actual money which the people have at their disposal is comparatively limited." True enough. It was a member of Mr. Kahn's firm who invented a monetary system which was promised to keep money in more equal relation to wealth.

But as he goes on telling what America will and will not do (the American people knowing nothing about it meanwhile) Mr. Kahn discovers with great enthusiasm a place where he thinks American capital can be placed, namely, "In the development of the vast and immensely rich colonial empire of France."

And pray where is that? Any Frenchman would tell you now, "In Syria." Syria—ah!—that part of the East where the natives are loudly complaining that the Jews are driving them out contrary to every written and moral law. The Jewish powers have already succeeded in getting French troops over there; bad blood has been caused between France and Great Britain; the Jews on both sides are playing for the middle; and here is Mr. Otto Kahn himself pledging American capital to the development of the French colonial empire! Talk to any Syrian who knows his country's present status, and he will interpret Mr. Kahn's words very vividly.

One of the nicest bits of work Mr. Kahn has done is to denounce "pro-German propaganda" which he says has exasperated Americans in favor of France. Next to committing the United States to an undying admiration for Briand, this is really his finest bit. Especially, with Partner Paul playing the German sympathy string! It is a great international orchestra, this Jewish financial firm; it can play The Star Spangled Banner, Die Wacht am Rhein, the Marseillaise, and God Save the King in one harmonious rendering, paying obsequious attention to the prejudices of each.

Next come the Warburgs. Their interest is, of course, in Germany. Paul stated in his testimony given at the beginning of the World War that he had interests in Hamburg and would dispose of them. The war came on. The Jewish government in the United States was augmented. Mr. Warburg was no mean figure, as previous articles have shown.

The Warburgs are three in number. Felix M. is the other one in America. He appears but slightly in public affairs although he is a member of the American Jewish Committee and of the firm of Kuhn, Loeb & Company. His retiring habit, however, does not argue lack of consequence. He was of sufficient consequence, Jewishly, to have bestowed upon him a sort of honorary rabbinical degree of "Haber" which entitles him to be known as "Haber Rabbi Baruch Ben Moshe." He is the only Jew in America upon whom the title has ever been conferred.

Max Warburg represents the family in its native land. Max Warburg had as much to do with the German war government as his family and financial colleagues in America had to do with the United States war government. As has been recounted in the press the world over, the brother from America and the brother from Germany both met at Paris as government representatives in determining the peace. There were so many Jews in the German delegation that it was known by the term "kosher," also as "the Warburg delegation," and there were so many Jews in the American delegation that the delegates from the minor countries of Europe looked upon the United States as a Jewish country which through unheard-of generosity had elected a non-Jew as its President.

Max Warburg is an interesting character also as regards the establishment of Bolshevism in Russia. The Jews had several objectives in the war, and one of them was "get Russia." To this end the German Jews worked very assiduously. Because Russia was a member of the Allies, the work of German Jews was made the easier. But the fact that Russia was an ally made no difference with the Jews who were resident in Allied countries. Win or lose, Russia must be destroyed. It is the testimony of history that it was not so much the German military prowess as the Jewish intrigue that accomplished the downfall of that empire.

In this work Max Warburg was a factor. His bank is noted in a dispatch published by the United States Government as being one whence funds were forwarded to Trotzky for use in destroying Russia. Always against Russia, not for German reasons, but for Jewish reasons, which in this particular instance coincided. Warburg and Trotzky—against Russia!

Poor John Spargo, who ought to know better, denies all this while every American who comes back from Russia, even those who went over there pro-Bolshevik, yes, and returned Jews themselves, proclaim it.

The crushing fact is that Bolshevism is not only Jewish in Russia, and in America, but it is Jewish in the higher regions of Jewry where better things ought to exist. Take Walter Rathenau, a German Jew on the plane of the Warburgs. Rathenau was the inventor of the Bolshevik system of centralization of industry, material and money. The Soviet Government asked Rathenau directly for the plans, and received them directly from him. Max Warburg's bank held the money; Walter Rathenau's mind held the plans—which makes it a pertinent question: If Bolshevism can be so Jewish outside of Russia, what hinders it being Jewish inside Russia?

It is a most significant fact that, as in Washington, the most constant and privileged visitors to the White House were Jews, so in Berlin the only private telephone wire to the Kaiser was owned by Walter Rathenau. Not even the Crown Prince could reach the Kaiser except through the ordinary telephone connections. It was the same in London. It was the same in Paris. It was the same in Petrograd—in Russia which so "persecuted" the race that controlled it then and controls it now.

Now, this sketchy outline of the internationalism of the firm of Kuhn, Loeb & Company is not offered as the result of keen research, for the facts are found on the very surface of the matter, for anyone to see. What is revealed by research is this: whether Mr. Schiff's interest in Russia had underground features which affected the welfare of nations; whether Mr. Kahn's flitting missions here and there, which he made with great freedom during the war, were wholly taken up with the business announced in the public notices; and whether Mr. Warburg, whose interest in Germany has not abated, to judge from his recent utterances, was able to retain complete neutrality of mind during the war. These are questions of value. Obviously, they are not easy to answer. But they can be answered.

It was a family enterprise, this international campaign. Jacob Schiff swore to destroy Russia. Paul M. Warburg was his brother-in-law; Felix Warburg was his son-in-law. Max Warburg, of Hamburg, banker of the Bolsheviks, was thus brother-in-law to Jacob Schiff's wife and daughter.

Speaking of the far-sighted manner in which the house of Kuhn, Loeb & Company disposes itself over world affairs, there is also the curious fact that in this Jewish firm is one who goes to a Christian church—a most heinous thing for a Jew to do. Split three ways in American politics and as many ways as international matters require, we find this firm split two ways with regard to religion. Mr. Kahn professes—at least he attends—a Christian church and is accounted an adherent of it. Yet he is not ostracized. His name is not taboo. The Jews do not curse him. He is not denounced as a renegade. The Jews have not buried him out of mind, as they do others who desert the faith.

This presents a strange situation when it is considered. Not to recount again the horror and reprehension and active antagonism with which Jews view such a desertion, suffice it to say that there is no greater marvel than that of Jacob H. Schiff retaining in the firm of Kuhn, Loeb & Company a "renegade" Jew. He could not have done it; every fiber of his intensely Jewish nature would have rebelled against it. Yet there it is!

Without going further into this ingenious system of covering all vital points from one center, enough has been said to show one busy Jewish financial firm with which political matters, national and international, is almost a profession. The family of Warburg high in the controlling group of two countries, and enemy countries at that. The family of Warburg high in the negotiations of world peace and the discussions of a League of Nations. The family of Warburg now advising the world from both sides of the earth, what to do next. It was probably with more reason than the general public surmised that a New York paper printed during the Peace Conference an article headed, "Watch the Warburgs!"

The fact seems to be that, as Mr. Pattullo is quoted as saying at the head of this article, the international financiers have been so engrossed in world money that the sense of national responsibility sometimes becomes blurred in their minds. They desire everyting—war, negotiations and peace—to be conducted in such a way as to react favorably on the money market. For that is their market: money is what they buy and sell: and because money has no fixed price, it is a market which offers the widest opportunity for the trickster and swindler. One cannot play such tricks with stone or corn or metals, but with money as the commodity everything is possible.

Mr. Warburg is already very much interested about the treatment to be accorded foreign securities in the next war. Readers of the daily newspapers may recall that recently a demand was made for the gold in the Reichsbank, which was resisted on the ground that the Reichsbank, although the central bank of Germany, was really a private concern—just as Paul Warburg said it was and just as he has insisted that our own Federal Reserve System should be, and which it is. There is far-sighted wisdom in that, with a view to possible defeat in war.

Mr. Warburg is apparently quite disapproving of the treatment accorded alien enemy property "by some countries." He quotes a French banker throughout—nationality not stated—and drives home his point. The French banker used as an illustration a possible war between England and France (this was only last year) and said that the bankers in each country would proceed to withdraw their mutual balances and securities, for fear of confiscation, and that such a course would precipitate a panic.

To which Mr. Warburg adds: "I think that our bankers ought carefully to study this very serious question. We have nothing to gain and much to lose by joining in a policy of disregarding the rights of private property. We shall probably, in the course of time, become the largest owners of foreign securities and properties, which would become endangered in case we were drawn into war. To me, however, it is of greater interest that nothing be done that might stand in the way of making the United States the gold reserve country of the world. . . ."

Such talk passes with too little scrutiny. It bears a strong reflection of recent events which should not be overlooked. Moreover, it presents a grandiose vision which is supposed to command instant agreement because of its appeal to superficial national pride and selfish ambition.

If what Mr. Warburg says is an intimation that the International Jews are planning to move their money market to the United States, it is safe to say that the United States does not want it. We have the warning of history as to what this would mean. It has meant that in turn Spain, Venice, Great Britain or Germany received the blame and suspicion of the world for what the Jewish financiers have done. It is a most important consideration that most of the national animosities that exist today arose out of resentment against what the Jewish money power did under the camouflage of national names. "The British did this," "the Germans did this," when it was the International Jew who did it, the nations being but the marked spaces on his checker board.

Today, around the world the blaming word is heard, "The United States did this. If it were not for the United States the world would be in better shape. The Americans are a sordid, greedy, cruel people." Why? Because the Jewish money power is largely centered here and is making money out of both our immunity and Europe's distress, playing one against the other; and because so many of the so-called "American business men" abroad today are not Americans at all—they are Jews, and in many cases as misrepresentative of their own race as they are of the Americans.

The United States does not want the transfer of All-Judaan to this soil. We do not desire to stand as a gold god above the nations. We would serve the nations, and we would protect them, but we would do both in the basis of real values, not in the name or under the sign of gold.

On the one hand Mr. Warburg recites pitiful facts about Germany in order to raise sympathy for her, and on the other hand he stimulates the gold lust of the United States. The plight of Germany is entirely due to the forces from which the United States has only narrowly escaped; and to harken to international Jewish plans for the rehabilitation of Germany is to be in danger of approving plans which will fasten Jewish domination more strongly on that unhappy country than it is now. Germany has paid dearly for her Jews. The Warburg voice that speaks for her would seem indeed to be the voice of Jacob, but the hand that proposes financial dealings is that of Esau.

The internationalism of the Warburgs is no longer in doubt, and cannot be denied. Felix Warburg hung on to the Hamburg connection longer than did Paul, but the breakage of either was probably perfunctory. At the same time that Felix left the Hamburg firm of his brother, Max, a Mr. Stern also left the Frankfort firm of Stern, and both became very active on the Allies side, taking sides against the German nation as lustily as anyone could. "Impossible!" say those who fancy that a German Jew is a German. Not at all impossible; the Jew's loyalty is to the Jewish nation; what the Jew himself refers to as his "cover nationality" may count or not as he himself elects.

This statement is always met with frothing wrath by the Jews' "gentile fronts" in the purchased pro-Jewish press. But here is an example: Do you remember "The Beast of Berlin," that lurid piece of war propaganda?

You did not, perhaps, know that its producer was a German Jew, Carl Laemmle. His German birth did not prevent him making money out of his film, and his film does not prevent him annually going back in state to his birthplace. This year he goes accompanied by Abe Stern, his treasurer; Lee Kohlmar, his director; and Harry Reichenbach—a list of names duplicable in any movie group.

Messrs. Stern and Warburg, of Frankfort and Hamburg, respectively, and away from home perhaps only temporarily, were not concerned about the fate of the "Huns," but they were immensely concerned about the fate of Jewish money power in Germany.

To indicate how blind the public has been to the inter-allied Jewish character of much of the world's important international financial activity, note this from the Living Age earlier in the year:

"According to the Svensk Handelstidning, the recent American loan of $5,000,000 to Norway was really the outcome of an agreement between the Hamburg firm of Warburg & Company and the New York bankers, Kuhn and Loeb. It is regarded as a significant sign of the times that a German firm should be responsible for an American loan to a neutral country.

"The conditions subject to which this money was borrowed, are not regarded as very favorable to Norway, and no marked effect on the rate of exchange between the two countries has followed."

Note, in the light of all the statements made about Kuhn, Loeb & Company, and the Warburgs in particular, the assumption in the above quotation that the transaction was really between a German and an American firm. It was principally an arrangement between the Warburgs themselves in family counsel. But the loan will pass in Norway as "an American loan," and the fact that the terms of the loan, "are not regarded as very favorable to Norway" will react upon Scandinavian opinion of this country. It goes without saying that "no marked effect on the rate of exchange between the two countries has followed," for that would not be the object of such a loan. The dislocation of exchange is not unprofitable.

It would be most interesting to know in how far Kuhn, Loeb & Company has endeavored to readjust the rate of exchange.

During the war, Kuhn, Loeb & Company made a loan to the city of Paris. Considerable German comment was occasioned by this naturally. And it is very well worthy of record that in the city of Hamburg, where Max Warburg does business, the chief of police issued this order:

"Further mention in the press of loans made by the firm of Kuhn, Loeb & Company to the city of Paris, and unfavorable comments thereon, are forbidden."

The following story is vouched for as reliable, and if in one or two minor details it does not represent the exact fact, it is a trustworthy illustration of how certain things were done:

"A Jewish international banking corporation bought up the mining and other similar concessions of Jugo-Slavia, and consequently the policy pushed at the Peace Conference was that which was most convenient for that group. An understanding on the Fiume question was in progress between Wilson and Nitti. Certain concessions had been agreed upon and Wilson was willing to negotiate, when Oscar Straus and one of the Warburgs appeared on the scene. Wilson changed his attitude over night and afterward insisted on the Jugo-Slavia solution of the problem. The way in which concessions had been bought through that territory was a disgrace, and observers expected that it would play an important part at the Peace Conference."

The financiers are not the only International Jews in the world. The revolutionary Jews, of all countries and none, are international also. They have seized upon the idea of Christian internationalism, which means amity between nations, and have used it as a weapon with which to weaken nationality. They know as well as anyone that there can be no internationalism except on the basis of strong nationalism, but they count on "cover words" to advance their plan.

Enough transpired between the lower and higher Jewish groups of every large center during the war to render it imperative that Jewry confess, repent and repudiate the madness that has ruled it, or else boldly assert and espouse it before the world.

Certainly enough has transpired to render it desirable that the American people look again into the purposes of those Jews who were instrumental in reorganizing our financial system at a most critical time in the world's history.

Max Warburg was apparently strong enough to suppress German discussion of his brothers' activity in America. The Warburgs at present resident in America must suffer it, therefore, that American comment be made as full as need be.

The Dearborn Independent, issue of 9 July 1921

61: Jewish Power and America's Money Famine

The international Jewish banker who has no country but plays them all against one another, and the International Jewish proletariat that roams from land to land in search of a peculiar type of economic opportunity, are not figments of the imagination except to the non-Jew who prefers a lazy laxity of mind.

Of these classes of Jews, one or both are at the heart of the problems that disturb the world today. The immigration problem is Jewish. The money question is Jewish. The tie-up of world politics is Jewish. The terms of the Peace Treaty are Jewish. The diplomacy of the world is Jewish. The moral question in movies and theaters is Jewish. The mystery of the illicit liquor business is Jewish.

These facts are unfortunate as well as unpleasant for the Jew, and it is squarely up to him to deal with the facts, and not waste time in trying to destroy those who define the facts. These facts are interpreted by the Jew and the anti-Semite with strange extremes of blindness. The Jew never gets the world's point of view at all; he always gets the anti-Semite's point of view; and the anti-Semite is equally at fault in always getting the Jew's point of view. What both need is to get society's point of view, which is the one being set forth in this present series of articles.

To say that the immigration problem is Jewish does not mean that Jews must be prohibited entry to any country; it means that they must become rooted to a country in loyal citizenship, as no doubt some are, and as no doubt most are not. To say that the money question is Jewish does not mean that Jews must get out of finance; it means that they must rid finance of the Jewish idea which has always been to use money to get a strangle-hold on men and business concerns, instead of using finance to help general business.

To say that the tie-up of world politics is Jewish does not mean that Jews, as human beings, are to be denied a voice in affairs; it means that they must give up trying to make the world revolve around the Jewish nation as its axis. To describe the influence of the Jew on the theater is not to demand that he leave the theater, but it is to demand that he rid the theater of his idea that sensualism is entertaining. The Jewish Question is first for the Jews to solve; if not, the world will have to solve it for them. They may stay in business, say the theater, for example, if they will cease spoiling the theater; if they do not cease, the theater will be taken away from them just as certainly as that day follows night. The world has been patient and the world will be fair, but the world knows the limit of imposition.

It is not the true Jewishness of the Jew, nor yet the nationalism of the Jew that is on trial, but his anti-national internationalism. A true Mosaic Jew—not a Talmud Jew—would be a good citizen. A nationalist Jew would at least be logical. But an international Jew has proved an abomination, because his internationalism is focused on his own racial nationalism, which in turn is founded on his ingrained belief that the rest of humanity is inferior to him and by right his prey. Jewish leaders may indulge in all the platitudes they possess, the fact which they cannot deny is that the Jew has for centuries regarded the "goyim" as beneath him and legitimately his spoil.

The internationalism of the Jew is confessed everywhere by him. Listen to a German banker: imagine the slow, oily voice in which he said:

"We are international bankers. Germany lost the war?—what of it?—that is an affair of the army. We are international bankers."

And that was the attitude of every international Jewish banker during the war. The nations were in strife? What of it? It was like a Dempsey-Carpentier bout in New Jersey, or a baseball game in Chicago an affair of the fighters—"we are international bankers."

A nation is being hamstrung by artificial exchange rates; another by the sucking of money out of its channels of trade; what of it to the international banker?—he has his own game to play. Hard times bring more plums tumbling off the tree into the baskets of the international bankers than does any other kind of times. Wars and panics are the Jewish international bankers' harvests.

Citizens wake up with a start to find that even the white nations are hardly allowed to see each other nowadays except through Jewish eyes. When the United States supposedly speaks to France, through whom does she speak? All that France sees is Otto H. Kahn! Why must a Jew represent the United States of America to France? When France supposedly speaks to the United States, through whom is it done? Through Viviani, Jewish in every thought and method. Now they are talking of sending Millerand over, another Jew. Britain sends Lord Reading. Germany sent Dr. Dernberg. And to other countries the United States sent Morgenthau, Strauss, Warburg, and lesser Jewlings.

It comes with something of a shock to learn that Foch is coming to the United States. We have not seen a Frenchman since Joffre visited us. It is good to see man of the white race come across the sea as if to reassure us that white men still live in those countries. The business of the Peace Conference was done by Jews—has it come to a point where international diplomacy is to become a Jewish monopoly also? Must the special conversations between France, Britain and the United States be held through Jewish interpreters, while Anglo-Saxons and true Frenchmen do the routine embassy work—or shall it be possible for the non-Jewish nations to see one another occasionally through non-Jewish representatives?

Internationalism is not a Jewish conviction, but a Jewish business device. It is most profitable. In diplomacy and at the immigrant station, internationalism pays. Jews interpret nation to nation in the high rites of special conversations between governments; Jewish interpreters swarm at the ports of every country also, where the poor swarm in. It was stated in the House of Lords the other day that most of the trouble in Palestine was caused by Jewish interpreters. It was charged that the Jewish administration added an extra language to the official list in order to make Jewish interpreters indispensable.

Go through the government of the United States, where the income tax secrets are kept, where the Federal Reserve secrets are kept, where the State Department secrets are kept—and you will find Jews sitting at the very spot where International Jewry desires them to sit, and where nothing is kept from their knowledge.

Go abroad and come back to your country, and a Jew will open the gate to let you in, or close it to keep you out—as he chooses.

"Will you be going to Detroit while you are here?" asked a Jewish government agent of a gentleman entering the country on a visit a few weeks ago.

"I may go to Detroit," was the reply.

"Well, you go to the damned *Dearborn Independent* and tell them a Jew let you into this country," said the government agent.

What the visitor replied is known, but had better not be quoted. The American Jewish Committee might shriek that the people were being incited to pogroms.

The incident, however, is but a sample of what is occurring every day. The truth about the Jewish Question in the United States is perhaps the one form of truth that cannot be indiscriminately told.

The international Jewish bankers regard themselves as in similar fashion "letting" the nations do this or that, regarding the nations not as fatherlands but as customers—and as customers in the Jewish sense. If an army wins or loses, if a government succeeds or fails, what of it? that is their affair—"we are international bankers," and we win, whoever loses.

For international Jewish bankers, the war is not over. The period of actual hostilities and the emergencies of the nations were but the opening of the trade. The ready cash was skimmed in then—all the cash the world had. True, some of it had to be distributed among the people as war wages and bonuses, in order to keep the struggle going, but this was soon recovered through the means of high prices, artificial scarcities and the orgy of extravagance deliberately organized and stimulated among the people. That phase over, and money disappeared.

Is there any more tragic joke than that diligently disseminated in this country—"The United States has more gold than any other country in the world"? Where is it? How long since you have seen a piece of gold? Where is all this gold—is it locked up in the Treasury of the United States Government? Why, that government is in debt, desperately trying to economize, cannot pay a soldier bonus because the finances of the country cannot stand it! Where is that gold? It may be in the United States, but it does not belong to the United States.

The American farmer, and those American industries which were not "wise" to the tricks of international Jewish bankers, and who were nipped by small loans, are wondering where all this money is. Furthermore, Europe, suffering from every possible lack, is looking to us and wondering where the money is.

This dispatch in a London paper may throw light on the matter: (italics are ours) "It is learned today that new gold shipments aggregating $2,800,000 are consigned to Kuhn, Loeb & Company, New York, making nearly $129,000,000 imported by that firm since the movement started. In responsible banking circles the belief is expressed that some of the German *coin recently imported by the firm is from Russia, instead of Germany,* as generally supposed."

This dispatch, coupled with one printed in a former article which showed Warburg & Company of Germany arranging with Kuhn, Loeb

& Company of New York for a $5,000,000 loan to Norway, is not devoid of light on the question—Where is the money?

The Jewish international banking system may be easily described. First, there is the international Jewish headquarters. This was in Germany. It had ramifications in Russia, Italy, France, Great Britain and the South American states. (South American Jewry is very menacing.) Germany and Russia were the two countries scheduled for punishment by the International Jewish bankers because these two countries were most aware of the Jew. They have been punished; that job is done.

Jewish political headquarters, as related to the internal affairs of the Jews, was also located in Germany, but the headquarters dealing with the "goyim" was in France. Statements have been made that the political center of Jewry has been transplanted to the United States. But these statements have been made by American Jews whose wish may have been father to the thought.

During the Wilson Administration it was possible for a Jew to think and to hope this, but affairs have slightly changed. The ousting of American Jews from the Zionist movement at the behest of Eastern Jews indicates that if the political center of world Jewry has shifted to the United States, the power is still in the hands of aliens resident here. The center is still in Jewry; the United States is merely a square on Jewry's world checker-board.

But, wherever the financial and political world centers may be, each country is separately handled. In every country—the United States, Mexico and the republics of South America; in France, England, Italy, Germany, Austria—yes, and in Japan—there is an international Jewish banking firm which stands at the head of the group for that country. Thus, the chief Jewish firm in the United States is Kuhn, Loeb & Company, of which one of the members is Paul M. Warburg, brother of M. Warburg & Company, of Hamburg; and another member of which is Otto H. Kahn, resident successively of Germany, Great Britain and the United States, and self-appointed financial spokesman for the United States to France and Great Britain. Great Britain and France seldom see a special American spokesman who is not a Jew. That may be the reason why they reciprocate by sending Jews to us, thinking perhaps that we prefer them.

Paul M. Warburg was the inventor, perfector and director of the Federal Reserve System of the United States. He is not the only Jew in the Federal Reserve System, but he was the chief Jew there. His mind counted for a great deal. There were others in the war government, of course; Bernard M. Baruch; Eugene Meyer, Jr.; Hoover's regiment of Jews; Felix Frankfurter; Julius Rosenwald—hundreds of them, and everywhere; but the financial group alone is receiving our attention just now, and they are not so notably successful in getting the country out of financial difficulty as they were in other lines of effort.

The Federal Reserve System may not be a bad system, in spite of the fact that it yields government monetary functions to private financial corporations, but there are all sorts of testimony that it has been badly manipulated. Mr. Warburg, the reader will remember, spoke about certain things being "overcome in an administrative way," showing that there was a certain amount of "play" or loose motion in the system which could be manipulated either way. The fact remains that the country went swimmingly through the war by reason of the assistance of the System, and is coming very lamely through the Peace, as the result, monetary experts say, of the hindrance of the same System. Mr. Warburg, whose name was so prominently connected with the advertisement of the glory of the System, must also stand being mentioned in connection with the criticism.

Whatever money we are said to have as the per capita in the United States, it is a false statement. The money per capita should always be figured on the basis of money in circulation. The statistical "per capita" is not always in circulation. Less than half of it, as a rule. The rest is being juggled.

Whatever the gold in the country, the wealth is still greater. There is more wealth in the United States than there is gold in the world. One year's products of the farms of the United States exceeds in money value all the gold in the world.

Yet, under our present system, the burgeoning bulk of the country's wealth must pass through the narrow neck of Money. And the Money must pass through the still narrower neck of Gold. And the controller of the Gold, under our present system, controls the world. There is more wealth than there is money; there is more money than there is gold; money exists at the pleasure of gold; wealth moves at the pleasure of money. Whoever sits at the neck of money, opening or closing as he will, controls the movement of the world's wealth. And the world's prosperity depends on the movement of that wealth. When wealth stands still and does not pass from hand to hand, the world's circulation has stopped; the world becomes economically sick.

The scarcity of cash in hand has led to Credit. Credit is a form of barter. It is a form of dealing by which many transactions are carried on, only the final one being cleared in money. It is a device which has its dangers, in spite of the efforts of apologists to exploit its advantages. But one thing the system of Credit indubitably does—it allows the money masters to hang on to the Cash. When the world is caught, it is caught with paper, not with Cash. The Cash is always in the hands of those who extol the advantage of the Credit System. Who holds money holds power, and will hold it, until real barter or real money comes in fashion again.

In 1919–1920, according to one of the best monetary authorities in the United States, the total shrinkage in values of the products of our fields, mines, factories, mills and forests represented a sum greater than the total gold supply of the world. It runs as high as the total amount of Liberty Bonds outstanding.

People say, "Well, the prices were too high." Certainly they were too high, but who and what made them too high? It was the generosity with which money was supplied by the private Federal Reserve System. There was plenty of money. People say, "Well, the shrinkage is only in paper values; the real value of the product is still there." Certainly, but when you live under a system in which "real" value and "money" value are so intimately intertwined that it affects your bread and butter, the tenure of your farm, and the steadiness of your job, it is pretty hard to separate the two. Moreover, when your prosperity was due to the readiness of a group of men to let out money, and your adversity is due to the unwillingness of the same group, and your own welfare and your country's welfare is thus see-sawed up and down without any reference to natural law but solely upon determinations taken in committee rooms, you naturally inquire, "Who is doing this? Where is all the money gone? Who is holding it? Here is the wealth of the country; here is the need of the country; where is the money to transfer the wealth to the need? Every condition remains as it was, except money."

We have a Federal Reserve System which still is benefiting by the assistance of its perfector and director, Paul M . Warburg. And what is the condition in the United States?

Some of the biggest industrial institutions in the country now in the hands of creditors' committees.

Farmers being sold out by the hundreds, their horses bringing about $3 each.

Cotton and wool enough to clothe the nation, spoiling in the hands of the men who raised it and cannot dispose of it.

Every line of business, railroading, newspaper publishing, storekeeping, manufacturing, agriculture, building, in depression. Why? For lack of money.

Where is the money? This is a country that is supposed to be the financial center of the world—where is the money?

It is in New York. The Federal Reserve System, which Mr. Warburg desired to head up in one central bank, has just about turned out that way. The money is in New York. Here is the charge made to the governor of the Federal Reserve Board by a responsible public official who knows:

While there is a scarcity of money for the producing sections of the West and Northwest, the South and Southwest, "we find that individual banks in New York City are borrowing from the Reserve System, in a number of cases, more than $100,000,000 each; and sometimes as much as $145,000,000 is loaned there to a single bank—twice as much as some of the Reserve Banks have been lending recently to all the member banks in their districts."

One bank in New York borrowed $134,000,000, or $20,000,000 more than the Federal Reserve Bank of Kansas City was advancing to 1,091 member banks in that Reserve District, which covers the states of Kansas, Nebraska, Colorado, Wyoming, and parts of Missouri, Oklahoma and New Mexico.

At the same time, another New York bank was borrowing from the Federal Reserve Bank about $40,000,000, which was more than the aggregate loans which the Federal Reserve Bank of Minneapolis was lending to its 1,000 member banks in the great states of Minnesota, North and South Dakota, Montana and part of Wisconsin.

Another New York bank borrowed from the Federal Reserve Bank a sum which was greater by $30,000,000 than the Federal Reserve Bank at Dallas was lending to all the banks in Texas, Louisiana and Oklahoma.

Still another New York bank got a loan which equaled the total loans allowed by the Federal Reserve Bank of St. Louis to the 569 member banks of that very important district, which includes the whole state of Arkansas, parts of Illinois, Indiana, Kentucky, Tennessee and Mississippi, and the larger part of Missouri.

Take the Fifth Federal Reserve District, served by the Federal Reserve Bank at Richmond, Virginia: one New York bank was able to borrow from the New York Reserve Bank more than the Richmond Reserve

Bank would lend to all its member banks in Maryland, Virginia, North and South Carolina and the larger part of West Virginia.

That is the situation. The twelve regional banks, which were supposed to make money serve all parts of the country equally, have apparently been "overcome in an administrative way" to such an extent that the New York Federal Reserve Bank is to all intents and purposes the Central Bank of the United States and serves the speculative part of the country with millions, while the productive part of the country is permitted to wilt with paltry thousands.

When it can occur that four New York banks can borrow from the New York Federal Reserve Bank as much money as the banks of 21 states were able to borrow from the five Federal Reserve Banks of St. Louis, Kansas City, Minneapolis, Dallas and Richmond—there would seem to be need of explanation somewhere.

Where did this money loaned in New York come from? It came from those parts of the country where money was scarcest. In May, 1920, the word went out over telephones—"The tie-up will come on the 15th." And it came. Credit was stopped. Payment was pressed. A stream of money, literally squeezed out of the producing sections of the country, began to roll toward New York. Otherwise those giant loans just recorded would have been impossible. It was pressure, Federal Reserve pressure, politely known as deflation, and that is the way it worked. The banks of the West were squeezed dry that the banks of New York might overflow.

"The money was withdrawn from legitimate business in various parts of the country to be loaned at fancy rates in Wall Street," says the official referred to above.

The speculative banks, it has been discovered, were able to borrow money at six per cent, which money they loaned at as high as 20, 25 and 30 per cent.

Federal Reserve deflation created a scarcity which speculative banks utilized. The Federal Reserve policy took the money out; New York banks borrowed the money taken out, and loaned it at tremendous rates—rates which people paid to stave off the ruin caused by the moneyless condition which the ill-measured deflation process brought on.

And all this time the Federal Reserve System was in the best financial condition of its whole career. In December, 1920, it had 45 per cent of its reserves, which was a higher reserve than it had in December, 1919. But at this writing (July, 1921) the reserve has reached 60 per cent.

The money is in New York. Go out through the agricultural states, and you will not find it. Go into the districts of silent factories and you will not find it. It is in New York. The Warburg Federal Reserve has deflated the country. A System that was intended to equalize the ups and downs of financial weather has been used "in an administrative" way to deplete the country of money.

The Federal Reserve Idea was doubtless right; if it had not been, it could not have been established. But it has been manipulated. It has not been a "federal" reserve; it has been a private reserve. It has been operated in the interest of bankers and not of everyone in general. Capable of being used to carry the country gradually back to a natural flow of business and to a natural level of prices, it was used to bludgeon business at a critical time and to bludgeon it in such a way that money-lenders profited when producers suffered.

If that is the fact, there is no American banker but will say that the method was wrong; economically wrong, logically wrong, commercially wrong, if not criminally wrong.

Today the Federal Reserve boasts of its own reserve as if that were a sign of national economic health. With the country struggling to live, the Federal Reserve ought to be low, not high. The height which the reserve has reached is a measure of the depth of the country's depression.

If the Federal Reserve would let out a part of that flood of money—a high financial authority suggests that less than 10 per cent would do it—it would be like an infusion of blood into the nation's veins.

Kuhn, Loeb & Company, the Speyers and the other Jewish moneylenders have money for Mexico, Norway, Germany, and all sorts of commercial companies being organized to do business overseas, and it is American money. The Warburg Federal Reserve System has been badly misused, badly manipulated, and the country is suffering from it.

Still, the people know not what to do. Money is still a mystery. Banking is still sacrosanct. What would be perfectly apparent if done in ordinary business intercourse with a $5 bill, is exceedingly complicated when the sum is five millions and the parties are (1) country banks, (2) Federal Reserve banks and (3) Wall Street speculative institutions. Yet they are only Tom, Dick and Harry with a $5 bill, after all.

The matter is somewhat affected by the gags that are placed on many men competent to criticize. High officials are more or less tied up, by campaign contributions in which all financial concerns have an interest. Legislative officials are, too many of them, indebted to these same interests. A schedule of the private debts of some of the men who have aspired to the Presidency in the last eight years would be very illuminating—almost as illuminating as a schedule of the names of Jews at whose homes they stayed while on journeys through the country. Men who are thus tied up with the present financial system cannot say what in their minds they know.

It is all illustrated in the testimony of T. Cushing Daniel before a committee of Congress. It shows to what an extent the power of this private corporation called the central bank can reach:

"When going through the Bank of England I presented a letter which I had from Secretary Hay, and the official of the bank was very polite. He took me through the bank and when we got back to the reception room I asked him if he would allow me to put a few leading questions to him. He said he would, and I asked him if he would give me a statement of the Bank of England. 'We do not issue statements.' 'Does not the House of Parliament sometimes call on you for some statement as to the condition of the bank?' 'No, sir; they do not call on us.' . . . . 'How is it that some of these revolutionists, so-called, do not get up in the House of Commons and raise the devil to know something about what is going on down here? That would be the condition in our country.' 'Oh most of them are large borrowers from the bank, and we have no difficulty with them.' (laughter.)"

The Dearborn Independent, issue of 16 July 1921

Volume 4: Aspects of Jewish Power in the United States

Preface

This is the fourth volume of reprinted studies in the Jewish Question as they appeared in *The Dearborn Independent*. The articles follow the same general line as the previous volume in showing the various angles of Jewish influence and achievement in the affairs of the people of the United States, but they do not by any means exhaust either the number of the angles nor the depth of the significance in the angles traced.

Deliberate public opinion has shown many signs of a new alertness to the movement which was proceeding deftly and unnoticed in the midst of America, and many checks have been put in operation. The work of *The Dearborn Independent* was undertaken at a disadvantage because of the tremendous emphasis of the American mind on racial peace and because of the ease with which racial propagandists can make a purely economic and political matter assume the aspects of a religious controversy. *The Dearborn Independent* opened the Question to public gaze, and was therefore assumed to be the attacker. In this country our sense of fairness always leaves the advantage with the attacked, and false accusations quickly fall. The country has seen, however, the truth of the statements and has observed the mild and unprejudiced manner in which they were made, so that it may now be said that truth has made its way. Most gratifying are the signs which Jews themselves have given that certain abuses must be quickly stopped. A Jewish leader has appealed for the removal of the exemption which nullifies the Constitution of the United States in favor of the Jew with reference to the use of liquor. Other Jewish leaders have sought to compel Jewish theatrical controllers to observe elementary decency in their productions.

These articles have always held that the cleansing must come from within Judah itself. It is recognized that racial pride might prevent many improvements being attempted under fire, but American Jews cannot afford to be ruled by a false pride in this respect. These are days of judgment for all the corruptive forces of society and the Jews cannot expect to escape responsibility for their part in these things.

May, 1922

"United, then, by the strongest feelings of solidarity, the Jews can easily hold their own in this disjointed and anarchic society of ours. If the millions of Christians by whom they are surrounded were to substitute the same principle of co-operation for that of individual competition, the importance of the Jew would immediately be destroyed. The Christian, however, will not adopt such a course, and the Jew must, inevitably, I will not say dominate (the favorite expression of the anti-Semites) but certainly possess the advantage over others, and exercise the supremacy against which the anti-Semites inveigh without being able to destroy it."—Lazare.

62: How Jews Gained American Liquor Control

To those who have been surprised and confounded by the widespread evidence, which even the newspapers have been unable to suppress, that the bulk of the organized bootlegging which is being carried on in this country is in the hands of Jews, it would have been less of a surprise had they known the liquor history of this country.

The claim made for the Jews, that they are a sober people, is undoubtedly true, but that has not prevented two facts concerning them, namely, that they usually constitute the liquor dealers of the countries where they live in numbers, and that in the United States they are the only people exempted from the operations of the Prohibition law.

Here as elsewhere the principle holds true that "the Jew is the key." The demoralization which struck the liquor business, causing its downfall, and the demoralization which has struck Prohibition enforcement for a time, cannot be understood without a study of the racial elements which contributed to both phenomena. If in what follows the Jews find objectionable elements, they should remember that their own people put them there. It is impossible to doubt that if the organized Jews of the United States were to make one-thousandth of the protest against the illegal liquor activities of their own people that they make against the perfectly legal and morally justifiable exposures being made in *The Dearborn Independent*, the result would be not only favorable but immediate.

There was a time when the term "whisky" had a much more respectable connotation than it has today. There was a time when to use whisky and even to make it, were customs sanctioned by the better class of public opinion. It is a common explanation of the difference between then and now, that people of the latter period became more sensitive morally than their forbears, that whereas the previous generation guzzled its whisky, innocently oblivious of the evil in it, the latter generation developed a stronger discrimination and banned the custom.

The truth is this: the people did not become better; the whisky became worse. When the entire story of the people's justifiable indignation is written, the competent historian will trace along with the people's rising disgust, the whisky's decreasing quality.

Attention to this matter will materially assist an understanding of the fact that Jews and bootlegging are so continuously and prominently connected in the public prints these days.

Readers of the old romances know how proud the master was of his wines. Vintages ripened under certain skies, on certain hills, where certain waters flowed, with cellarage in certain soils, had a faculty of aging gracefully, mellowing to a smoothness and purity and desirableness that made for cheer and health without the alloy of sordid inebriety. The bouquet of wine, the perfected essence of the grape subjected to the further courses of nature, has been a theme of praise for centuries. If it were uttered today the source of the utterance would be suspected, and very probably with good reason, of being in pay of the "wets." For the vile stuff which civilization threw out is not at all the wine of popular custom and century-long esteem.

Nevertheless, it is not difficult for even a modern to grasp the fact that there was an art in making wine and strong drink, in which art men took pride. That art required time, experience, a love of good quality.

It is a little difficult to speak of this art in connection with whisky—wine being a more poetic word—yet it is a matter of knowledge that three places in the world have devoted to the production of whisky the same spirit which France and Portugal devoted to their wines. These three districts are Glenlivet in Scotland, the region of Dublin in Ireland, and the Blue-Grass region of Kentucky. Why in these three regions? First, because there were men—non-Jews, of course—who were willing to wait ten years to produce a good article. Second, the waters of these regions are of a quality which is beautifully adapted to the making of pure goods. Pure whisky, it should be remembered, is a vegetable product matured by natural forces and no other. Grain, water, and time—not even artificial heat added, nor any other thing—completes the best whisky product.

In older times in America there were men who were as choice of their whiskies as of their horses or books. There was then such a thing as quality. But there was no such thing as delirium tremens. That came later, with the disappearance of pure whisky. A distiller seldom grew rich—he was too engrossed in maintaining the quality of his product; and it consumed much time.

There were certain brands known nationally because of their mildness and purity—purest wine of the choicest grapes, aged in the best adapted cellars, was not more mild or pure. There are names that remain until this day—Pepper, Crow, Taylor, and others—the names of men who took time and pains, whose names became "brands" which guaranteed quality and purity. These men were distillers in the true sense, not manufacturers nor compounders, but distillers in a time when distilling was both a science and an art, and not a mere name to conceal a gigantic fraud on the public.

In time to come, when the people's justifiable moral indignation will permit a study of the steps by which the reputation of whisky came to its present low degree, they will see how much better it would have been, how much more efficacious and clarifying, if the attack on whisky had included an exposure of the men who had driven whisky out of the country and were selling rank poison as a substitute. The saloon, the brewer, the man who used strong drink were all of them made the target for attack; the Jews who demoralized the whole business went on collecting their enormous and illegitimate profits without so much as their identity being revealed.

Whisky ceased to be whisky and beer grew less like beer; the results upon humanity became apparent and deplorable. So society raised the license fee and increased the restrictions. To meet this, the Jewish compounders turned out still cheaper stuff, and still more vicious mixtures. Licenses went up, and quality went down; the Jewish compounders always getting a larger margin of profit. And through the long, long fight, no one, with one or two notable exceptions, had the sense and the courage to point a finger at the solid racial phalanx lined up behind the whole rotten combination.

Distilling is one of the long list of businesses which has been ruined by Jewish monopoly. Those who favor Prohibition will probably thank the Jew for his work in that direction. It may be that the Jew is destiny's agent to demoralize the business that must pass away. But set against that the fact that it is Jewish influence that demoralizes Prohibition, too, and both "wets" and "drys" have an interesting situation to consider. In general, the Jews are on the side of liquor and always have been. They are the steadiest drinkers of all. That is why they were able to secure exemption from the Prohibition laws; their religious ceremonies require them to drink an amount which the law has considered to equal ten gallons a year. And so the Prohibition law of the United States—a part of the Constitution of the United States—is made legally ineffective to the extent of ten gallons of year a Jew. The amount, of course, is very much more; it is always easy to get 100 gallons through a 10-gallon loophole. In fact, thousands of gallons have come through that 10-gallon loophole.

It will come to many people as new knowledge that the liquor business of the world has been in the hands of Jews. In the United States the liquor business was almost exclusively in the hands of Jews for 25 years previous to Prohibition, during the period, in fact, when the liquor trade was giving point and confirmation to Prohibition arguments. This knowledge has an important bearing on the interpretation of our times.

In the volume, "The Conquering Jew," published by Funk & Wagnalls Company in 1916, John Foster Fraser writes:

"The Jews are masters of the whisky trade in the United States. Eighty per cent of the members of the National Liquor Dealers' Association are Jews. It has been shown that 60 per cent of the business of distilling and wholesale trade in whisky is in the hands of the Jews. As middlemen they control the wine product of California. Jews visit the tobacco-growing States and buy up nearly all the leaf tobacco, so that the great tobacco companies have to buy the raw product from them. The Jews have a grip on the cigar trade. The American Tobacco Company manufactures about 15 per cent of the cigars smoked in the United States. The Jews provide the rest."

It was also true in Russia, Poland, Rumania. The *Jewish Encyclopedia* states that "The Establishment of the government liquor monopoly (in Russia in 1896) deprived thousands of Jewish families of a livelihood." They controlled the liquor traffic, the vodka business which undermined Russia. The government made the liquor business a national monopoly in order to abolish it, which was done. Liquor in Russia was Jewish, as the Encyclopedia testifies. Anyone reading carefully the article on Russia, especially pages 527 and 559 in the *Jewish Encyclopedia*, will be in no doubt as to the fact. In Rumania the whole "Jewish Question" was the liquor question. The land of the peasants came into control of the liquor sellers, and the business of handling liquors was a strict Jewish monopoly for years. In Poland the same was true. It is not surprising, therefore, that in the United States whisky also became Jewish.

For convenience in detailing this story, most of the observations made will center in the state of Kentucky. Almost every one of age knows the phrase "fine old Kentucky whiskies." It was once a phrase that meant something. Kentucky produced, in her limestone regions, the kind of water that served best with the grain ingredients of whisky. The word "Bourbon," known mostly as a kind of whisky, is really the name of a county in Kentucky where "Bourbon whisky" was first made. How profoundly the region in which whisky is manufactured affects the product may be gathered from the fact that a primitive Kentucky distiller named Shields, who became famous for a brand of Bourbon made from the waters of Glen's Creek, conceived of the idea of lowering his costs by transferring his distillery to Illinois, where he would be nearer the rich cornfields. He was disappointed. Illinois water would not make Bourbon. "The rule of the region" is supreme. Jamaica rum owes its characteristic to the waters of Jamaica. Port wine is best produced in the region of Duro in Portugal, champagne in the region of Rheims in France, and beer in Bavaria. And so, in Kentucky there was the right combination of elements which made the whisky product of that state world famous.

An alcoholic spirit from grain may be made in any climate and by many methods. Neutral spirits, high wines and alcohol, are not indigenous anywhere. They can be made in any back room or cellar, in very little time. Little care is required. A concoction of drugs and spirits, properly colored and flavored, fraudulently labeled "whisky" and passed out over the bar, is a crime against the art of distilling, against the human nervous system, and against society.

Readers may recall that in 1904, Dr. Wiley, then chief of the United States Bureau of Chemistry, had a great deal to say about this. But because he did not point out that the evil he was attacking was fostered by a single class of men bent on gain at the cost of ruin to an American industry and to countless thousands of American citizens, few paid any attention to him. The public supposed that Dr. Wiley was discussing a technical question which interested American distillers only. It vastly more interested the American citizen, if he had but known it, if anyone had but had the clear vision and the courage to expose the great Jewish whisky conspiracy.

The difference between the non-Jewish and the Jewish method, as illustrated in the history of American whisky, is thus described by Dr. Wiley:

"The aging of whisky takes years of time. It is expensive. The whisky leaks out. It is allowed to stand for four years at least. The object of this is to permit the oxidation of the alcohols. . . . There is a loss of interest on the value of the whisky while it is aging; hence it is an expensive process.

"But the manufacture of compounded, or artificial whisky has for its purpose the avoiding of this long and expensive process. The makers begin with the pure article of spirits which can be made in a few hours. . . . To this is added enough water to dilute it to the strength of whisky. The next step is to color it. . . . this is done by adding burnt sugar and caramel. The next thing is to supply the flavors. . . . By the way I have described, in two or three hours the compounder can make a material which looks like, smells like, tastes like, and analyzes like genuine whisky, but it has a different effect on the system. The people who drink this whisky are much more liable to receive injury from it than those who drink the genuine article."

All sorts of practices were resorted to. Drugs and raw "crops" of whisky were bought up and the business of "rectifying," as it was called, began the ruin of the natural and wholesome process of distilling. Quick money, regardless of what happened to the customer: that was the motive of the rectifying business.

This rectifying business was mostly Jewish. Here and there a non-Jew was associated with Jewish partners, but rarely. The way had been found to trade on the reputation of the term "whisky" by compounding a liquid which looked and tasted like whisky but the effect of which was harmful.

That was the capital fraud—the capture of the name "whisky" for a synthetic poison. There was a concealment of the meaning of "rectified spirits," a deceptive use of the word "blend," and even a most fraudulent misrepresentation concerning aging. If chemical deception could be used to make a whisky taste as if it were nine years old, then it was advertised as "Nine Years in the Wood." Here is a bit of Jewish court testimony:

Q. Is your make of whisky nine years old?

A. Nine years old, but I want to explain in that respect that the whisky may not have existed nine years before it was put into that bottle. . . .

That brand of whisky which we brand as nine years old blended, means that it is equal to a nine-year-old whisky in smoothness and quality.

Q. How did you arrive at the fact which you put upon this bottle that the whisky was nine years old?

A. Because it is comparatively nine years old.

Q. How do you arrive at that result?

A. By sampling. You take the whisky that is allowed to remain in the original package for nine years and compare it with our nine-year-old blend and you will find them in smoothness the same. Therefore, we class it as nine-year-old whisky.

Let the reader form his own judgement on that type of mind. The whisky bore a name resembling a time-honored brand of pure goods, and it flaunted the name Kentucky, when it was not whisky at all, was not a Kentucky product, but was compounded of neutral spirits from Indiana, prune juice from California, rock candy from anywhere, and raw Illinois whisky from Peoria to give it flavor.

Although Louisville, Kentucky, became headquarters of whisky men, it was Cincinnati, Ohio, a thoroughly Judaized city, which became a greater headquarters for the pseudo-whisky men, the compounders, mixers and rectifiers. The list of Cincinnati liquor dealers reads like a directory of the Warsaw ghetto. In Louisville the Judaic complexion of the city, as well as society, is very noticeable; indeed, most of the leading Jews in the whisky business are now Kentucky "Colonels."

The Jewish character of the whisky business since the Civil War may be visualized, by the simple expedient of noting how many of the better known brands have been at various dates under Jewish control:

There is "Old 66," owned by Straus, Pritz & Co.

"Highland Rye," owned by Freiberg & Workum.

"T. W. Samuel Old Style Sour Mash," owned by Max Hirsch, the Star Distilling Company.

"Bridgewater Sour Mash and Rye Whiskies," "Rosewood and Westbrook Bourbon Whiskies," distilled by J. & A. Freiberg.

"T. J. Monarch" and "Davies County Sour Mash Whiskies," controlled by J. & A. Freiberg.

"Louis Hunter 1870," "Crystal Wedding," and "Old Jug," blended by J. & A. Freiberg.

"Gannymede '76," put out by Sigmund and Sol H. Freiberg. "Jig-Saw Kentucky Corn Whisky," "Lynndale Whisky,"

"Brunswick Rye and Bourbon," by Hoffheimer Brothers Company.

"Red Top Rye" and "White House Club," by Ferdinand Westheimer & Sons.

"Green River" came into the control of E. La Montague.

"Sunnybrook," a widely advertised brand, on whose advertising matter a man in a United States inspector's uniform stood behind as if endorsing it, was at the time owned by Rosenfield Brothers & Co.

"Mount Vernon," as from the Hannis Distilling Company, was at the time owned by Angelo Meyer.

"Belle of Nelson" came into control of the Jewish trust, which was brought to legal birth by Levy Mayer and Alfred Austrian, the latter being the Chicago attorney whose name will be recalled in connection with the baseball articles in this series.

"James E. Pepper" was owned by James Wolf.

"Cedar Brook" was owned by Julius Kessler & Co. It was formerly the old "W. H. McBrayer" brand, but the real W. H. McBrayer, knowing the new methods that were arising in liquor-making, requested in his will that his name should not be used as a brand after he had ceased to see that the product was worthy of his name.

In the Pittsburgh and Peoria districts, the same story held true; the alleged whisky made in those districts was controlled, with one exception, by Jews.

The Great Western Distillery, in Peoria, is owned by a corporation of Jews. Two of its brands were "Ravenswood Rye" and "Ravenswood Bourbon." The Woolner Distillery made "Old Grove Whisky" and "Old Ryan Whisky," and "Bucha Gin."

In the city of Peoria alone there are fifteen great fortunes, all held by Jews, and for the most part made in what passed in Peoria for Whisky.

Take the city of Cincinnati alone and note what even an incomplete list reveals as to the names of the men classified as "distillers":

Bernheim, Rexinger & Company; Elias Bloch & Sons; J. & A. Freiberg; Freiberg & Workum; Helfferich & Sons; Hoffheimer Brothers Company; Elias Hyman & Sons; Kaufman, Bare & Company; Klein Brothers; A. Loeb & Co.; H. Rosenthal & Sons; Seligman Distilling Company; Straus, Pritz & Company; S. N. Weil & Company, and F. Westheimer & Sons; with many other Jews concealed under fancy trade names and corporation designations. It is the same throughout Ohio, which state, incidentally, is one of the most Jew-ridden states in the Union.

The lists here given do not by any means begin to indicate the numbers of the Jews who were engaged in the liquor business, they only indicate the complexion which the business takes on when a search is made behind the "brands" and the trade names. Any citizen in any city of size will have no trouble in confirming the statement that most of the rectifiers and wholesalers and brokers in the whisky trade of his city also were Jews.

But it is not only the fact that the liquor business was controlled by Jews that assumes importance. That is a fact which no one will deny not even the Jewish defenders. But it is the additional fact that there was spread over this country the machinery of a vicious system which while it was destined to ruin the liquor business—as perhaps it deserved to be ruined—also ruined hundreds of thousands of citizens who trusted that "pure and unadulterated" meant what the words were intended to convey. It would be a separate story to tell of all the manipulation of labels, the piracy of brand names, the conscienceless play upon words "pure and unadulterated" of which the un-American "compounded liquor" combine was guilty. Of course, the stuff was "pure and unadulterated"—so is carbolic acid—but it was not whisky! There were law violations galore, and it was well enough recognized in the rectifying business as a regular practice to appropriate annually a certain sum to pay the fines that were bound to be assessed against it. A riot of adulteration and chicanery ensued, with whisky being made in many saloon cellars and the dangerous secrets of synthetic booze-making being peddled abroad among the customers of the trust.

Presently the saloon men became aware of the fact that they were the goats of the game. Seldom was the Jew engaged in dishing out five-cent beers or ten-cent whiskies; it remained for the "boob Gentile" to do that; the Jew was at the wholesale end where the real profits were made. But it was the saloon man who took the brunt of the blame. The Jewish "distillers," as the compounders and blenders of the Louisville and Peoria districts were called, wore silk hats and their respectability was unquestioned. The saloon men made an eleventh hour effort to save their business, but the stuff they were pouring out had not improved, and Prohibition came, sweeping the saloon away, but, as the sequel will show, not depriving the Jewish compounder of his profits.

How much of the liquor business of the United States was in whisky and how much in rectified spirits?

The Twelfth Census of the United States, 1900, said: "Most of the distilled liquors consumed as a beverage by the American people pass through rectifying houses. The different classes of rectified spirits range from the cheapest concoctions of neutral spirits and drugs to the simple blending of young and old whisky."

Twenty years ago statistics showed that 80 per cent of the so-called whisky put up in the United States was imitation whisky. Chief Chemist Wiley, whose concern was not with the quantity but with the quality, gave it as his information "that over half the whisky in this country was compounded whisky. Less than half was genuine; and while they usually mix a little old whisky with it, they often sell it purely and simply as it is, whisky which has no claim to be called whisky under the real meaning of that term."

But all that was only a beginning. The time came when the vision of a great liquor combination rose in certain minds in this country. It was planned to sweep the good brands and the bad brands alike into one common management—whose control the reader will by this time suspect—and thus not only capitalize the reputation which the old-time American distillers had made through years of honest distilling, but use the trade names of pure goods as a mask for a deluge of the dishonest kind of liquor which left a trail of suicide, insanity, crime and social wreckage in its path.

This, with independent testimony as to the Jewish direction of it all, will form the subject matter of a separate story.

The Dearborn Independent, issue of 17 December 1921

63: Gigantic Jewish Liquor Trust and its Career

It has been shown how the American Whisky business became Jewish. The distillers of pure whisky which required years to make, were driven out by the manufacturers of drugged and chemicalized liquors which could be made in three or four hours. The latter, being cheaper and more intoxicating, so completely usurped the market that the public never knew that it was not whisky. It had stolen the name of whisky, and under that name the righteous indignation of the people prohibited it; and under that name still it is being sold by bootleggers at an advance of 1,000 per cent. The use of the fraudulent label is not new, it is not a product of Prohibition days; it began with the advent of Jewish capital into the liquor business. Whisky, carefully and scientifically made, purified by long years of repose in the warehouse, was an American product; "red eye," "forty rod stuff," "knock 'em dead" and "squirrel whisky" mixed and sold the same day, were Jewish products.

The Pure Food Law came into the fight to protect the American industry, but it was flouted at every turn. Bad liquor was in such a deep state of public disgrace that the people paid little attention to Chief Chemist Wiley's efforts. They thought when he said "whisky" he meant the stuff that they knew as "whisky," and they disregarded him. The degeneracy of the liquor business became deeper and deeper, to the amazement of both its friends and its foes, and no one had the key to the situation because no one saw, or seeing, had the courage to expose, the Jewish program behind the scenes.

To resume the story: Even after the cheap compounded liquors which masqueraded as "whisky" had won a commanding place in the market, to the serious detriment of the business in pure brands, the Jewish compounders were far from satisfied.

There remained a few American brands whose names, by reason of their dependability, topped the list. Their very quality, though of limited quantity, was a constant challenge to the vicious mixtures of which the rectifiers produced millions of gallons a year. How to remove those standard American brands, with their honest labels, from the market?—

that was the problem which the leaders of the Jewish compounding business tackled. The first resort was, characteristically, to trickery. Shipments of pure goods would be sidetracked somewhere en route, while the rectifiers drew off half the whisky and refilled the barrels with mixed compounds. People who have been amazed at the stunts of the bootleggers—the sidetracking of whisky shipments, the "robbery" of loaded trucks, and so on—would not be so surprised if they knew that every trick was used by the compounders of bad liquor twenty years ago! It was Jewish then, as it is Jewish now, but no one dared say so. Merely to list the tricks would require too much space. It was a nasty business from any point of view.

But still the standard brands held their place in public confidence. The Jew who claims to be the superior of the American in skill did not think of making a better whisky and thus winning the market; he thought to get rid of the better whisky that the vicious, adulterated product might own the field.

It was the day of Trusts. Big Business was amalgamating. It occurred to the leaders of the compounding business that if they could sweep all the honest distilleries into a combine with all the backroom rectifying places, put them all under one management and run down the quality of famous brands to the standard of cheap ones—cashing in on the names of the brands, and doubly profiting by decreasing the cost which quality requires—they could thus accomplish in a financial way what had been formerly tried by less respectable methods.

The inception of the idea of a "whisky combine" was legitimate. The Kentucky distillers (who must at all times be distinguished from compounders and rectifiers) endeavored in 1898 to establish a combination that would unite all the legitimate distilleries in the fight against the flood of counterfeit whisky. It is, however, significant that there was not enough capital in the legitimate whisky business to finance the plan. But when the idea was picked up by the makers of spurious liquor, there were millions of dollars at their command—just as today, with industry suffering, there are millions of Jewish capital at the disposal of the motion picture business!

In the *Louisville Courier-Journal,* February, 1899, the story of the first operations toward a combine is told, the language being inflated, of course, that hesitant distilleries might be stampeded. "Absorbed Kentucky Distilleries in a Mammoth Combine. Capital Stock $32,000,000. Some of the Biggest Plants in the State Involved. Sixteen in

Louisville. Controls 90 per cent of the Product and Nearly All Standard Brands."

"Levy Mayer, of Chicago, has acted as counsel in the drawing up of the papers. He becomes the general counsel of the new company."

This article contained a list of Kentucky distilleries, all of them American—that is, non-Jewish. It was the well-established brands, the names of quality, that were sought. These names were all non-Jewish.

"Levy Mayer, the general counsel of the new company, said tonight: 'The Kentucky Distilleries and Warehouse Company is a reality and will bring prosperity to the state of Kentucky where depression has prevailed for some years on account of the discord which has existed among the distillers of Bourbon whisky, who for a generation prior enjoyed a great prosperity.'"

A most ingenuous statement. But Mr. Mayer is a most ingenuous man. However, there is some truth in his statement: it was true that the legitimate distillers had suffered from depression, not because the American people were not consuming liquor, however, but because the American people had been turned from pure whisky to "red eye"; and Mr. Mayer's smooth statement that this depression was "on account of the discord which has existed among the distillers of Bourbon whisky" needs revision to "the fight between the non-Jewish makers of real whisky and the Jewish makers of compounded liquor."

In the story of the combine a great deal is heard of Mr. Mayer and Alfred Austrian. Mayer is a Chicago Jew who is worth a story by himself. He is one of those Jews with whom candidates for the American presidency—mostly those candidates who are in debt—feel it is necessary to stay, when he invites them. Mr. Austrian is sufficiently well known by his connection with the baseball scandal. He was attorney for Rothstein, the gambler, whose name figured so prominently in that scandal, and who is credited with doing things to the grand jury testimony in a way that makes a pretty tale. Austrian also appeared for two St. Louis Jew gamblers, implicated in the baseball scandal, who were afterward indicted. Austrian is also credited with being the author of the so-called "Lasker Plan" of baseball reorganization. The services of Mayer and Austrian to the liquor interests of Chicago and Cook County, were and are important.

There were Jewish names previously appearing. About 1889 Nathan Hoffheimer had tried to bring all the Kentucky whisky business under one head, and later Morris Greenbaum tried it. It will probably be conceded that both these men are Jews, and it is provable by the records that they were endeavoring to consolidate the whisky business. But the big stunt was really pulled off under the guidance of the two Chicago Jews, Mayer and Austrian.

"The various companies forming the Trust are:

"American Spirits Manufacturing Company, $35,000,000; Kentucky Distilling and Warehouse Association, $32,000,000; The Rye Whisky Distillers Association $30,000,000; the Standard Distilling Company, $28,000,000; and the Spirits Distributing Company, $7,500,000.

"The forerunner of the gigantic combination of the whisky interests of the country was the organization of the American Spirits Manufacturing Company upon the ruins of the old whisky trust which was controlled and directed by Joseph Greenhut. . . .

"Attorney Levi Mayer, of Chicago, who has been legal adviser of the whisky people from the inception of the American Spirits Manufacturing Association, was called to New York Saturday last to confer over the legal form of the charter and the closing of the negotiations."

The italicized portions indicate the connection, and it was a connection maintained to the end, and may indeed be continued yet.

Then, in the current accounts of this merger of the liquor business under Jewish control, another name appears. On March 15, 1899:

"Angelo Meyer, a big whisky buyer of New York, is in Louisville trying to buy a big lot of whiskies." It appears that Mr. Meyer put on a poor mouth and told how hard it was to buy whisky in big lots.

And then on March 17, two days later, this appeared: "Mr. Angelo Meyer, the wealthy Philadelphia whisky man, has been appointed one of the general managers of the business of the Kentucky Distilleries Company, and is engaged in appointing men to take charge of the various departments of the combine's affairs."

The discrepancy in the above two paragraphs need not be charged to the untruthfulness of the newspaper reporter. Reporters as a rule faithfully report what they are told; but sometimes what they are told is not true.

"Mr. Meyer has commonly been called the Napoleon of the whisky trade. He is largely interested in the recently formed combine.

"'We intend to make plenty of whisky. No brand will be killed.' said Mr. Meyer."

Henceforth the names of Levi Mayer, Alfred Austrian and Angelo Meyer appear most frequently in the reports.

"Alfred Austrian, who is Levy Mayer's legal representative, says that all the distilleries now negotiated for will be absorbed in three weeks more."

"In an interview today Mr. Angelo Meyer said, 'I believe confidently that in the next five years a business calling for 10,000,000 gallons of whisky a year will be built up.'"

In April, 1899, another Jewish movement appeared: "Joseph Wolf, the Chicago whisky dealer, who is said to own more Kentucky whisky, independent of the Kentucky Distilleries and Warehouse Company, than any other individual or corporation, is behind the new whisky combine formed in Chicago with a capital stock of $3,000,000. The purpose of the new trust, which it is said will be given the title of the Illinois Distilleries and Warehouse Company, is to fight the Kentucky Distilleries and Warehouse Company."

The few remaining Kentucky Distillers were wary; they regarded Wolf, probably with reason, as simulating enmity to the other part of the Jew-made whisky trust in order to sweep into his net the remaining independents.

"Alfred Austrian and C. H. Stoll, attorneys for the Kentucky Distilleries and Warehouse Company, will leave Louisville today for Chicago to confer with Levy D. Mayer, chief counsel for the trust; and in fact, counsel for three big whisky and spirits combines."

"Alfred Austrian, of Chicago, left last night for Cincinnati to close the deal for the celebrated Sam Clay distillery of Bourbon County."

Under an exciting headline detailing the departure of the Jew lawyer Austrian to Chicago to see the Jew lawyer Mayer, there is the story of a still greater whisky combine:

"The projected combination of all the whisky interests of the country will probably be completed in Chicago today. A rye whisky trust is now being formed, and will soon be ready for incorporation and presentation to men with capital. . . . It is said that the capitalization of the rye whisky trust will be $60,000,000, and the combined capitalization of the five companies will amount to about $175,000,000. . . . Levy Mayer, of Chicago, Alfred Austrian, of Chicago, and C. H. Stoll, of New York, are the attorneys for the three trusts, Mr. Mayer being the chief counsel."

And still later, a statement by Levy Mayer:

"The new rye distillery combination will be the largest individual whisky amalgamation in the world. It is controlled and is being financed by the same people and the same trust companies of New

York and Philadelphia now controlling and financing the Kentucky Distilleries and Warehouse Company, whose capital is $32,000,000; the Standard Distilling and Distributing Company, with a capital of $28,000,000; the American Spirits Manufacturing Company, with a capital of $35,000,000; and the Spirits Distributing Company, with a capitalization of $15,000,000.

"Rumor has it," and Mr. Mayer smiled as he patted a big bundle of legal documents, "that after the rye consolidation has been perfected all the separate companies will be merged into one central company, which will have an aggregate capital close to $200,000,000. A whisky combination of that size will certainly hold foremost place among the world's liquor trusts and organizations."

Another dispatch: "Alfred Austrian today returned to Louisville from New York, where he assisted in forming the combine of the American Spirits Manufacturing Company (and the three other companies).

"Mr. Austrian leaves tonight for Chicago, where he expects to close the deal with Elias Bloch & Sons to purchase the Darling distillery in Carroll County, and with Freiberg and Workum to secure their two plants in Boone County."

Here it is possible to see the Jewish agents of Jewish capital hurrying to and fro with every assurance of success, working along well-defined lines, known to themselves but concealed from the public, building up a colossal structure which public opinion was to hurl down in two decades. But two decades were enough for enormous revenues to be derived from the criminal debasement of all kinds of liquor, which became more apparent from the time of the giant consolidation.

Whisky became so rotten that in Kentucky, the pioneer whisky state, there were only four whole "wet" counties by 1908. The first decade of absolute Jewish control put even the first whisky state in the "dry" column.

The Jewish compounders did not care how they marketed their goods, so long as they could sell them in quantities. The cheap "barrel house" appeared with its windows full of gleaming bottles and gaudy labels and "cut rate" whisky prices. The compounders became saloon owners toward the end of the saloon era, and many Jews went into the "barrel house" business for a quick cleanup. The proportion of vicious dives increased everywhere, and the moral guardians of society were amazed at "the wave of vice" that was "sweeping over the country"; but they did not have the key that explained it. The whisky business was riding to a wild finish, but the men at the helm knew exactly what they were doing every moment of the time. To look back upon that period, with all the facts at hand, makes it more and more apparent how fitting is the term, "boob Gentile."

Why, even Norman Hapgood knew how bad it was, and *Collier's Weekly*, under his editorship, was the first journal in the land to print the names of Jews in connection with the liquor debauchery of the country. But those were the good old days, when Hapgood could tell the truth even about Hearst, the man for whom he now writes his graceless palaver of pro-Jewish propaganda.

In *Collier's Weekly*, during the year 1908, solid truths appeared, which are in point today as proofs of what was transpiring. There was a specially scathing attack on what was called "nigger gin," a peculiarly vile beverage which was compounded to act upon the Negro in a most vicious manner. Will Irwin spoke of this gin as "the king iniquity in the degenerated liquor traffic of these United States." This author and Collier's started a new fashion in giving publicity not only to the names of certain brands of liquors, but also the names of the men who made them. It turned out that the maker of a brand of "nigger gin" which had spurred certain Negroes on to the nameless crime, was one Lee Levy. Mr. Irwin wrote:

"Because the South is not through with Lee Levy, and because its citizens may at least drive him out of business—if they cannot get him behind the bars—one declaration of the Commercial Appeal is worthy of reply. That paper raises a question of fact—it charges that Levy's gin, Dreyfuss, Weil & Company's gin, Bluthenthal & Blickert's gin, the Old Spring Distilling Company's gin, do not exist; or that, if they exist, their sales are insignificant. Let me present my own evidence on that point."

Mr. Irwin then details some of this experiences. The gin which he was discussing was provocative of peculiar lawlessness, its labels bore lascivious suggestions and were decorated with highly indecent portraiture of white women. "I bought, for evidence, many other brands, some emanating from the big liquor cities and some put up by local people; but I could always get Levy's. I never saw it in any saloon which bars the Negro.

"In Galveston, which prides itself on its clean government, some brand or other was for sale in nearly all the corner grocery 'drums.'

"In a Negro street of New Orleans I saw five saloon shop windows in one block which displayed either Lee Levy's or Dreyfuss, Weil &

Company's. This latter firm is more clever in its work than the others, much more delicate and subtle in its labeling policy. It takes one who understands the Negro and his slang to appreciate the enigma of their wording; it all comes in a 'caution label' on the obverse of the bottles.

". . . Such gins were sold everywhere in Birmingham . . . . a bottle of the stuff, half empty, had been taken from a Pickens County Negro just after his arrest for the nameless crime.

"Levy—so the gossip of the liquor trade has it—grew rich through this department of his business. Dreyfuss, Weil & Company advertise everywhere that theirs is 'the most widely sold brand in the South.' And more and more one hears of tragedies that lie at the end of this course."

That is a sample—an expurgated sample—of what went on in every part of the country. Newspaper reporters will remember how the police used to wonder about the change that came over certain foreign communities. "They come here nice people," the experienced police captain would say, "but in a short time they are giving us all sorts of trouble. They don't do that in their own country."

"It's the drink," somebody would suggest.

"No, they drink in their own country, they drink all the time there. It's the kind of drink they get here that does it—the 'rot-gut,' that drives them wild." That was the captain's diagnosis, made a thousand times, but no one was the wiser. No one saw the key, which was the Jew.

In the South a terrible lynching period came and divided the country into pro-lynching and pro-Negro parties, but still no one saw the reason for it all. The race question rose to threatening proportions, the Americans of the North and South looked at each other askance, there was a cooling of sympathy between the regions. Northerners were inclined to look at Southerners as unjust and inhuman in their treatment of the Negro, and Southerners were inclined to look upon Northerners as temperamentally unsympathetic and stupidly ignorant of what the conditions were.

Behind it all were the products of men like Lee Levy and Dreyfuss, Weil & Company, to use only the names quoted from Collier's.

The ancient Jewish policy of Divide-Conquer-Destroy was in operation. Jewish policy favors disunion as a preparation to the kind of union which Jewish leaders want. Jewish influence was strong for disunion in the Civil War. Jewish influence is directly behind the present attitude of the Negro toward the white man—look at the so-called "Negro welfare societies" with their hordes of Jewish officials and patrons! Jewish influence in the South is today active in keeping up the memory of the old divisions. And, with reference to the Negro question, "nigger gin," the product of Jewish poisoned liquor factories, was its most provocative element.

Trace the appearance of this gin as to date, and you will find the period when Negro outbursts and lynching became serious. Trace the localities where this gin was most widely sold and you will find the places where these disorders prevailed.

It is extremely simple, so simple that it has been overlooked. The public is being constantly deceived by an appearance of complexity, where there is none. When you find the fever-bearing mosquito, yellow fever is no longer a mystery.

The same policy of "Divide-Conquer-Destroy" tells the story of the liquor traffic. Jewish influence divided between distilling and compounding, drove out distilling, and in the end destroyed the traffic as a legalized entity.

It needs to be said, however, that the destruction is not part of the Jewish intention. "Divide and Conquer" is the formula as the Jewish leaders conceive it, as, indeed, it is stated in the Protocols. The "destroy" comes as Nemesis upon Jewish achievements. Russia was divided and conquered, but just as the Jews had conquered it, the canker worm of fate began to consume their conquest. The story is repeated wherever Jewish intrigue has succeeded. Whatever the Jews can succeed in making Jewish, falls!

It may be fate. It may be Destiny's way to the survival of the fittest. That which succumbs to complete Judiazation, as Jewish leaders conceive it, may deserve to fall. The justification of its destruction may appear in the possibility of its Judaization. Anything that can be Judaized is to that extent sentenced to oblivion.

The story of Jewish control of liquor has now been carried through two stages, the "Divide and Conquer" stages. The third stage follows with swift and relentless steps. Blind though the country was to the Jewish character of the liquor business, it was not blind to the ravages of that business upon society.

There came a sentiment that moved ceaselessly through the country, and mounted to stormy power; people could only speak of it as a "wave." The term became hackneyed by overuse, but it was accurately descriptive. The indignation of the people, the arousal of their just moral resentment was as a flood which rose to cleanse the land. The attack was on liquor, and the attack was just. The attack was on liquor and it came none too soon. The country was drenched in vile concoctions which rapidly undermined large sections of the population. Crime increased and domestic misery was everywhere. The people attacked the only thing they could see—they attacked the stuff and the places that distributed it. They did not see the $200,000,000 Jewish whisky combination, they did not see the sinister devices by which strong drink was made vile and viler with the growth of Jewish control.

The people rose and swept away the saloon. They did not sweep away the stocks of liquor. They did not sweep away Jewish interest in liquor. They left the source untouched. And that source is still existent.

There remains another chapter of the narrative: the coming of Prohibition and of the illicit traffic in liquor. It remains to be seen whether the same thread carries through the latter phases.

The Dearborn Independent, issue of 24 December 1921

64: The Jewish Element in Bootlegging Evil

A student of the liquor history of the United States is left wondering, not that Prohibition came, but that the authorities ever allowed matters to go so far as to compel the people to take the issue into their own hands. That is the point where those who believe in "personal liberty" and those who believe in "public safety" ought to meet each other. It cannot be contended that every believer in Prohibition is a crank, nor can it be contended that every believer in "personal liberty" is a drunkard or a liquor guzzler; each of them stands for a principle that is a principle of right. But the Prohibitionist has been able to command victory over the "personal liberty" advocate because the stuff that the Prohibitionist is against ought not to be sold nor used under any circumstances, whereas the stuff the "personal liberty" advocate thinks he favors is not the stuff he thinks it is at all.

If the element in question were poisoned tooth paste, or opium, or any other concededly dangerous substance, both the Prohibitionist and the "personal liberty" advocate would agree. What the honest "personal liberty" advocate needs to learn is that the liquor which caused the adoption of Prohibition was most dangerous to the individual and society. The question was not one of "liberty" but of safety.

It is scarcely to be hoped that all the "personal liberty" groups will come to agree with this, because most of them are formed of the very men who made and profited by the drugged and chemicalized substances which were sold over the bar and in bottles.

Liquor men themselves must agree with the facts. Even Bonfort's Wine and Spirits Circular admitted years ago that "the bulk of spirits sold today in glass under well-known brands is not what it is represented to be." "The truth of the matter is (we dislike to say it) the wine and spirit trade of this country is honeycombed with fraud, and the most radical measure should be applied and applied vigorously." "Many a dealer prominent socially, morally, religiously and in philanthropic circles will take a lot of neutral spirits, only a few days old, flavor them with a little heavy-bodied whisky, and brand them on the label or glass with the name of any state or county desired, and with any age, and this he will do with all smiles and glee and inward delight that is said to characterize the bold buccaneer when he cuts a throat and scuttles a ship."

These excerpts show how near the official publications of the liquor trade could come to describing the practice and indicating the Jew. The last quotation was a direct hit at Louisville liquor Jews, one of which compounders furnished a room at the Y.M.C.A. of that city, another of whom adorned the town with public gifts, all of whom are Kentucky "Colonels"; though their ancestry is not exactly Kentuckian, nor even American.

The wine companies of Ohio, whose vineyards on Kelleys Island and elsewhere had built up a standard business, joined in the protest. They pointed out that counterfeit wines were flowing out of factories in Cleveland and Cincinnati, while the legitimate wine districts of Sandusky and Put-in-Bay were being saddled with the stigma of poisoned goods. As all the counterfeit business was in the hands of Jews, the statement is unavoidable that the whole movement of the degradation of liquor was Jewish.

Then came Prohibition. The Constitution of the United States was amended, the amendment being ratified by 45 states. The issue had been actively before the nation longer than any other issue except the slavery question, so that the people's action on it must be regarded as deliberate. And the liquor business was legally ended. BUT

What was the Jewish attitude toward Prohibition while it was being argued before the nation? What has been the Jewish attitude toward Prohibition since it has been adopted?

Both questions can be answered the same way. There are, of course, Kentuckians and others who have convinced themselves that the Jewish compounders foresaw Prohibition and welcomed it, because they saw that it would increase their profits 1,000 per cent. But whatever the truth of that may be, there are no available records to support it. The Jews destroyed the business—that is true; but whether intentionally, for greater illegitimate profits, we cannot say.

There are, however, records of Jewish activity during the reform agitation. The Jews were against Prohibition. Their press and pulpit were against it. Their whole influence in politics and finance were against it. They were the backbone of the entire "wet" propaganda, and are today. The great temperance organizations will tell you that Jews did not contribute to their work. One national Prohibition organization admits a gift of $5 in many years. Will Irwin, investigating the early Prohibition movement in the South for Collier's in 1901, found that *The Modern Voice,* a Jewish religious weekly which is still published, was engaged in carrying the "wet" propaganda into the southern states. *The Modern Voice* lost more votes than it made for its lack of taste in printing a halftone picture of Christ endorsing the liquor traffic. J. K. Baer, one of the editors of this Jewish paper, explained his activity in this direction by saying, "We are a Jewish weekly, and the Jews are opposed on moral grounds to prohibition." A Mr. Rosenthal was associated in the work. This was typical of the Jewish press everywhere. The Jewish stage was enlisted, every man and every girl, just as it is now, to deride those who protested against the destruction of the American people by counterfeit whisky and wine. Jazz music, the movies, fake medical "experts"—every agency under Jewish control was mobilized to assist the fight for a continuance of the privilege of drugging the people's drink.

This will scarcely be denied, at least by Jews. Some "Gentile fronts" may feel obliged to rush to the defense of the Jews by denying it, but their work is unnecessary. Jews themselves make no bones about it. They did not favor Prohibition, but they did not fear it; they knew that they would be exempt, they knew that it would bring certain illegitimate commercial advantages; they would be winners either way. Jewish luck!

It is not surprising, therefore, that violation and evasion of the Prohibition law has had a deep Jewish complexion from the very beginning. *The Dearborn Independent* would be glad to be excused from making the raw statement that bootlegging is a 95 per cent controlled Jewish industry in which a certain class of rabbis have been active; we, therefore, avail ourselves of the report of an address of Rabbi Leo M. Franklin, of Detroit, president of the Central Conference of American Rabbis, as given before that body at Washington in April, 1921, confirming the general fact:

"In making the recommendation I gave you in my message in regard to this matter, and in going to the extreme in suggesting that we appeal to the government to rescind that part of the Prohibition law which gives rabbis permission to issue permits for the purchase and distribution of wine for ritual purposes, I did so after very mature consideration. I am sure that after (his successor) shall have been in the chair of the conference for any length of time, he will come to exactly the same conclusions as I did.

"You gentlemen, members of the conference, who have dealt with this situation as a local question have had, here and there, some small question to solve; but when you become president of the conference and have letters from every part of the country, almost day by day, asking you as president of the conference to give the necessary authority to all sorts of men in all sorts of conditions, to purchase and distribute wine for ritual purposes, then you will take a different angle on this whole situation.

"I pointed out to one of my colleagues, next to whom I was just now sitting, that within the past month I have received requests from three different men calling themselves rabbis in their communities, for authorization to purchase and distribute wine. I know that I am not exaggerating when I say that during this last year I received requests from not less than 150 men in all parts of the country for permits to distribute wine. . . . I had the applicants investigated, and I may say to you that in nine cases out of ten we found those who were attempting to use this conference, through its executive officers, for the obtaining of this authority, were men who had not the slightest right to stand before their communities as rabbis.

"What were they for the most part? They were men without the slightest pretense at rabbinical training or position who, for the purpose of getting into the wholesale liquor business, if you will, organized congregations. Nothing on God's earth could prevent them from doing so. They simply gathered around them little companies of men; they called them congregations; and then, under the law as it now exists, they were privileged to purchase and distribute wine to these people. And I call your attention to the fact that many of the so-called members of these congregations were not members of one congregation only! (Laughter.) This is not a laughing matter. They were not only members of one congregation, but members of two, three, four and upward. Why, you don't know what good Jews many have become since this law has gone into effect!

"What is more, gentlemen, perhaps some of you don't realize what popularity has come to the—sermon, and how many Jews have suddenly come to realize the beauty and the duty of the Kiddush on Friday night. I tell you it is a mighty serious problem, and say what you will, our conference, under present conditions, is being used as a medium by unscrupulous men, by the dozens and by the hundreds, to carry on a bootlegging business in the name of religion. . . .

"Now you say there have been just small scandals here and there. A wine company in New York was raided last week and a quarter of a million dollars' worth of wine was taken away by the authorities, supposed to be for ritual purposes. Don't forget that rabbi after rabbi last week in New York, a few of whom I happen to know, and in Rochester, Buffalo, Flint, Michigan, and Port Huron, Michigan—in any number of small towns throughout the country, if you have read your papers carefully, you will find that Rabbi So-and-So has been arrested as a bootlegger."

The discussion of this subject by the other rabbis present was very interesting. There was a request that "personal experiences be debarred," but some crept in. Rabbi Cohen, for example, was quite explicit.

"Being one of those who opposed the whole Prohibition law, I am not in sympathy with the whole Prohibition law. . . . It seems to me that we rabbis ought not to stand in the way of our own members in their legitimate ways of getting wine for their homes. . . . If a member wants the wine, I would like to be in a position that he may have the wine, even though he may not absolutely have to have it."

Rabbi Cohen pronounced the typical Jewish view. If the fool Gentiles want to prohibit themselves from having liquor, let them do it, but if there is a loophole for the Jews such as the rabbinical permit offers, it should be used generously for any "member," "even though he may not absolutely have to have it."

The pre-Prohibition Jewish liquor business is also the post-Prohibition Jewish liquor business. That fact is established by mountainous evidence. This does not mean, of course, that every bootlegger you meet is a Jew, nor that you will ever meet a Jew serving as an itinerant bootlegger. Unless you live in Chicago, New York or other large cities, an actual meeting with the Jew in this minor capacity will not be frequent. The Jew is the possessor of the wholesale stocks; he is the director of the underground railways that convey the stuff surreptitiously to the public; seldom does he risk his own safety in being the last man to hand the goods to the consumer and to take the money.

But notwithstanding all the carefulness, the bulk of the arrests made in the United States have been among Jews. The bulk of the liquor permits—a guess at 95 per cent would not be too high—are in the hands of Jews. More and more the Jews are being appointed as Prohibition enforcement officers at the central points of distribution. It is a fact, as Rabbi Franklin showed, that part of the trouble arises over the abuse of what has been called "rabbinical wine," but big as it seems by itself, it is really a small part in comparison with the whole. Numbers of lesser rabbis have profited from the sale of liquor, no doubt of that. And not only among their own people, but from any people making the demand. "If you sign a Jewish name you can get it," is the watchword. Newspaper offices have been kept "wet" in some cases by "rabbinical wine," which accounts for the dribble of "wet" propaganda in the so-called humorous and other columns of the evening journals.

It happens that "rabbinical wine" is a euphemism for whisky, gin, Scotch, champagne, vermouth, absinthe, or any other kind of hard liquor. The stocks that existed when Prohibition went into force have not only not deceased, but have actually increased, because of the increase in the "doctoring" of the stuff. It has been cheapened, its bulk has been increased and it has been made, if anything, more deadly than before. "As fatal as bootleg whisky" is a saying founded on thousands of deaths.

The wholesale stocks of compounded liquor remained in the hands of the men who owned them, while the retail stocks in stores and saloons had to be disposed of. That was one of the first big mistakes— that the little fellow was compelled to get rid of his stock, while the big fellow was permitted to keep his. The so-called rabbis who had advance information of the special privileges which the Jews were to enjoy under the Prohibition law, were very active in buying up the smaller stocks and storing them away. Of course, no one could prevent them. Was it not "ritual wine"?—Even though it was any kind of liquor, it went under the "cover name" of "ritual wine," and of course, as everybody knows, great scandal resulted.

Protests like that of Rabbi Franklin indicate that a part of Jewish public opinion resents the policy of exempting Jews from the Prohibition law, but this is minority opinion. What the Central Conference of American Rabbis may think is of little consequence to the mass of Jews in America. The people to scrutinize with regard to this are not the Rabbi Franklins, who are amenable to the significance of American opinion, but those Jews who do not consult with Americanized rabbis, but run the political end of Jewry as they choose.

There is no reason why the Jews should be exempt from the operation of the Constitution of the United States at all, yet the Constitution is suspended in their favor when the Ten-Gallon Permit is given.

But it would be a great mistake to suppose that there is or could be any objection to the Jews' ritualistic use of wine, or that the present scandal with regard to law violation rises from that. It is not a religious question at all. It is purely a commercial question. The people who are breaking the Prohibition law are the same people who broke the Pure Food law with regard to the ingredients of whisky. They are essentially a lawbreaking class.

The "Gentile boobs" who patronize bootleggers today are being sold a liquor which is never what it is represented to be, in spite of names blown in the bottles, in spite of seals and in spite of labels. The most conscienceless fraud is being perpetrated on gullible people at an increase in profit from 400 to 1,000 per cent. The stuff brought from Havana is Jew whisky shipped there, "doctored" still more and shipped back at increased prices—the "Gentile boobs" fancying they are getting something extra special "just brought in from Havana."

Twenty hears ago Jewish liquor dealers of Chicago were using genuine James E. Pepper bottles refilled with vile ingredients compounded in back rooms. Twenty years ago there were counterfeit whiskies sold in the United States bearing forged Canadian Government stamps. The forgers of the labels were Jewish liquor houses. Twenty years ago there was unlimited faking of liquor labels, a Chicago printing house furnishing Jewish liquor houses with clever imitations of any reputable label in use, to be placed on bottles containing doped goods. Foreign, American and Canadian labels were unscrupulously adopted and brazenly advertised everywhere.

These abuses did not wait for Prohibition; they were daily Jewish practices twenty years ago.

The only difference now is that the stuff which is sold is still worse.

The enforcement of the Prohibition law ought to be rigidly complete, for the same reason that the enforcement of the Pure Food law should have been complete years ago—it is necessary to prevent the wholesale harming of an ignorant public.

The maintenance of the idea of drink in the minds of the people is due to Jewish propaganda. There is not a dialog on the stage today that does not drip with whisky patter. As all the plays making much noise this year are not only Jew-written, Jew-produced and Jew-controlled, but also Jew-played (the stage swarms with Jewish countenances this year), the drip of whisky patter is constant. If theatergoers were at all observant they would see that most of their money goes to support pro-Jewish propaganda in one form or another, which, is of course, a tribute to Jewish business genius—what other people could embark on a pro-racial propaganda and make the opposite race pay for it?

This idea of drink will be maintained by means of the Jewish stage, Jewish jazz and the Jewish comics until somebody comes down hard upon it as being incentive of treason to the Constitution. When a Jewish comedian can indulge in a 15-minute monologue "panning" the United States, defaming Liberty, heaping contempt upon the Pilgrims, and openly praising a violation of a portion of the Constitution of the United States—and when choruses sing this sort of thing, and slap-stick artists take it up, and it becomes evident that the country is being ringed around every week by repeated attacks upon what the people have established—it is certain not to be very long before a heavy hand will be laid on the whole business.

The Department of Justice should pay some attention to the treason nightly spouted on the legitimate stage before Americans who pay as high as $5 each in support of the propaganda.

First and last, the illicit liquor business in all its phases, both before and after Prohibition, has always been Jewish. Before Prohibition it was morally illicit, after Prohibition it became both morally and legally illicit.

And it is not a cause for shame among the majority of the Jews, sad to say; it is rather a cause for boast. The Yiddish newspapers are fruitful of jocular references to the fact, and they even carry large wine company advertisements week after week.

As before Prohibition the key to the steady degeneration of the liquor business was the fact of Jewish domination, so now the key to the organized and lawless rebellion against a recently enacted article of the Constitution is also Jewish. Prohibition enforcement officers will find a short-cut to successful enforcement along this line. And if law-abiding Jews would help with what they know, the work could be soon accomplished.

The Dearborn Independent, issue of 31 December 1921

65: Angles of Jewish Influence in American Life

The Jewish Question exists wherever Jews appear, says Theodor Herzl, because they bring it with them. It is not their numbers that create the Question, for there is in almost every country a larger number of other aliens than of Jews. It is not their much-boasted ability, for it is now coming to be understood that, give the Jew an equal start and hold him to the rules of the game, and he is not smarter than anyone else; indeed, in one great class of Jews the zeal is quenched when opportunity for intrigue is removed.

The Jewish Question is not in the number of Jews who here reside, not in the American's jealousy of the Jew's success, certainly not in any objection to the Jew's entirely unobjectionable Mosaic religion; it is in something else, and that something else is the fact of Jewish influence on the life of the country where Jews dwell; in the United States it is the Jewish influence on American life.

That the Jews exert an influence, they themselves loudly proclaim. One is permitted to think that they really claim a stronger influence than they possess, especially in those higher regions where excellent and determinative influences have been at work. The Jews claim, indeed, that the fundamentals of the United States are Jewish and not Christian, and that the entire history of this country should be rewritten to make proper acknowledgment of the prior glory due to Judah. If the question of influence rested entirely on the Jewish claim, there would be no occasion for doubt; they claim it all. But it is kindness to hold them to the facts; it is also more clearly explanatory of conditions in our country. If they insist that they "gave us our Bible" and "gave us our God" and "gave us our religion," as they do over and over again with nauseating superciliousness throughout all their polemic publications—not a single one of these claims being true—they must not grow impatient and profane while we complete the list of the real influences they have set at work in American life.

It is not the Jewish people but the Jewish idea, and the people only as vehicles of the idea, that is the point at issue. As it was Prussianism and not the German people that was the objective in the recent war, so in this investigation of the Jewish Question, it is Jewish influence and the Jewish Idea that are being discovered and defined.

The Jews are propagandists. This was originally their mission. But they were to propagate the central tenet of their religion. This they failed to do. By failing in this they, according to their own Scriptures, failed everywhere. They are now without a mission of blessing. Few of their leaders even claim a spiritual mission. But the mission idea is still with them in a degenerate form; it represents the grossest materialism of the day; it has become a means of sordid acquisition instead of a channel of service.

The essence of the Jewish Idea in its influence on the labor world is the same as in all other departments—the destruction of real values in favor of fictitious values. The Jewish philosophy of money is not to "make money," but to "get money." The distinction between these two is fundamental. That explains Jews being "financiers" instead of "captains of industry." It is the difference between "getting" and "making."

The creative, constructive type of mind has an affection for the thing it is doing. The non-Jewish worker formerly chose the work he liked best. He did not change his employment easily, because there was a bond between him and the kind of work he had chosen. Nothing else was so attractive to him. He would rather draw a little less money and do what he liked to do, than a little more and do what irked him. The "maker" is always thus influenced by his liking.

Not so the "getter." It doesn't matter what he does, so long as the income is satisfactory. He has no illusions, sentiments or affections on the side of work. It is the "geld" that counts. He has no attachment for the things he makes, for he doesn't make any; he deals in the things which other men make and regards them solely on the side of their money-drawing value. "The joy of creative labor" is nothing to him, not even an intelligible saying.

Now, previous to the advent of Jewish socialistic and subversive ideas, the predominant thought in the labor world was to "make" things and thus "make" money. There was a pride among mechanics. Men who made things were a sturdy, honest race because they dealt with ideas of skill and quality, and their very characters were formed by the satisfaction of having performed useful functions in society. They were the Makers. And society was solid as long as they were solid. Men made shoes as exhibitions of their skill. Farmers raised crops for the inherent love of crops, not with reference to far-off money-markets. Everywhere The Job was the main thing and the rest was incidental.

The only way to break down this strong safeguard of society—a laboring class of sturdy character—was to sow other ideas among it; and the most dangerous of all the ideas sown was that which substituted "get" for "make." With the required manipulation of the money and food markets, enough pressure could be brought to bear on the ultimate consumers to give point to the idea of "get," and it was not long before the internal relations of American business were totally upset, with Jews at the head of the banking system, and Jews at the head of both the conservative and radical elements of the Labor Movement, AND, most potent of all, the Jewish Idea sowed through the minds of workingmen. What Idea? The old idea of "get" instead of "make."

The idea of "get" is a vicious, anti-social and destructive idea when held alone; but when held in company with "make" and as second in importance, it is legitimate and constructive.

As soon as a man or a class is inoculated with the strictly Jewish Idea of "getting"—("getting mine;" "getting while the getting is good;" "honestly if you can, dishonestly if you must—but get it"—all of which are notes of this treasonable philosophy), the very cement of society loses its adhesiveness and begins to crumble. The great myth and fiction of Money has been forced into the place of real things, and the second step of the drama can thus be opened up.

Jewish influence on the thought of the working men of the United States, as well as on the thought of business and professional men, has been bad, thoroughly bad. This is not manifested in a division between "capital" and "labor," for there are no such separate elements; there is only the executive and operating departments of American business. The real division is between the Jewish idea of "get" and the Anglo-Saxon idea of "make," and at the present time the Jewish idea has been successful enough to have caused an upset.

All over the United States, in many branches of trade, Communist colleges are maintained, officered and taught by Jews. Those so-called colleges exist in Chicago, Detroit, Cleveland, Rochester, Pittsburgh, New York, Philadelphia and other cities, the whole intent being to put all American labor on a "get" basis, which must prove the economic damnation of the country. And that, apparently, is the end sought, as in Russia. Until Jews can show that the infiltration of foreign Jews and the Jewish Idea into the American labor movement has made for the betterment in character and estate, in citizenship and economic statesmanship, of the American workingman, the charge of being an alien, destructive and treasonable influence will have to stand.

The last place the uninstructed observer would look for traces of Jewish influence is in the Christian church, yet if he fail to look there he will miss much. If the libraries of our theological seminaries were equipped with complete files of Jewish literary effort in the United States during the past 15 years, and if theological students were required to read these Jewish utterances, there would be less silly talk and fewer "easy marks" for Jewish propaganda in the American pulpit. For the next 25 years every theological seminary should support a chair for the study of Modern Jewish Influence and the Protocols. The fiction, that the Jews are an Old Testament people faithful to the Mosaic Law, would then be exploded, and timid Christians would no longer superstitiously hesitate to speak the truth about them because of that sadly misinterpreted text: "I will bless them that bless thee, and curse him that curseth thee."

There is a mission for the pulpit to liberate the Church from what the New Testament Scriptures call "the fear of the Jews."

The pulpit has also the mission of liberating the Church from the error that Judah and Israel are synonymous. The reading of the Scriptures which confuse the tribe of Judah with Israel, and which interpret every mention of Israel as signifying the Jews, is at the root of more than one-half the confusion and division traceable in Christian doctrinal statements.

The Jews are not "The Chosen People," though practically the entire Church has succumbed to the propaganda which declares them to be so. The Jewish tinge of thought has of late years overspread many Christian statements, and the uninstructed clergy have proved more and more amenable to Jewish suggestion.

The flaccid condition of the Church, so much deplored by spokesmen who had regard for her inner life, was brought about not by "science," not by "scholarship," not by the "increase of light and learning"—for none of these things are antagonistic even to incomplete statements of truth—but by Jewish-German higher criticism.

The defenders of the faith have fought long and valiantly against the inroads made by the so-called Higher Criticism, but were sadly incapacitated in their defense, because they did not see that its origin and purpose were Jewish. It was not Christian; it was not German; it was Jewish. It is almost wholly discounted today in the practical life of the church, but it still adheres to the darker corners of the colleges, along with the Red Bolshevism which is taking root there under Jewish influences.

Let the Christian minister who wishes to know the source of Jewish influence in the church look over the names of the more notorious "German" Higher Critics of the Bible, and consider their race. Add to them one Frenchman, an atheist and a Jew, and you have modern "liberal" sources very complete:

Wellhausen - Kuehne
Strauss — Hitzig
Ewald — Renan

It is perfectly in keeping with the Jewish World Program that this destructive influence should be sent out under Jewish auspices, and it is perfectly in keeping with non-Jewish trustfulness to accept the thing without looking at its source. A great many so called "liberals" played the Jewish game for a time; they are now coming back to the old citadel which stood in its own strength and without their patronage while the fever of the Higher Criticism raged.

The church is now victim of a second attack against her, in the rampant Socialism and Sovietism that have been thrust upon her in the name of flabby and unmoral theories of "brotherhood" and in an appeal to her "fairness." The church has been made to believe that she is a forum for discussion and not a high place for annunciation. She has been turned from a Voice into an echo of jangling cries. Jews have actually invaded, in person and in program, hundreds of American churches, with their subversive and impossible social ideals, and at last became so cocksure of their domination of the situation that they were met with the inevitable check.

Clergymen ought to know that seven-eighths of the economic mush they speak from the pulpit is prepared by Jewish professors of political economy and revolutionary leaders. They should be informed that economic thought has been so completely Judaized by means of a deliberate and masterly plan of camouflaged propaganda, that the mass thought of the crowd (which is the thought mostly echoed in "popular" pulpits and editorials) is more Jewish than Jewry itself holds.

The Jew has got hold of the church in doctrine, in liberalism, so-called, and in the feverish and feeble sociological diversions of many pulpits and adult classes. If there is any place where a straight study of the Jewish Question should be made, with the Bible always in hand as the authoritative textbook, it is in the modern church which is unconsciously giving allegiance to a mass of Jewish propaganda.

It is not reaction that is counseled here; it is progress along constructive paths, the paths of our forefathers, the Anglo-Saxons, who have to this day been the World-Builders, the Makers of cities and commerce and continents; and not the Jews who have never been builders or pioneers, who have never peopled the wilderness, but who move in upon the labors of other men. They are not to be blamed for not being Builders and Pioneers, perhaps; they are to be blamed for claiming all the rights of pioneers; but even then, perhaps, their blame ought not to be so great as the blame that rests upon the sons of the Anglo-Saxons for rejecting the straightforward Building of their fathers, and taking up with the doubtful ideas of Judah.

Colleges are being constantly invaded by the Jewish Idea. The sons of the Anglo-Saxon are being attacked in their very heredity. The sons of the Builders, the Makers, are being subverted to the philosophy of the destroyers.

Young men in the first exhilarating months of intellectual freedom are being seized with promissory doctrines, the source and consequences of which they do not see. There is a natural rebelliousness of youth, which promises progress; there is a natural venturesomeness to play free with ancient faiths, both of which are ebullitions of the spirit and significant of dawning mental virility. It is during the periods when these adolescent expansions are in process that the youth is captured by influences which deliberately lie in wait for him in the colleges. True, in after years a large proportion come to their senses sufficiently to be able "to sit on the fence and see themselves go by," and they come back to sanity.

They find that "free love" doctrines make exhilarating club topics, but that the Family—the old-fashioned loyalty of one man and one woman to each other and their children—is the basis, not only of society, but of all personal character and progress. They find that Revolution, while a delightful subject for fiery debates and an excellent stimulant to the feeling of supermanlikeness, is nevertheless not the process of progress.

And, too, they come at length to see that the Stars and Stripes and the Free Republic are better far than the Red Star and Soviet sordidness.

When a Supreme Court Justice addressed one of the greater American universities, a student came to him after a lecture and said: "It gave me so much pleasure to hear your lectures, for they were the first kindly words

I have heard said about our government since the commencement of my university career."

For years the secular magazines have been carrying articles on the question, "What Is Wrong With the Colleges?" The answer is perfectly clear to those who can discern Jewish influence in American life.

The trouble with the colleges has progressed along precisely the same lines that have been described above in connection with the churches. First, Jewish higher criticism in the destruction of young men's sense of respect for the ancient foundations; second, Jewish revolutionary social doctrines. The two always go together. They cannot live apart. They are the fulfillment of the Protocol's program to split non-Jewish society by means of ideas.

It is idle to attack the "unbelief" of college students, idle to attack their "radicalism"—these are always the qualities of immaturity. But it is not idle to show that social radicalism ("radicalism" being a very good word very sadly misused) and antagonism to the religious sanctions of the moral law, both come from the same source. Over the fountain of Revolutionism and Anti-Christian belief place the descriptive and definitive term "Jewish," and let the sons of the Anglo-Saxons learn from what waters they are drinking. That source is not Mosaic, but Jewish—there is a world of difference between them.

The central groups of Red philosophers in every university is a Jewish group, with often enough a "Gentile front" in the shape of a deluded professor. Some of these professors are in the pay of outside Red organizations. There are Intercollegiate Socialist Societies, swarming with Jews and Jewish influences, and toting Jewish professors around the country, addressing medics and lits and even the Divinity schools, under the patronage of the best civic and university auspices. Student lecture courses are fine pasture for this propaganda. Intercollegiate Liberal Leagues are established everywhere, the purpose evidently being to give students the thrill of believing that they are taking part in the beginning of a great new movement, comparable to the winning of Independence or the Abolition of slavery. As stein parties gradually cease as a college diversion, Red conferences will come in; it is part of the effervescence of youth.

The revolutionary forces which head up in Jewry rely very heavily on the respectability which is given their movement by the adhesion of students and a few professors. It was so in Russia—everyone knows what the name "student" eventually came to signify in that country. And as a result, while Sovietists are glorifying the "success" of the Revolution, men like Maxim Gorky are sending out appeals for food to prevent the intelligentsia from starving to death.

The Jewish Chautauqua, which works exclusively in colleges and universities, together with Bolshevism in art, science, religion, economics and sociology, are driving straight through the Anglo-Saxon traditions and landmarks of our race of students. And these are ably assisted by professors and clergymen whose thinking has been dislocated and poisoned by Jewish subversive influences in theology and sociology.

What to do about it? Simply identify the source and nature of the influence which has overrun our colleges. Let the students know that their choice is between the Anglo-Saxons and the Tribe of Judah. Let the students decide, in making up their allegiance, whether they will follow the Builders or those who seek to tear down.

It is not a case for argument. Radicalism and religious indifferentism are states of mind. Normal men usually grow out of them in good time. Others are caught and held to the end. But the treatment is not argument.

The only absolute antidote to the Jewish influence is to call college students back to a pride of race. We often speak of the Fathers as if they were the few who happened to affix their signatures to a great document which marked a new era of liberty. The Fathers were the men of the Anglo-Saxon-Celtic race. The men who came across Europe with civilization in their blood and in their destiny; the men who crossed the Atlantic and set up civilization on a bleak and rock-bound coast; the men who drove west to California and north to Alaska; the men who peopled Australia and seized the gates of the world at Suez, Gibralter and Panama; the men who opened the tropics and subdued the arctics—Anglo-Saxon men, who have given form to every government and a livelihood to every people and an ideal to every century. They got neither their God nor their religion from Judah, nor yet their speech nor their creative genius—they are the Ruling People, Chosen throughout the centuries to Master the world, by Building it ever better and better and not by breaking it down.

Into the camp of this race, among the sons of the rulers, comes a people that has no civilization to point to, no aspiring religion, no universal speech, no great achievement in any realm but the realm of "get," cast out of every land that gave them hospitality, and these people endeavor to tell the sons of the Saxons what is needed to make the world what it ought to be.

If our sons in college follow this counsel of dark rebellion and destruction, it is because they do not know whose sons they are, of what race they are the scions.

Let there be free speech to the limit in our universities and free intercourse of ideas, but let Jewish thought be labeled Jewish, and let our sons know the racial secret.

The warning has already gone out through the colleges. The system of procedure is already fully known. And how simple it is:

First, you secularize the public schools—"secularize" is the precise word the Jews use for the process. You prepare the mind of the public school child by enforcing the rule that no mention shall ever be made to indicate that culture or patriotism is in any way connected with the deeper principles of the Anglo-Saxon religion. Keep it out, every sight and sound of it! Keep out also every word that will aid any child to identify the Jewish race.

Then, when you have thus prepared the soil, you can go into the universities and colleges and enter upon the double program of pouring contempt on all the Christian landmarks, at the same time filling the void with Jewish revolutionary ideas.

The influence of the common people is driven out of the public schools, where common people's influence can go; but Jewish influence is allowed to run rampant in the higher institutions where the common people's influence cannot go.

Secularize the public schools, and you can then Judaize the universities.

This is the "liberalism" which Jewish spokesman so much applaud. In labor unions, in church, in university, it has tinctured the principles of work, faith and society. This will not be denied, because the proof of it is too thickly written over Jewish activities and utterances. Indeed, it is in exerting these very influences that Jewry convinces itself it is fulfilling its "mission" to the world. The capitalism attacked is non-Jewish capitalism; the orthodoxy attacked is Christian orthodoxy; the society attacked is the Anglo-Saxon form of society, all of which by their destruction would redound to the glory of Judaism.

The list could be extended—the influence of the Jewish idea on Anglo-Saxon sports and pleasure, on the Anglo-Saxon-Celtic idea of patriotism, on the Anglo-Saxon-Celtic conception of the learned professions; the influence of the Jewish idea runs down through every department of life. "Well," one very badly deluded Anglo-Saxon editor, wrapped up in Jewish advertising contracts, was heard to say, "if the Jews can get away with it, then they have a right to." It is a variant of the "answer" of Jewish origin, which runs thus: "How can a paltry 3,000,000 run the 100,000,000 of the rest of us? Nonsense!"

Yes, let it be agreed; if the Jewish idea is the stronger, if the Jewish ability is greater, let them conquer; let Anglo-Saxon principles and Anglo-Saxon power go down in ruins before the Tribe of Judah. But first let the two ideas struggle under their own banners; let it be a fair struggle. It is not a fair fight when in the movies, in the public schools, in the Judaized churches, in the universities, the Anglo-Saxon idea is kept away from Anglo-Saxons on the plea that it is "sectarian" or "clannish" or "obsolete" or something else. It is not a fair fight when Jewish ideas are offered as Anglo-Saxon ideas, because offered under Anglo-Saxon auspices. Let the heritage of our Anglo-Saxon-Celtic fathers have free course among their Anglo-Saxon-Celtic sons, and the Jewish idea can never triumph over it, in university forum or in the marts of trade. The Jewish idea never triumphs until first the people over whom it triumphs are denied the nurture of their native culture.

Judah has begun the struggle. Judah has made the invasion. Let it come. Let no man fear it. But let every man insist that the fight be fair. Let college students and leaders of thought know that the objective is the regnancy of the ideas and the race that have built all the civilization we see and that promise all the civilization of the future; let them also know that the attacking force is Jewish.

That is all that will be necessary. And it is against this that the Jews protest. "You must not identify us," they say, "you must not use the term 'Jew'" Why? Because unless the Jewish idea can creep in under the assumption of other than Jewish origin, it is doomed. Anglo-Saxon ideas dare proclaim themselves and their origin. A proper proclamation is all that is necessary today. Compel every invading idea to run up its flag!

The Dearborn Independent, issue of 21 May 1921

66: The Jews' Complaint against "Americanism"

From the earliest record of the Jews' contact with other nations, no long period of years has ever passed without the charge arising that the Jews constitute "a people within a people, a nation within a nation." When this charge is made today it is vehemently denied by men who pose as the defenders of their people, and the denial is more or less countenanced by all the Jews of every class.

And yet there is nothing more clearly stated in Jewish teaching, nor more clearly indicated in Jewish life, than that the charge is true. But whether the truth should be used against the Jews is quite another question. If the Jews are a nation, their nationality founded upon the double ground of race and religion, it is certainly outside the bounds of reason that they should be asked or expected to de-racialize, denationalize and dereligionize themselves; but neither is it to be expected that they should bitterly denounce those who state the facts. It is only upon a basis of facts that a solution of any problem can come. Where blame attaches is here: that the evident facts are denied, as if no one but the Jews themselves knew that there are such facts.

If the Jews are to be continuously a nation, as they teach, and if the condition of "a nation within a nation" becomes more and more intolerable, then the solution must come through one of two things: a separation of the "nation" from the rest of the nations, or an exaltation of the "nation" above the rest of the nations. There is a mass of evidence in Jewish writings that the leaders expect both of these conditions to come—a separate nation and a super-nation; indeed the heart of Jewish teaching is, as quite fully illustrated in the last article, that Jewry is a separate nation now, and on the way to becoming a super-nation. It is only those appointed to address the Gentiles who deny this: the real rabbinate of Israel does not deny.

Now, in any investigation of the Jewish Question, the student is struck over and over again by the fact that what the Jews most complain of, they themselves began. They complain of what they call anti-Semitism; but it must be apparent to the dullest mind that there could never have been such a thing as anti-Semitism were there not first such a thing as Semitism.

And then take the complaint about the Jews having to live in ghettos. The ghetto is a Jewish invention. In the beginning of the invasion of European and American cities the Jews always lived by themselves because they wanted to, because they believed the presence of Gentiles contaminated them. Jewish writers, writing for Jews, freely admit this; but in writing for Gentiles, they refer to the ghetto as a surviving illustration of Gentile cruelty. The idea of contamination originated with the Jews; it spread by suggestion to the Gentiles.

And so with this fact of the separate "nation"; it was the Jews who first recognized it, first insisted upon it and have always sought to realize that separateness both in thought and action.

Nay, more, the true and normal type of Jew today believes that the influence of Americanism, or of any civilized Gentile state, is harmful to Judaism.

That is a serious statement and no amount of Gentile assertion will be sufficient to confirm it. Indeed, it is such a statement as the Gentile mind could not have evolved, because the trend of Gentile feeling is all in the opposite direction, namely, that Americanization is a good thing for the Jew. It is from authoritative Jewish sources that we learn this fact, that what we call civilizing influences are looked upon as being at enmity with Judaism.

It is not the Gentile who says that the Jewish ideals, as ideals, are incompatible with life in our country; it is the Jew who says so. It is he who inveighs against Americanism, not the American who inveighs against Judaism.

As this article is one with the last, the same method of impassive presentation of the testimony will be followed. Readers of this study of the Jewish Question should know that neither rhetoric nor emotion will contribute a single element to the solution of the Question. We prefer to leave rhetoric and emotion to the anti-Semites who call names and to the pro-Semites who are apparently reduced to the same necessitous level.

Now, the first thing to know is this: that though Americanism is yet unfinished, Judaism has been complete for centuries; and while no American would think of pointing to any part of the country or to any group as representing the true and final type of Americanism, the Jews quite unhesitatingly point to parts of the world and to certain groups as representing the true type of Judaism. Where is the type to be found which Jewish writers recognize as the true one?

The Jew of the ghetto is held up in Jewish treatises as the norm of Judaism.

The visitor in New York has perhaps seen on Central Park west the massive synagogue of the Spanish and Portuguese Jews. Its famous rabbi was the Rev. Dr. D. de Sola Pool. He is the author of the following words:

"In the ghetto the observance of Judaism was natural and almost inevitable. The regimen of Jewish life was the atmosphere that was breathed. . . . Not only did public opinion make it possible for men to go bearded, to keep the head covered at all times, to carry the palm branch in the public street, or to walk the street in stockinged feet on fast days, but public opinion made it almost impossible for a Jew to profane the Sabbath or the Passover regulations, or openly to transgress any of the main observances"—and, as we shall later see, the learned rabbi considers these conditions more preservative of Judaism than are American conditions.

Rev. Dr. M. H. Segal expresses the view that Jewry in the more modern portions of Europe and America was really kept alive by the infusions of immigrants from Poland and Lithuania. Asserting, in agreement with other Jewish leaders, that the Jewish center of the world has been, until now, in Russia and Poland, Dr. Segal says:

"The war has destroyed the last traces of the declining Jewish society which has dragged out its feeble existence in the semi-medieval ghettos of Poland and Lithuania. With all their growing feebleness, these communities were yet the last refuge of Judaism in the Dispersion. In them there had still survived something of the old Jewish life, some of the old Jewish institutions, practices and traditions. These communities also supplied such vitality as they could afford to the attenuated and atrophied Judaism in the communities of the more modern states of Europe and America."

The idea is not at all uncommon—that large infusions of "real Jews" from the Old World ghettos are desirable and necessary in order to keep Judaism alive in countries like the United States.

Israel Friedlaender, whose name just at present is held in peculiar honor by the Jews, and justly so, was a man of most enlightened intellect, and he too recognized the service of the ghetto stream to Judaism. In his lecture, "The Problem of Judaism in America," he speaks about the deJudaizing tendency of absolute freedom, such as the Jew has always enjoyed in the United States. This tendency, he says, is corrected in two ways—by anti-Semitic influences and "by the large stream of Jewish emigration, on the other hand, which, proceeding from the lands of oppression to the lands of freedom, carries with it, on or under the surface, the preserving and reviving influences of the ghetto."

The same authority, in an article entitled "The Americanization of the Jewish Immigrant," frankly prefers the Jew fresh from the ghetto to the Jew who has been influenced by American life.

He says that he "prefers the kaftan-clad, old-fashioned Jew, with his unattractive appearance and ungainly manners, whose whole life is dominated by the ideals and mandates of an ancient religion and civilization . . . to that modernized, amphibious creature, the gaudily attired, slang-using, gum-chewing, movie-visiting, dollar-hunting, vulgar and uncultured, quasi-Americanized 'dzentleman.'"

The "kaftan-clad, old-fashioned Jew" of whom Mr. Freidlaender writes, is the Polish Jew, 250,000 of whom are coming to the United State as "a preserving and reviving influence" upon Judaism in the United States.

Not to use more space, however, on the identity of the normal type of Jew as precisely stated by those who have expressed themselves on this subject, it is possible to preserve the idea and add its logical complement, by quoting some testimony on the Jewish view of Americanization.

What now follows is of special interest because it is so generally stated and received throughout Jewish circles, that the center of Jewry has shifted to America. That is the form in which Jewish spokesmen make the statement: they say "America," not the United States.

A little story—a true one—may be worth while here. It may throw a sidelight on the use of the word "American" as used in the testimony. A certain editor of an American newspaper gave a trifling bit of publicity to this series of articles. Jewish advertising was withdrawn from his columns by the chairman of the Anti-Defamation Committee of the local lodge of B'nai B'rith, which chairman was also an advertising agent who handled all the Jewish advertising in that city. The editor, not being a wise man, yielded to the bulldozing methods used upon him, and in a half-hearted bit of editorial praise for the Jews used the word "Americanism." The advertising agent toyed with the word in the manner of one who, having a weak Gentile in his power, would make the best of it.

"Why did you say, 'Americanism'? Why did you not say 'civilization'?" he asked.

The editor to this day thinks it was a bit of captiousness. It was not. There is meaning in it.

To "Americanize" means, in our ordinary speech, to bring into sympathy with the traditions and institutions of the United States, but the Jews do not mean only the United States when they say "America." They mean also South and Central America—where so many revolutions have occurred. There are large numbers of Jews in Argentina, and many are found in other countries. The next place to be extensively colonized will be Mexico. If the people of the United States see a Jewish ambassador sent to represent them in Mexico, they must know that the invasion of that country is about to begin. If the ambassador is not himself a Jew, it will be well to scrutinize his connections; there may be reasons which will make it necessary to employ a "Gentile front" for a time.

Now, it would probably give a wrong twist to the fact to say that the Jewish leaders are anti-American, but it is true that they are against the "Americanization" of the Jewish immigrant stream. That is, the trend of "Americanism" is so different from the trend of "Judaism" that the two are in conflict. This does not indicate treason toward American nationalism, perhaps, so much as it indicates loyalty toward Jewish nationalism.

But the reader must himself be the judge as to how far the difference goes. The testimony which will now be given divided itself into two parts: first, that relating to the American state in particular; second, that relating to any Gentile state.

After he had spoken in praise of the old type of Jew, as seen in the foreign ghettos, Dr. D. de Sola Pool added:

"To a large extent the adult Jewish population of the United States has been reared in Jewish communities of this type of Jewish inevitableness. To a large extent the young generation is being reared in an atmosphere in which this type of Jewishness is unknown, or at least strange and impossible. Jewish religious observance in the United States is becoming increasingly difficult and increasingly rare."

Describing the antagonism between the American and the Jewish tendencies, he continues with this reference to the effect of "Americanism" on Jewish modes of worship:

"On the platform officiate a cantor and a preacher, who turn their backs to the ark and address themselves to their congregation. The tallith and similar externals are un-American, and have consequently been sacrificed. The 'American' worships with bare head; therefore the American of Jewish persuasion must also doff his headgear when at worship. Hebrew, an Oriental language, is not an American tongue. The American prays in English, which all understand, and accordingly the American of Jewish faith has Anglicized his ritual. Such a ritual is not susceptible of being chanted with traditional Jewish Chazzanuth, and the music of the temple has therefore been brought up to date by the introduction of an organ, sacred music borrowed from non-Jewish neighbors, and mixed choirs in which non-Jewish singers are almost the rule . . . The Jewish Sabbath is out of keeping with the environment, and the only way in which it seemed to be possible to save it was by celebrating it with a Friday evening temple service after supper, and resting, and sometimes also attending temple on Sunday."

It is not difficult to detect underneath these words the tone of criticism for such "Americanization." It is a criticism which is fully justified by conditions. And it must be remembered that it was not uttered by a "kaftan-clad, old-fashioned Jew," but by a learned rabbi with a magnificent temple on Central Park west, a man whom our government has seen fit to honor.

But that is not all that Dr. de Sola Pool objects to. Nor does he mince words in making his objections known: "If so far, Reform has avoided the logical end of the process and has stopped short of identifying itself with Christianity, it has Americanized Judaism by dropping the elements that are characteristically Jewish and un-American, and has thereby created an almost non-sectarian Judaism housed in an almost non-sectarian Temple."

It will be noticed that the learned doctor uses the word "American" as one accustomed to quite another atmosphere. A further illustration is found in this:

"Neglect of the un-American dietary laws is usually the first step that the Americanizing Jew takes in asserting his Americanism."

The "un-American dietary laws" are, of course, the Jewish dietary laws. But if any Gentile writer had so referred to them, he would have been abused as a hostile witness.

It is very curious indeed to read the long list of complaints against modern conditions in their power to bring about the "decay of Judaism." The ghetto, which makes for separateness, is frequently heralded as the true safeguard of Judaism. Intercourse with the world is dangerous. "Americanizing" influences are distrusted. No doubt many and many a Gentile parent in New York, Boston, Louisville, Dallas and other American cities has witnessed the spectacle of Jewish teachers and "welfare workers" instructing Gentile children in the principles of Americanism, but did anyone ever see a Gentile teacher instructing Jewish children in Americanism?

Recently when the American Legion asked permission of the government to establish Americanization classes at Ellis Island, where tens of thousands of Polish Jews gain entry into the United States, the reply was a refusal, and the reason was that all the space for charitable institutions was already taken. What charitable institutions? How many of them were Jewish?

"The beginning of this decay," says Israel Friedlaender, referring to the effect of modern life on Judaism, "is obviously coincident with the beginning of Jewish emancipation, that is to say, with the moment when the Jews left the ghetto to join the life and culture of the nations around them."

Mr. Friedlaender even went so far as to say that pogroms against the Jews were "fortunate" in that they drove the Jews back to their Judaism— "Fortunately, however, Russian Jewry was halted on its downward rush toward national self-annihilation. The process of assimilation was cut short by the pogroms, and ever since then the Jews of Russia have stood firmly their ground . . . "

That may be the reason why some Jewish spokesmen of the Jews in America are trying to make this series of articles appear as a "pogrom." There is plenty of evidence to indicate that Jewish leaders have regarded "pogroms," in modern times at least, as very useful in preserving the solidarity of Jewry. However, those who are responsible for the present series of articles, much as they hope to benefit the general situation of the humbler Jews by showing the use which the leading Jews are making of them, must decline to be counted among those who justify "pogroms" on any ground whatsoever.

Justice Brandeis, of the United States Supreme Court, is also an exponent of the idea that, released from ghetto influences, the Jew becomes less of a Jew. He says:

"We must protect America and ourselves from demoralization, which has to some extent already set in among American Jews. The cause of this demoralization is clear. It results, in large part, from the fact that in our land of liberty all the restraints by which the Jews were protected in their ghettos were removed and a new generation left without necessary moral and spiritual support."

Justice Brandeis is a Zionist on these very grounds. He wants the land of Palestine because there the Jews, as he says, "may live together and lead a Jewish life."

Not the United States, but Palestine, is Justice Brandeis' hope for the Jews; he says of Palestine that "there only can Jewish life be fully protected from the forces of disintegration."

Arguing the same question, the Rev. Mr. S. Levy says: "I shall probably be told that the re-establishment of Jews as a nation would mean the recreation of the ghetto. I am frankly prepared to admit the force of the criticism, but with an important qualification dependent on the interpretation of the word 'ghetto.'

"In so far as the national center will insure the existence of this Jewish environment, Jewish atmosphere, and Jewish culture, there will be a *recreation of the ghetto.*" (The italics are Mr. Levy's.)

"The continuance of Judaism, then, is dependent on the existence of an area with an aggregation of Jews living in a Jewish environment, breathing a Jewish atmosphere and fostering a Jewish culture, and these factors must predominate over all other influences."

It is therefore plain that, however startling and improbable the statement may seem when made by a Gentile, the Jews themselves regard the influences of modern lands as inimical to Judaism.

But there is still a further consideration, which is distinctly set forth in Jewish writings, namely, that the trend of the modern State is harmful to all that Judaism holds to be essential to its moral and spiritual welfare.

The modern State is changing, and Jewish observers sense the fact more readily than do the rest of the people, because Jews see in the change both an opportunity and a menace. If the State continues to change according to the trend of the general mind of the world, Jewish ideas of supremacy will find less and less opportunity to be realized—that is the menace. If the change, or the spirit of change, can be seized and twisted to Jewish purposes, as was done in Russia, and a Jewish type of State erected on the ruins of the old—that is the opportunity. Readers of these articles know that stimulation of "the spirit of change" is one of the clearest planks in the World Program.

As Cyril M. Picciotto points out in his "Conceptions of the State and the Jewish Question," there is a tendency to "increase the control of the State over the individual." This, of course, has nowhere been done so thoroughly as in Russia under the Jewish-Bolshevik regime, but it is not of this that Mr. Picciotto speaks, it is of the tendency observed in the Gentile states; and he asks: "In the face of such a tendency in political development (which it is not rash to assume will be more pronounced in the future than in the past) how does the Jew stand?"

He adds: "The time is not far distant when the development of the State will continue on organic and collectivist lines. The central authority will embrace an ever wider area, and will make such a penetration into the recesses of individual freedom as would have been thought inconceivable thirty or forty years ago. Compulsory military service, compulsory education, compulsory insurance are but milestones on the road which logically leads to the adoption of a State morality, a State creed, and of a common way of life. To say this is merely to indicate the probable trend, not to approve it."

"How, then, is the State of the future going to deal with a people in its midst which largely preserves its separateness of blood, which in its fasts, its day of rest, its dietary laws, its marriage ceremony, suggests a distinct historic entity?"

The question is a disturbing one to Jews, as is shown by Rabbi Segal's words in "The Future of Judaism." He even says that "the medieval State, with all its tyranny and obscurantism" was more favorable to the Jews than the modern type of State. "Its defective organization permitted both individuals and whole classes to live their life in their own way. Hence the medieval State enabled the Jews to organize themselves on semi-national lines, and, as far as circumstances permitted, to create afresh in their dispersion the national institutions and practices of their ancient commonwealth."

They did this, of course, by establishing the ghetto.

"But this has become an absolute impossibility in the modern State," continues the rabbi. "The rise of democracy and the transference of the ultimate power of government from the oligarchy to the majority involves the practical suppression of weak minorities. The identification of the State with the culture and aspiration of a particular nationality leads inevitably to the crippling of and gradual extinction of those classes who do not share that particular culture and those aspirations. The State, moreover, enforces a system of education which is purposely designed to fashion and mold all the inhabitants . . . It also maintains a thoroughgoing organization which embraces all the departments of the public and private life of all its inhabitants, irrespective of class, race or tradition. There is thus no room in the modern State for Jewish culture, for Jewish national life, or for a specifically Jewish society, with its own specific institutions, customs and practices . . .

"Therefore, Judaism can live and work only with a specifically Jewish society and within a Jewish national organization. The medieval ghetto, with all its narrowness, with all the unhealthy and abnormal conditions of its existence, yet contained such a semi-national society: therefore, Judaism flourished in the medieval ghetto. The modern State, on the other hand, has broken up that specifically Jewish society . . . "

Now, there are the reactions of leading Jewish minds to conditions in America particularly, and to conditions in the modern Gentile State generally. The statement of the antagonism which exists between the two is clear and complete. The Gentiles do not notice that antagonism, but the Jews are always and everywhere keenly aware of it. This throws a light, a very strong light, on all the revolutionary programs to break up the present control of society, by sowing dissensions between capital and labor so-called, by cheapening the dignity of government through corrupt politics, by trivializing the mind of the people through theaters and movies and similar agencies, and by weakening the appeal of distinctively Christian religion. A breakdown of Gentile seriousness is the opportunity of the Jew. A colossal war is also his opportunity, as witness his seizure of the United States Government during the recent war. Judaism says that Americanism and Gentile nationalism generally, are harmful to it. Judaism has therefore the alternative of changing and controlling Gentile nationalism, or of constructing a nationalism of its own in Palestine. It is trying both.

This all harks back to what Lord Eustace Percy is quoted in the Jewish press as saying: that the Jew participates in revolutions "not because the Jew cares for the positive side of radical philosophy, not because he desires to be a partaker in Gentile nationalism or Gentile democracy, but because no existing Gentile system of government is ever anything but distasteful to him."

And the same author—"In a world of completely organized territorial sovereignties, he (the Jew) has only two possible cities of refuge: he must either pull down the pillars of the whole national state system or he must create a territorial sovereignty of his own. In this perhaps lies the explanation both of Jewish Bolshevism and of Zionism, for at this moment Eastern Jewry seems to hover uncertainly between the two."

The Dearborn Independent, issue of 23 October 1920

67: The Jewish Associates of Benedict Arnold

As the Jewish propagandists in the United States cannot be trusted to give the people all the facts—even though these propagandists have the facts in their possession—it devolves upon some impartial agency to do so. The Jewish propagandists are accorded the utmost freedom of the newspapers of the United States—by reason of Jewish advertising being more than 75 per cent of all the advertising done in this country—and thus a wide web of false impressions is constantly being woven around the Jewish Question.

The most recent is the widespread publication of a new "exposure" of the origin of the Protocols. This makes the sixth "final" and "complete" exposure that the Jews have put forth for public consumption. The Jews have still time to repent and tell the truth. Suppose they make the seventh the whole truth with a true repudiation of the Protocols.

It is *The Dearborn Independent*'s purpose to open up from time to time new angles of the Jewish Question, so that the candid reader who would be informed of the extensive character of Jewish influence may obtain a general view of it.

The part taken by Jews in the wars of the United States has been a subject of considerable boasting by Jewish publicists. It is a most interesting subject. It deserves the fullest possible treatment. It is not *The Dearborn Independent*'s present purpose to challenge the Jewish boast; it is, however, our purpose to fill in the omitted parts of the story, and supply the missing links in several of the most interesting episodes in American history. This will be done on the basis of unquestioned historical authority, mostly of a Jewish character, and solely in the interests of a complete understanding of a matter which Jewish leaders have brought to the front.

The first subject which will be treated in this series is the part of Jews in the treason of Benedict Arnold.

Benedict Arnold, the most conspicuous traitor in American history, has been the subject of considerable comment of late. Among the commentators have been American Jews who have failed to make known to the American public the information which may be found in Jewish archives concerning Benedict Arnold and his associates.

To begin with, the propensity of the Jews to engage in the business of supplying the needs of armies and to avail themselves as far as possible of war contracts, is of long standing and notice.

An authority on this matter, Werner Sombart, says in his "Jews and Modern Capitalism" (pp. 50–53):

"The Jews throughout the sixteenth, seventeenth, and eighteenth centuries were most influential as army-purveyors and as the moneyed men to whom the princes looked for financial backing . . . we cannot attempt to mention every possible example. We can only point the way; it will be for subsequent research to follow.

"Although there are numerous cases on record of Jews acting in the capacity of army-contractors in Spain previous to 1492, I shall not refer to this period, because it lies outside the scope of our present considerations. We shall confine ourselves to the centuries that followed, and begin with England.

"In the seventeenth and eighteenth centuries the Jews had already achieved renown as army-purveyors. Under the Commonwealth the most famous army contractor was Antonio Fernandez Carvajal, 'the great Jew,' who came to London some time between 1630 and 1635, and was very soon accounted among the most prominent traders in the land. In 1649 he was one of the five London merchants intrusted by the council of state with the army contract for corn. It is said that he annually imported into England silver to the value of £100,000. In the period that ensued, especially in the wars of William III, Sir Solomon Medina ('the Jew Medina') was 'the great contractor,' and for his services he was knighted, being the first professing Jew to receive that honor.

"It was the same in the wars of the Spanish Succession; here, too, Jews were the principal army-contractors. In 1716 the Jews of Strassburg recall the services they rendered the armies of Louis XIV by furnishing information and supplying provisions. Indeed, Louis XIV's army-contractor-in-chief was a Jew, Jacob Worms by name; and in the eighteenth century Jews gradually took a more and more prominent part in this work. In 1727 the Jews of Metz brought into the city in the space of six weeks, 2,000 horses for food and more than 5,000 for remounts. Field Marshall Maurice, of Saxony, the victor of Fontenoy, expressed the opinion that his armies were never better served with supplies than when the Jews were contractors. One of the best known of the army-contractors in the time of the last two Louises was Cerf Beer, in whose patent of naturalization it is recorded that '. . . in the wars which raged in Alsace in 1770 and 1771 he found the opportunity of proving his zeal in our service and in that of the state.'

"Similarly the house of Gradis, of Bordeaux, was an establishment of international repute in the eighteenth century. Abraham Gradis set up large store-houses in Quebec to supply the needs of the French troops there. Under the Revolutionary Government, under the Directory, in the Napoleonic wars it was always the Jews who acted as purveyors. In this connection a public notice displayed in the streets of Paris is significant. There was a famine in the city and the Jews were called upon to show their gratitude for the rights bestowed upon them by the Revolution by bringing in corn. 'They alone,' says the author of this notice, 'can successfully accomplish this enterprise, thanks to their business relations, of which their fellow citizens ought to have full benefit.' A parallel story comes from Dresden. In 1720 the Court Jew, Jonas Meyer, saved the town from starvation by supplying it with large quantities of corn. (The Chronicler mentions 40,000 bushels.)

"All over Germany, the Jews from an early date were found in the ranks of the army-contractors. Let us enumerate a few of them. There was Isaac Meyer in the sixteenth century, who, when admitted by Cardinal Albrecht as a resident of Halberstadt in 1537, was enjoined by him, in view of the dangerous times, 'to supply our monastery with good weapons and armour.' There was Joselman von Rosheim, who in 1548 received an imperial letter of protection because he had supplied both money and provisions for the army. In 1546 there is a record of Bohemian Jews who provided great-coats and blankets for the army. In the next century another Bohemian Jew, Lazarus by name, received an official declaration that he 'obtained either in person or at his own expense, valuable information for the imperial troops, and that he made it his business to see that the army had a good supply of ammunition and clothing.' The Great Elector also had recourse to Jews for his military needs. Leimann Gompertz and Solomon Elias were his contractors for cannon, powder and so forth. There were numerous others: Samuel Julius, remount contractor under the Elector Frederick Augustus of Saxony; the Model family, court-purveyors and army-contractors in the Duchy of Aensbach in the seventeenth and eighteenth centuries are well known in history. In short, as one writer of the time pithily expresses it, 'all the contractors are Jews and all the Jews are contractors.'

"Austria does not differ in this respect from Germany, France and England. The wealthy Jews, who in the reign of the Emperor Leopold received permission to resettle in Vienna (1670)—the Oppenheimers, Wertheimers, Mayer Herschel and the rest—were all army-contractors. And we find the same thing in all the countries under the Austrian Crown.

"Lastly, we must mention the Jewish army-contractors who provisioned the American troops in the Revolutionary and Civil wars."

Sombart's record ceases there. He does not go on to mention "the Jewish contractors who provisioned the American troops in the Revolutionary and Civil wars." That task shall be *The Dearborn Independent*'s from time to time in the future.

It is in the study of Jewish money-making out of war that the clues are found to most of the great abuses of which Jews have been guilty. In the present instance, it was in the matter of profiteering in war goods, that the Jewish connections of Benedict Arnold were discovered.

"Wars are the Jews' harvests" is an ancient saying. Their predilection for the quartermaster's department has been observed anciently and modernly. Their interest being mostly in profits and not in national issues; their traditional loyalty being to the Jewish nation, rather than to any other nation; it is only natural that they should be found to be the merchants of goods and information in times of war—that is, the war profiteers and the spies. As the unbroken program is traced through the Revolutionary War, through the American Civil War, and through the Great War of recent occurrence, the only change observable is the increasing power and profit of the Jews.

Although the number of Jews resident in the American colonies was very small, there were enough to make a mark on the Revolutionary War; and while there was no wholesale legislation against Jews as there was in the Civil War, there were actions against individuals for the same causes which in 1861-5 obtained more extensively.

The Journals of the Continental Congress contain numerous entries of payments made to Jews, as well as the records of various dealings with them on other scores. For drums, for blankets, for rifles, for provisions, for clothing—these are the usual entries. Most of the Jewish commissars were Indian traders (the extent to which the Jews dealt with the American Indians has not as yet been made a subject of research it deserves). The Gratz family of Pennsylvania carried on a very extensive Indian trade and amassed a vast fortune out of it. A most curious lot of information concerning the dealings of the Colonies with the Jews is obtainable by a search through the old records.

The Jews of Colonial New York were both loyalists and rebels, as the tide turned. They profited under loyalism by the contracts which they secured, and by buying in the confiscated property of those who were loyal to the American cause. It is interesting to note that some of the purchasers of the extensive Delancey properties were Jews. Delancey was a patriot whom New York City afterward honored by giving his name to an important thoroughfare. That same New York has recently by official action separated the name of Delancey from that thoroughfare, and substituted the name of Jacob H. Schiff, a Jew, native of Frankfort-on-the-Main.

We enter immediately into the limits of the Benedict Arnold narrative by making mention of the Franks family of Philadelphia, of which family several members will claim our attention.

The Franks were Jews from England who settled in America, retaining their English connections. They were in the business of public contracts, principally army contracts. They were holders of the British army contracts for the French and Indian wars, and for the succeeding Revolutionary War.

To get the picture, conceive it thus, as it is taken from Jewish sources:

Moses Franks lived in England, doing business with the British Government direct. He had the contract for supplying all the British forces in America before military trouble between the Colonies and the Home Government was thought of. He was the principal purveyor of the British Army in Quebec, Montreal, Massachusetts, New York and in the country of the Illinois Indians. It was all British territory then.

Jacob Franks lived in New York. He was American representative of Moses Franks of England. He was the American agent of the Franks Army Purveyors Syndicate—for that is what it was.

In Philadelphia was David Franks, son of Jacob, of New York. David was the Franks' agent for the state or colony of Pennsylvania. He was at the seat of the colonial government, the center of American politics. He was hand in glove with many of the fathers of the American Government. He was an immensely rich man (although but an agent) and carried a high hand at Philadelphia.

At Montreal was another Franks—David Solesbury Franks also in the business of army contractor. He was a gay young man, described as "a blooded buck," who knew all the arts of turning an honest penny out of the needs of armies and the distress of nations. This young man was a grandson or grand nephew of the Moses Franks of England, as he was a nephew of the David Franks of Philadelphia.

Here and there were other Franks, all intent on business with the non-Jewish government, but the four here mentioned carry along the main parts of the tale.

A moment's digression will give us at once a view of the looseness of the liberalism of some of the Fathers of the Country, and a view of the equanimity with which David Franks, of Philadelphia, could pass from one role to another—a facility which cost him dearly when war came on.

John Trumbull, an artist of considerable note at the time, whose paintings still adorn the National Capitol, was invited to dine at Thomas Jefferson's home, among the guests being Senator Giles, from Virginia, Trumbull tells the story:

"I was scarcely seated when Giles began to rally me on the Puritanical ancestry and character of New England. I saw there was no other person from New England present, and, therefore, although conscious that I was in no degree qualified to manage a religious discussion, I felt myself bound to defend my country on this delicate point as well as I could. Whether it had been prearranged that a debate on the Christian religion, in which it should be powerfully ridiculed on the one side and weakly defended on the other, was to be brought forward as promising amusement to a rather free-thinking dinner party, I will not presume to say, but it had that appearance, and Mr. Giles pushed his raillery, to my no small annoyance, if not to my discomfiture, until dinner was announced.

"That I hoped would relive me by giving a new turn to the conversation, but the company was hardly seated at the table when he renewed the assault with increased asperity, and proceeded so far at last as to ridicule the character, conduct and doctrines of the Divine Founder of our religion; Mr. Jefferson in the meantime smiling and nodding approval on Mr. Giles, while the rest of the company silently left me and my defense to our fate, until at length my friend David Franks took up the argument on my side. Thinking this a fair opportunity for avoiding further conversation on the subject, I turned to Mr. Jefferson and said, 'Sir, this is a strange situation in which I find myself; in a country professing Christianity and at a table with Christians, as I supposed, I find my religion and myself attacked with severe and almost irresistible wit and raillery, and not a person to aid in my defense but my friend Mr. Franks, who is himself a Jew.'"

This episode throws a curious light on the character of Thomas Jefferson's "philosophical unbelief," the unlovely fashion of that day; it also illustrates a certain facility in David Franks.

Relations between the Colonies and the Mother Country became strained. Political feelings ran high. The lines of division between "American" and "British" began to appear for the first time. At first there was a degree of agreement among all the population, except the government officials, that a protest against governmental abuses was justified and that strong representations should be made in behalf of the Colonists. Even loyalists and imperialists agreed with that. It was a question of domestic politics. But when presently the idea of protest began to develop into the idea of rebellion and independence, a cleavage came. It was one thing to correct the Empire, another thing to desert it. Here is where the people of the Colonies split.

Mr. Jacob Franks in royalist and loyalist New York, was, of course, royalist and loyalist. As army-contractor for the British Government, he had no choice.

Mr. David Franks, down in Philadelphia, was a little nearer the heart of the new American sentiment, and could not be so royal and loyal as was his kinsman north. In fact, David Franks tried to do what is modernly called "the straddle," attempting to side with the Empire and with the Colonies, too.

It was natural. His business was in Philadelphia. He may also have wished to remain as long as possible in the position of a spy, and send information of the state of public feeling to the royalists. Moreover, he was received in good society and his reputation for wealth and shrewdness won him attentions he could not otherwise have commanded.

So, in 1765 we find him joining the merchants of Philadelphia in the pact not to import articles from England while the hated Stamp Act was in force. In 1775 he favors the continuance of the colonial currency.

He was enjoying his accustomed life in the city—and his acquaintance with the Shippen family into which the dashing young Benedict Arnold married.

There is a strange intermingling of all the tragic figures of the play: Benedict Arnold marries the girl for whom Major André wrote a parlor play. Major André, during his period of captivity as an American prisoner of war and before his exchange, was often at the home of David

Franks. And David Solesbury Franks, at his post as agent of the Franks syndicate at Montreal, is placed by a strange turn of the wheel of destiny in the military family of Benedict Arnold for a considerable period preceding and including the great treason.

So, for the moment let us leave the Jewish family of Franks—all of them still stationed as we first described them: Moses in England, Jacob at New York, David at Philadelphia, David S. at Montreal—and let us scrutinize the young American officer, Benedict Arnold.

These facts would most of them be lost, had they not been preserved in the Jewish archives, by the American Jewish Historical Society. You will read any history of Benedict Arnold without perceiving the Jews around him. The authors of the accepted histories were blind.

The principal defect in Benedict Arnold's character was his love of money. All of the trouble which led up to the situation in which he found himself with reference to the American Government and Army, was due to the suspicion which hung like a cloud over many of his business transactions. There have been attempts to paint Arnold as a dashing martyr, as one who was discouraged by the unmerited slights of the Continental Congress, as a victim of the jealousy of lesser men, as one from whom confidence was unjustly withheld. Nothing could be further from the fact. He was a man to whom men were instinctively drawn to be generous, but so general was the knowledge of his looseness in money matters that, while admiring him, his brother officers acted upon the protective instinct and held aloof from him. He was tainted by a low form of dishonesty before he was tainted with treason, and the chief explanation of his treason was in the hard bargain he drove as to the amount of money he was to receive for his guilty act.

Arnold's own record makes this clear. Let us then take up his career at a certain point and see how the Franks strand and the money strand weave themselves through it like colored threads.

Extraordinary efforts have been made in recent years to extenuate Arnold's treason by the recital of his daring services. These services need not be minimized. Indeed, it was his great achievement of the winter march to Montreal and Quebec in 1775-6 that seems to begin the chapter of his troubles. To rehearse this feat of courage and endurance would be to tell a tale that has thrilled the American schoolboy.

It was at Montreal that Benedict Arnold came into contact with the young Jew, David Solesbury Franks, the Canadian agent of the Franks army-purveying syndicate. And the next thing known about young

Franks is that he returns to the American Colonies in the train of Benedict Arnold as an officer of the American Army.

How this change was effected is not explained in any of the records. There is a moment of darkness, as it were, in which the "quick change" was made, which transformed the young Montreal Jew from an army-contractor for the British into an officer of Benedict Arnold's staff.

But as it is impossible for every fact to be suppressed, there are here and there indications of what might have been, what indeed most probably was, the basis of the attraction and relation between the two. It was very probably—almost certainly—the opportunities for graft which could be capitalized by a combination of General Arnold's authority and young Franks' ability in the handling of goods.

From the day they met in Montreal until the hour when General Arnold fled, a traitor, from the fort on the Hudson, young David Solesbury Franks was his companion.

In one of the numerous court-martials which tried General Arnold for questionable dealings in matters pertaining to army supplies, Franks, who was aid-de-camp to Arnold, and by rank of major, testified thus:

"I had, by being in the army, injured my private affairs very considerably, and meant to leave it, if a proper opportunity of entering into business should happen. I had several conversations on the subject with General Arnold, who promised me all the assistance in his power; he was to participate in the profits of the business I was to enter in."

This testimony was given by Major Franks in 1779; the two men had met in the winter of 1775–1776, but, as the records will show, Major Franks was always General Arnold's reliance on getting out of scrapes caused by questionable business methods in which Arnold's military authority was used quite freely. Major Franks admits that he was to enter business and General Arnold was to share the profits. On what basis this arrangement could exist, is another point not known. Arnold had no capital. He had no credit. He was a spendthrift, a borrower, notorious for his constant need of money. The only credible inducement for Franks to accept a partnership with him was on the understanding that Arnold should use his military authority to throw business to Franks. Or, to state it more bluntly, the "profits" which Benedict Arnold was to receive were payments for his misuse of authority for his own gain.

A complete opening of the records will show this to be the most reasonable view of the case. It was at Montreal that Benedict Arnold's name first became attainted with rumors of shady dealing in private and public property. General George Washington had laid down the most explicit instructions on these matters, with a view to having the Canadians treated as fellow-Americans and not as enemies. General Washington had cashiered officers and whipped soldiers who had previously disobeyed the order against looting and theft.

General Arnold had seized large quantities of goods at Montreal and had hurried them away without making proper account of them. This he admits in his letter to General Schuyler: "Our hurry and confusion was so great when the goods were received, it was impossible to take a particular account of them." This means only that Arnold seized the goods without giving the Canadian citizens proper receipts for them, so that he had in his hands a large amount of wealth for which he was under no compulsion to account to anybody. This mass of goods he sent to Colonel Hazen at Chambley, and Colonel Hazen, evidently aware of the conditions under which the goods were taken, refused to receive them. This disobedience of Colonel Hazen to his superior officer, especially in a question relating to goods, made it necessary for Arnold to take some self-protective action, which he did in his letter to General Schuyler.

Meantime, a very ugly rumor ran through the American Army that General Benedict Arnold had tried to pull a scurvy trick of graft, but had been held up by the strict conduct of Colonel Hazen. Moreover, it was rumored (and the fact was admitted by Arnold in his letter) that in the transfer the goods were well sorted over so that when they finally arrived a great part of them was missing. All the principal facts were admitted by Arnold, who used them, however, to throw blame on Colonel Hazen. He even went so far as to prefer charges against Colonel Hazen, forcing the matter into a court-martial. The court was called and refused to hear the witnesses chosen by General Arnold in his behalf, on the ground that the witnesses were not entitled to credibility. Whereupon General Arnold flouted the court, who ordered him arrested. General Gates, to preserve the useful services of Arnold to the United States Army, dissolved the court-martial, to that extent condoning the conduct of Arnold. Before the court-martial dissolved, however, it informally acquitted Colonel Hazen with honor.

Here then, almost immediately, as it would seem, upon his new connection with David Solesbury Franks, Benedict Arnold is involved in a bad tangle concerning property which had come into his possession irregularly and which disappeared soon after. His attempt to throw the blame on an officer whose disobedience was the factor that disclosed the true state of affairs, failed. It was his bold scheme to forestall an exposure which must inevitably have come.

While it is true that on this Montreal case, no verdict stands recorded against Benedict Arnold, for the theft of goods, it is also true that the American Army became suspicious of him from that day.

Had Benedict Arnold been innocent then and had he kept his hands clean thereafter, the Montreal episode would have been forgotten. But as a matter of fact such affairs came with increasing frequency thereafter, all of them strangely enough, involving also the Jew whom he associated with himself at the time of that first exposure.

The story of this Jew's relations with Benedict Arnold all through the period ending with the great treason, may now be taken up with greater consecutiveness, for now their formerly separate courses run together. In another article this relationship and all that it meant will be illustrated from the government records.

The Dearborn Independent, issue of 8 October 1921

68: Benedict Arnold and Jewish Aid in Shady Deal

While Benedict Arnold was in Canada and David Solesbury Franks, the Jew of Montreal and a British subject, was serving as quartermaster to the American troops, David Franks, of Philadelphia, a member of the same Jewish family and of the same Jewish syndicate of army-contractors, was also engaged in an interesting business.

It has already been shown that this David Franks, the Philadelphia Jew, had gone part way with the colonists in their protests against British colonial rule. That this was not sincerity on his part, his subsequent actions proved. He first comes into the purview of this narrative in 1775, the year in which Benedict Arnold performed the remarkable feat of marching into Canada, whence he was sending back into the colonies numerous Canadian prisoners. These prisoners were kept in the New England colonies for a time, but were later collected into Pennsylvania, some of them being quartered in the city of Philadelphia.

How inspired it is impossible now to tell, but presently a committee of the Continental Congress proposes that Mr. David Franks be commissioned to feed and otherwise care for these British prisoners, and be allowed to sell his bills for as much money as may be necessary for the purpose. Of course, in accepting this proposal, Franks was not only pursuing the course for which he and his numerous relatives had come to America. He was really doing business with and for Moses Franks, the head of the family syndicate in London. Shortly afterward we read of David under the mouth-filling title of "Agent to the Contractors for Victualing the Troops of the King of Great Britain," and to check him up, a British officer was allowed to pass the lines once a month and spend a few hours with David. That this was a dangerous practice may be deduced from his further story.

In the records of the Continental Congress is a request from Franks that he be permitted to go to New York, then the British headquarters; and such was the power of the man that his request was granted on condition that he pledged his word "not to give any intelligence to the enemy" and to return to Philadelphia.

In January, 1778, six months before Benedict Arnold took command of Philadelphia, David Franks got himself into trouble. A letter of his was intercepted on its way to England. The letter was intended for Moses Franks, of London, and was concealed under cover of a letter to a captain in a regiment commanded by a British general who had married Franks' sister. It appears on the record of the American Congress "that the contents of the letter manifest a disposition and intentions inimical to the safety and liberty of the United States."

Whereupon it was "Resolved, that Major General Arnold be directed to cause the said David Franks forthwith to be arrested and conveyed to the new gaol in this city (Philadelphia), there to be confined until the further order of Congress."

Thus Benedict Arnold comes into contact with another member of the Franks family, whose name was to be closely associated with the great treason.

And now begins a serpentine course of twistings and turnings which are so delightfully Jewish as to be worth restating if only to show how true the race remains to its character through the centuries. It is in October, about the eleventh day of the month. Franks is imprisoned and remains a week. Then by strange reasoning it is discovered that the United States has no jurisdiction over the charge of treason against the United States (!) and that the prisoner should be handed over to the Supreme Executive Council of the state of Pennsylvania. It follows that the state of Pennsylvania has nothing to do with the crime of treason against the United States either, and in spite of the contents of the letters and the findings of the Congressional Committee thereon, David Franks smiles pleasantly and goes free! It was a time, of course, when much money was lent by Jews to public officials. The Jew, Haym Salomon, was credited with having most of the "fathers" on his books, but he did not charge them interest nor principal. He grew immensely wealthy, however, and was recipient, in lieu of interest and repayment, of many official favors. David Franks, likewise a wealthy man, charged with treason, has his case transferred and finally dismissed. It is a trick not unknown today.

The Jewish records give much credit to Mr. Franks for not being daunted by this experience. Whether he is entitled to particular credit for his courage when he was master of so much influence, is a matter for the reader to decide, but that he was undaunted his subsequent actions show. He is very soon on the records again with an appeal for permission for his secretary to go again to New York within the British lines. He appeals to the Council of Pennsylvania. The Council refers him to Congress. Congress says it has no objection, if the secretary will be governed by General George Washington's orders in the matter. Washington's aid-de-camp gives permission, and the secretary gives sufficient bonds and sets out for New York.

Arrived in New York, the secretary discovers that Mr. Franks' presence is necessary and has made all arrangements for his master to go to New York, having even secured British permission to pass the lines. It was made very easy for Congress, it had only to say yes. But this time Congress said "no."

The former escape of Franks made people aware of an un-American influence at work. After his first arrest he was regarded as dangerous to the American cause. He apparently succeeds in living well in Philadelphia in spite of his difficulties, living even gayly with the society of the city.

Up to this time, David Franks had come into contact with the two principal figures in Arnold's treason. As purveyor to the captured troops, Franks had met and entertained, in 1776, the young and engaging Major André, who in 1780 was to become the tragic victim of Arnold's perfidy. And in 1778 Franks had been the subject of an order of arrest given to General Benedict Arnold. Jacob Mordecai "mentions that it was at Mr. Franks' house that he met Major André, then a paroled prisoner, who was passing his idle hours and exercising his talents in the most agreeable ways by taking a miniature likeness of the beautiful Miss Franks." (American Jewish Historical Society, Vol. 6, page 41.)

In the meantime, Benedict Arnold was pursing his career, a career strangely checkered with brilliant bravery and subtle knavery, a career sustained by the confidence of noble friends who believed in Arnold even against himself. Except for this strange power of holding friends in spite of what they knew about him, Arnold's career would have terminated before it did.

That psychic gift of his, and the desperate need of the Continental cause for military leaders, held him on until his moral turpitude matured for the final collapse. As before stated, there is no intention to minimize Arnold's services to his country, but there is a determination to show what were his associations during the period of his moral decline, and thus fill in the gaps of history and account for the distrust with which the American Congress regarded the young general.

David Solesbury Franks, the Montreal Jew, who was an agent of the Franks army-contractor syndicate in Canada, came south to the American colonies with Arnold when the American Army retreated. In his own account of himself, written in 1789—eight years after the treason—he makes so little of his association with Arnold that were it not for the reports of certain courts-martial it would be impossible to determine how close the two men had been. In his record of himself, as preserved in the tenth volume of the American Jewish Historical Society's publications, he admits leaving Canada with the Americans in 1776 and remaining attached to the American Army until the surrender of Burgoyne, which occurred late in 1777. He then lightly passes over an important period which saw the command of Philadelphia bestowed on General Arnold. He mentions simply that he was "in Arnold's military family at West Point until his desertion," which was in 1780. Reference to the first court-martial of Arnold, in which Colonel David Solesbury Franks was Arnold's chief witness, will show, however, that Franks and Arnold were more closely associated than the former would care to admit after Arnold's name had become anathema. Indeed, as the Jewish Historical Society's note correctly observes, the account of this court-martial "is of much interest, as it bears directly upon the relations of General Arnold and his aid, Major David S. Franks, before the traitor's final flight in September, 1780."

There were in all eight charges preferred against Arnold, the second one being—"In having shut up the shops and stores on his arrival in the city (Philadelphia), so as even to prevent officers of the army from purchasing, while he privately made considerable purchases for his own benefit, as is alleged and believed."

Follows a supporting affidavit, printed in the style of the original, with emphatic italics added:

"On the seventh day of May, A. D. 1779, before me, Plunket Fleeson, Esq., one of the justices, etc., for the city of Philadelphia, comes colonel John Fitzgerald, late aid de camp to his excellency general Washington, and being duly sworn according to law, deposeth and saith: That on the evening of the day on which the British forces left Philadelphia, he and Major David S. Franks, aid de camp to major Arnold, went to the house of miss Brackenberry, and lodged there that night; and the next morning, major Franks having gone down stairs, the deponent going into the front room of the said house, to view colonel Jackson's regiment then marching into the city, saw lying in the window two open papers;

that on casting his eye on one of them, he was surprised it contained instructions to the said major Franks to purchase European and East Indian goods in the city of Philadelphia, to any amount, for the payment of which the writer would furnish major Franks with the money, and the same paper contained also a strict charge to the said Franks not to make known to his most intimate acquaintance that the writer was concerned in the proposed purchase; that these instructions were not signed, but appeared to the deponent to be in the hand-writing of major general Arnold, whether or not there was a date to it the deponent doth not recollect; that the other paper contained instructions signed by major general Arnold, directing major Franks to purchase for the said general Arnold some necessaries for the use of his table; that the deponent compared the writing of the two papers and verily believes that they were both written by major general Arnold's own hand; and soon afterward major Franks came into the room and took the papers away, as the deponent supposes.

"And further the deponent saith not.

"Sworn, etc. John Fitzgerald."

That such a charge involved as much the trial of Major Franks as General Arnold, will at once appear. The statements in the charge argue close association between Arnold and Franks. Yet in Franks' written record of himself in 1789 he passes over this Philadelphia period thus lightly: "In 1778, after the evacuation of Philadelphia by the British Army & on the arrival of Count D'Estaing I procured Letters of recommendation from the Board of War. . . . . and joined him off Sandy Hook, I continued with that Admiral until he arrived at Rhode Island, where on the failure of the Expedition I returned to Philadelphia where my military duty called me."

No reference here, nor anywhere in his record, to a closeness of bond between the two which his testimony, now offered from the records, amply proves to have existed.

"The judge-advocate produced major Franks, aid-de-camp to major General Arnold, who was sworn.

"Q. On General Arnold's arrival in Philadelphia, do you know whether himself or any person on his account, made any considerable purchases of goods?

"A. I do not.

"Q. At or before general Arnold's arrival in Philadelphia did you receive orders from general Arnold to purchase goods, or do you know of general Arnold's having given orders to any other person to make purchases of goods?

"A. I did receive from general Arnold that paper which colonel Fitzgerald has mentioned in his deposition. There are circumstances leading to it which I must explain. I had, by being in the army, injured my private affairs very considerably, and meant to leave it, if a proper opportunity to enter into business should happen. I had several conversations on the subject with General Arnold, who promised me all the assistance in his power; he was to participate in the profits of the business I was to enter into. At that time, previous to our going to Philadelphia, I had several particular conversations with him, and thought that the period in which I might leave the army with honor and enter into business (had come). I received at that time, or about that time, I think several days before the enemy evacuated the city, the paper mentioned in colonel Fitzgerald's deposition that was not signed, as well as the other. Upon our coming into town we had a variety of military business to do. I did not purchase any goods, neither did I leave the army. That paper was entirely neglected, neither did I think anything concerning it until I heard of colonel Fitzgerald's deposition. General Arnold has told me since, which is since I came from Carolina some time in August last, that the reason for his not supporting me in business was, supposing I had left the army, it was incompatible with his excellency's instructions and the resolution of Congress."

This testimony, seemingly straightforward in form, is rather damning to the characters of both the men involved. Arnold, upon taking command of Philadelphia, ordered the stores and shops to be closed and no goods sold. He stopped business outright. It was a most unpopular order, because it prevented the merchants profiting by the new order of things, the return of the Americans.

The very first day the closing law is in force, Arnold writes an order to Franks to make large purchases of European and East Indian goods "to any amount" and to keep the transaction secret from his most intimate acquaintance. That is, Benedict Arnold and the Jewish major on his staff, have an understanding that under cover of the military closing, they will loot the city of its most profitable goods at the enforced low selling prices—for the obvious purpose of selling at higher prices when the military order was rescinded.

These are undisputed facts. Colonel Fitzgerald saw the papers and knew the unsigned one to be in Arnold's handwriting, even as the signed one was. They were both addressed to the Jewish Major Franks. In his testimony, Major Franks admits the existence of the unsigned order as Colonel Fitzgerald saw it, and admits also its character.

Even Benedict Arnold admitted the order, but he endeavored to show that having exhibited General Washington's orders to him (Arnold) to command Philadelphia, that fact would be a sufficient countermand to the order given to Franks to load up on valuable goods.

"General Arnold to Major Franks. Did you not suppose my showing you the instructions from general Washington to me, previous to your going into the city, a sufficient countermand of the order I had given you to purchase goods?

"Major Franks. I did not form any supposition on the subject."

This admission that he wrote the order, and the fact that no large purchases of goods could be shown, constituted Arnold's defense. It requires no keen legal mind to show its weakness. If the order was countermanded several days before they entered the city, what was it doing in Miss Brackenberry's house in Philadelphia on the first morning of Arnold's command and the first morning of the operation of his order to close the stores? And why did Franks come in search of it? Discarded orders are not thus carried around and preserved.

Probably no purchases were made. Probably the order was not carried out. When Colonel Fitzgerald walked into the room early in the morning and saw the papers, and when soon thereafter Major Franks walked into the room and saw both Colonel Fitzgerald and the papers, there was nothing else to do than to call the plan off. It had become known. Colonel Fitzgerald waited in the room to see what became of the papers.

He saw the Jew Franks come and get them. He saw him go out with them. He knew what those papers directed the Jew to do, and he knew that the directing hand was Benedict Arnold's. Doubtless with this clue he kept his eyes open in Philadelphia during the operation of the closing order. And doubtless Franks lost no time in transmitting to General Arnold the fact that he found Colonel Fitzgerald in the room where the papers had been left. The inadvertent visit of Colonel Fitzgerald is the key-fact in that phase of the matter.

But the Jewish major becomes talkative in his effort to explain the situation. "There are circumstances which I must explain," he says. And then, in words that were frequently in the mouth of Arnold, he represents that his service in the army was injuring his private affairs very seriously, and that he was contemplating retiring from the army and going into business.

It is worth noting at this point that numerous opportunities were given Franks to retire, both before and after the Arnold treason, but he developed into a persistent clamorer after official jobs. In spite of his testimony, he could not be shaken loose from public employment.

And then Franks revealed the whole secret of his relations with Arnold. They were in close association in profiteering matters. "I had several conversations on the subject with general Arnold . . . . he was to participate in the profits of the business I was to enter into." Arnold was to remain a general in the army; his aide was to get out of the army and work with him privately, sharing the profits.

But what had all this to do with the orders to close the stores at Philadelphia? What had this to do with the papers found by Colonel Fitzgerald? For after all, this was the "circumstance" which Major Franks had set out to explain. At last he reaches it: "At that time, previous to our going into Philadelphia, I had several particular conversations with him. . . . I received at that time, or about that time, the paper mentioned in Colonel Fitzgerald's deposition which was not signed, as well as the other."

The paper authorized him to get the most merchantable goods out of the closed stores. It followed upon "several particular conversations" about the business of which Arnold was to "participate in the profits." But, apparently, the deal did not go through. Colonel Fitzgerald's untimely appearance, and the carelessness of some one in leaving the papers about, were most unfavorable to the Arnold-Franks project.

There can be no question of the intimacy of the relations between the Jew and Arnold and the use that both made of their relationship. There can be no question, either, that these relationships must have been the result of continuous acquaintance and testing.

Merely to show that a Jew once crossed the path of Benedict Arnold and was implicated with him in a discreditable scheme that probably did not fully mature, means nothing. But that this Jew was involved in Arnold's fortunes from the time the two first met in Canada until the day that Arnold betrayed his country, may mean something. And that is the case. From the time of their first meeting, their lines run along together Franks always being relied upon by Arnold as the credible witness who extricates him from his scrapes, and Franks usually doing it with a sort of clumsy success, as in the instance just cited.

The reader may refer now to the reference made above to Franks' record of himself in which he mentions having joined Count d'Estaing, the French admiral, at Sandy Hook. This was just a month after Arnold took command at Philadelphia, just a month after the events on which the above charge was based. Evidently Franks got out of town for a little while. He would notice the coolness of his fellow officers among whom reports of Colonel Fitzgerald's discovery must have circulated. There would be no prejudice against him because he was a Jew, it would be solely due to the suspicions concerning him. Indeed, readers of the ordinary history will never learn that Arnold had Jews around him. There were David Franks, moneyed man and merchant in the city, and David Solesbury Franks on Arnold's staff—both outstanding figures, yet wholly passed over by the historians, with one or two exceptions, and even these have never caught the Jewish clue. In that day there was no prejudice against Jews as Jews, even as there is none now.

Franks, then, easily gains letters which permit him to join the French fleet of d'Estaing, within a month after the Philadelphia business. And strange to relate, at precisely the same time, Benedict Arnold conceived the notion that he too should go into the navy, and a month after his appointment to Philadelphia he writes to General Washington suggesting nothing less than that he be given command of the American Navy!—at precisely the time Major Franks takes to the water.

". . . . being obliged entirely to neglect my private affairs since I have been in the service," Arnold writes to General Washington, "has induced me to wish to retire from public business, unless an offer, which my friends have mentioned, should be made to me of the command of the navy . . . . I must beg leave to request your sentiments respecting a command in the navy."

So far as the historians have been able to discover, no one ever proposed such a thing as making Arnold the admiral of the American Navy. But, then, the historians did not know David S. Franks. He, a landsman, had gone for a few weeks with the French ships. Perhaps he was the friend who "mentioned" the matter. At any rate, when Franks came off the ships again, it was to serve as witness once more for Benedict Arnold.

The charges against Arnold were such as these: Permitting an enemy ship to land, and buying a share of her cargo; imposing menial service on soldiers (a charge brought about by an action of Major Franks); issuing passes unlawfully—the case in point being that of a Jewess, named Levy; the use of army wagons for his private affairs, and so forth.

This is Major Franks' testimony concerning Arnold's permitting "The Charming Nancy" to land at a United States port, contrary to law:

"Q. (by the court) Do you know whether general Arnold purchased any part of the Charming Nancy or her cargo?

"A. I do not know of my own knowledge, but I have heard general Arnold say he did, and I have also heard Mr. Seagrove say he did.

"Q. Was it previous or subsequent to general Arnold's granting the pass?

"A. It was subsequent."

Here is a complete admission of all the facts, but the defense consisted in laboriously showing, by means of quite leading questions addressed to Franks, that the owners of "The Charming Nancy" were indeed good Americans, though residing and doing business in enemy territory. Franks was rather useful in this part of the business, and the court, overlooking the other elements, simply found that the permission which Arnold gave to "The Charming Nancy" was illegal. The fact that a major general of the United States Army speculated in the cargo of the ship which had come into port in violation of the law and on his military permission, was not considered at all. Neither was the fact, stated in the charge, that he gave his permission while he was in camp with General Washington at Valley Forge, whom he did not consult in any way.

But here again the fact is established that Major Franks was privy to the whole matter, and was the chief witness for Arnold's defense.

If it had occurred but once, as at Montreal, that Arnold had been charged with irregularities involving profitable goods; or if it had occurred but once, as at Philadelphia, that Major Franks happened to be the chief available witness, no serious notice could be taken of it.

But time and again Arnold is caught in shady acts involving profitable goods, and time and again the Jewish Major Franks is his accomplice and chief witness. And this partnership in shady transactions, extending from the time Arnold first met Franks till the time Arnold betrayed his country, is significant, at least as a contribution to history, and possibly as a side light on the gradual degeneration of Benedict Arnold.

Arnold could no longer wholly escape. But still the good fortune that seemed patiently to accompany him, as if waiting for his better nature to recover from some dark spell, remained with him; the court could not exonerate him entirely, but neither could they punish him as he deserved; and so it was given as a verdict that General Arnold should be reprimanded by General Washington, his best friend.

Washington's reprimand is one of the finest utterances in human record. It would have saved a man in whom a shred of moral determination remained:

"Our profession is the chastest of all; even the shadow of a fault tarnishes the luster of our finest achievements. The least inadvertance may rob us of the public favor, so hard to be acquired. I reprimand you for having forgotten that in proportion as you have rendered yourself formidable to our enemies, you should have been guarded and temperate in your deportment toward your fellow-citizens. Exhibit anew those noble qualities which have placed you on the list of our most valued commanders. I will myself furnish you, as far as it may be in my power, with opportunities of regaining the esteem of your country."

It was a bad day for Benedict Arnold when he got into touch with the Jewish syndicate of army-contractors. There was hope for him even yet, if he would cast off the evil spell. But time pressed; events were culminating; the alien, having gripped him, was about to make the best of the baleful opportunity. The closing chapter was about to be written in glory or in shame.

The Dearborn Independent, issue of 15 October 1921

69: Arnold and His Jewish Aides at West Point

After General Washington had delivered the reprimand to Benedict Arnold, he proceeded at once to make good the intimation which he had given the unhappy officer—"I will myself furnish you, as far as may be in my power, with opportunities of regaining the esteem of your country." It was late in July, 1780, that General Washington had learned of the British plan to march to Newport and attack re-enforcements of the American cause before they could land and entrench themselves. Washington therefore decided to harry the British and perhaps prevent the attack by crossing the Hudson and marching down the east shore to menace New York, the British headquarters.

It was the last day of July, and General Washington was personally seeing the last division over at King's Ferry, when Benedict Arnold appeared. It is true that he had been wounded, it is also true that his accounts had not been allowed by Congress; but his wound was the fortune of war, and the delay in allowing his accounts was due to his already acquired reputation for shady dealing in money matters, neither of which justified him in betraying his country, but both of which might have stimulated him to recover the status he had so early lost.

It was thus that Benedict Arnold appeared before George Washington, that last day of July, 1780—a man whom Congress rightly distrusted, a man who had just been rightly reprimanded, a man whose fellow-officers looked at him askance.

Yet it was to such a man that Washington made good his word. The army was on the way to New York to attack the British. As Arnold rode up, General Washington said to him, "You are to command the left wing, the post of honor."

Those who were present report that, at Washington's words, Arnold's countenance fell. The magnanimity of the First American meant nothing to him. The opportunity to retrieve his good name had somehow lost its value.

So patent was Arnold's disappointment, that Washington asked him to ride to headquarters and await him there. At headquarters Arnold disclosed to Washington's aid, Colonel Tilghman, that his desire was not for a command in the army, but for the command of West Point. West Point was then but a post up the Hudson River, far outside the zone of important fighting, and certainly the last place it was thought the intrepid Arnold would desire to be. The inconsistency between Arnold's desire for action and West Point's lack of action struck General Washington very forcibly. He had offered Arnold a chance to rehabilitate his reputation; Arnold hung back, asking for a place where no distinctive service could then be rendered.

Now let the reader take note of this fact: it may be important, it may be unimportant; it may have some bearing on Benedict Arnold's action, it may have none; but the fact nevertheless is this: The Forage Master, that is, the quartermaster at West Point, was Colonel Isaac Franks, a member of the same family which we have been considering in these articles. This Colonel Isaac Franks, we are informed by the Jewish records which make a great deal of the fact, was once confidential aide-de-camp to General Washington, though for what reason the relationship was dissolved we are not informed.

The reader will recall that the narrative of Benedict Arnold has already included two members of the Franks family—David, of Philadelphia, and David Solesbury Franks, who came down from Montreal.

The third Franks is now in view—Colonel Isaac Franks. He is in charge of supplies at the post of West Point. It is to West Point that Benedict Arnold wishes to go, even though General Washington is offering him the post of honor in the forward movement which the Continental Army is about to make. It is the last day of July, 1780.

On August 3, General Washington gave Arnold his orders and allowed him to proceed to take command of West Point. Accompanying him, of course, was Colonel David Solesbury Franks, his aide-de-camp, whose testimony had been so useful at the court martial. There were then two Franks at West Point—Colonel D. S. Franks, aid to the commandant, and Colonel Isaac Franks, in charge of supplying the post.

It appears that Arnold had already been in communication with the enemy and had asked for the command at West Point, not for any of the reasons he alleged to General Washington, but because he had already chosen it as the gateway through which he was to let the British through into the weakened American territory. For two months Arnold had been writing to "Anderson," or John André. He had been reaching out toward the enemy for a longer time than that, and had at length requested that a man equal to himself be appointed to negotiate with him. Major John André, adjutant general of the British Army in America, was chosen as one of rank sufficiently high to deal with Arnold. They had already come into touch with each other before Arnold asked General Washington for the post at West Point. And André, as we have previously seen, knew the Franks.

Apologists for Arnold have said that the reason he showed so deep a disappointment when General Washington offered him the command of the left wing of the army, was that he had never expected such magnanimous treatment, and for the moment was conscience-stricken that he had gone so far with the enemy when his own country offered him such fine prospects. If that were the true state of Arnold's mind, he need only have taken command of the left wing, or, having been committed to take West Point, he need only have gone there and performed his soldierly duty.

The history and personality of Major John André, who completed the negotiations with Arnold, and lost his life as a spy, while Arnold lived long as a traitor, have been the object of much interest and research. His descent is obscure. His parentage was known as "Swiss-French." It is thought that the first André came to England in the train of a Jewish family. André himself had those accomplishments which were most highly prized in the society of the day. In any event, of Jewish or non-Jewish descent, he was a far finer character than Benedict Arnold.

On Arnold's staff at West Point, besides the two Jewish Franks Isaac and David—there was Lieutenant Colonel Richard Varick. This Varick was a wise young fellow who preferred to have as little as possible to do with Arnold's affairs. He refused to take any responsibility connected with Arnold's dealings with money or goods. For some apparently good reason, which will not be difficult for the reader to surmise, Varick adopted the strict policy of keeping his hands off all supplies. Thus it was left to Major Franks to attend all such matters, to which he was apparently nothing loath. In fact, Major Franks even looked after General Arnold's private cupboard.

Not to delay longer over details, suffice it to say that on September 22, 1780, less than two months after assuming command at West Point, the treason of Benedict Arnold was accomplished. One more day, and it was discovered and foiled.

Instant inquiry was made to detect accomplices. Major Franks is placed under arrest. David Franks, of Philadelphia, is arrested. It may or may not be significant, but it is nevertheless a fact, that upon the accomplishment of Arnold's treason the authorities ordered that the two Jews, David Franks and David Solesbury Franks, be put under arrest.

The experience of David Franks adds a bit of Jewish comedy to this serious scene. It appears that he still has influence to save him from severe treatment and to gain him time. On the occasion of his previous arrest in 1778, Benedict Arnold was commander of the city of Philadelphia and David Solesbury Franks was on Arnold's staff, and if Arnold and Franks could concoct a scheme of profiteering off the closed stores of the city, it was probably not beyond them to see that the elder David Franks received favor in his case. At least, as the reader of previous articles knows, David Franks went free, although caught in the act of communicating with the enemy.

But this time there is no Benedict Arnold to help him, and his nephew, like himself, is under arrest because of Arnold's treason. Yet the Philadelphia Jew discloses a marvelous facility of playing horse with the law.

He remained in jail until October 6, and then, strange to relate, he is given two weeks to get within the enemy's lines. Investigation somehow has been stopped; prosecution has been sidetracked. But David found 14 days too brief a time to wind up his affairs, and he petitions for an extension of time. It is denied. Then when one week of the time had passed, Franks asks for a pass to New York for himself, daughter, manservant and two maid-servants; this is refused and passes are authorized for himself, daughter, and one maid-servant, "provided she be an indented servant." But David does not use these passes. He applies again for an extension of time on account of an "indisposition of body." Thus, by keeping officials busy with his evasions and his counter-suggestions the record finds him still in Philadelphia on November 18, a month after he was supposed to be out of the country.

He makes application for another pass. The Council obediently sends him one, the secretary making this observation in his note: "The Council are much surprised that you still remain in this city, and hope that you will immediately depart this state, agreeable to their late order, otherwise measures will be taken to compel you to comply with the same."

Does David go? He does not. He writes an extremely polite letter. Incidentally he gives a hint of what may be keeping him. In his letter to the Council he says:

"Being apprehensive that a report raised and circulated that I had depreciated the currency by purchase of specie may have given rise to prejudice against me with the Honorable Council . . . ."

More than likely this is precisely what David was doing. It was done later by another Jew in American history, Judah P. Benjamin, and it was done everywhere by Jews during the recent war. With David's racial itch for money and his disloyalty to the American cause, there was probably sound foundation for the report.

And then, in the last line of his letter, he finds fault with his pass, and asks for another. All this time, of course, he is gaining time, and is fulfilling his purpose with regard to the specie.

This, by the way, is a common Jewish stratagem. It is very much observed in lawsuits. The non-Jew can always be depended on to desire justice and humanity, and these traits are systematically played upon. The non-Jew is also inclined to take men's word at its face value, which is also a trait which can be used to his hurt. If, for example, in a business transaction which is to be consummated a week hence, the non-Jew could absolutely fortify himself if he had the slightest suspicion of sharp dealing, it is to the advantage of the Jew who tries to "do" him to give him his word as to exactly what steps will be taken a week hence at the final settlement. If the non-Jew believes that word, he is quieted for a week. He does nothing. He rests implicitly on the given word. Then the morning comes, and the dishonest Jew steps up without warning and drives through ruthlessly to a tricky gain. This is so common that thousands who have been tricked by it have told the full details. Keep the Gentile so busy, or satisfy him so fully, that he will not bother—that's the strategy. David knew it even in his day, and it was ancient then.

His request for a new pass is refused. But still he does not go. Finally, an aroused Council sends him notice to be gone by the next day. And he then goes, but not, we may well believe, until he had done all he intended to do. David is delightfully Jewish, and the Council are naively Gentile.

Up at West Point other matters are proceeding. When General Washington arrived and heard the startling news, he asked Colonel Varick to walk with him. He spoke to the young officer most considerately, told him he did not question his loyalty, but under the circumstances he would ask him to consider himself under arrest. It was very like Washington to do this, to make the arrest himself, gently. There is no record, however, that a like courtesy was shown the Jewish

Major David Solesbury Franks. Washington probably remembered him as the witness for Arnold in the case which led to Arnold's court-martial and reprimand.

On that frontier post (as West Point then was) there were no witnesses. Franks and Varick were confronted with the necessity of testifying for each other. That is, the Jewish major was his own representative in court and practically his own witness. Franks put Varick on the stand to testify for him, and Varick put Franks on the stand to testify for him. The resulting testimony shows that Franks knew much and was eager to tell how much he knew of Arnold's traitorous intentions—but he did not tell it until Arnold's treason was exposed and he himself under arrest.

The purpose of this article being merely to fill up the gaps which are left in the Jewish propagandist boasting of the part they have played in public affairs in the United States, the reader must himself be a judge as to how far Major David Solesbury Franks was in Arnold's secret. (The "Smith" mentioned in the testimony was Joshua Hett Smith, who did secret work for Arnold and rowed André ashore for the night conference with Arnold.) Following are vital extracts from the testimony:

Major Franks—"What was my opinion of Joshua H. Smith's character and conduct, and of his visits at Arnold's headquarters. . . .?"

Colonel Varick—"When I first joined Arnold's family . . . . Arnold and yourself thought well of him as a man, but I soon prevailed on you to think him a Liar and a Rascal; and you ever after spoke of him in a manner his real character merited. . . . ."

Arnold, of course, knew what Smith was. Arnold and Smith were already partners in treason. But Varick did not know of this partnership. All that Varick knew was that both Arnold and Franks appeared to hold the same opinion, that Smith was all right. Here Arnold and Franks appear as agreed again. Varick regarded them as holding the same opinion. Varick says so to Franks' face in answer to Franks' question. He does it, however, from a friendly purpose. But the fact is significant that Franks and Arnold are found holding the same front—"Arnold and yourself thought well of him as a man."

Now, Arnold knew what Smith was, knew enough about Smith to hang him. Smith was one of the tools of his long extended treason. The question is, did Franks also know? Was Franks kept in ignorance of Arnold's real knowledge of Smith, or was Franks actually deceived as regards Smith? It may be, but let this be observed, that Varick, who was not at all in Arnold's confidence, nevertheless was not deceived about

Smith, but saw through him at once. Did not Franks see through him, too? Until the time that Varick dared speak out about the matter, Franks and Arnold were preserving the same appearance of opinion—they "thought well of him as a man."

Then Varick honestly spoke out. He got hold of the Jewish Franks and told him all that he knew and suspected about Smith. The evidence was too overwhelming for Franks to scoff at. Any man scoffing at Varick's tale would himself be under suspicion. Varick was given to understand that he had changed Franks' opinion of Smith. Thereafter Franks comported himself in a manner to convince Varick that he regarded Smith as a "Liar and a Rascal."

It is permissible to ask, was this pretense or reality? If Varick knew things, Varick was a man to handle wisely. If Varick knew things, it would be foolish to lose touch with him and thus lose the benefit of knowing how much was known or surmised outside. These, of course, are the arguments of suspicion, but they are made concerning the same Jewish officer who, on finding that Colonel Fitzgerald had discovered the profiteering venture in which Franks and Arnold were partners, was wise enough to inform Arnold and permit the plan to drop. Major Franks' previous behavior, like Benedict Arnold's, arouses the suspicion. Benedict Arnold appeared to Varick to regard Smith as a good man; Franks appeared to Varick to share Arnold's opinion; but whether Franks really knew, as Arnold knew, and only pretended to change his opinion that he might keep the confidence of Varick, is a point on which Franks' previous conduct compels the mind to waver.

How well Franks knew Arnold may be gathered from other points brought out in this testimony:

Major Franks—"How often did Arnold go down the river in his barge, whilst I was at Robinson's House (Arnold's headquarters)? Did I even attend him, and what were our opinions and conduct on his going down and remaining absent the night of the twenty-first of September?" (This was the night of his meeting André.)

Colonel Varick—(answers that Franks, to his knowledge, never accompanied Arnold) "But when I was informed by you or Mrs. Arnold, on the twenty-first, that he was not to return that evening, I suggested to you that I supposed he had gone to Smith's, and that I considered Arnold's treatment of me in keeping up his connection with Smith, in opposition to the warning I had given him, as very ungenteel, and that I was resolved to quit his family" (meaning his staff). "We did thereupon concert the plan of preventing their further intimacy by alarming Mrs. Arnold's fears. . . .

"You did at the same time inform me that you could not account for his connections with Smith—that you knew him to be an avaricious man and suspected he meant to open trade with some person in New York, under sanction of his command, and by means of flags and the unprincipled rascal Smith; and that you were induced to suspect it from the letter he wrote to Anderson in a commercial style as related to you by me. We thereupon pledged to each our word of honor that if our suspicions should prove to be founded in fact, we would instantly quit him."

It is the honest Varick talking. Franks questioning him. It will be observed that it is Franks who tells Varick of Arnold's absence and that he will not return that night. Franks knew, but Varick did not. It will be observed also, that it was Varick who protested and threatened to quit Arnold. It was indeed the second time he had threatened to quit, but the Jewish major seems never to have had a similar thought. But most important to observe is Varick's statement in answer to Franks, and in Franks' presence, that it was Franks who opened up with information regarding Arnold's character—that Arnold was an avaricious man, that Franks suspected him of opening up trade with the enemy "under sanction of his command" (just as he had planned to misuse his authority at Philadelphia) and that Smith was to be the go-between. Then he mentions a letter to "Anderson in a commercial style"—this "Anderson" being none other than Major John André of the British Army.

Here we find Major Franks intimate with every element of the conspiracy—every element of it!—and giving a certain explanation of it to Varick. Did Franks know more than he told, and was he quieting Varick with an explanation which seemed to cover all the facts, and yet did not divulge the truth? It is a question that occurs, directly we recall the close collusion of Arnold and Franks at Philadelphia.

There is other testimony, that it was Varick, not Franks, who prevented Arnold selling supplies of the government for his own profit. Time and again this occurred, but never with Franks, the long-time aid and confidant of Arnold, in the role of actor. But every time Varick did it, Franks knew of it, as he testified. Now we approach the "Day of his Desertion," as the records call the day of Arnold's treason.

Major Franks—"What was Arnold's, as well as my conduct and deportment on the Day of his Desertion, and had you the slightest reason to think I had been or was party or privy to any of his villainous practices and correspondence with the enemy, or to his flight? Pray relate the whole of our conduct on that day to your knowledge."

Colonel Varick—"I was sick and a greater part of the time in my bed in the morning of his flight. Before breakfast he came into my room" (and talked about certain letters) "and I never saw him after it but betook myself to my bed. I think it was about an hour thereafter when you came to me and told me Arnold was gone to West Point—also a considerable time thereafter you came to the window of my room near my bed and, shoving it up hastily told me with a degree of apparent surprise that you believed Arnold was a villain or rascal, and added you had heard a report that one Anderson was taken as a spy on the lines and that a militia officer had brought a letter to Arnold and that he was enjoined secrecy by Arnold. I made some warm reply, but instantly reflecting that I was injuring a gentleman and friend of high reputation in a tender point, I told you it was uncharitable and unwarrantable even to suppose it. You concurred in opinion with me and I lay down secure in the high idea I entertained of Arnold's integrity and patriotism. . . ."

Here is a record of Major Franks' conduct, told at his own solicitation before a court of inquiry. It reveals that Arnold told Franks, but did not tell Varick, where he was going. It reveals also that Franks knew of the message that came to Arnold, the bearer of which had been bound by Arnold to secrecy.

(For the reader's benefit it is recalled that Arnold's treason was prematurely exposed by André being lost in the woods at night after his interview with Arnold, and his consequent inability to get back to the British ship. He was sighted and halted in daylight, and discovery was made of the West Point plans in his stockings. The innocent soldiers sent word to Benedict Arnold, their commanding officer, that they had captured a spy named Anderson. This gave Arnold information that the plot had fallen through. Enjoining absolute secrecy on the messenger, Arnold made off hastily as if to investigate, but really to rush to the ship to which André had failed to return.) But observe: the messenger arrived and immediately Franks appears to be informed what the message contains. He is informed also that Arnold is going to West Point. He is informed of "Anderson's" capture. Once again Franks is in instant touch with all the points of the matter, but this time he goes further and accuses Arnold. In the peculiar phraseology of Varick, which may or may not be significant, Franks "hastily told me with a degree of apparent surprise" that he believed Arnold to be a villain or rascal.

Then the difference between these two men appeared again; it shines out luminously. When it was possible to save Arnold, it was Varick who was most concerned, while Franks appeared to be hand-in-glove with the traitor. But when it was apparent that something irrevocable had happened, it was the Jew who was first and bitterest to denounce, while Varick remembered the conduct expected of gentlemen. Likewise, as at first, the Jewish major changed his opinion of Smith to agree with Varick's opinion, so now he "concurred in opinion" with Varick, although he had just violently uttered the opposite opinion concerning Arnold.

Varick was charitable because he did not have the facts. Was Franks outspoken as he was because he had all the facts? If so, where did he get them? From Arnold?

How much did Franks know? That question will probably never be answered. There is, however, this additional testimony of his on record:

"I told you that I thought Arnold had corresponded with Anderson or some such name before from Philadelphia, and had got intelligence of consequence from him."

David Solesbury Franks was implicated in every major crime of Benedict Arnold and in the great treason he gave evidence of knowing every movement of the game, from its far beginning in Philadelphia.

Franks was exonerated by the court.

From his safe retreat on the British man-of-war, Benedict Arnold wrote a letter in which he exculpated Smith, Franks and Varick, writing that they were "totally ignorant of any transactions of mine, that they had reason to believe were injurious to the public."

Smith was neither ignorant nor innocent. He had rowed out to the British ship and brought André ashore for his conference with Arnold. He had been a go-between on many shady missions. Yet Arnold in his letter exonerates Smith. That fact seriously affects his exoneration of Franks. If Arnold can lie about Smith's innocence, why cannot he lie about Franks' innocence? As to Varick, he is the only one of the three who can do without Arnold's exoneration; to Varick it is an insult to have Benedict Arnold vouch for him. Franks, however, was always afterward inclined to lean upon Arnold's letter. An impartial study of the testimony, upon the background of a knowledge of Frank's history, leaves grave doubts as to the unimpeachability of his relations with

Benedict Arnold. So much so, indeed, that in the study of Arnold's treason it is a grave omission to pass over Franks' name.

The reader who will make a complete study of Franks' character as revealed in the records will testify to this: the present study has been exceedingly charitable to his character; he could easily have been prejudiced in the reader's mind by the presentation of a series of facts omitted here; the object has been to judge him solely on his acts with relation to Benedict Arnold.

Rightly or wrongly, Franks was suspected ever afterward. It was the Philadelphia incident that stamped his reputation. The suspicion of perjury on that occasion never left him. Franks insisted on having himself vindicated all around, but he was never satisfied with his vindications, he always wanted more. Jewish propagandists have misrepresented his subsequent work as a diplomatist. It was of the merest messenger-boy character, and he was entrusted with it only after the most obsequious appeals. He peddled petitions reciting his services and asking for government favor. The man who asserted in his defense at Philadelphia that he was eager to leave the army and enter business, could not be induced to leave the public service, until the allotment to him of 400 acres of land seems to have effectually weaned him from public life. What his end was, no one appears to know. His present-day use, however, is to furnish Jewish and pro-Jewish propagandists with a peg on which to hang extravagant praise of the Jew in Revolutionary times.

There can be no objection whatever to Jewish propagandists making the most of their material, but there is strong objection to the policy of concealment and misrepresentation. These impositions on public confidence will be exposed as regularly as they occur.

The Dearborn Independent, issue of 22 October 1921

70: The Gentle Art of Changing Jewish Names

The Madansky brothers—Max, Solomon, Benjamin, and Jacob—have written that their names henceforth will be May. It is a good old Anglo-Saxon name, but the Madanskys are of Asiatic origin.

Elmo Lincoln, a movie actor, comes into a Los Angeles court on the motion of his wife, and it is discovered that he is only Otto Linknhelt.

A large department store owner was born with the name Levy. He is now known as Lytton. It is quite possible he did not like Levy as a name; but why did he not change it for another Jewish name? Or perhaps it was the Jewishness of "Levy" that displeased him.

A popular tenor star recently brought suit against his wife, who married him after allowing him to believe that she was of Spanish origin. "I understood from her misleading stage name that she was Spanish when I married her. Later I found that she was Jewish and that her real name was Bergenstein."

One of the biggest and best known stores in the United States goes under an honored Christian name, though every one of the owners is Jewish. The public still carries a mental picture of the good old merchant who established the store, which picture would speedily change if the public could get a glimpse of the real owners.

Take the name Belmont, for example, and trace its history. Prior to the nineteenth century the Jews resident in Germany did not use family names. It was "Joseph the son of Jacob," "Isaac ben Abraham," the son being designated as the son of his father. But the Napoleonic era, especially following upon the assembly of the Great Sanhedrin under Napoleon's command, caused a distinct change in Jewish customs in Europe.

In 1808 Napoleon sent out a decree commanding all Jews to adopt family names. In Austria a list of surnames was assigned to the Jews, and if a Jew was unable to choose, the state chose for him. The names were devised from precious stones, as Rubenstein; precious metals, such as Goldstein, Silberberg; plants, trees, and animals, such as Mandelbaum, Lilienthal, Ochs, Wolf, and Loewe.

The German Jews created surnames by the simple method of affixing the syllable "son" to the father's name, thus making Jacobson, Isaacson; while others adopted the names of the localities in which they lived, the Jew resident in Berlin becoming Berliner, and the Jew resident in Oppenheim becoming Oppenheimer.

Now, in the region of Schoenberg, in the German Rhine country, a settlement of Jews had lived for several generations. When the order to adopt surnames went forth, Isaac Simon, the head of the settlement, chose the name of Schoenberg. It signifies in German, "beautiful hill." It is very easily Frenchified into Belmont, which also means beautiful hill or mountain. A Columbia University professor once tried to make it appear that the Belmonts originated in the Belmontes family of Portugal, but found it impossible to harmonize this theory with the Schoenberg facts.

It is noteworthy that a Belmont became American agent of the Rothschilds, and that the name of Rothschild is derived from the red shield on a house in the Jewish quarter of Frankfort-on-the-Main. What the original family name is has never been divulged.

The Jewish habit of changing names is responsible for the immense camouflage that has concealed the true character of Russian events. When Leon Bronstein becomes Leo Trotsky, and when the Jewish Apfelbaum becomes the "Russian" Zinoviev; and when the Jewish Cohen becomes the "Russian" Volodarsky, and so on down through the list of the controllers of Russia—Goldman becoming Izgoev, and Feldman becoming Vladimirov—it is a little difficult for people who think that names do not lie, to see just what is transpiring.

Indeed, there is any amount of evidence that in numberless cases this change of names—or adoption of "cover names," as the Jewish description is—is for purposes of concealment. There is an immense difference in the state of mind in which a customer enters the store of Isadore Levy and the state of mind in which he enters the store of Alex May. And what would be his feeling to learn that Isadore Levy painted up the name of Alex May with that state of mind in view? When Rosenbluth and Schlesinger becomes "The American Mercantile Company," there is justification for the feeling that the name "American" is being used to conceal the Jewish character of the firm.

The tendency of Jews to change their names dates back very far. There was and is a superstition that to give a sick person another name is to "change his luck," and save him from the misfortune destined upon his old name. There was also the Biblical example of a change of nature being followed by a change of name, as when Abram became Abraham and Jacob became Israel.

There have been justifiable grounds, however, for Jews changing their names in Europe. The nationalism of that continent is, of course, intense, and the Jews are an international nation, scattered among all the nations, with an unenviable reputation of being ready to exploit for Jewish purposes the nationalistic intensity of the Gentiles. To mollify a suspicion held against them wherever they have lived (a suspicion so general and so persistent as to be explainable only on the assumption that it was abundantly justified) the Jews have been quick to adopt the names and colors of whatever country they may be living in. It is no trouble at all to change a flag, since none of the flags is the insignia of Judah. This was seen throughout the war zone; the Jews hoisted whatever flag was expedient at the moment, and changed it as often as the shifting tide of battle required.

A Polish Jew named Zuckermandle, emigrating to Hungary, would be anxious to show that he had shuffled off the Polish allegiance which his name proclaimed; and the only way he could do this would be to change his name, which would very likely become Zukor, a perfectly good Hungarian name.

Originally the Zukors were not Jews; now the usual guess would be that they are. In the United States it would be almost a certainty. Such a change as Mr. Zuckermandle would make, however, would not be for the purpose of concealing the fact that he was a Jew, but only to conceal the fact that he was a foreign Jew.

In the United States it has been found that Jews change their names for three reasons: first, for the same reason that many other foreigners change their names, namely, to minimize as much as possible the "foreign look" and the difficulty of pronunciation which many of those names carry with them; second, for business reasons, to prevent the knowledge becoming current that So-and-So is "a Jew store"; third, for social reasons.

The desire not to appear singular among one's neighbors, when stated in just these words, very easily passes muster as being a natural desire, until you apply it to yourself. If you were going abroad to Italy, Germany, Russia, there to live and engage in business, would you cast about for a changed name immediately? Of course not. Your name is part of you, and you have your own opinion of an alias. The Jew, however, has his own name among his own people, regardless of what "cover name" the world may know him by, and, therefore, he changes his outside name quite coolly. The only likeness we have to that in America is the changing of men's pay numbers as they move their employment from place to place. John Smith may be No. 49 in Black's shop and No. 375 in White's shop, but he is always John Smith. So the Jew may be Simon son of Benjamin in the privacy of the Jewish circle, while to the world he may be Mortimer Alexander.

In the United States it is hardly to be doubted that business and social reasons are mostly responsible for the changes in Jewish names. The designation "American" is itself much coveted, as may be gathered by its frequent use in firm names, the members of which are not American in any sense that entitles them to blazon that name throughout the world.

When Moses is changed to Mortimer, and Nathan to Norton, and Isadore to Irving (as for example Irving Berlin, whose relatives, however, still know him as "Izzy"), the concealment of Jewishness in a country where so much is done by print, must be regarded as a probable motive.

When "Mr. Lee Jackson" is proposed for the club there would seem to be no reason, as far as reading goes, why anything unusual about Mr. Jackson should be surmised, until you know that Mr. Jackson is really Mr. Jacobs. Jackson happens to be the name of a President of the United States, which names are quite in favor with the name-changers, but in this case it happens also to be one of the "derivatives" of an old Jewish name.

The *Jewish Encyclopedia* contains interesting information on this matter of derivatives.

Asher is shaded off into Archer, Ansell, Asherson. Baruch is touched up into Benedict, Beniton, Berthold. Benjamin becomes Lopez, Seef, Wolf (this is translation). David becomes Davis, Davison, Davies, Davidson. Isaac becomes Sachs, Saxe, Sace, Seckel.

Jacob becomes Jackson, Jacobi, Jacobus, Jacof, Kaplan, Kauffmann, Marchant, Merchant.

Jonah becomes by quite simple changes, Jones and Joseph, Jonas. Judah (the true Jewish name) becomes Jewell, Leo, Leon, Lionel, Lyon, Leoni, Judith.

Levi becomes Leopold, Levine, Lewis, Loewe, Low, Lowy. Moses becomes Moritz, Moss, Mortimer, Max, Mack, Moskin, Mosse.

Solomon becomes Salmon, Salome, Sloman, Salmuth. And so on through the list of Jewish "changelings"—Barnett, Barnard, Beer,

Hirschel, Mann, Mendel, Mandell, Mendelsohn, with various others which are not even adaptations but sheer appropriations.

The millinery business, which is one of the principal Jewish grafts off American women, shows, the liking of the Jews for names which do not name, but which stand as impressive insignia—"Lucile," "Mme. Grande," and the like. Reuben Abraham Cohen is a perfectly good name, and a good citizen could make it immensely respected in his neighborhood, but Reuben thinks that the first round in the battle of minds should be his, and he does not scruple at a little deceit to obtain it, so he painted on a window of his store, R. A. Le Cán, which, when set off with a borrowed coat of arms, looks sufficiently Frenchified for even observant boobs among the Gentiles. Similarly a Mr. Barondesky may blossom out as Barondes or La Baron.

Commonly, Mr. Abraham becomes Miller. Why Miller should have been picked on for Judaization is not clear, but the Millers of the white race may yet be compelled to adopt some method of indicating that their name is not Jewish. It is conceivable that a Yiddish and an American form of the same name may some time be deemed necessary. Aarons becomes Arnold—there are a number of Jewish Arnolds. Aarons became Allingham. One Cohen became Druce, another Cohen became Freeman. Still another Cohen became a Montagu; a fourth Cohen became a Rothbury and a fifth Cohen became a Cooke.

The Cohens have an excuse, however. In one ghetto there are so many Cohens that some distinction must be observed. There is Cohen the rag gatherer, and Cohen the schacet (ritual meat killer), and Cohen the rising lawyer, as well as Cohen the physician. To make the matter more difficult their first names (otherwise their "Christian" names) are Louis. It is not to be wondered at, therefore, that the young lawyer should become Attorney Cohane (which does all the better if thereby certain Irish clients are attracted), and that the young doctor should become Doctor Kahn, or Kohn. These are some of the many forms that the priestly name of Cohen takes.

The same may be said with reference to Kaplan, a very common name. Charlie Chaplin's name was, in all probability, Caplan, or Kaplan. At any rate, this is what the Jews believe about their great "star." Non-Jews have read of Charlie as a "poor English boy."

There is the Rev. Stephen S. Wise, for another example. He booms his way across the country from one platform to the other, a wonder in his way, that such pomposity of sound should convey such paucity of sense. He is an actor, the less effective because he essays a part in which sincerity is requisite. This Rabbi, whose vocal exercise exhausts his other powers, was born in Hungary, his family name being Weisz. Sometimes this name is Germanized to Weiss. When S. S. Weisz became S. S. Wise, we do not know. If he had merely Americanized his Hungarian name it would have given him the name of White. Apparently "Wise" looked better. Truly it is better to be white than to be wise, but Dr. Stephen S. is a fresh point in the query of "what's in a name?"

The list of Jews in public life whose names are not Jewish would be a long one. Louis Marshall, head of the American Jewish Committee, for example—what could his old family name have been before it was changed for the name of the Chief Justice of the Supreme Court of the United States?

Mr. Selwyn's name, now so widely known in motion pictures, was originally Schlesinger. Some of the Schlesingers become Sinclairs, but Selwyn made a really good choice for a man in the show business. A rabbi whose real name was Posnansky became Posner. The name Kalen is usually an abbreviation of Kalensky. A true story is told of an East Side tinsmith whose name was very decidedly foreign-Jewish. It is withheld here, because *The Dearborn Independent* prefers in this connection to mention only the names of those who can take care of themselves. But the tinsmith moved to a non-Jewish section and opened a new shop under the name of Perkins, and his luck really did change! He is doing well and, being an industrious, honest workman, deserves his prosperity.

Of course, there are lower uses of the name-changing practice, as every employer of labor knows. A man contracts a debt under one name, and to avoid a garnishee, quits his job, collects his pay, and in a day or two attempts to hire out under another name. This was once quite a successful trick, and is not wholly unknown now.

There is also much complaint among the stricter observers of the Jewish ritual requirements that the word "Kosher" is greatly misused, that indeed it covers a multitude of sins. "Kosher" has come to signify, in some places, little more than a commercial advertisement designed to attract Jewish trade. For all it means of what it says, it might just as well be "The Best Place in Town to Eat"—which it isn't, of course; and neither is it always "strictly" Kosher.

It must be conceded, however, that the tendency to mislabel men and things is deep set in Jewish character. Jews are great coiners of catchwords that are not true, inventors of slogans that do not move.

There is a considerable decrease in the power they wielded by such methods; their brilliancy in this respect is running to seed. This may be explained by the fact that there are so many song titles to write for the Jewish jazz factories, and so much "snappy" matter for screen descriptions. Their come-back is painfully thin and forced. Without peers in dealing with a superficial situation like a dispute over the beauty of two rival "stars," or the amount and method of distributing confetti, they are the veriest dubs in dealing with a situation like that which has arisen in this country.

Immediately upon the appearance of the Jewish Question in the United States the Jews reverted naturally to their habit of mislabeling.

They were going to fool the people once more with a pat phrase. They are still seeking for that phrase. Slowly they are recognizing that they are up against the Truth, and truth is neither a jazzy jade nor a movie motto, which can be recostumed and changed at will.

This passion for misleading people by names is deep and varied in its expression. Chiefly due to Jewish influences, we are giving the name of "liberalism" to looseness. We are dignifying with names that do not correctly name, many subversive movements. We are living in an era of false labels, whose danger is recognized by all who observe the various underground currents which move through all sections of society. Socialism itself is no longer what its name signifies; the name has been seized and used to label anarchy. Judaistic influence creeping into the Christian church has kept the apostolic labels, but thoroughly destroyed the apostolic content; the disruptive work has gone on quietly and unhindered, because often as the people looked, the same label was there as the same old merchant's name stays on the store the Jews have bought and cheapened. Thus there are "reverends" who are both unreverend and irreverent, and there are shepherds who flock with the wolves.

Zionism is another misnomer. Modern Zionism is not what its label would indicate it to be. The managers of the new money collection—millions of it, badly used, badly accounted for—are about as much interested in Zionism as an Ohio Baptist is in Meccaism. For the leading so-called "Zionists," Mt. Zion and all that it stands for has next to no meaning; they see only the political and real estate aspects of Palestine, another people's country just at present.

The present movement is not religious, although it plays upon the religious sentiments of the lower class of Jews; it is certainly not what

Judaized orators among the Christians want the Christians to think it is; Zionism is at present a most mischievous thing, potentially a most dangerous thing, as several governments could confidentially tell you.

But it is all a part of the Jewish practice of setting up a label pretending one thing, while quite another thing really exists.

Take anti-Semitism. That is a label which the Jews have industriously pasted up everywhere. If ever it was an effective label its uses are over now. It doesn't mean anything. Anti-Semitism does not exist, since the thing so named is found among the Semites, too. Semites cannot be anti-Semitic. When the world holds up a warning finger against a race that is the moving spirit of the corruptive, subversive and destructive influences abroad in the world today, that race cannot nullify the warning by sticking up a false label of "Anti-Semitism," anymore than it can justify the sign of gold on a $1.50 watch or the sign of "pure wool" on a $11.50 suit of clothes.

So with the whole group of labels which the Jews have trotted out like talismen to work some magic spell upon the aroused mind of America. They are lies. And when one lie fails, how quickly they hitch their hopes to another. If "Anti-Semitism" fails, then try "Anti-Catholic"— that might do something. If that fails, try "Anti-American"—get the biggest talent that can be hired for a night on the B'nai B'rith platform to shout it. And when that fails, as it has—?

The American Jewish Committee is itself a misnomer. The committee is not exclusively American, and its work is not to Americanize the Jews nor even to encourage real Americanization among them. It is a committee composed of Jews representing that class which profits most by keeping the mass of the Jews segregated from Americans and in bondage to the "higher ups" among the Jews. They are the "big Jews," as Norman Hapgood used to call them, who say to the "little Jews," "You hang closely together; we will be your representatives to these foreign peoples, the Americans and others." If the American Jewish Committee would change its name to this:

"The Jewish Commission for America," it might be nearer the truth. It has dealt with America in the recent past very much as the Allied Commissions deal with Germany.

There are certain things we may do, and certain things we may not do, and the Jewish Commission for America tells us what we may and may not do. One of the things we may not do is to declare that this is a Christian country.

There is one absolutely safe rule in dealing with anything emanating from the American Jewish Committee. Don't rely on the label, open the matter up. You will find that the Kehillah is not what it pretends to be; that the Jewish labor union is not what it pretends to be; that Zionism is a camouflage for something entirely different; that the name and the nature are nearly always different, which is the reason for a particular name being chosen. It runs all the way through Jewish practice, and presents another little job for the Jewish reformer.

The Dearborn Independent, issue of 12 November 1921

"What the American Jew needs to develop is the habit of self-criticism. If the spokesmen of the Jewish people would devote one-half the energy they now expend in answering attacks to attacking the evils that stare everyone in the face, they would make a real contribution to American life. But judged by their public utterances, they seem to be supersensitive to trivial prejudice in non-Jews and extraordinarily insensitive to the faults of Jews. They are hypochondriac and morbidly defensive about their critics, and indulgent and complacent about what the Jewish people is and does. Races, not cursed with a sense of inferiority, do not shrink from criticism. They initiate it."—Walter Lippmann, in *The American Hebrew.*

71: Jewish "Kol Nidre" and "Eli, Eli" Explained

I have looked this year and last for something in your paper about the prayer which the Jews say at their New Year. But you say nothing. Can it be you have not heard of the Kol Nidre?

"Lately in three cities I have heard a Jewish religious hymn sung in the public theaters. This was in New York, Detroit and Chicago. Each time the program said 'by request.' Who makes the request? What is the meaning of this kind of propaganda? The name of the hymn is 'Eli.'"

The Jewish year just passed has been described by a Jewish writer in the *Jewish Daily News* as the Year of Chaos. The writer is apparently intelligent enough to ascribe this condition to something besides "anti-Semitism."

He says, "the thought that there is something wrong in Jewish life will not down," and when he describes the situation in the Near East, he says, "The Jew himself is stirring the mess." He indicts the Jewish year 5681 on 12 counts, among them being, "mismanagement in Palestine," "engaging in internal warfare," "treason to the Jewish people," "selfishness," "self-delusion."

"The Jewish people is a sick people," cries the writer, and when he utters a comfortable prophecy for the year 5682, it is not in the terms of Judah but in the terms of "Kol Yisroel"—All Israel—the terms of a larger and more inclusive unity which gives Judah its own place, and its own place only, in the world. The Jewish people are sick, to be sure, and the disease is the fallacy of superiority, with its consequent "foreign policy" against the world.

When Jewish writers describe the year 5681 as the Year of Chaos, it is an unconscious admission that the Jewish people are ripening for a change of attitude. The "chaos" is among the leaders; it involves the plans which are based on the old false assumptions. The Jewish people are waiting for leaders who can emancipate them from the thralldom of their self-seeking masters in the religious and political fields. The enemies of the emancipation of Judah are those who profit by Judah's bondage, and these are the groups that follow the American Jewish Committee and the political rabbis. When a true Jewish prophet arises—and he should arise in the United States—there will be a great sweeping away of the selfish, scheming, heartless Jewish leaders, a general desertion of the Jewish idea of "getting" instead of "making," and an emergence of the true idea submerged so long.

There will also be a separation among the Jews themselves. They are not all Jews who call themselves so today. There is a Tartar strain in so-called Jewry that is absolutely incompatible with true Israelitish raciality; there are other alien strains which utterly differ from the true Jewish; but until now these strains have been held because the Jewish leaders needed vast hordes of low-type people to carry out their world designs. But the Jew himself is recognizing the presence of an alien element; and that is the first step in a movement which will place the Jewish Question on quite another basis.

What the Jews of the United States are coming to think is indicated by this letter—one among many (the writer is a Jew):

"Gentlemen:

"'Because you believe in a good cause,' said Dr. Johnson, 'is no reason why you should feel called upon to defend it, for by your manner of defense you may do your cause much harm.'

"The above applying to me I will only say that I have received the books you sent me and read both with much interest.

"You are rendering the Jews a very great service, that of saving them from themselves.

"It takes courage, and nerve, and intelligence to do and pursue such a work, and I admire you for it."

The letter was accompanied by a check which ordered *The Dearborn Independent* sent to the address of another who bears a distinctively Jewish name.

It is very clear that unity is not to be won by the truth-teller soft-pedaling or suppressing his truth, nor by the truth-hearer strenuously denying that the truth is true, but by both together honoring the truth in telling and in acknowledging it. When the Jews see this, they can take over the work of truth-telling and carry it on themselves. These articles have as their only purpose: First, that the Jews may see the truth for themselves about themselves; second, that non-Jews may see the fallacy of the present Jewish idea and use enough common sense to cease falling victims to it. With both Jews and non-Jews seeing their error, the way is opened for cooperation instead of the kind of competition (not commercial, but moral) which has resulted so disastrously to Jewish false ambitions these long centuries.

Now, as to the questions at the beginning of this article: *The Dearborn Independent* has heretofore scrupulously avoided even the appearance of criticizing the Jew for his religion. The Jew's religion, as most people think of it, is unobjectionable. But when he has carried on campaigns against the Christian religion, and when in every conceivable manner he thrusts his own religion upon the public from the stage of theaters and in other public places, he has himself to blame if the public asks questions.

It is quite impossible to select the largest theater in the United States, place the Star of David high in a beautiful stage heavens above all flags and other symbols, apostrophize it for a week with all sorts of wild prophecy and all sorts of silly defiance of the world, sing hymns to it and otherwise adore it, without arousing curiosity. Yet the Jewish theatrical managers, with no protest from the Anti-Defamation Committee, have done this on a greater or smaller scale in many cities. To say it is meaningless is to use words lightly.

The "Kol Nidre" is a Jewish prayer, named from its opening words, "All vows," (kol nidre). It is based on the declaration of the Talmud:

"He who wishes that his vows and oaths shall have no value, stand up at the beginning of the year and say: 'All vows which I shall make during the year shall be of no value.'"

It would be pleasant to be able to declare that this is merely one of the curiosities of the darkness which covers the Talmud, but the fact is that "Kol Nidre" is not only an ancient curiosity; it is also a modern practice. In the volume of revised "Festival Prayers," published in 1919 by the Hebrew Publishing Company, New York, the prayer appears in its fullness:

"All vows, obligations, oaths or anathemas, pledges of all names, which we have vowed, sworn, devoted, or bound ourselves to, from this day of atonement, until the next day of atonement (whose arrival we hope for in happiness) we repent, aforehand, of them all, they shall all be deemed absolved, forgiven, annulled, void and made of no effect; they shall not be binding, nor have any power; the vows shall not be reckoned vows, the obligations shall not be obligatory, nor the oaths considered as oaths."

If this strange statement were something dug out of the misty past, it would scarcely merit serious attention, but as being part of a revised Jewish prayer book printed in the United States in 1919, and as being one of the high points of the Jewish religious celebration of the New Year, it cannot be lightly dismissed after attention has once been called to it.

Indeed, the Jews do not deny it. Early in the year, when a famous Jewish violinist landed in New York after a triumphant tour abroad, he was besieged by thousands of his East Side admirers, and was able to quiet their cries only when he took his violin and played the "Kol Nidre." Then the people wept as exiles do at the sound of the songs of the homeland.

In that incident the reader will see that (hard as it is for the non-Jew to understand it!) there is a deep-rooted, sentimental regard for the "Kol Nidre" which makes it one of the most sacred of possessions to the Jew. Indefensibly immoral as the "Kol Nidre" is, utterly destructive of all social confidence, yet the most earnest efforts of a few really spiritual Jews have utterly failed to remove it from the prayer books, save in a few isolated instances. The music of the "Kol Nidre" is famous and ancient. One has only to refer to the article "Kol Nidre" in the *Jewish Encyclopedia* to see the predicament of the modern Jew: he cannot deny; he cannot defend; he cannot renounce. The "Kol Nidre" is here, and remains.

If the prayer were a request for forgiveness for the broken vows of the past, normal human beings could quite understand it. Vows, promises, obligations and pledges are broken, sometimes by weakness of will to perform them, sometimes by reason of forgetfulness, sometimes by sheer inability to do the thing we thought we could do. Human experience is neither Jew nor Gentile in that respect.

But the prayer is a holy advance notice, given in the secrecy of the synagogue, that no promise whatever shall be binding, and more than not being binding is there and then violated before it is ever made.

The scope of the prayer is "from this day of atonement, until the next day of atonement." The prayer looks wholly to the future, "we repent, aforehand, of them all."

The prayer breaks down the common ground of confidence between men—"the vows shall not be reckoned vows; the obligations shall not be obligatory, nor the oaths considered as oaths."

It requires no argument to show that if this prayer be really the rule of faith and conduct for the Jews who utter it, the ordinary social and business relations are impossible to maintain with them.

It should be observed that there is no likeness here with Christian "hypocrisy," so-called. Christian "hypocrisy" arises mostly from men holding higher ideals than they are able to attain to, and verbally extolling higher principles than their conduct illustrates. That is, to use Browning's figure, the man's reach exceeds his grasp; as it always does, where the man is more than a clod.

But "Kol Nidre" is in the opposite direction. It recognizes by inference that in the common world of men, in the common morality of the street and the mart, a promise passes current as a promise, a pledge as a pledge, an obligation as an obligation—that there is a certain social currency given to the individual's mere word on the assumption that its quality is kept good by straight moral intention. And it makes provision to drop below that level.

How did the "Kol Nidre" come into existence? Is it the cause or the effect of that untrustworthiness with which the Jew has been charged for centuries?

Its origin is not from the Bible but from Babylon, and the mark of Babylon is more strongly impressed on the Jew than is the mark of the Bible. "Kol Nidre" is Talmudic and finds its place among many other dark things in that many-volumed and burdensom invention. If the "Kol Nidre" ever was a backward look over the failures of the previous year, it very early became a forward look to the deliberate deceptions of the coming year.

Many explanations have been made in an attempt to account for this. Each explanation is denied and disproved by those who favor some other explanation. The commonest of all is this, and it rings in the overworked note of "persecution": The Jews were so hounded and harried by the bloodthirsty Christians, and so brutally and viciously treated in the name of loving Jesus (the terms are borrowed from Jewish writers) that they were compelled by wounds and starvation and the fear of death to renounce their religion and to vow that thereafter they would take the once despised Jesus for their Messiah. Therefore, say the Jewish apologists, knowing that during the ensuing year the terrible, bloodthirsty Christians would force the poor Jews to take Christian vows, the Jews in advance announced to God that all the promises they would make on that score would be lies. They would say what the Christians forced them to say, but they would not mean or intend one word of it.

That is the best explanation of all. Its weakness is that it assumes the "Kol Nidre" to have been coincident with times of "persecution," especially in Spain. Unfortunately for this explanation, the "Kol Nidre" is found centuries before that, when the Jews were under no pressure.

In a refreshingly frank article in the Cleveland Jewish World for October 11, the insufficiency of the above explanation is so clearly set forth that a quotation is made:

"Many learned men want to have it understood that the Kol Nidre dates from the Spanish Inquisition, it having become necessary on account of all sorts of persecution and inflictions to adopt the Christian religion for appearances' sake. Then the Jews in Spain, gathering in cellars to celebrate the Day of Atonement and pardon, composed a prayer that declared of no value all vows and oaths that they would be forced to make during the year. . . .

"The learned men say, moreover, that in remembrance of those days when hundreds and thousands of Maranos (secret Jews) were dragged out of the cellars and were tortured with all kinds of torment, the Jews in all parts of the world have adopted the Kol Nidre as a token of faithfulness to the faith and as self-sacrifice for the faith.

"These assertions are not correct. The fact is that the formula of Kol Nidre was composed and said on the night of Yom Kippur quite a time earlier than the period of the Spanish Inquisition. We find, for instance, a formula to invalidate vows on Yom Kippur in the prayer book of the Rabbi Amram Goun who lived in the ninth century, about five hundred years before the Spanish Inquisition; although Rabbi Amram's forumla is not 'Kol Nidre' but 'Kol Nidrim' ('All vows and oaths which we shall swear from Yom Kippurim to Yom Kippurim will return to us void.')"

The form of the prayer in the matter of its age may be in dispute; but back in the ancient and modern Talmud is the authorization of the practice: "He who wishes that his vows and oaths shall have no value, stand up at the beginning of the year and say: 'All vows which I shall make during the year shall be of no value.'"

That answers our reader's question. This article does not say that all Jews thus deliberately assassinate their pledged word. It does say that both the Talmud and the prayer book permit them to do so, and tell them how it may be accomplished.

Now, as to the Jewish religious hymn which is being sung "by request" throughout the country: the story of it is soon told.

The name of the hymn is "Eli, Eli"; its base is the first verse of the Twenty-second Psalm, known best in Christian countries as the Cry of Christ on the Cross.

It is being used by Jewish vaudeville managers as their contribution to the pro-Jewish campaign which the Jew-controlled theater is flinging into the faces of the public, from stage and motion picture screen. It is an incantation designed to inflame the lower classes of Jews against the people, and intensify the racial consciousness of those hordes of Eastern Jews who have flocked here.

At the instigation of the New York Kehillah, "Eli, Eli" has for a long time been sung at the ordinary run of performances in vaudeville and motion picture houses, and the notice "By Request" is usually a bald lie. It should be "By Order." The "request" is from Jewish headquarters, which has ordered the speeding up of Jewish propaganda. The situation of the theater now is that American audiences are paying at the box office for the privilege of hearing Jews advertise the things they want non-Jews to think about them.

If even a vestige of decency, or the slightest appreciation of good taste remained, the Jews who control the theaters would see that the American public must eventually gag on such things. When two Jewish comedians who have been indulging in always vulgar and often indecent antics, appear before the drop curtain and sing the Yiddish incantation, "Eli, Eli," which, of course, is incomprehensible to the major part of the audience, the Jewish element always betrays a high pitch of excitement. They understand the game that is being played: the "Gentiles" are being flayed to their face, and they don't know it; as when a Yiddish comedian pours out shocking invectives on the name of Jesus Christ, and "gets away with it," the Jewish portion of his audience howling with delight, and the "boob Gentiles" looking serenely on and feeling it to be polite to laugh and applaud too!

This Yiddish chant is the rallying cry of race hatred which is being spread abroad by orders of the Jewish leaders. You, if you are a theatergoer, help to pay the expense of getting yourself roundly damned. The Kehillah and the American Jewish Committee, which for more than ten years have been driving all mention of Christianity out of public life, under their slogan "This Is Not a Christian Country," are spreading their own type of Judaism everywhere with insolence unparalleled.

"Eli, Eli" is not a religious hymn! It is a racial war cry. In the low cafés of New York, where Bolshevik Jews hang out, "Eli, Eli" is their song. It is the Marseillaise of Jewish solidarity. It has become the fanatical chant of all Jewish Bolshevik clubs; it is constantly heard in Jewish coffee houses and cabarets where emotional Russian and Polish Jews—all enemies to all government—shout the words amid torrential excitement. When you see the hymn in print you are utterly puzzled to understand the excitement it arouses.

And this rallying cry has now been obtruded into the midst of the theatrical world.

The term "incantation" here used is used advisedly. The term is used by Kurt Schindler, who adapted the Yiddish hymn to American use. And its effect is that of an incantation.

In translation it is as follows:

"My God, my God, why hast thou forsaken me? With fire and flame they have burnt us, Everywhere they have shamed and derided us, Yet none amongst us has dared depart From our Holy Scriptures, from our Law.

"My God, my God, why hast thou forsaken me?
By day and night I only yearn and pray,
Anxiously keeping our Holy Scriptures
And praying, Save us, save us once again!
For the sake of our fathers and our fathers' fathers!

"Listen to my prayer and to my lamenting, For only Thou canst help, Thou, God, alone, For it is said, 'Hear, O Israel, the Lord is Our God, The Lord is One!'"

The words of the hymn are so much resembling a lament that they strangely contrast with the spirit which the hymn itself seems to arouse; its mournful melody inspires a very different spirit among the Jewish hearers than the same sort of melody would inspire among other people. Those who have heard its public rendition can better understand how a hymn of such utterly quiet and resigned tone could be the wild rage of the anarchists of the East Side coffee houses.

The motive, of course, for the singing of the hymn is the reference to non-Jewish people.

"With fire and flame *they* have burnt us, everywhere *they* have shamed and derided us?" Who are "they"? Who but the goyim, the Christians who all unsuspectingly sit nearby and who are so affected by the Jewish applause that they applaud too! Truly, in one way of looking at it, Jews have a right to despise the "gentiles."

"*They* have burnt us; *They* have shamed us," but we, the poor Jews, have been harmless all the while, none among us daring to depart from the Law! That is the meaning of "Eli, Eli." That is why, in spite of its words of religious resignation, it becomes a rallying cry. "They" are all wrong; "we" are all right.

It is possible, of course, that right-minded Jews do not approve all this. They may disapprove of "Kol Nidre" and they may resent the use which the Jewish leaders are making of "Eli, Eli." Let us at least credit some Jews with both these attitudes. But they do nothing about it. These same Jews, however, will go to the public library of their town and put the fear of political or business reprisal in the hearts of the Library Board if they do not instantly remove *The Dearborn Independent* from the library; these same Jews will form committees to coerce mayors of cities into issuing illegal orders which cannot be enforced; these same Jews will give commands to the newspapers under their patronage or control—they are indeed mighty and active in the affairs of the non-Jews. But when it is a matter of keeping "Eli, Eli" out of the theater, or the "Kol Nidre" out of the mouths of those who thus plan a whole year of deception "aforehand," these same Jews are very inactive and apparently very powerless.

The Anti-Defamation Committee would better shut up shop until it can show either the will or the ability to bring pressure to bear on its own people. Coercion of the rest of the people is rapidly growing less and less possible.

The "Kol Nidre" is far from being the worst counsel in the Talmud; "Eli, Eli" is far from being the worst anti-social misuse of apparently holy things. But it will remain the policy of *The Dearborn Independent*, for the present at least, to let all such matters alone except, as in the present case, where the number of the inquiries indicates that a knowledge of the facts has been had at other sources. In many instances, what our inquirers heard was much worse than is stated here, so that this article is by way of being a service to the inquirer to prevent his being misled, and to the Jew to prevent misrepresentation.

The Dearborn Independent, issue of 5 November 1921

72: Jews as New York Magistrates See Them

The Dearborn Independent has been frequently importuned to make exposure of the Jewish crime record in New York and other cities, but up to this time has chosen not to do so. The material is mountainous and the facts are damaging, but *The Dearborn Independent* will continue to assume that the majority of the Jewish people do not approve of criminal acts, even against non-Jewish life and property. This paper prefers to confine its attention to those matters which are plainly within the purpose and approval of the Jewish leaders. There is a decided criminal element in the Jewish Question, and no small part of the criminality flows directly or indirectly from the attitude of the Jewish leaders, but the Great Crime is the introduction of corruptive and anti-American ideas into American life, and Jewish leaders cannot escape responsibility for that.

The magistrates of every city with a considerable Jewish population know the facts. In practically every state in the Union there is today a celebrated case where some Jew, through money or influence, is playing horse with American law. It is locally known, but not generally, except in two or three instances.

The local press—deriving 80 per cent of its support from Jewish advertising—is usually very discreet, preferring to leave the matter to the courts. Strange things occur in the courts, such as judges being taken into very lucrative partnerships after giving decisions favorable to wealthy Jewish defendants.

The following extracts of opinions given *The Dearborn Independent* by magistrates of the City of New York are offered in the hope that the Jewish leaders will read and digest them, and see, if possible, what a hopeless game they are playing. The Jewish Question of today is turning about in the direction of the Jewish Question of tomorrow—which is, When are the Jewish Leaders going to admit that their game is a losing one? They see it now; but they must admit it and quit it. And it will not be surprising if a mass movement of the Jewish people compels them to do so.

"The Jewish race," said one of the magistrates, "seems deliberately blind to its own faults. Some twelve years ago General Bingham, then police commissioner, found it necessary to call attention to certain criminal tendencies of the East Side Jews. His criticisms were bitterly resented. I venture to say, however, that there are few men who preside in our inferior courts who will not readily indorse those views of General Bingham in their application to the conditions of the present day."

(It was because of General Bingham's criticisms that the New York Kehillah was increased in power—not to clean up conditions, but to shut up the critics.)

"The different groups, racial or religious, of New York City, have always each supported institutions for the care of its fallen women. We have the Magdalen Home, the Protestant Episcopal House of Mercy and the Catholic House of the Good Shepherd. The Jews alone are the exception. Yet it does not require more than short experience in the Magistrates' Courts to convince one that more than two-thirds of the fallen women in the metropolis are of the Jewish race. This fact and the urgent necessity of caring for these unfortunates was laid before some prominent Jews. They gave the assurance that ample provision was being made by a group of wealthy Jewish families to endow an institution of the kind. However, nothing was done or even contemplated. The Jews absolutely ignored the issue. And today we magistrates are compelled, as usual, to commit such Jewish women to the Protestant Episcopal and Catholic homes.

"This is indicative of a strange refusal to look facts in the face, if the facts reflect on the Jews. A lawyer, once highly prominent in Jewish circles here, became involved in a blackmailing scandal with a notorious member of his race known as the 'Wolf of Wall Street.' The 'Wolf' was convicted and sent to a Federal prison. The lawyer was scathingly denounced by the Appellate Court and only escaped disbarment because of his age.

The Jews of New York deliberately refused to condemn this man's nefarious acts. Only the other day they 'honored' him by dedicating a library to him in one of their charitable institutions, and hanging his portrait on the wall. An action such as this smacks a great deal of an absence of moral sense."

One magistrate prefaced his remarks by stating that he had no desire to dwell upon any special misdemeanors or crimes that might be considered peculiar to the Jewish race. But he pointed out that a more serious situation than one caused by sporadic criminality had been created by reason of a persistent class movement among the Jews.

"Any law," he said, "which appears to be obnoxious to the self-centered Jewish element, is deliberately ignored by them, or opposed with a stubborn resistance which neither time nor education seems to mitigate. The result is that our Magistrates' Courts and the Court of Special Sessions are crowded with cases of violations of that character. The newly arrived Jews especially are apparently determined to subordinate this country to their own desires, rather than to accommodate themselves to the conditions here as other races do.

"The most blatant example of this attitude is in connection with the law relating to Sabbath breaking. Our Penal Law is plain and specific on this matter. It states:

The first day of the week, being by general consent set apart for rest and religious uses, the law prohibits the doing on that day of certain acts hereinafter specified, which are serious interruptions of the repose and religious liberty of the community.

A violation of the foregoing prohibition is Sabbath breaking.

"Sabbath breaking is a misdemeanor, punishable by a fine or by imprisonment in a county jail, and where the offense is aggravated by a previous conviction, the fine and jail sentence are doubled. Yet the various acts specified as Sabbath breaking are violated openly and with insolent impunity by thousands of Jews every Sunday in New York. Their race has much to say about its own religious liberty, but it thinks nothing of outraging the religious liberties of other races. If any serious attempt were made to enforce this statute in the Jewish districts, the police would be compelled to arrest the larger part of the population.

"These Jews are determined to trade and traffic and to keep their factories and workshops going on the American Sunday. They impose their will upon the greatest city in the United States, through silent resistance and the sheer force of numbers.

"The Jews of whom I am speaking are mostly from Eastern Europe—Russia, Galicia, and Poland. They are of the first or second generation of immigrants. They generally speak and read only the Yiddish tongue. But it is a deplorable fact that Americanized Jews of prominence, openly encourage these ignorant people in their defiance of the law. Whenever Yiddish tradesmen and manufacturers are arrested for Sabbath breaking, hosts of Jewish lawyers spring to their defense, and powerful Jewish societies intervene to protect them. The Jewish Sabbath

Alliance, with offices on Fifth Avenue, conducts a constant propaganda among the ghetto people, urging them to insist upon their alleged legal right to pursue their ordinary vocations on the American Sunday. And it provides them with legal counsel with they get into trouble.

"Jewish lawyers set up the specious claim that these people from Eastern Europe observe another day as 'holy time,' and therefore have a right to labor and traffic on Sunday. Some of the Jewish magistrates encourage this contention by discharging such lawbreakers. But there is no question of religion in these Sunday violations. It is merely money greed. These Jews are so hot after money that they are afraid of losing some if they close their shops on Sunday. This is easily proved by the fact that when the Jews find it to their interest or convenience to observe Sunday closing, they do it by agreement among themselves.

"This was demonstrated during last summer. In Rivington and Delancey streets, and in fact throughout the ghetto, there were signs posted in the shop windows of Jews, authorized by an organization calling itself 'The Independent Ladies' Garment Merchants Association, Incorporated.' The notices read:

This Store will be
closed on
SUNDAYS
from
JUNE 26th until the end of AUGUST
The Independent Ladies' Garment
Merchants Association, Incorporated.

"In other words these shopkeepers were spending week-ends at the Yiddish summer resorts. They didn't want any of their competitors to steal the trade of customers during their absence. So they all agreed to close up. The question of religion did not enter their minds.

"Jews of the more intelligent and well-to-do class are also constantly attempting to break the Sabbath laws in sections of the city where their race does not predominate. Non-Jewish merchants have had to organize associations to protect themselves against this unfair competition. If a non-Jew is arrested for Sabbath-breaking, he suffers. The Jewish Sabbath-breaker goes free. This gives the Jew an unfair advantage.

"Not long ago there was a large advertising sign posted conspicuously on the platforms of the elevated railroad. A Jewish wholesale house on Fifth Avenue notified buyers that its salesrooms would be open from 2 p.m. to 5 p.m. every Sunday afternoon. I thought this was going a little too far, and I called the attention of several of the protective associations to the methods practiced by this firm. The signs soon afterward disappeared. However, such tactics are continually being attempted by Jewish merchants and manufacturers in the Bronx and on the West Side of the city, in an effort to gain a business advantage over their non-Jewish competitors. But there are means of putting an immediate and effective stop to all this rascality. This would be by enforcing Section 2149 of the Penal Law, which provides for the forfeiture of commodities exposed for sale on Sunday. The section reads:

In addition to the penalty imposed by section 2142, all property and commodities exposed for sale on the first day of the week in violation of the provisions of this article shall be forfeited. Upon conviction of the offender by the justice of the peace of a county, or by a police justice or magistrate, such officer shall issue a warrant for the seizure of the forfeited articles, which when seized shall be sold on one day's notice, and the proceeds paid to the overseers of the poor, for the use of the poor of the town or city.

"This statute is not enforced. But I believe we shall yet be compelled to enforce it in New York. The seizure of the stocks of some of these Jewish shopkeepers would be the most effective lesson one could administer in teaching them to respect the law."

Another magistrate expressed himself still more forcibly on the Jewish question. "These people from Eastern Europe," he said, "are tending to destroy all American conceptions of right and justice. Day after day my court is crowded with Jewish people. I am compelled to fine and warn them. The attitude of the women is especially truculent. They have adopted a misconception of woman's suffrage. They say to me: 'This is a woman's country. Woman can do what she likes—men can't.'

"There is no denying the fact that New York is falling more and more under the dominance of Jews. Americans are gradually being driven from public life. It will not be long before we shall have a Jewish mayor and a Jewish board of aldermen. This in itself should be no great misfortune were it not for the tendency of the Jew to abuse his power. He is ambitious and restless to obtain authority. But the moment he gets it, he becomes oppressive. This is evident already wherever the Jews are obtaining monopolies. A friend, a young man, came to me the other day, complaining bitterly that he was deliberately being driven out of business by the Jews. He was the owner of a prosperous laundry. But the large machine laundries of the city are now mostly in the hands of the

Jews. They refuse to do his work for him, saying: 'You are not a member of our syndicate.' (This is one of the new phases of the Jewish invasion—the almost complete absorption of the laundry business.)

"We all remember the time when the Jews began to clamor for special news stand privileges. They formed Jewish organizations of news dealers, until the business was entirely in their hands. While they still had non-Jewish competition they were obliging and attentive enough. They did anything to curry favor. But today they carry themselves like lords. No Jewish news dealer in New York will deliver newspapers to his non-Jewish customers on Jewish holidays.

"In the New York post office, where there are now some 11,000 employees, about one-half of whom are Jews, the same conditions exist. The Jewish postal employees complained that they were being deprived of their constitutional rights if they were compelled to work on Rosh Hashana, the Jewish New Year, and on Yom Kippur, the Jewish Day of Atonement. The postmaster was compelled to grant their demands, at the same time pointing out that leaves of absence could not be granted to Christian employees on Christmas, New Year's and Good Friday, otherwise the post office would be swamped with mail."

Another phase of this Jewish insistence upon special rights was emphasized by one of the magistrates. "I have often observed," he said, "that there is generally a good result when a Jew settles in a small New England town where there are only three or four stores. The situation develops social stimulus and competitive spirit. Too often there is a tendency toward dry-rot among the native population. They stagnate.

"But where Jews assemble in large numbers, as they do in New York City and the industrial towns of New Jersey, they immediately develop a class and racial consciousness that is unfortunate. It is not surprising that Jews should cling to their traditional customs. But it is a peculiar fact that of the forty different nationalities in New York, it is only one race, the Jewish, which persistently tries to impose its own modes of life upon the mass of the people.

"One dangerous feature of this tendency is a constant effort to put upon the statue books laws which favor the Jewish race, and placing weapons into the hands of the mischievous and litigious.

"In the Penal Law of the state of New York there is a statute which is outrageous in its import and should be stricken from the code. In effect it renders a man guilty of a misdemeanor if he ventures to have a process served upon a Jew on Saturday. He is equally guilty if he dares to serve a process which is made returnable on Saturday. It is a notorious fact that a large percentage of Jews deliberately alter their names in order to conceal their race. Yet if a man should induce his lawyer to procure a civil action to which such a Jew is a party to be adjourned to Saturday for trial, in ignorance of the fact that the borrowed American name conceals a Jew, that man renders himself liable to fine or imprisonment.

"This is Section 2150 of the Penal Law. Its exact wording is as follows:

Maliciously serving process on Saturday on person who keeps Saturday as holy time—Whoever maliciously procures any process in a civil action to be served on Saturday, upon any person who keeps Saturday as holy time, and does not labor on that day, or serves upon him any process returnable on that day, or maliciously procures any civil action to which such person is a party to be adjourned to that day for trial, is guilty of a misdemeanor.

"Advantage was taken of this statute by a Jew in the city of Rochester to evade the payment of goods which had been delivered to him. The summons which had been served upon him was made returnable upon a Saturday, and upon the return day the Jewish defendant, evidently at the instigation of his Jewish lawyer, appeared in the action for the sole purpose of objecting to the jurisdiction of the court upon several grounds, but more especially for the reason that the defendant was a Jew, and that as such he uniformly observed Saturday of each week as 'holy time.'

"This case was used to tie up the business of two courts until it was finally taken to the appellate division of the Supreme Court, where Judge Adams rendered a decision in which he said:

"'In order to give to this section the construction claimed by the defendant's counsel, we must hold that the legislature has not only utterly ignored this elementary principle (that to constitute a crime there must be not only the act itself, but a criminal intent must accompany the act), but, in violation thereof, has declared that, while in the case specified, malice or intent must exist in order to constitute the crime of procuring a process to be served on Saturday or of procuring a civil action to be adjourned to that day, the crime of serving a process which is returnable on Saturday may be committed without any intent accompanying the act.

"'This proposition, it seems to us, has only to be stated to render its absurdity manifest; for the person who served the summons in this action, as is generally the case, was a public officer; and it is fair to assume that he performed his official duty in this instance without knowing, or having any reason to suppose, that the party served regarded one day of the week as more sacred than another.

"'It is true that the defendant is a Jew, and certain racial characteristics may have manifested themselves to such an extent as to acquaint the officer with that fact, but there are other religions than the Jewish that require the observance of the seventh day of the week as "holy time," and, consequently, if the rule contended for is to obtain, an officer must somehow ascertain, in every instance before serving a process, that the party upon whom it is to be served does not come within the favored class; otherwise he renders himself amenable to the statute.

"'It is inconceivable that the legislature intended that a person thus serving a process returnable on Saturday, in ignorance of the fact that he was in any way interfering with the religious liberty of the party served, should be regarded as a criminal and it is equally certain that a conviction under such circumstances would be absurd and unjust, if not impossible. A construction of a statute, therefore, which leads to such a result should manifestly be avoided if practicable.'

"Judge Adams thereupon reversed the judgement of the county court and of the municipal court, with costs."

"Now Jewish politicians and Jewish lawyers are clever enough, as a rule," continued this magistrate. "Therefore it seems the more surprising that they should waste their time and efforts in placing such laws on the statute books, and trying to establish precedents by means of them. It is very stupid business. The ultimate effect is calculated to bring ridicule upon the Jew, and awaken suspicion, dislike and enmity against his race."

Another of the magistrates commented on the fact that in London, Jews were permitted to trade on Sunday by Act of Parliament, but only within the circumscribed limits of their ghetto. "When I was in London several years ago," he continued, "I was shown one of the Jewish Sunday markets in full swing. Opposite it was an English church. But trade was confined to the Yiddish district."

"But compared with New York, there is only a small Yiddish population in the British metropolis. Our millions of Jews are scattered throughout the city, and if we were to relax our Sunday laws in their favor, it would mean goodby to the Christian Sabbath. I cannot understand the attitude of the Jews on this question. They cheapen their own status by their conduct."

The Dearborn Independent, issue of 10 December 1921

73: Jews are Silent, the National Voice is Heard

By order of Louis Marshall, the American Jewish Committee and the B'nai B'rith, American Jewry has muffled the calculated furioso of its outcry, and contents itself now with occasional yelps. No longer do the syndicated sermons of the rabbis take their course across the country, saying the same old untrue things in the same old insincere way. No longer do editorial echoes spew vilification across pages supported by advertising blackmail levied upon the community. The outcry has ceased. Suddenly, on order, orderly as a regiment on parade, American Jewry has been turned from a termagant in action to a silent mystery. A most impressive illustration of the inner control exercised by Jewish leaders.

The psychology of it all, of course, is false. Jewry decided that it was the attention which it paid to *The Dearborn Independent* which gave these articles vogue. The leaders asserted, indeed, that had the Jews of the United States paid no attention, no one would have known that they were under scrutiny. It is a rather flattering criticism to lay upon their inability to meet the situation, but it lacks the merit of being true.

The Jews of the United States issued the order of silence, not out of wisdom but out of fear. And not out of fear of injustice, but out of fear of the truth. As soon as *The Dearborn Independent* issued it first articles on the New York Kehillah (and only the outer edges of the facts concerning that institution have as yet been set forth) it became evident to Jewish leaders that something had to be done. They did not challenge a public investigation; rather they used discretion, refused to answer even the questions of local reporters, made absurdly untrue denials, and gave every evidence of panic. Thereafter their safest course was silence.

Not that they are inactive. Fearing a sudden investigation by the authorities, the New York Kehillah has grown extremely busy and has doubled the guards all round. Why?

The reason is that there is a resolution in the United States Senate which points directly at the New York Kehillah. Prominent Jews have invaded Washington on one pretext or another, but only to turn their influence against that resolution. Why? The reason is that the resolution provides for an investigation by a Senate Committee into certain matters which have already been set forth in *The Dearborn Independent.*

Senate Resolution No. 60, introduced by Senator George H. Moses, of New Hampshire, provides that the Amalgamated Clothing Workers (a Jewish Bolshevik organization that is the feeder of Red activity throughout this country) be thoroughly investigated. In the official language of the Resolution: "The purposes, objects, methods and tactics of the Amalgamated Clothing Workers of America and its relations, if any, with other political organizations and quasi-political groups, and to make a report to the Senate of such findings."

Why has the New York Kehillah closed the portholes and called in help—"Gentile," by the way—to face a possible storm?

Why have the most prominent Jews in the United States hurried to Washington to hold conferences with Senators, their object being to bring pressure to bear against the Resolution?

Why should the American Jewish Committee, or members of it, why should Jewish clothing manufacturers who are the principal sufferers from the Amalgamated, why should Jewish members of the Baruch "war government" go to Washington to interfere with a proposed investigation? Why?

Because such an investigation of the Amalgamated, honestly conducted, would led straight through to the New York Kehillah and the American Jewish Committee and would rip the Jewish program in the United States clean open to the public gaze—if honestly conducted.

Next to stopping the investigation, the Jews will try to control it. That is really the greater danger. The country does not need the investigation to get the facts. Most of the facts can be given now. The country does need an investigation that will give the facts a governmental exposure. But a pro-Jewish investigation, an investigation conducted by elective office-holders who quake under "the fear of the Jews," would simply be an additional crime.

If the Jews lose their fight to kill the resolution, they have already started on their plans to control the initiative of, divert the course of, and defeat the purpose of the investigation.

If, therefore, the Jews are silent, they are not inactive.

But, the gain has been general. For instance, the country has been given quiet and leisure to hear what the non-Jews think. During the Jewish clamor, which was nothing more nor less than an attempt to stampede the public opinion of the United States, it was impossible to hear the voice of the people. Ministers who poured adulation upon the Jews were reported in the Press; but ministers who seriously handled the Jewish Question were not reported. Publications which could be induced to act as Judah's mouthpieces, were worked to the limit; publications which desired to preserve the value of their opinions, did not join the general hue and cry. In the succeeding lull, the still, small voice of American conviction, both Jewish and non-Jewish, began to be heard.

In public propaganda, after having felt it inadvisable to print any more telegraphic news from Palestine, because even the Jews could no longer juggle the truth, the spotlight was turned on Russia, and now the newspapers are filled with headlines intended to prepare the public for a new exodus when the Russian people awake to take back their land from the Jewish usurpers.

We are told that 6,000,000 Jews in Russia are in danger of violence. It is true. Much truer than the miles of telegraphic lies which have been printed about alleged "pogroms" in Russia and adjacent countries. *The Dearborn Independent* knows that in Eastern Europe the Jew has not been persecuted, but has consistently acted as persecutor. The proof of it is in the Jews' ability to flee; they have taken all the wealth of the people of those countries. Poles cannot flee, Rumanians cannot flee, Russians cannot flee; but after having squeezed the life out of those nations the Jews see the dark clouds of justice rolling toward them, and they are able to flee, filling the ships of the sea with their hosts. In fact, their desertion of the Jew-spoiled countries of Europe is as precipitate as was their desertion of Woodrow Wilson and the Democratic party last autumn—Barney Baruch ostentationsly staying behind to cover, if possible, the shamefulness of it. When the Jew has fried the fat and skimmed the cream, he's off. Gratitude and loyalty mean nothing to his people. They are persecutors in Poland. They are persecutors in Russia. They are persecutors in Palestine. They were the arch religious persecutors of history, as the best historians testify. They will be persecutors here as soon as they think they can start it. It is possible, however, that in the United States their anti-social career will be rolled back upon itself.

American magazines have begun to pay attention to the Jewish Question. If is a good sign. Even magazines cannot long ignore what all the people know. It is a good sign of the degree of freedom the Press still enjoys.

It is true, of course, that this freedom is not very great; indeed, not so great as it was a few years ago. But insofar as the Press is American it is impossible for Americans to think it will consent to be permanently gagged even by the Jews. There have been, it is true, some rather sad instances of editorial weakness. We know that of two oldest publishing firms, both of New York, one of them published a most scurrilous Jewish defense by a non-Jewish socialist who, if he has not deliberately lied, has shown too dark an ignorance of facts to command the confidence of a great publishing firm; and we know that that publication was made with a view to the value of the publisher's imprint and that Jews would undertake to buy tens of thousands of copies for gratuitous circulation.

Of the other old New York firm it is known that an American diplomat was advised if not compelled by it to eliminate from his forthcoming book nearly one third of its material because it dealt in an honest, straightforward American way with what this diplomat had seen with his own eyes of the development of the Jewish subjugation of Russia. Had this diplomat been dealing with his own opinions about the Jews or Russia, it might have been different; but he dealt with his official observations on the spot—observations literally invaluable to history. But this New York firm dared not, even in the interest of history, print the truth.

The experience of G. P. Putnam's Sons, of New York, is familiar to students of the question in recent months. The name of this firm is used because it has already appeared in public print with regard to a controversy it had with the American Jewish Committee.

The Putnams, acting on the ancient and honorable principle of the freedom of the Press, nay more, the duty of the Press to inform the people, reprinted last year "The Cause of World Unrest," which had first appeared as a series of articles in the London Morning Post and was later put into book form by the publishing house of Grant Richards, London. Both the newspaper and the publishing house are of the highest respectability and standing, as was also the house of Eyre and Spottiswoode which brought out the Protocols. Major George Haven Putnam, head of the firm of G. P. Putnam's Sons, is an American, a fair man, a careful publisher, and one who would not stoop to propagate a lie for any wealth.

This is not a defense of "The Cause of World Unrest." In the main the book is true. But it is not the result of original research. It does not make those small but important discriminations on which the Jews always rely to lead the people astray. It too often links in the downfall of Jewry those things which shall stand independently and gloriously when freed of their present insidious Jewish connections. On the whole, however, it maintains a correct view of world affairs. But it was not a book on which the Putnams could feel obliged to make a final stand, except as regards their right to print it.

However, a proper understanding of the book called for the Protocols, to which the book made frequent reference. So, like serviceable publishers, the Putnams announced that the Protocols would follow.

Whereupon the American Jewish Committee—which means Louis Marshall—got busy, and an interesting correspondence ensued. It is included in the report of the American Jewish Committee for 1921. Throughout the correspondence Louis Marshall was the dictator, but Major Putnam's position and statement of principles were correctly maintained. However, there were personal conferences which are not reported in the American Jewish Committee's report and there were Jews crowded into those personal conferences whose names do not appear in the correspondence, and there were fists banged on the table and loud threats—"boycott," of course—and altogether a rather typical scene enacted. The upshot of that passage was that, upon Major Putnam discovering that the Boston house of Small, Maynard & Company had published the Protocols, he decided that there was no call for his firm to do so. And now, in a letter to these same people, G. P. Putnam's Sons has decided to discontinue supplying copies of "The Cause of World Unrest" to the book trade.

It is a rather interesting story.

In Britain, of course, publications of the highest standing like "Blackwood's" and the "Nineteenth Century Review" can publish articles on the Jewish Question without regard to dictatorial Jewish attempts at control of the Press. In this country, however, the spies of Jewry are on the alert for every printed letter and syllable, and attempt to make editors feel uncomfortable, as if they were the instigators of pogroms, whenever they present an intelligent view of the question. Yet editors have not been able entirely to ignore it.

The reader is rather impressed with one quality common to all the articles that have been written, namely, the facts used are always those that have been given in *The Dearborn Independent*. Not that they necessarily have been copied from this magazine, but the facts are so well established that anyone who attempts even to "defend" the Jews must necessarily appeal to the same facts. Thus in "New York and the Real Jew," by Rollin Lynde Hartt, in the *New York Independent* for June 25, 1921, this is illustrated. It is pure Jewish publicity, but it must use the facts that have been used in this series. It must use them in order to extol the Jews. Mr. Hartt is not to be considered as a contributor to the Question; the article is mentioned merely as indicating what the American magazine editor is up against—and perhaps it is not quite fair to be hard on the editor of the New York Independent just at this time. The one flash of value in the entire article is this paragraph:

"Ambassador Page, then editor of the *Atlantic*, once remarked to me, 'The most interesting fellow in America is the Jew, but don't write about Jews; without intending it, you may precipitate the calamity America should be most anxious to prevent—I mean Jew-baiting'"

That is a strange assertion. The Jews must not be written about. To write about them, even with good intent, may bring evil upon them.

Not only a strange assertion, but a strange situation. To mention the Jew has always been dangerous to the non-Jew; but why also dangerous to the Jew? The Jewish explanation of anti-Semitism, that it is in the blood of the other races, that the moment they see a Jew they hate him, cannot be defended. Most non-Jews can testify that it is untrue of them. But it is a most amazing condition if even a mention of Jews arouses this feeling. Why should it?

However, the statement is of doubtful fact value. The Jew himself should be the first to protest against having to go concealed all his days. He should welcome the use of his definite racial name, and he should not demand that it always be used in laudatory connections. A Jew should not be a Jew when he is elected to the United States Senate, and a "Russian" or a "Pole" when he is caught bootlegging. He should take the luck of life with the other races, and this would come to him without discrimination if he did not first arouse the spirit of discrimination by insisting on discrimination in his own favor.

It is probably much nearer the truth to say that publicity is a preventive of "Jew-Baiting." People should not be confined in a condition which makes the use of the word "Jew" unusual. It should attract no more attention than does the use of any other racial name.

Mr. Page was, before his ambassadorial days, an editor of the *Atlantic Monthly*, a magazine which is an integral part of American life. To read the *Atlantic* is a certificate of character. It is one of the few publications that preserve the American spirit in literature. It is still worthy of the glory of the group that first made its name known wherever sound thought expressed in good writing is appreciated. The *Atlantic* is not in need of this appraisal, it is too well established in the regard of the class of minds that give color and sinew to our intellectual life. In Mr. Page's day the *Atlantic* may never have touched the Jewish Question with even so much as the tip of a discreet pen.

Nevertheless the *Atlantic* has in more recent years done its duty toward this as toward other questions. As far back as 1917, and that is very far back in view of the crowded years between, this old Boston magazine contained an article relating to the Jewish Question. The fact that the article was written by a Jew does not militate against it, but rather adds to its value. It contained valuable suggestions which the New York Kehillah and the American Jewish Committee might well devote the remaining years of their activity to disseminating and actualizing among the Jews of this country. Even today its counsel would save them from much of the folly which marks their attempts to combat what they call "persecution," and which is nothing but rather plain and charitable truth-telling.

This year the *Atlantic* has contained three articles of value on the Jewish Question. The first was by Professor Clay upon the situation in Palestine. Now, Professor Clay is not an anti-Semite, and certainly the *Atlantic* is not, and yet the article was received with a good deal of abuse from Jewish quarters. It told nothing but the truth, and it was rather pertinent truth too, which intelligent Jews doubtless welcomed. Professor Clay knew what he was writing about and his conclusions are not challenged by any authority on the subject.

In the May *Atlantic*, Ralph Philip Boas, who is understood to be of Jewish descent, wrote an article on "Jew-Baiting in America." He speaks rather disdainfully of publications which have endeavored to air the Jewish Question, but after having thus paid his tax to the Jews' prejudice, he proceeds in commendable fashion to contribute his thoughts to the matter. On the whole what he says is true, and the facts he uses as his foundation are of course the facts with which *The Dearborn Independent* has made its readers familiar.

He sets up his straw man of "Anti-Semitism" and after having valiantly destroyed it, to the applause of all of us, he gets down to serious business, and says some things which all could hope would pierce the Jewish consciousness to its innermost stronghold and set up new vibrations there.

And in the July *Atlantic*, Paul Scott Mowrer, Paris representative of the *Chicago Daily News*, has an article on "The Assimilation of Israel." Mr. Mowrer has won the respect of students of world affairs by the conscientious ability with which he has observed and reported big events in Europe. In his news reports he has not hesitated, when the facts justified it, to cable a story of Jewish participation in this or that movement. It was reported at one time that an attempt on his job had been made by certain Jewish influences, and it is certain that sections of the Jewish press bitterly attacked him. Yet Mr. Mowrer is probably no more interested in the Jewish Question than the many other big problems which have come within his journalistic ken, and it would be extremely unfair to regard him as in any way a propagandist for anything.

Mr. Mowrer talks about Israel when, of course, he means Judah. There is a deep distinction there. And he talks also about assimilation, which the Jew will not admit as a solution. He protects himself fore and aft by attacking the "anti-Semites," whoever they are, and by expressing his confidence in the Jews, but on all the decks of his article he gives the facts—and they are the same facts. It ought to be pretty well settled by this time that there are facts, not two sets of facts, but only one set of facts, concerning Jewish influence and activity.

The *World's Work* has taken the liberty of setting before the people the only real anti-Jewish article that has appeared in the United States since the present discussion of the Question began, and that article was written by Henry Morgenthau, a Jew whom the government is accustomed to honor whenever it would pay a compliment to the Jews. It turns out that he attacks Jewry in its most tender spot—Zionism. Most people have read it, for it was immediately turned into propaganda and published in hosts of newspapers, in many of them as first-column, first-page news. Mr. Morganthau said that Zionism was not a solution but a surrender. He attacks the whole Palestinian plan from every angle, and not only attacks but belittles it.

Of course, this is very interesting. But one doesn't understand the heat displayed. If the Jews wish to go back to Palestine, why all this objection? Mr. Morgenthau does not wish to go back, it is true; it is extremely difficult to find a Jew who does want to go back; but to desire a national land for the Jews is quite another thing, and most Jews desire that. The pity is that they carry into Palestine the same method which puts them upon question here, and they are in danger of tipping over the apple cart in their imperious disregard of the rights of men in Palestine.

Mr. Morgenthau's motive in writing the article must remain a mystery, because it would seem to leave him practically outside of American Jewry, and of course he is not outside. Not at all. Watch and see. His article was printed in a magazine read and supported by non-Jews and was intended for non-Jews; it was not a plea to his people, it was a kind of confidential explanation, whispered from behind the hand, to non-Jews.

Mr. Morgenthau knows that Zionism is the core of Jewry in this country. The Zionists rule. The Zionists, and not the Americans, dictate the policy of American Jewry. The Zionist program was the only program that went unaltered through the Peace Conference at Versailles. Zionism is the heart of Jewish aspiration. "Not of American Jews," Mr. Morgenthau may retort. But who are the American Jews? Inquire of the recent convention of Zionists at Cleveland for information.

That convention is worth a story by itself, but it explains why the World's Work stopped its press for the July issue and made an insertion of eight extra pages for the accommodation of Mr. Morgenthau's article. The Jews who call themselves Americans had been thrown down and out by the Cleveland convention, and Russian Jews proved themselves the stronger.

It was an event that called for quick explanation. The humiliation of the Americans was something to be covered as speedily as possible. Why the *World's Work* should have been chosen as the vehicle is not known. But the presses were stopped and the Morgenthau backfire started.

Mr. Morgenthau's article as a Jewish pronouncement is negligible, but the Editor's Note that preceded it has the value of unbiased testimony. Referring to the world organization of Zionists, whose chief officer stepped over here from Europe and simply slammed the American Jewish leaders out of office, the editor of the *World's Work* has this to say:

"This world organization has a highly centralized form of government. This consists of an international committee, including representatives from all countries that have a local organization. But the real control is vested in what is known as the 'Inner Actions Council.' This is a compact body of only seven men and it is dominated by the Jews of Europe."

The "Jews of Europe" might be still more definitely described as the "Jews of Russia." And "Dr. Chaim Weizmann, from London" might more accurately be described as from Pinsk, Russia.

The Russian Jews won, as they have always won, for they are the originators and corruptors of the false political Zionism which is leading so many Jews to disappointment and distress.

The point in all this is that in the silence of the Jewish regimented protest, the voice of the country has had a chance to be heard. The religious press has not been mentioned here, for it deserves a separate account, nor have the many newspapers which have reacted from the previously imposed burden of Jewish propaganda. Editorial speech is becoming freer. Jews themselves are coming to see that the call is not for abuse, but for a clean-up. The expression of the press of the country indicates that there is a Jewish Question and that the Jews used the worst possible tactics in trying to suppress the knowledge of it. They behaved in a way to show what bad masters they would be if given the chance, and what essential cowardice controls their actions. One by one the holds they gained by force of fear, are being loosened. And if the Jews would lay up capital on which to draw—the capital of public confidence in their desire to do the right thing—they would go around and loosen the holds they still have. This, however, is not expected of them. It requires too much foresight.

The Dearborn Independent, issue of 30 July 1921

74: What Jews Attempted Where They Had Power

The time of the year has come when Christians implore the tolerance of Jews while Christmas is being celebrated. If the Jews will only permit the Christians to celebrate Christmas in their schools, their homes, their churches—in their city squares and country villages—there will be more disposition on the part of the public to believe the Jewish boasts of tolerance.

It is not yet announced whether the Jews will give their permission or not. But that there are inquiries being made into the matter is indicated by this article in the *Brooklyn Eagle*, of October 31:

"Canon William Sheafe Chase today made public a letter he has sent to the secretary of the Board of Education asking for a copy of rules and regulations which, he alleged, forbid the telling of a Christ story at Christmas time in the public schools. Canon Chase said that the attention of the Federation of Churches has been called to a statement of a kindergarten teacher who last year said she had told such a story and had been notified that 'she will be removed from her position if she repeats such an exercise this Christmas.'

"He said that the Supreme Court of the United States has said that this is a Christian country and 'the courts in the State of New York have said that Christianity is the common law of our land.'" Dr. Chase added:

"'This government has treated the Hebrew more generously than any other nation in the world. I believe that the people generally, Hebrew as well as Christian, are very glad to enter into the spirit of Christmas time. Any attempt, therefore, to eliminate Christ from the hymns of our country, from the reading books, and from the religious holidays of the Christian people, I believe, is not instigated by the Hebrews as a whole, but by certain misguided leaders of Jewish religion.'"

This is a variation of the Christmas theme. Instead of looking forward to Christmas, it is a spirit of inquiry as to how far we can go at Christmas. We are asking whether we dare, as Christians in a Christian land, whisper the Name that gives Christmas its meaning. That is, the Christians are doing the Christmas asking early this year. Christian teachers want to know if they will be discharged if they give their classes a bit of Christmas flavor, as all our teachers gave us when we were young.

The contrast between the schools which we of the mature generation attended when we were young, and the schools of today whose pupils are carefully screened from the fact that Christmas celebrates Christ, is such a contrast as ought to give mature Americans a pause.

But, if past experience be the standard of judgement, the appeal to Jewish tolerance in New York will be futile. If Christians do not take their rights, it is certain the Jews will never grant them. It would be un-Jewish to do so; and the ceaseless cry of the leaders is, "Be Jewish!"

Any number of instances could be cited of the whip which Jewish leaders crack across the educational and political systems of the City of New York, but one or two must serve for the present.

The first case to be considered is that of Rev. William Carter, D.D., given in "Who's Who in America" as pastor of the Throop Avenue Presbyterian Church, Brooklyn; author of "The Gate of Janus," an epic story of the War; also of "Milton and His Masterpiece" and "Studies in the Pentateuch." He is an extensive traveler and a lecturer of reputation, his specialty being history and literature. At an important Y.M.C.A. center he has lectured for thirty consecutive weeks a year on "Current Events," which course was so successful that he was asked by the New York Board of Education to start a similar one at the Erasmus High School. For ten years, he has been engaged by the New York Board of Education as special lecturer in the popular evening extension courses.

The course Dr. Carter undertook was badly run down, but in six weeks the regular audience had been increased from 35 to 350. The plan of the lectures was to discuss a major topic selected by the Board, a second period was devoted to the discussion of current events, and a third period to questions from the audience.

Now it happened that for the week of November 15, 1920—just a year ago—the topic selected by the Board of Education was "The Racial Origins of the American People," a study of immigration. That is to say, Dr. Carter was asked to study that matter and discuss it publicly before his weekly lecture audience at Erasmus School. He did so, taking time to make a serious investigation of all phases of the subject.

He showed that just before the war—thirty days before the war—the highest peak of immigration was reached; the year ending June 30, 1914, having seen 1,403,000 aliens enter this country. Analyzing this great flood, he showed that whereas six per cent came from Great

Britain and two per cent came from Scandinavian countries, over ten per cent were Jews. The doctor's subject was "The Racial Origins of the American People."

Again, on the subject, "What Has Immigration Done for America?"—this subject also scheduled by the Board of Education Dr. Carter showed that some parts of Europe had given their worst instead of their best, and stated that the lowest percentage of immigration came from the best developed and most desirable countries, while the largest percentage came from the least desirable. For example, he differentiated between the desirable Italians and those who form the material for Black Hand activities. Speaking of Russia and Austro-Hungary, he made a reference to the Jews.

But Dr. Carter made a mistake—perhaps two. It is always difficult to tell just where the line falls between fear of giving offense and fear of being unfair. In any event, Dr. Carter gave every evidence of, let us say, fear of being unfair. But it is fear, and a Jew scents fear a long way; the man who fears even though he fear to be unfair is already marked by the Jew who may happen to be stationed to watch him.

So Dr. Carter, to avoid giving offense by this part of his lecture, did the usual thing which has always drawn sneers from the Jewish press; he began to pay compliments to the Jews on their good points. He spoke of their contributions to Art, Science, and Philosophy; to Statesmanship, Religion, and Philanthropy. He lauded their distinguished men by name, such as Disraeli, Rubinstein, Schiff, Kahn, even Rabbi Wise! He referred to his pride in counting many Jews among his personal friends. With all respect to Dr. Carter, it was the same old stuff usually handed out in such circumstances. Madison C. Peters made it unjustly famous, and American clergymen have been spouting it ever since.

If Dr. Carter will study the alleged contributions of the Jews to the Arts and Sciences, study this as carefully as he did the immigration theme, he may omit the praises from future lectures. And he may also revise his list of great Jews. But that is neither here nor there.

"As we have found bad elements in these other peoples," said Dr. Carter in this portion of his lecture, "so they are to be found in the Jew, and as the majority of these 143,000 Jews who came here the year before the war were from Russia, or Russian countries, let us not forget that the Jews themselves admit the Russian Jew is the worst of his race."

Apparently the audience remained unshocked. The question period came round and two Jews, a woman and a man, asked the lecturer why he had picked out the Russian Jew in particular for criticism. Dr. Carter replied that he had only given the evidence of the Jews themselves, that he was merely quoting what the Jews themselves had alleged time and again to explain certain matters. He added that the statement was universally accepted except by some who came from Russia.

A few days afterward the Board of Education sent word to Dr. Carter that complaints had been received against him for certain statements against the Jews, and calling upon him to explain. Dr. Carter is said to have replied that as only two Jews out of 400 people had objected at the lecture, he regarded that as evidence that the proprieties had not been violated.

Within a week, however, a more insistent communication was sent out by the Board of Education, stating that more letters of complaint had been received and citing Dr. Carter to meet his accusers at a special meeting of investigation.

Now begins as strange a proceeding as American may hope to see in this land of the free. It is really not as rare as some might think. It can be duplicated in a number of known and proved cases. The way the Carter case worked out was this:

Dr. Carter arrived, as summoned. There were seven Jews there before him. Four of these Jews admitted they had not attended the lecture, and one had never even heard of Dr. Carter before. The minister was alone. Not knowing what was afoot, and not having been told to bring witnesses who had heard his lecture, he was there—a lone Gentile before a Jewish tribunal.

The Jewish delegation was headed by a certain Rabbi C. H. Levy, who was referred to as secretary of the Board of Jewish Ministers, a union of rabbis in connection with the New York Kehillah, which is part of the general spy system of American Jewry. Rabbi Levy admitted that he had not attended the specific lecture complained of, nor any other lecture in the course, but declared he was there to "represent my people."

Well, Rabbi Levy's "people" were pretty well represented. There was hardly any other kind of people there except the Christian clergyman who was on trial for telling the truth as to public opinion, and Jewish opinion particularly, about the Russian Jew.

So the Inquisition upon the Gentile began. Six letters were read, most of them having been addressed to Dr. W. L. Ettinger, Superintendent of New York Schools. One of these letters asked Dr. Ettinger as a Jew not to allow his people to be maligned and misrepresented, but to see that this Gentile was stopped! After the reading of the letters, Dr. Carter was permitted to speak. He called attention to the similarity of the style in all the letters, a similarity which suggested to him the possibility of their having been dictated by one person.

At which Rabbi Levy flew into a passion—though no had mentioned his name. Dr. Carter also observed that as Dr. Ettinger had been appealed to on racial, religious and prejudiced grounds, it would be right to permit Dr. Carter time to get witnesses on his side. This was not permitted. He was on trial!

Even the Jews admitted, under straight questioning, that what Dr. Carter had said was not uttered invidiously. They admitted that he had referred to the undesirable elements of other races as well as of the Jews. It was admitted that the subject was not of his own choosing, but was assigned to him by the Board of Education. There was very little left at the end of the examination except to assume that the Jews were a sacrosanct race, with special privileges, a race whom no non-Jews should presume even to mention in anything but awe-filled tones.

That was the issue as it appeared that day. With half the Jewish population of the United States centered in the city of New York, they had assumed control of American education at its source. The group of Jews sitting in judgement on Dr. Carter were as serene in their control of the education of the Christians, as if they had been a Soviet court sitting in Moscow. They had succeeded in driving everything Christian out of the schools; they had succeeded in introducing the most sickening praise of their own race; they had looked forward to the teaching of Judaism as the universal morality!

It was further brought out that this Christian minister had been one of the men who had preached in favor of the Jews. He had been one of those public men on whom Jewish leaders could depend to respond with typical Christian generosity. He had delivered blows at race prejudice.

He had lauded the Jewish race and its leading figures. He had interpreted its commanding influence as the reward of diligence and ability. He had thundered against what Jewish reports had led him to believe was "the Crime at Kishineff." And for this he had been duly complimented by the Jewish Publication Society, and others. *But* he had now spoken a word of truth which the Jews disliked, and he was before them for trial and condemnation.

In the course of the examination it developed that he had been a citizen of the United States for thirty years, having come to this country from England at the age of 15. Rabbi Levy apparently missed the full fact, getting only the fact that Dr. Carter was born in England.

"May I inquire as to whether the gentleman is or is not a citizen of the United States?" said the rabbi in the air of one who was innocently uncovering a great exposure.

"I became a citizen over thirty years ago, as soon as the law allowed—as I trust you did," was Dr. Carter's straight thrust.

The rabbi dropped the subject. He did not take up the challenge as to his own citizenship. But that the matter burned in him is evidenced by his later remark:

"I'll see to it, notwithstanding all this, that you shall never speak again from any platform in New York, you dirty Englishman!"

Dr. Carter called the attention of the committee to the hatred and malignity expressed in the face, attitude and words of the enraged rabbi, and said he did not know whether it was a threat against his life, his pastorate, or his position as lecturer for the New York Board of Education.

The term "dirty" is rather an unusual one to apply to a race that has so long astonished Semitic countries by its insistence on its "bawth." That is to say, the accuracy of Rabbi Levy's description would draw about the same degree as would an appraisal of his gentlemanliness.

There was, fortunately, one other non-Jew present, namely, Ernest L. Crandall, supervisor of lectures, who was American enough to enter the fray. He addressed the hysterical little rabbi:

"I never have seen nor heard such bitterness and hatred expressed by any human being toward another as you have manifested here. You ought to be ashamed of yourself, and if I hear another word from you along such lines, I will have you thrown out!"

The future of Mr. Crandall should be worth watching. If he is apologetic for his principles, they will "get" him. If not, he may be the instrument of "getting" some things that are wrong with New York.

At any rate, Mr. Crandall acquitted Dr. Carter, and the Jews went out muttering.

It is rather an unusual and noteworthy fact, the acquittal of a man against whom the Jews had moved the charge and against whom the secretary of the Board of Jewish Ministers had uttered the aforesaid threat.

Dr. Carter went back to Erasmus school. He received from the Board of Education his appointments for the ensuing months. Affairs seemed to be going along as before. Then one day all the lecturers on "Current Events" in New York public schools received simultaneous notice that they must refrain from discussing the Jewish and Irish questions. With Zionism crowding the newspapers, and breeding a war in Mesopotamia, and dictating the policy of the diplomatic departments of Great Britain and the United States; with the Irish Question uppermost in the minds of millions and coloring the politics of the United States as well as challenging the full ability of the British Government—that is, with the two foremost "Current Events" seething throughout the world, orders were given through the New York Board of Education that lecturers must remain mum.

It was plain to be seen what had happened. Rabbi Levy, and those who worked with him, having failed in their personal attack, had achieved what they wanted another way—by an order given to lecturers not to speak about the Jewish or the Irish question.

Why lug in the Irish? The Irish were not protesting against discussion of the Irish Question. The Irish wanted the Irish Question discussed; they believed that the successful issue of the matter depended on wide and free discussion. It is beyond the realm of imagination that the Irish should ever ask, desire or sanction a gag on popular discussion of Irish affairs.

As to Dr. Carter, his audiences had been asking him questions about the Irish Question for three years. In Y.M.C.A., in public school, in people's forum, everywhere he had been asked for information about one or another phase of the Irish Question; and being a well informed man he was able to give answers. And no one had ever complained before. Indeed, it is said that at the next lecture he gave at Erasmus School, following the encounter with Rabbi Levy, the audience had asked questions touching the Irish Question, and Mr. Crandall was present and found no ground for criticism.

Yet soon thereafter came the order to observe complete silence on the Irish Question. Why?

Even the tyro in Jewish policy knows the answer. The Irish Question was lugged in to camouflage the order regarding the Jewish Question. That is a very common Jewish practice: any Gentile name will serve for concealment!

Imagine an Irishman and his family attending an evening lecture on "Current Events" and asking a question about the Irish situation. Imagine the lecturer saying, "I am forbidden to mention Ireland, or the

Irish, or the Irish Question on these premises." The Irishman, being a white man, would not be slow to see that somehow he was being discriminated against. He would demand to be told why the lecturer dared not mention the matter. And, being forbidden to mention the Jews either, the lecturer would not be able to say, "Those Jews down at the Board of Education have put their taboo on both the Jews and the Irish!" He would be breaking the rules even in giving the explanation.

But imagine the Irishman being classed with the Jew—the Irishman who wants publicity, with the Jew who fears it! How long would it take an Irishman to see that what was intended to be discrimination in favor of the Jew was discrimination against the Irish.

Yet that was precisely what the Jews of New York brought about in the public lecture system to make their point against a Christian clergyman who had told a very well-known truth about the Jews.

Of course, there is nothing in such an order that would appear to the Jew as being subversive. Suppression is his first thought. Suppress the paper! Suppress the investigation! Suppress the out-and-out speaker! Suppress the immigration discussion! Suppress the facts about the theater, about the money system, about the baseball scandal, about the bootlegging business! Suppress the lecturers of the City of New York! Fire them from their jobs unless they stand up like phonographs and recite what men like the sentinel rabbis of New York dictate!

The order was Jewish in every element of it. And as an American citizen who did not believe that American free speech should be a plaything of a crowd of aliens, Dr. Carter resigned his lectureship. It meant serious inconvenience and financial loss to him to do so at the end of December, when it was late to make further plans for the winter, but a principle was at stake, and he resigned.

Immediately the matter came into the newspapers and there was the usual ado—the Jewish writers throwing threats about recklessly; a few timid Americans asking what New York was coming to! One newspaper came out with an American editorial defending the right of free speech, but changed its tone somewhat upon receiving a deluge of Jewish protests threatening the paper with the displeasure of the Jews.

A man of less ability and of lower standing than Dr. Carter might have been overwhelmed by the storm. But he had at last struck rock and there he stood. At that time he was not known to have said anything detrimental to the Jews, and he is not known to have made subsequent remarks upon his experience. That is, being attacked by the Jews, he is not known to have attacked them in return. It is quite possible that he might be induced to do the Madison C. Peters stunt again and speak in praise of them, giving them the usual laudation which they themselves first prepared for our consumption. But nevertheless he has been, through no fault of his own, the focus of the vindictive policy which pursues the truth-teller. It may be distasteful to Dr. Carter to have his story thus told, but if he will begin anew his studies of the history and character of the International Jew, he will find his own experience a valuable commentary thereon.

Dr. Carter is only one of many. There are teachers in New York who could a tale unfold that would stir indignation to its depths—but there has never been any one to tell their story or take their side. Many of these stories are in the possession of *The Dearborn Independent.*

The Dearborn Independent, issue of 19 November 1921

75: The Jewish Question in Current Testimony

The Jewish Question continues to attract more and more attention. In many quarters a new tendency toward freedom of the press is observed, and the long-concealed truth is getting itself spoken bit by bit. It has been thought worth while, before going on to other phases of the study of the Jewish Question, to present in this article a few of the informative or confirmatory articles that have appeared in the public press. It need not be said that, with a single possible exception, none of the writers or publications here quoted could be called "anti-Semitic." Not even the most unreasonable Jew could append that term to any writer or publication here cited.

The Associated Press sent out a dispatch which was printed in American papers of August 24, as follows:

"Thousands of Russian Jews are crossing the Esthonian, Lithuanian and Polish borders every month, many sent from Soviet territory under protection of high Bolsheviki officials, according to travelers in the border states who recently have returned here. The opinion in neighboring states is that the exodus is prompted by fear of an approaching crisis. The fact that no appreciable organized Russian anti-Bolshevik movement has appeared since Baron Wrangel's forces were dissipated, leads observers of the situation here to believe that, should the overthrow of the Soviets occur this winter, it will take the nature of a popular uprising, supported by such troops as are not at the front. Many fear it will result in a widespread anti-Jewish program.

"For these reasons every Jewish family of means, and many that are destitute, are attempting to get out of Russia. They have no desire to tarry in Lithuania or Esthonia, but are seeking to enter Germany, with the idea of eventually reaching America."

To give the reader the background of this fear, we offer part of a letter from Kishinev which was received by a North Dakotan:

"My Dear Friend Gutsche:

"For one month no fugitives arrived, but now again many of them are coming from the Ukraine to Bessarabia, most of whom are Jews. They are a different lot than the former fugitives were; for they are wearing costly clothes, furs, precious stones, jewels, and so on, such as were seen before the war only by very well-to-do people, landowners and the like; they have money and money's worth. There is no doubt that these fugitives had leading positions in the Bolshevik régime, perhaps they were commissars, or even 'judges' on the 'Blood and Inquisition courts' of the so-called 'Tschreswytschaika' or short 'Tscheka'—their purses and pockets are filled, not with worthless paper money—for they themselves have manufactured that, millions and billions of it, which they have thrown before the Christian brood, the 'goies'—no, filled with money and precious jewels which no more show traces of blood and tears, but shine and glitter the same as in those happy hours of their rightful owners.

"But the people over there (in Russia.—Ed.) are awakening; they wonder about the source of all this terror. The children of Judah know the answer thereto, but they prefer to leave the ground which is becoming unsafe to stand upon; it is getting too hot for them. The Nemesis is raising her head from out the blood of innocence which calls to heaven for revenge. Yes, they fear the result of their actions and wish to save their skins before it is too late. In this they succeed, but not always are they allowed to keep their furs, their stones and precious metals; they overlooked the Rumanians. These people are very vain and greedy for costly things! The newcomers are on their way to America and the doors on all borders are willingly opened them, even to the soldier in the army. Only on again! The faster, the better! I think that some day America will have so many Semites that they (the Semites) will be looked upon the same as the colored, the black, yellow and brown races.

"Imagine for a moment that there were no Semites in Europe. Would the tragedy be so terrible now? Hardly! They have stirred up the people in all countries, have incited them to war, revolution and communism. They believe in the saying that 'there is good fishing in troubled waters.'

"But enough of 'the chosen people.' Some day they will reap what they have sown . . . .

". . . . Another picture—Every three or four days a 'razzia' (domiciliary search, graze) is being conducted in the city. Terror, fear and oppression drive the people from the streets, looking for hiding places. The people do not work, eat or sleep. Only stamping, cursing patrouilles are seen on the streets with their victims. In this manner 200 or 300 persons are often driven together: former civil and military officials, teachers, landlords, business men, and so on (only Christians, seldom Jews); among them also women. This group is then led to the 'Tschreswytschaika.' In front of the group are 40 to 50 armed red guards, infantry and on horses, right and left about the same number of guards, in the rear several carriages or an automobile with machine gun, and behind that again infantry and horseback riders. When this group is seen on the streets, everyone flees terrified; occupants of houses peep through cracks and press their hands to their hearts to see—what?—Father, brother, son or other relatives led away from their once happy homes, perhaps never to return again. This they know, those behind doors and windows, where occur hysterical spells, heart failures and deaths. Words cannot express the terror of it all.

"And then at the 'Tschreswytschaika'? There are youths, mostly circumcised, often half or wholly drunk! Should there be personal enemies among the 'judges,' the unfortunate ones are executed either the same day or the next one, but are sometimes also 'tried' like they 'tried' the heretics in the Inquisition chambers. Several of these creatures of the 'Tschreswytschaika' and especially a certain Wichmann—a Jew, of course—carry on terribly; he is the terror of the city and the flat land; he even kills Bolshevist Commissars and their wives should they now and then reveal a more humane feeling.

"They fear the reprisal and hasten across the borders, laden down with valuables.

"More suffering is caused in the cities by hunger and cold. The dead bodies are buried without coffins and often without clothes. How the people dwell in houses I shall, perhaps, relate next week. Enough for today. F. Horch."

The freedom of the Balkan Jew from the hunger and suffering which afflict the native peoples is vividly set forth in the words of an American:

"Our ship is the first to enter Libau on a peaceful mission since the war, they say. At any rate, our arrival has caused a great excitement, on account of the food cargo we have for these people. At present, we are tied up to a quay, in a narrow stream that seems to be also a sewer. Unloading our flour is a ticklish piece of work, due to the terrible hunger of the crowd that watches us. Whenever a bag breaks, people fight to scrape up the loose flour, which they put in cans along with a good portion of dirt that is mixed into it. . . . Everyone has a tin can and at noon there was almost a riot over a bucket of potato peelings that were tossed into the water. The people tied strings to their cans and went fishing for the peelings. They stand all day and beg us for food . . . . It is not a very pleasant sight—this crowd of emaciated, white-faced men and women, and big-eyed children.

"The most damnable thing about it all is the dozen Jews who flit like magpies through the crowd. They are young, soft, well-groomed and prosperous. They carry canes, wear new straw hats, and resemble the kind you see in the States. They have nothing in common with the other people. They have money, plenty of it, and they seem to think this ship is a floating pedlar's cart and tobacco store. They come up the gangway and wave British five-pound notes in the air, offering them for a carton of cigarettes. Or, they have gold watches that they will trade for a few pounds of soap. From the looks that other people favor them with, I do not wonder that we hear about periodic slaughters of the Jews in Russia. These fellows look too prosperous in comparison with the rest of the population to suit me."

The peculiar character of the Jewish cruelty in Russia is so little in accord with the character of the Jews as we propagandized Americans have been taught to conceive it, that even *The Dearborn Independent*, in its desire to present a consistent account of Jewish activities as they relate to the United States, has not opened this special phase of the study of the Jewish psychology. The Sadism displayed throughout the Russian Terror has been discussed briefly in "*The World Significance of the Russian Revolution*," by George Pitt-Rivers.

There is, however, American Jewish testimony on the same point. It is found in the April, 1921 number of the Hebrew Christian Alliance Quarterly. In an article entitled "Persecution Is Not the Monopoly of Christianity and Is Contrary to Its Principles," the Rev. M. Malbert, B.A., of Ottawa, Ontario, says:

"We must now proceed to deal with our last point. The Jews blame Christianity for its persecuting spirit. They consider it a monstrous thing to persecute another person for his convictions. Now, the question is, are they themselves free from the persecuting zeal? I am going to show that real religious persecution is uniquely Jewish, and that they themselves have been the relentless persecutors. In the year 120 B.C., John Hyrcanus, son of Simon, the last of the Maccabean brothers, who fought against the Syrian hosts in defense of their religion, persecuted other religions. He destroyed the Samaritan Temple on Mount Gerizin. Next, he conquered the Idumeans and bade them choose between exile or Judaism. They chose the latter. That he made a mistake in forcing his religion on an unwilling people, may be seen in the treacherous Herodian dynasty, Idumean converts, who were a curse on the Jewish nation.

"The intolerant religious spirit among the Jews themselves is unique in history. In the Maccabean princes the royalty and the high priesthood were united in one person, King Alexander, third son of John Hyrcanus, who was a Sadducee. The Pharisees therefore hated him. In the year 95 B.C., on the Feast of Tabernacles, as he was officiating in his high priestly capacity in the Temple, instead of pouring the water on the altar, he spilled it at his feet. The congregation worshiping with the palm branches and citrons in their hands, noticing the water spilled at the high priest's feet, started to pelt him with them. The king's life was in danger and he was constrained to summon to his aid the Pisidian and Cilician mercenaries. Those fell on the people and slew 6,000 within the precincts of the Temple. The hostility of the Pharisees was more bitter against the king, and their hatred knew no bounds. But the king endeavored to make peace with them. He therefore summoned their chief men and told them that he was tired of the feuds and that he desired peace. What were their conditions? They replied, the death of the king.

"Then they actually set out to betray their country. They invited the Syrian king, Eucaerus, to invade Palestine and treacherously offered him their aid. Eucaerus advanced upon Judea with 43,000 men. The Pharisees kept their promise and fought in the camp of their country's enemy against their king, who was eventually defeated. The poor king, the descendant of the heroic Maccabees, wandered about in the mountains of Ephraim. At last, 6,000 Pharisees, conscience-stricken, returned to him from the Syrian camp. With these 6,000 penitents, he was able to force the Syrians from Judea. But the majority still remained hostile and made war against him, but they were finally defeated and reaped the fruits of punishment that they deserved.

"The Jewish king himself was intolerant and he forced many heathen cities to embrace Judaism; those who refused were destroyed. Simon ben Shetach, president of the Synhedrion, condemned 80 women to be crucified for witchcraft. The son of Simon ben Shetach was accused by his enemies of some breach of a religious precept and although the father himself knew him to be innocent, he nevertheless sentenced him to death and allowed him to be executed.

"Between the school of Hillel and Shammai there was constantly bloodshed. The trial and execution of Jesus were the natural outcome of religous intolerance. The greatest service to God a Jew thought possible was to persecute the Christians. Rabbi Tarphon said that the Gilion, that is, the Gospels and all the writings of the Minim, that is, the Apostolic Epistles, should be burned even with the holy name of God in them. He maintained that Christianity was more dangerous than paganism and he would rather fly to a heathen Temple than to a meeting house of the Minim.

"A curse against the Minim was inserted into the Jewish daily prayers at that time, which is still used by the congregations. Bar-Kosibah, the false Messiah, persecuted the Christians without mercy. Even in the time of Justinian, in the sixth century, the Jews massacred Christians in Caesarea and destroyed their churches. When Stephanus, the governor, attempted to defend the Christians, the Jews fell on him and slew him. In 608, the Jews of Antioch fell upon their Christian neighbors and killed them with fire and sword. The Patriach Anastasius, surnamed the Sinaite, was disgracefully illtreated by them and his body dragged through the streets, before he was finally put to death. About 614, the Persians advanced upon Palestine and the Jews, after joining their standard, massacred the Christians and destroyed their churches. Ninety thousand Christians perished in Jerusalem alone. The Jews expected fair play from the Persians as a reward, but were treated worse by them than by the Christians.

"In 628, the Emperor Heraclius had retaken Palestine from the Persians and when marching through Tiberius, he was entertained by a wealthy Jew named Benjamin, the same man who invited the Jews to join the Persians against the Byzantines; the emperor asked him what had induced him to betray so great an animosity against the Christians, to which he replied that they were the enemies of his religion. Yet they claim the prophecy of Isaiah in the fifty-third chapter, to have been fulfilled in them. 'He was oppressed, and he was afflicted yet he opened not his mouth.' They even persecuted Mohammed in the incipient stages of his career. They prejudiced the chief Arabs against him, helped his enemies to discredit him and endeavored to alienate his followers."

The article continues to give in detail the persecution to which the Jews subjected their own people who were progressive. It reminds one of the warning given to Rabbi Isaac M. Wise by Rabbi Lilienthal, when the former was urging the reform of Judaism: "If you want to be Christ you must expect to be crucified." ("Isaac Meyer Wise," p. 92) Readers of Gibbons' "Rise and Fall of the Roman Empire" will recall that in Volume 1, Chapter 16, he wrote severe words about the cruelty of the Jews. It will be agreed that only records of the most staggering cruelty could have driven the calm historian to the use of such terms. Readers will also observe, in the passage herewith quoted, that the desire for "the empire of the earth" which actuated the Jews of that period is the same as that discovered in the Protocols:

"From the reign of Nero to that of Antonius Pius, the Jew discovered a fierce impatience of the dominion of Rome, which repeatedly broke out in the most furious massacres and insurrections. Humanity is shocked at the recital of the horrid cruelties which they committed in the cities of Egypt, of Cyprus and of Cyrene, where they dwelt in the treacherous friendship with the unsuspecting natives; and we are tempted to applaud the severe retaliation which was exercised by the arm of the legions against a race of fanatics, whose dire and credulous superstitions seemed to render them the implacable enemies not only of the Roman Government, but of human kind. The enthusiasm of the Jews was supported . . . . by the flattering promise which they derived from their ancient oracles, that a conquering Messiah would soon arise, destined to break their fetters and to invest the favorites of heaven with the empire of the earth."

In footnotes to this passage, Gibbons gives revolting details of the methods used by the Jews of that period.

In all this work the Jewish Idea has the assistance of certain Christian sects who gloss over the inhumanity and immorality of certain courses of actions by saying that "these are doubtless the means by which God is giving the Jew his promised control of the world." This is one form of the un-Biblical conception, the un-Scriptural teaching, that the Jews are God's Chosen People.

Of all the sects following this error, none is more active than the so-called "Russellites," the followers of Pastor Russell, and officially known as the International Bible Students' Association.

It has been reported to *The Dearborn Independent* by numerous witnesses that Jewish interpreters at points of debarkation in Canada and the United States have circulated Russellite literature. The fact that a Jew would circulate any kind of Christian literature is sufficiently astonishing to cause inquiry. It is explained by the elaborate pro-Jewish propaganda which Russellism is conducting.

Not to go into this extensively at this time, suffice it to refer to handbill advertising in the Russian quarters of American cities. The fact that the literature is circulated among Russians and that meetings are held in Russian sections of our cities would seem to indicate a desire to explain to credulous Russians that Bolshevism, too, should be received as part of the circumstance by which the Jews are to obtain world rule. The handbills are headed "The Fifth Universal Kingdom," and in every meeting reported the speakers have declared that in 1914 the rule of the world was taken away from "us"—that is, the non-Jews who are the so-called "Gentiles"— and was given to God's Chosen People, who, according to this sect, are the Jews. Thus acquiescence in Bolshevism and every other form of revolutionary overturning is acquiescence in the will of God.

The teaching that world rule is already in the hand of the Jew is so novel, so unrelated to Biblical sources, as to warrant careful scrutiny for possible pro-Jewish connections.

But Palestine is not yet a fact, and other Bible students see in the present political movement a daring and God-defiant scheme destined to failure. Certainly there are great obstacles in the way—moral obstacles, matters of honor and humanity—which do not promise easily to disappear. The Jews of the world are discovering that they read too much into the Balfour Declaration and that Great Britain is not ready to violate her obligations to the Arabs. Jewish leaders are beginning to feel the weight of realities in the settlement of the land itself. The Jews are not going back. Those who have gone back are, a considerable and influential number of them, tainted with Russian Bolshevism.

The English people themselves are becoming dubious about the situation as is shown by the dispatch of the London correspondent of the *Detroit News* printed in the August 14 issue of that paper:

"Then there is the scarcity of accurate information from Palestine. The high commissioner, Sir Herbert Samuel, transmits reports to the British Government, but they are not published. Even the report which he made on going to Palestine two years ago to inquire into the exact status of affairs never has been made public. Lord Sydenham asked for it in the House of Lords, and, though Lord Curzon replied that the report contained nothing unsuitable for publication, it has never been given out. It is also charged that the Zionist Commission maintains a strict censorship; that even a petition to the king disappeared in transit; that letters have to be written guardedly. A series of articles by the special correspondent of the Times suddenly ceased, though the last, May 17, bore the line, 'To Be Continued.'

"News from Palestine is exceedingly scanty, and no one knows whether what does come through is trustworthy. It has been printed that Sir Herbert Samuel does not dare ride through the streets of Jerusalem without an armored car in attendance. For these reasons there is a great deal of suspicion in England that all is not well in Palestine."

The most outspoken word that has yet been uttered on the political dilemma in which Zionism places the Jew, appeared in an editorial entitled, "Political Judaism" in the Christian Century, of Chicago, a publication of weight and character:

"Political loyalty is one. Under the present world order it does not admit of division. The citizens of any nation may maintain a Platonic admiration for the political systems of neighboring nations, but their ultimate loyalty cannot be 'Platonized.' Spiritual Judaism is one thing. A Palestinian state, or a Jewish political organization anywhere else, is a very different thing—at least in Gentile estimation. . . .

"Once a Jewish state is set up in Palestine, in so far as it is accepted as the proper expression of Judaism, the Jew of the diaspora must surrender his religion. Is there any escape from this issue? The Jew can be a Jew anywhere, so long as his religious adherence carries with it no political implications. At least he can be an acknowledged Jew in every land were religious freedom is guaranteed or practiced. And even in states where an established religion other than Jewish debars him from the fullest and highest participation in the affairs of state, he can still hold to his religion without too serious embarrassment.

"But what would be the status of the Jew in any land of the present world when the profession of his religion would inevitably identify him with the fortunes and aspirations and diplomacy, even with the military policies, of a political state alien to the society of his residence and citizenship? The status seems, at least to the Gentile mind, altogether impossible. A revival of anti-Semitism, and its spread to lands where heretofore it has not prevailed, is not the least embarrassing of the inevitable results of such a move. How can the Jewish outlander maintain his own spiritual and mental integrity? It is not even necessary to imagine a possible precipitation of war between the new Jewish state and the land of his citizenship. War is not, let us hope, the necessary condition or even potentiality among separate political states. But it remains true, by the very nature of the present system of political organization, that political loyalty is one, and cannot be divided. Hyphenation, discriminating Americans are by this time well aware, must remain spiritual, or racial, or sentimental; it dare not become political under any circumstances.

"If the proposed new Jewish state in Palestine is to be and remain a province or dominion of the British Empire the way is smoothed for any Jew residing and claiming citizenship in any portion of the British Empire. But the way is decidedly roughened for the Jew elsewhere. The Briton is honored, especially in times of peace, in most regions of the world for his connection with so magnificent a political structure, but for that very reason his political loyalty is the more emphasized in his own mind and scrutinized by citizens of other political units. A Jew indentified with so insignificant a power as an independent Palestinian state must forever be, would, in many lands and on many occasions, be in a far more advantageous position when a resident of an outlying nation, than if he were recognized as a Briton. The anticipated dependence of a new Palestine upon British sovereignty thus fails to relieve the embarrassment of Zionism; it would seem rather to compound it."

The Dearborn Independent, issue of 27 August 1921

76: America's Jewish Enigma—Louis Marshall

Something of an enigma is Louis Marshall, whose name heads the list of organized Jewry in America, and who is known as the arch-protester against most things non-Jewish. He is head of nearly every Jewish movement that amounts to anything, and he is chief opponent of practically every non-Jewish movement that promises to amount to something. Yet he is known mostly as a name—and not a very Jewish name at that.

It would be interesting to know how the name of "Marshall" found its way to this Jewish gentleman. It is not a common name, even among Jews who change their names. Louis Marshall is the only "Marshall" listed in the *Jewish Encyclopedia*, and the only Jewish "Marshall" in the index of the publications of the American Jewish Historical Society. In the list of the annual contributors to the American Jewish Committee are to be found such names as Marshutz, Mayer, Massal, Maremort, Mannheimer, Marx, Morse, Mackler, Marcus, Morris, Moskowitz, Marks, Margolis, Mareck—but only one "Marshall," and that is Louis. Of any other prominent Jew it may be asked, "Which Straus?" "Which Untermeyer?" "Which Kahn?" "Which Schiff?"—but never, "Which Marshall?" for there is only one.

This in itself would indicate that Marshall is not a Jewish name. It is an American, or an Anglo-Saxon name transplanted into a Jewish family. But how and why are questions to which the public as yet have no answer.

Louis Marshall is head of the American Jewish Committee, and the American Jewish Committee is head of all official Jewish activity in the United States.

As head of the committee, he is also head of the executive committee of the New York Kehillah, an organization which is the active front of organized Jewry in New York, and the center of Jewish propaganda for the United States. The nominal head of the Kehillah is Rabbi Judah L. Magnes, a brother-in-law of Louis Marshall. Not only are the American Jewish Committee and the Kehillah linked officially (see chapter 33, s), but they are linked domestically as well. Louis nt of all the Jewish Committees of the world at Conference, and it is charged now, as it has been the Jewish Program is the only program that went es conference as it was drawn, and the so-called busily carrying out its terms today. A determined by Jews to have the Washington Conference take up the same ... olonel House was Louis Marshall's chief aid at Paris in forcing the Jewish Program on an unwilling world.

Louis Marshall has appeared in all the great Jewish cases. The impeachment of Governor Sulzer was a piece of Jewish revenge, but Louis Marshall was Sulzer's attorney. Sulzer was removed from the office of governor. The case of Leo Frank, a Jew, charged with the peculiarly vicious murder of a Georgia factory girl, was defended by Mr. Marshall. It was one of those cases where the whole world is whipped into excitement because a Jew is in trouble. It is almost an indication of the racial character of a culprit these days to note how much money is spent for him and how much fuss is raised concerning him. It seems to be a part of Jewish loyalty to prevent if possible the Gentile law being enforced against Jews.

The Dreyfus case and the Frank case are examples of the endless publicity the Jews secure in behalf of their own people. Frank was reprieved from the death sentence, and sent to prison, after which he was killed. That horrible act can be traced directly to the state of public opinion which was caused by raucous Jewish publicity which stopped at nothing to attain its ends.

To this day the state of Georgia is, in the average mind, part of an association of ideas directly traceable to this Jewish propaganda. Jewish publicity did to Georgia what it did to Russia—grossly misrepresented it, and so ceaselessly as to create a false impression generally. It is not without reason that the Ku Klux Klan was revived in Georgia and that Jews were excluded from membership.

Louis Marshall is chairman of the board and of the executive committee of the Jewish Theological Seminary of America, whose principal theologian, Mordecai M. Kaplan, is the leading exponent of an educational plan by which Judaism can be made to supersede Christianity in the United States. Under cover of synagogal activities, which he knows that the well-known tolerance of the American people will never suspect, Rabbi Kaplan has thought out and systemized and launched a program to that end, certainly not without the approval of Mr. Marshall.

Louis Marshall is not the world leader of Jewry, but he is well advanced in Jewry's world counsel, as is seen by the fact that international Jewry reports to him, and also by the fact that he headed the Jews at the "kosher conference"—as the Versailles assemblage was known among those on the inside. Strange things happened in Paris. Mr. Marshall and "Colonel" House had affairs very well in hand between them. President Wilson sent a delegation to Syria to find out just what the contention of the Syrians was against the Jews, but that report has never seen the light of day. But it was the easiest thing imaginable to keep the President informed as to what the Jews of New York thought (that is, the few who had not taken up their residence in Paris). For example, this prominent dispatch in the *New York Times* of May 27, 1919:

"Wilson gets Full Report of Jewish Protest Here.

"Copyright, 1919, by the *New York Times* Co.

"By Wireless to The *New York Times.*

"Paris, May 26.—Louis Marshall, who has succeeded Judge Mack as head of the Jewish Committee in Paris, was received by President Wilson this afternoon, and gave him a long cabled account of the Jewish mass meeting recently held in Madison Square Garden, including the full text of the resolutions adopted at the meeting . . . . and editorial comment in The Times and other papers . . . ."

When Russia fell, Louis Marshall hailed it with delight. The *New York Times* begins its story on March 19, 1917:

"Hailing the Russian upheaval as the greatest world event since the French Revolution, Louis Marshall in an interview for the *New York Times* last night said"—a number of things, among which was the statement that the events in Russia were no surprise. Of course they were not, the events being of Jewish origin, and Mr. Marshall being the recipient of the most intimate international news.

Even the new Russian revolutionary government made reports to Louis Marshall, as is shown by the dispatch printed in the *New York Times* of April 3, 1917, in which Baron Gunzburg reports what had been done to assure to the Jews the full advantage of the Russian upheaval.

This glorification of the Jewish overthrow of Russia, it must be remembered, occurred before the world knew what Bolshevism was, and before it realized that the revolution meant the withdrawal of the whole eastern front from the war. Russia was simply taken out of the war and the Central Powers left free to devote their whole attention to the western front. One of the resulting necessities was the immediate entrance of America into the conflict, and the prolongation of the hostilities for nearly two more years.

As the truth became known, Louis Marshall first defended, then explained, then denied—his latest position being that the Jews are against Bolshevism. He was brought to this position by the necessity of meeting the testimony of eye-witnesses as given to congressional investigation committees. This testimony came from responsible men whom even Mr. Marshall could not dispose of with a wave of his hand, and as time has gone on the testimony has increased to mountainous proportions that Bolshevism is Jewish in its origin, its method, its personnel and its purpose. Herman Bernstein, a member of Mr. Marshall's American Jewish Committee, has lately been preparing American public opinion for a great anti-Semitic movement in Russia. Certainly, it will be an anti-Semitic movement, because it will be anti-Bolshevist, and the Russian people, having lived with the hybrid for five years, are not mistaken as to its identity.

During the war, Mr. Marshall was the arch-protestor. While Mr. Baruch was running the war from the business end ("I probably had more power than perhaps any other man did in the war; doubtless that is true"), Mr. Marshall was running another side. We find him protesting because an army officer gave him instructions as to his duties as a registration official. It was Mr. Marshall who complained to the Secretary of War that a certain camp contractor, after trying out carpenters, had advertised for Christian carpenters only. It was to the discrimination in print that Mr. Marshall chiefly objected, it may be surmised, since it is the policy of his committee to make it impossible, or at least unhealthy, to use print to call attention to the Jew.

It was Mr. Marshall who compelled a change in the instructions sent out by the Provost Marshal General of the United States Army to the effect that "the foreign-born, especially Jews, are more apt to malinger than the native-born." It is said that a Jewish medical officer afterward confirmed this part of the instruction, saying that experience proved it. Nevertheless, President Wilson ordered that the paragraph be cut out.

It was Mr. Marshall who compelled the revision of the Plattsburg Officers' Training Manual. That valuable book rightly said that "the ideal officer is a Christian gentleman." Mr. Marshall wrote, wired, demanded, and the edition was changed. It now reads that "the ideal officer is a courteous gentleman," a big drop in idealism. There was nothing too unimportant to draw forth Mr. Marshall's protest. To take care of protests alone, he must have a large organization.

And yet with all this high-tension pro-Jewish activity, Mr. Marshall is not a self-advertising man, as is his law partner, Samuel Untermyer, who has been referred to as the arch-inquisitor against the Gentiles. Marshall is a name, a power, not so much a public figure.

As an informed Jew said about the two men:

"No, Marshall doesn't advertise himself like Sam, and he has never tried to feature himself in the newspapers for personal reasons. Outside his professional life he devotes himself exclusively to religious affairs." That is the way the American Jew like to describe the activities referred to above—"religious affairs." We shall soon see that they are political affairs.

Mr. Marshall is short, stocky, and aggressive. Like his brother-in-law, Rabbi Magnes, he works on the principle that "the Jew can do no wrong." For many years Mr. Marshall has lived in a four-story brownstone house, of the old-fashioned type, with a grilled door, in East Seventy-second street. This is an old-time "swell" neighborhood, once almost wholly occupied by wealthy Jews. It was as close as they could crowd to the choice Fifth Avenue corners, which had been pre-empted by the Yanderbilts, the Astors, and other rich families.

That Mr. Marshall regards the whole Jewish program in which he is engaged, not in its religious aspect alone, but in its world-wide political aspect, may be judged from his attitude on Zionism. Mr. Marshall wrote in 1918 as follows:

"I have never been identified and am not now in any way connected with the Zionist organization. I have never favored the creation of a sovereign Jewish state."

But Mr. Marshall says, "Let the Zionists go on. Don't interfere with them." Why? He writes:

"Zionism is but an incident of a far-reaching plan. It is merely a convenient peg on which to hang a powerful weapon. All the protests that non-Zionists may make would be futile to affect that policy."

He says that opposition to Zionism at that time would be dangerous. "I could give concrete examples of a most impressive nature in support of what I have said. I am not an alarmist, and even my enemies will give me credit for not being a coward, but my love for our people is such that even if I were disposed to combat Zionism, I would shrink from the responsibilities that might be entailed were I to do so." And in concluding this strange pronouncement, he says: "Give me the credit of believing that I am speaking advisedly."

Of course, there is more to Zionism than appears on the surface, but this is as close as anyone can come to finding a Jewish admission on the subject.

If in this country there is apprehension over the Jewish Problem, the activities of Louis Marshall have been the most powerful agents to evoke it. His propagandas have occasioned great resentment in many sections of the United States. His opposition to salutary immigration laws, his dictation to book and periodical publishers, as in the recent case of G. P. Putnam's Sons, who modified their publishing program on his order; his campaign against the use of "Christological expressions" by Federal, State and municipal officers; all have resulted in alarming the native population and harming the very cause he so indiscreetly advocates.

That this defender of "Jewish rights," and restless advocate of the Jewish religious propaganda, should make himself the leader in attacking the religion of the dominant race in this country, in ridiculing Sunday laws and heading an anti-Christianity campaign, seems, to say the least, inconsistent.

Mr. Marshall, who is regarded by the Jews as their greatest "constitutional" lawyer, since the decline of Edward Lauterbach (and that is a tale!) originated, in a series of legal arguments, the contention that "this is not a Christian country nor a Christian government." This argument he has expounded in many writings. He has built up a large host of followers among contentious Jews, who have elaborated on this theme in a variety of ways. It is one of the main arguments of those who are endeavoring to build up a "United Israel" in the United States.

Mr. Marshall maintains that the opening of deliberative assemblies and conventions with prayer is a "hollow mockery"; he ridicules "the absurd phrase 'In the name of God, Amen,'" as used in the beginning of wills. He opposes Sunday observance legislation as being "the cloak of hypocrisy." He advocates "crushing out every agitation which tends to introduce into the body politic the virus of religious controversy."

But Mr. Marshall himself has spent the last twenty years of his life in the "virus of religious controversy." A few of his more impertinent interferences have been noted above. These are, in the Jewish phrase, "religious activities" with a decidedly political tinge. The following extracts are quoted from the contentions of Mr. Marshall, published in the Menorah Journal, the official organ of the Jewish Chautauqua, that the United States is not a Christian country:

IS OURS A CHRISTIAN GOVERNMENT?

BY LOUIS MARSHALL

When, in 1892, Mr. Justice Brewer, in rendering the decision of the Supreme Court of the United States in the case of the Church of the Holy Trinity against the United States (144 U.S. 457), which involved an interpretation of the Alien Labor Law, indulged in the obiter remark that "this is a Christian nation," a subject was presented for the consideration of thoughtful minds which is of no ordinary importance.

The dictum of Mr. Justice Story in Vidal against Girard's Executors (2 How. U.S., 198), to the effect that Christianity was a part of the common law of Pennsylvania, is also relied upon, but is not an authoritative judicial determination of that proposition. The remark was not necessary to the decision.

The remarks of Mr. Justice Brewer, to which reference has already been made, were also unnecessary to the decision rendered by the court.

The fact that oaths are administered to witnesses, that the hollow mockery is pursued of opening deliberative assemblies and conventions with prayer, that wills begin with the absurd phrase "In the name of God, Amen," that gigantic missionary associations are in operation to establish Christian missions in every quarter of the globe, were all instanced. But none of these illustrations affords any valid proof in support of the assertion that "this is a Christian nation."

Our legislation relative to the observance of Sunday is such a mass of absurdities and inconsistencies that almost anything can be predicated thereon except the idea that our legislators are impressed with the notion that there is anything sacred in the day. According to the views of any section of the Christian church, the acts which I have enumerated as permitted would be regarded as sinful. Their legality in the eye of the law is a demonstration that the prohibitory enactments relating to Sunday are simply police regulations, and it should be the effort of every good American citizen to liberalize our Sunday legislation still more, so that it shall cease to be the cloak of hypocrisy.

As a final resort, we are told by our opponents that this is a Christian government because the majority of our citizens are adherents of the Christian faith; that this is a government of majorities, because government means force and majorities represent the preponderance of strength. This is a most dangerous doctrine . . . .

If the Christianity of the United States is to be questioned, the last person to initiate the inquiry should be a member of that race which had no hand in creating the Constitution or in the upbuilding of the country. If Christian prayers in public are a hollow mockery, and Sunday laws unreasonable, the last person in the world to oppose them should be a Jew.

Mr. Marshall has the advantage of being an American by birth. He was born in Syracuse, New York, in 1856, the son of Jacob and Zilli Marshall. After practicing law in Syracuse, he established himself in New York, became a Wall Street corporation lawyer, and his native country has afforded him generous means to win a large fortune.

The question arises whether it is patriotic for Mr. Marshall to implant into the minds of his foreign-born co-religionists the idea that this is not a Christian country, that Sunday laws should be opposed, and that the manners and customs of the native-born should be scorned and ridiculed. The effect has been that thousands of immigrant Jews from Eastern Europe are persistently violating Sunday laws in the large industrial centers of the country, that they are haled to court, lectured by judges, and fined. American Jews who are carrying into practice the teachings of Mr. Marshall and his followers are reaping the whirlwind of a natural resentment.

Mr. Marshall was the leader of the movement which led to the abrogation of the treaty between the United States and Russia. Whenever government boards or committees are appointed to investigate the actions, conduct or conditions of foreign-born Jews, great influences are immediately exerted to have Mr. Marshall made a member of such bodies to "protect" the Jewish interests.

As head of millions of organized Jews in the United States, Mr. Marshall has invariably wielded this influence by means of a campaign of "protests," to silence criticisms of Jewish wrongdoing. He thus protested when testimony was made before the Senate Sub-Committee in Washington, in 1919, that the Jewish East Side of New York was the hotbed of Bolshevism. Again he protested to Norman Hapgood against the editorial in *Harper's Weekly*, criticizing the activities of Jewish lobbyists in Washington.

Mr. Marshall describes himself in "Who's Who" as a leader in the fight for the abrogation of the treaty with Russia. That was a distinct interference in America's political affairs and was not a "religious activity" connected with the preservation of "Jewish rights" in the United States.

The limiting expression "in the United States" is, of course, our own assumption. It is doubtful if Mr. Marshall limits anything to the United States. He is a Jew and therefore an internationalist. He is ambassador of the "international nation of Jewry" to the Gentile world.

The pro-Jewish fights in which Mr. Marshall has been engaged in this country make a considerable list:

He fought the proposal of the Census Bureau to enumerate Jews as a race. As a result, there are no official figures, except those prepared by the American Jewish Committee, as to the Jewish population of the United States. The Census has them listed under a score of different nationalities, which is not only a non-descriptive method, but a deceptive one as well. At a pinch the Jewish authorities will admit of 3,500,000 Jews in the United States. The increase in the amount of Passover Bread required would indicate that there are 6,000,000 in the United States now! But the Government of the United States is entirely at sea, officially, as to the Jewish population of this country, except as the Jewish government in this country, as an act of courtesy, passes over certain figures to the government. The Jews have a "foreign office" through which they deal with the Government of the United States.

Mr. Marshall also fought the proposed naturalization laws that would deprive "Asiatics" of the privilege of becoming naturalized citizens. This was something of a confession!

Wherever there were extradition cases to be fought, preventing Jewish offenders from being extradited, Mr. Marshall was frequently one who assisted. This also was part of his "religious activities," perhaps.

He fought the right of the United States Government to restrict immigration. He has appeared oftener in Washington than any other Jew on this question.

In connection with this, it may be suggested to Mr. Marshall that if he is really interested in upholding the law of the land and restraining his own people from lawless acts, he could busy himself with profitable results if he would look into the smuggling of Jews across the Mexican and Canadian borders. And when that service is finished, he might look into the national Jewish system of bootlegging which, as a Jew of "religious activities," he should be concerned to break up.

Louis Marshall is leader of that movement which will force the Jew by law into places where he is not wanted. The law, compelling hotel keepers to permit Jews to make their hotels a place of resort if they want to, has been steadily pushed. Such a law is practically a Bolshevik order to destroy property, for it is commonly known what Jewish patronage does for public places. Where a few respectable Jews are permitted, others flock. And when one day they discover that the place they "patronize" is becoming known as "a Jew hotel" or a "Jew club," then all the Jews abandon it—but they cannot take the stigma with them. The place is known as "a Jew place," but lacks both Jew and Gentile patronage as a result.

When Louis Marshall succeeded in compelling by Jewish pressure and Jewish threats the Congress of the United States to break the treaty with Russia, he was laying a train of causes which resulted in a prolongation of the war and the utter subjugation of Russia. Russia serves the world today as a living illustration of the ruthlessness, the stupidity and the reality of Jewish power—endless power, fanatically mobilized for a vengeful end, but most stupidly administered. Does Mr. Marshall ever reflect on the grotesque stupidity of Jewish leadership?

It is regretted that space does not permit the publication here of the correspondence between Mr. Marshall and Major G. H. Putnam, the publisher, as set forth in the annual report of the American Jewish Committee. It illustrates quite vividly the methods by which Mr. Marshall secures the suppression of books and other publications which he does not like. Mr. Marshall, assisted by factors which are not mentioned in his letter, procured the suppression of the Protocols, after the house of Putnam had them ready to publish, and procured later the withdrawal of a book on the Jewish Question which had attracted wide attention both here and in England.

Mr. Marshall apparently has no confidence in "absurdities" appearing absurd to the reader, nor of "lies" appearing false; but he would constitute himself a censor and a guide of public reading, as well as of international legislation. If one might hazard a guess—Mr. Marshall's kind of leadership is on the wane.

The Dearborn Independent, issue of 26 November 1921

James Russell Lowell always declared "that he was of Jewish extraction and proud of his ancestry." If anybody has achieved an exceptionally high grade in a difficult course, he or she was probably Jewish.—*Syracuse Jewish Monthly.*

77: The Economic Plans of International Jews

The strength of Jewish money is in its internationalism. It stretches a chain of banks and centers of financial control across the world and plays them on the side of the game that favors Judah. This center was, and for the moment is, in Germany, at Frankfort-on-the-Main, but feverish anxiety now accompanies the fear that it may have to be moved. Destiny is overtaking the Jewish World Power. The gold which is their god—"the God of the living" is what they call their gold—is being brought overseas on every available ship and locked up in the vaults of Jewish bankers in North and South America, not to enrich this hemisphere but to mobilize Jewish financial power for any desperate stroke. Financial Jewry is afraid. It has a right to be afraid. Its conscience, still bloody from the war whose gains have not yet stopped, is in a troubled state.

Single Jewish banking houses in any country, however great such banks should grow, would be no menace. In spite of the fact that the richest bankers in the world are Jews, as mere bankers in their several countries they would not occasion alarm. In straight out-and-out banking, the Jew is not a success. The Rothschilds were never bankers in a proper sense; they were money-lenders to nations whose representatives they had corrupted to seek the loans. They did business precisely on the plane of the money-lender in the side street who induces the rich man's son to borrow a large sum, knowing that the father will pay. That is scarcely banking. Brains of that sort may "get" money, but will not "make" money. The deposit banking of the world is not done in Jewish banks anyway, even Jewish depositors preferring banks which are managed by non-Jews.

It is not, therefore, the success of the individual Jewish banking house that concerns us. Flabby-minded non-Jews who have been blinded by pro-Jewish propaganda find difficulty in seeing that point. They say that the individual Jewish business man has as much right to his business success as has anyone else. Which is a perfect Jewish platitude! Certainly he has. Who ever stated that he had not? But when you are dealing with a world chain of financial consulates, all of them linking up in a world system, none of them to be regarded as American banks, or British banks, or French banks, or Italian banks, or German banks, but all of them members of the Jewish World Banking System, you are obviously not dealing with individuals who are trying to make a living. You are then dealing with a mighty force for good or ill, and thus far, sad truth to know, the ill is mountainous in comparison.

Nor does this Jewish banking system require that in each country a Jewish house be the most important. It is not the wealth and importance of single houses, but the wealth and importance of the world chain, that gives the strength. Kuhn, Loeb & Company is far from being the most important financial house in the United States, but with its foreign connections, all Jewish, it takes on a new aspect. Kuhn, Loeb & Company is far from being the most important banking house in the United States, and yet it was an idea that came out of Kuhn, Loeb & Company's office that now dominates the monetary system of the United States. Paul Warburg, a German Jew, scion of the Jewish world banking group, is boosted into undue prominence and power through the pressure of banker-bought prestige in government circles. It is his connections Jewish ones—that count.

The Warburg idea in the United States, dovetailing with the Sterns, the Furstenbergs, the Sonnenscheins and the Sassoons and Samuels and Bleichroeders overseas, was something to wonder at. Jewish bankers ran this war as they have run every great war. No informed Jew will deny that. Most informed Jews have boasted of it as indicating the importance of their people. Above the nations at war was an international financial committee, all Jewish, looking down upon all the ruction and blood as serenely as American baseball league directors look down upon a pennant series. Separated, each man tied to his country by ties of undivided nationalistic loyalty, none of these would have amounted to much. United, as a super-national financial board, knowing the secrets of all the nations, conferring one with another in all sorts of ways, even during the hardest days when all communication between countries was supposed to be locked by war, deciding the duration of the war and the hour of so-called peace, these groups constitute a danger which no one doubts after once having clearly seen it.

Men who can thus manipulate money in time of war can do so in time of peace. The United States is living under some of that peace manipulation now.

The reader of the Protocols is much impressed by the financial notes that are sounded throughout their proposals. The Jewish defense against the Protocols, that they were written by a criminal or madman, is intended only for those who have not read the Protocols, or who have overlooked the financial plans they offer. Madmen and criminals do not coolly dissect one money system and invent another, as do the Protocolists.

It will be worth while, in view of the sidelights that these articles have thrown on the money question, to recall some of the forecasts and plans made in these most remarkable documents which have been attributed to the Wise Men of Zion, the world leaders of the inner council.

"When we sink, we become a revolutionary proletariat, the subordinate officers of the revolutionary party; when we rise, there rises also our terrible power of the purse." So wrote the great Jewish Zionist leader, Theodor Herzl, in his work, "A Jewish State," (p. 23). It is precisely that union of revolutionary tendencies and financial power that the world is facing now. Look at Russia, and look at the people who swarmed at Versailles and made the Peace Treaty. The Peace Treaty was written by financiers; it is the bill presented, not to a beaten foe, but to the world. Very few people have ever read it; but its operation is evident everywhere. The Jewish bankers the world over are shoveling in the gold.

Protocol VI is interesting in this connection:

"We shall soon begin to establish huge monopolies, colossal reservoirs of wealth, upon which even the big Gentile properties will be dependent to such an extent that they will all fall, together with the government credit, on the day following the political catastrophe."

Although these words were written with Europe in view (the United States not yet having been Judaized) their import is clear. At the present moment the number of business concerns in the hands of Jewish creditors, through "loans," is very large. The Jewish idea in business is to "borrow," instead of making the business stand on its own two feet. The trail of that idea is seen all over our land today.

"At the same time it is necessary to encourage trade and industry vigorously, and especially speculation, the function of which is to act as a counterpoise of industry. Without speculation, industry will cause private wealth to increase and tend to improve the position of agriculture by freeing the land from indebtedness for loans by the land banks. It is necessary for industry to deplete the land both of laborers and capital, and, through speculation, transfer all the money in the world into our hands. . . . .

"To destroy Gentile industry, we shall, as an incentive to this speculation, encourage among the Gentiles a strong demand for luxuries, all-enticing luxuries."

There is the Idea—Extravagance and Debt support the Jewish money-lender's power. He does not lend to build industry, but to drain it.

Independent industrial or agricultural wealth menaces his rule. Industry must be curbed by speculation; speculation must be encouraged by extravagance; an industrious people soon works itself free of its debt slavery; therefore invent new excitements to keep it in debt. Entice people from the farms, and so forth, and so forth, all which devices are now well known to the world.

"We will force up wages, which, however, will be of no benefit to workers, for we will at the same time cause a rise in the price of prime necessities, pretending that this is due to the decline of agriculture and cattle raising. We will also artfully and deeply undermine the sources of production by instilling in the workmen ideas of anarchy and encourage them in the use of alcohol. . . . ."

That wages were forced up, that they were of little profit to the workers, that prices did rise, that the above excuses were given, that anarchistic ideas now being circulated among the workers are Jewish and are circulated by Jews, that the illicit liquor business (as once was the legal liquor business) is entirely in the hands of Jews—these things everyone knows to be true.

The Protocols have been in non-Jewish knowledge since 1896. The British Museum has possessed a copy since 1906. Were they written by a prophet who foresaw, or by a power that foreordained?

The Jewish World Program is shown in these Protocols to be largely dependent on the false economic ideas it can induce the governments and peoples to accept. The false economic ideas—not only false, but cruelly deceptive and impossible—which are being sown among the masses of the people are the counterpart of the other false economic propaganda being sown in the upper circles of banking and government.

Jewish economic ideas are quite different from the ones which Jewish thinkers put out for others to follow.

Jewish bankers know better than anyone else the utter falsity of the present system, but they profit by that falsity, and they are ruining non-Jewish rule by that falsity, and they are establishing Judah by that falsity, and they will try to maintain that falsity until it brings the inevitable collapse, after which they hope to reorganize the world on Jewish monetary principles. So at least, the Protocols indicate. This bad régime is for the so-called Gentile period only.

The temporary nature of the present Jewish system, and the destruction it is meant to work in the world, is shown in the Third Protocol, where, after discussing ways and means to make the lower classes hate the well-to-do, it says:

"This hostility will be still more accentuated as the result of crises which will close stock exchange operations and stop the wheels of industry. Having organized such a general economic crisis by all the underground means available to us, and thanks to the assistance of gold, all of which is in our hands, we will throw whole crowds of workingmen into the streets simultaneously in all the countries of Europe. These crowds will gladly shed the blood of those whom they, in the simpicity of their ignorance, have envied since childhood and whose property they will then be able to loot."

All this, as the world knows, has occurred in Europe. The weapons first used were economic. The subjection of the people, the revolution, was first economic. The Jewish program profited by the split which Jewish ideas had been able to make between the upper and lower classes of "Gentile" society. "Divide and Rule," is the Jewish motto, as quoted in the Protocols.

"Divide the working class from the directing class. Divide the Catholic and Protestant churches." In brief, divide Christendom on economic, creedal, social and racial lines, while the Jew remains a solid body, able because of his solidarity to handle a divided world. And this plan has succeeded. Out of the disorder of the World War look how high the government of Judah has been placed in Russia, Austria, Germany, France, Italy, England and in the United States.

All the Jewish bankers are still in Russia. It was only the non-Jewish bankers who were shot and their property confiscated. Bolshevism has not abolished Capital, it has only stolen the Capital of the "Gentiles." And that is all that Jewish socialism or anarchism or Bolshevism is designed to do. Every banker who is caricatured with dollar marks on his clothes is a "Gentile" banker. Every capitalist publicly denounced in Red parades is a "Gentile" capitalist. Every big strike—railroad, steel, coal—is against "Gentile" industry. That is the purpose of the Red movement. It is alien, Jewish and anti-Christian.

Now, one of the interesting points about the Jewish financial scheme for the future as shown in the Protocols is the way in which it contrasts with the financial scheme which the Jewish groups now favor. As before stated, what the Protocolists now advise is not what they will adopt when their present advice has worked its hoped-for results.

The Protocols which detail the future financial plan of Jewish control are numbered XX and XXI. Protocol XX opens thus:

"Today we will speak of the financial program, the discussion of which I have postponed to the close of my report as it is the most difficult, decisive and concrete of our plans."

Throughout the recital the Protocolist harks back to the old (our present) financial system, and some of his remarks are worth transcribing here:

"You know that the gold standard destroyed the governments that accepted it, for it could not satisfy the demand for currency, especially as we removed as much gold as possible from circulation."

Whether the first statement is true remains to be seen; the others are demonstrably true. The gold in the ground and the gold that is money is under Jewish control, and they withdraw it when they will.

The stupid so-called "Gentile" says, "Why should they withdraw it? They cannot make any money that way!" Once again remember the distinction: it is not a matter of "making" money but of "getting" it; panics are more quickly profitable than is a long period of prosperity for men whose commodity is money. Indeed, men who deal in money as a commodity and on the Jewish plan, lose their prestige if prosperity continues too long. The banker who is a banker, who lives to serve industry and the community—he profits by prosperity, but not so the money sharks.

"We created economic crises for the Gentiles by the withdrawal of money from circulation. Mass capital stagnated, money was withdrawn from use by the various governments, and they in turn were obliged to turn back to the capitalists for loans. Such loans naturally embarrassed the governments owing to the payment of interest charges, and made them subservient to the capitalists. . . . ."

The withdrawal of money from circulation will create panics; everyone knows that. Such withdrawal of money is within the decision of a very small group of men. Here in the United States we have been for a long fifteen months witnessing such a withdrawal and its effects. The word went by wire across the land, setting a date. On that date values began to crash all over the country, and honest bankers tried to help, while others who knew the game profited hugely. As shown in the last article, money was withdrawn from legitimate use, that it might be lent to money speculators at six per cent, who in turn lent it to desperate people at rates as high as 30 per cent.

No intelligent person will attempt to explain such events on the ground of natural law or of honest practice. These things occurred in this country within recent days. It is the "elastic" system, you know, with the public as a monkey on one end of the "elastic." A splendid idea, no doubt, if administered by the non-Jewish method of doing the greatest possible good to the greatest number, but a deliberate assassination of life and property as it has been administered.

The Protocolists then pay their respects to governmental finance with the keenness that is well justified:

"Owing to methods allowed by irresponsible Gentile governments, their treasuries became empty. Then came the period of contracting loans and using up the assets that remained. This brought all the Gentile governments to bankruptcy."

As operating groups, the governments are bankrupt now. Only their power of confiscation keeps them up. The United States, commonly referred to as the richest country in the world, is just as poor as a government as is any other. It has nothing; it is in debt and borrowing. And its creditors are constantly discounting their obligations and are putting it into worse hands than ever. Even the Liberty Bonds are almost passed out of the hands of the people into the hands of Jewish fiscal agents who "get" money out of the necessities of the people who sell and out of the necessities of the government which borrowed. And if all signs do not fail, we shall one day be hearing in Congress pleas for special legislation in behalf of "the poor bond-holders." It is to be hoped when that day comes, some one will have mettle enough to stand up and declare who the "poor bond-holders" are. A list should be made now, for future reference.

"Every loan proves government inefficiency and ignorance of governmental rights. Loans, like the sword of Damocles, hangs above the heads of the rulers, who, instead of placing temporary taxes on their subjects, stretch forth their hands and beg for charity at the hands of our bankers. Essentially, foreign loans are leeches, which in no instance can be removed from the government body until they fall off of their own accord or the government itself removes them. But Gentile governments, instead of removing them, continue to place more. They must perish inevitably through exhaustion by voluntary blood-letting."

This is the plainly expressed criticism of the Jewish World Government upon the governments of the nations, and the truth of it cannot be gainsaid. It represents a statement of common wisdom upon which the Jewish World Program hopes to commend itself to the common people.

"Then why do not the Jewish world financiers help the nations out of this false financial policy?" Why, indeed? Jewish financiers are the inventors of such loans as they here describe, the barriers to such direct taxes as they here recommend. Listen—in the same page as above:

"You may well understand that such a policy, although inspired by us, cannot be followed by us."

That is historically true, whether it will prove prophetically true or not. Compromising loans and interest are Jewish devices, historically Jewish. Practically and at present the Jew prefers not to borrow except in such a way as to place all business risks on other people's money while he keeps his own safely, and the payment of interest is an abomination to him. These statements of the Protocols have at least these historical and racial confirmations.

The whole stupidity of the "Gentile" system by which Jewish International Financiers are enriched is clearly set forth in the same XXth Protocol:

"What is the effect of a loan, especially of a foreign loan, other than this? A loan is the issuance of government notes, pledging interest in proportion to the sum of borrowed capital. If the loan pays five per cent then in twenty years the government has paid the interest in vain, for it is equal to the sum of the loan; in forty years it has paid out an amount equal to the loan twice over; and in sixty years, three times, while the original debt remains unpaid."

Extremely simple, and yet it is the most generally ignored fact of all.

We live in a democracy, yet loans are contracted that always cost more than the amount of the loan, and no one has a word to say about it. We Americans do not know how much interest we pay every year, and we don't know to whom we pay it. We are still living under the lie that "A National Debt Is a National Blessing," the most delusive doctrine ever promulgated.

The amount of our National Debt is the measure of our enslavement to Jewish World Finance. The reader may observe in passing that Jewish apologists, John Spargo, Herman Bernstein, and others, say that the Protocols were put out by the secret police of the Russian Czarist régime. It is very unusual, is it not, to find the Czar's police interested in plans to remove graft from high finance, and preaching doctrines exactly contrary to the established system? The reader will find some amusement in searching for Russian police spies in the further development of the Jewish financial philosophy.

The purpose of Protocols XX and XXI is not to describe the present financial chaos in which the Gentiles are encouraged to continue; that system was described in previous Protocols; their purpose is rather to describe how the Jewish World Power plans to run things when the time comes.

This is well worth considering, for there are portions of the plan which would be worth adopting. The Jewish expectation of World Rule is, of course, absurd, although the mass of Jews sincerely hold it. Their condemnation is that they regard every degeneracy in society as bringing them a step nearer their goal, which explains the great assistance they give to all degenerative processes.

"When we ascend the thrones of the world, such financial expediencies, not being in accord with our interest, will be definitely eliminated."

That is the opening note. It is another version of the statement— "You may well understand that such a policy, although inspired by us, cannot be followed by us."

What, then, did the Protocolists, looking for world power, propose to eliminate?

(1) "The stock exchanges will be permanently suppressed, for we will not allow the prestige of our authority to be shaken by price fluctuations on our stocks. We will fix the full value legally without permitting any power to raise or lower it. Raising prices gives the pretext for lowering them—which was what we started with the stocks and bonds of the Gentiles."

(2) "The lawful confiscation of money in order to regulate its circulation."

(3) "We must introduce a unit of exchange based on the value of labor units regardless of whether paper or wood are used as the medium. We will issue money to meet the normal demands of every subject (citizen), adding a total sum for every birth and decreasing the total amount for every death."

(4) "Commercial paper will be bought by the government, which, instead of paying tribute on loans as at present, will grant loans on a

business basis. A measure of this character will prevent the stagnation of money, parasitism and laziness, qualities which were useful to us as long as the Gentiles maintained their independence, but which are not desirable to us when our kingdom comes."

(5) "We will replace stock exchanges by great government credit institutions, whose functions will be to tax trade paper according to government regulations. These institutions will be in such a position that they may market or buy as many as half a billion industrial shares a day." (The reader will bear in mind that "police spies" of agricultural Russia "forged this document" in 1896. As a gentleman remarked: If this is a forgery, what must the original have been!—Ed.) "Thus all industrial undertakings will become dependent on us. You may well imagine what power that will give us."

The Protocolist now being quoted also gives his attention to taxation (observe again the "Russian police spy" doing some "forging"). The builders of this plan for World Rule recognize that when the overturn comes they will have to be in a position to offer the people something extremely good in order to win their favor. This, of course, was the plan in Russia, although Russia presents no parallel to what the Protocolists hope to do for what they call their "kingdom." Russia was simply tortured in punishment. Russia was a passover offering. Russia is an example of Jewish vengeance, destruction, rage, not of the rule which International Jewry hopes to put over a world economically conquered through its own weakness and lust. Hear then the taxation plan:

(1) "When we become rulers, our autocratic government, as a first principle of self-protection, will avoid burdening the people with heavy taxes. It must not forget to play the part of father and protector. But as government organizations are costly, it is necessary to raise money for maintenance. Consequently, it is necessary to study carefully in this particular the problem of checks and balances."

(2) Kinds of taxes to be raised: (a) "The best method of taxation is to establish a progressive tax on property." (b) The receipt of purchase money or an inheritance will be subjected to a progressive stamp tax." (c) "Any transfer of personal property, whether in money or other form of value . . . ." (d) A luxury tax—"the latter will be taxed through the medium of a stamp impost."

The rich are to be taxed in proportion to their wealth: "A tax on a poor man is the seed of revolution and it is detrimental to the government which loses the big things in its pursuit of the small." But there are other shrewd reasons for thus taxing the rich (a) "Aside from this, the tax on capitalists will lessen the growth of wealth in private hands, where we have concentrated it at present as a counterweight to the governmental power of the Gentiles. . . . (b) "Such a measure will destroy the hatred of the poor toward the rich, who will be regarded as the financial support of the government and the exponents of peace and prosperity. The poor will realize that the rich are paying the money necessary to attain these things."

This was written at least as early as 1896. How many forms of taxation have come precisely as here outlined!

How illuminating also the following remark: "Money should circulate; and to hinder free circulation has a fatal effect upon the government mechanism, which it lubricates. That thickening of the lubricator may stop the correct functioning of the whole machine. The substitution of a part of money exchange by discount paper has created just such an impediment."

Remember that when next you hear the Jewish plan that "Gentiles" shall do business with their own bits of paper, while Jews keep the gold reserve safely in their own hands. If the crash comes, "Gentiles" have the paper and Jews the gold. If bits of paper serve ordinarily, the world may some time decide to do away with the gold. Certainly a system which rests on Cash yet works with Not-Cash, has disadvantages which depression and panic reveal. Says Protocol XXII— "We hold in our hands the greatest modern power—gold; in two days we could free it from our treasuries in any desired quantities."

The Jews are economists, esoteric and exoteric; they have one system to tangle up the "Gentiles," another which they hope to install when "Gentile" stupidity has bankrupted the world. The Jews are economists. Note the number of them who teach economics in the state universities. Says Protocol VIII:

"We will surround our government with a whole world of economists. It is for this reason that the science of economics is the chief subject of instruction taught by the Jews."

The Dearborn Independent, issue of 23 July 1921

78: A Jew Sees His People as Others See Them

This week we present another Jew's comment on his race and for the good of the race. Bert Levy has said these things before Jewish Women's Councils, and B'nai B'rith lodges, and they will assist readers of this series to an understanding of some of the truer, though minority, influences which are at work in American Jewry. He sincerely exposes every obvious defect, and it is to be hoped that one day, with as sincere a pen, he will go deeper. Mr. Levy's chosen title is:

FOR THE GOOD OF THE RACE

> From a far-off land I came, a sad-eyed, pale-faced, poetic young Jew, with an unspeakable love of my people burning in my heart. Of Polish-Russian parentage, there was implanted in my nature an indefinable sorrow (born perhaps of my father's and mother's persecution), which left me high-strung and sensitive to the anti-Semitic taunts of my schoolmates. Given to idle dreaming by some old abandoned shaft or roaming the deserted alluvial diggings of the little mining town of my youth, I would conjure up visions of that new world I had so often read about— that great country where there was no prejudice against my race—the New Jerusalem.
>
> Shyly hugging to my breast some borrowed American book or magazine I would seek the shadows of the huge decaying poppet legs and dream over the pages containing many Jewish faces, and I read with pride and gratitude of the high places occupied by my people in music, art, literature and the drama. Filled with Jewish names and good Jewish deeds was the story of this new Zion, and a longing to be among the great ones of my people took possession of me. Between my dear father and myself there was a bond of love too sacred for words, and when I looked upon his dear face for the last time in this world and bade him a sorrowful goodbye before my departure for the New Jerusalem, he held me close to his breast and whispered:

"Don't forget that you are a Jew, and if you need sympathy, love or help, go to your own race and show your Arba Kanfoth." (According to Deuteronomy XXII, 12, the Jews are commanded to wear fringe upon four corners of their vestures and this command is observed to the present day by wearing a special garment with these fringes, generally hidden by the ordinary clothes.)

I carried my father's words across the ocean in my heart and the memory of his tear-dimmed eyes and the pressure of his big loving arms has never left me; in fact, it is so strong at times that I find it hard to believe that he is not by my side telling me, in spite of many disappointments, that after all the Jews are still my brethren and sisters.

Words fail to describe my feelings as the beauties of the New World unfolded to me. In wonderful contrast to the melancholy aspect of my own country was the joyous color of Samoa, with its hallowed memories of Robert Louis Stevenson, lifted like some fairy veil out of the midst of the Pacific to give me a glimpse, as it were, of my dream of America—the New Jerusalem.

Oh, the wonderful days and wonderful nights out on that vast blue expanse, where God and His stars seemed so near that one formed a good resolution with every throb of the great engine far down below. On one of those nights I sat listening to some one playing in the music salon and I was inwardly thanking the Creator that there was a Puccini in the world and that he had given us "La Boheme."

There we were, thousands of miles from anywhere, languidly rolling under a perfect moonlit sky, listening to the plaintive airs that Puccini had coined for Mimi. There was hardly a sound but the gentle lapping of the waves breaking against the vessel's side till a slight commotion on deck up ahead caused some of the listeners to investigate. One of the passengers, an ex-Harvard man, returned with the remark:

"Oh it's only some damned Jew. He's fallen and hurt himself pretty badly."

Like a smudge on some beautiful picture was this anti-Semitic sentiment on such a night, and considering its source I felt deeply grieved. As I was the only other Jew in the first cabin I made my way to the stateroom where they had carried the victim of the accident and found him to be a tender-hearted old man who I subsequently learned had spent a long life in acts of charity toward his fellow men and women, regardless of creed. He was returning to end his days in Jerusalem (his Jerusalem, not the one of my dreams), where he could touch again the beloved stones of the wailing wall. Something in the old man's face, that "something" which was in the face of my father, my brother, that "something" which is in the face of every Jew, drew me to him, as it has drawn me to all Jews always, and I spent many intellectual hours by his bedside, picking up grains of wisdom which he had translated from the Talmud. I wished that the ex-Harvard man could have known that the old man's wrinkles were but the pathetic records of the massacres of his kith and kin which he had witnessed in his homeland and that he daily prayed for death to efface the awful memories.

Later on, the ex-Harvard man asked me to join in a deck game. I reminded him that I also was a "damned Jew."

"I'm sorry," he said. "I know what you refer to—that was an unfortunate slip I made the other night—merely a figure of speech, I assure you."

I found him a charming companion and soon in a cozy corner of the smoking room we became fast friends and I tried to win him over to think better of our people.

"I would like to hear your opinion of your fellow Jew after you have spent, say, twelve months in America," he said.

Since then I have walked the length and breadth of the great cities of America, and my very soul cried out to my fellow Jew: "Suppress Thyself!" The day I arrived in New York I learned that my dearest friend, my father, had passed away, and naturally my first thought was to say the kaddish, a prayer of the Jewish liturgy recited by orphans for the welfare of the souls of their deceased parents, somewhat after the fashion of the Catholic mass. Every male of Jewish blood at some time of his life recites this beautiful prayer. It does not matter how far one strays from the fold or how much one has denied the faith, there comes a time when the Jew in him asserts itself and he says the kaddish.

Public prayer among Jews can be recited only in the presence of ten males above the age of religious maturity, and this assembly is called minyan. Surely in this great city I would easily find a minyan, I thought; so I followed the line of least resistance, like any stranger in a strange land, and sought out the Jewish names best known to the public. I called at a business house uptown with the name of a great Hebrew over the door. He was the great man of whom I read with such pride in the little mining town at the other end of the world. Yes! The same Jewish face depicted in the huge photograph in the lobby I had seen in the magazine I had hugged so lovingly at home.

I made my way, full of hope, to his office and was asked by a doorkeeper my mission. I explained—the doorkeeper was a Hebrew that I desired to say kaddish for my father and that I wanted to form a minyan. With a sly wink he passed me on to several Hebrew clerks and office boys, each of whom smiled, sneered, and made his little joke about "greenhorns." Then I was ushered with many grimaces into the presence of the big man.

Just a minute's conversation convinced me that he was a Jew in appearance only, and that he had never known anything of the traditions, the romance, the art or the literature of our race. He didn't exactly know what minyan was, or pretended he didn't, but recommended me to "one of our people," as he put it, who ran a very popular chophouse close by. I began to realize that I was a stranger among my own people and that night I walked the streets of great New York with an aching heart. Everywhere in the hurrying crowds I saw the faces of my brethren and sisters, thousands, hundreds of thousands of them, hurrying, pushing, shoving brethren they were, with all the tenderness, the friendship and the Semitic look gone from their eyes.

"Oh God!" I thought, "are these the children of Israel? Is this the persecuted race—that people who had been scattered to the four corners of the earth?"

Hungry and weary, I made my way as if in a dream to the café of a great hotel. Everything in the huge room was glaringly false—marble pillars, oak beams, flowers, were all imitation: a big orchestra sat in a balcony with an artificial moon and a painted sky as a background; everywhere were lights, lights and more lights.

From table to table I went but I was roughly reminded that "this" was reserved and "that" was reserved. Presently glaringly gowned, bediamonded Jewish women, accompanied by equally vulgar Jewish men, filed in and occupied every seat, and between mouthfuls of food and drink their bodies would sway to the voices of other Jews who sang only of "Mississippi" and "Georgia." How these people did laugh when they caught sight of my foreign clothes and my pale, poetic face, and how they would have screamed with laughter had I shown them my Arba Kanfoth, that beautiful little token which my poor father fondly imagined would have made me understood in the New World.

Out in the night I went and found myself struggling in a torrent of humanity. Every time I received an extra bump or hard push I looked only to see that my antagonist was a Hebrew. On the street, in the cars, in the subway, or at the soda fountain, wherever I saw my fellow Jews blatantly shouting and rudely pushing, I, in spite of my indignation, felt the love of my race uppermost in my heart, and I wanted to cry out:

"Oh, Jew; dear brothers and sisters, suppress yourselves for the good of the race! Stand back! For the good of the race!"

Never in the world have our people known such a free country as this, and it is a privilege to be here, but at times a great fear comes over me that we are abusing that privilege. Amid the din of Jewish music and laughter, the newsboys are shouting the names of Jewish murderers (the Rosenthal case), the gunmen of the city. The bribe givers and the bribe takers depicted in the news sheets have Jewish countenances. The gambling house keepers—yes! yes! I know that there are Christians who are murderers, gamblers and informers, but the Jew is a marked man. He is distinct, apart, so distinct that in a crowd he is the first noticed.

It is for this reason that I would have my brethren and sisters suppress themselves, stand back! I would have real Jews take the worst of a bargain once in a while for the sake of the race. I would have them once in a while give up their seats in public conveyances, behave modestly in cafés, dress quietly, and give up the use of assumed Christian names.

There is nothing so pathetic as the man who, with Hebrew face, assumes a Christian name. I never go to a public place without wishing that my fellow Jew would talk less and appear less ostentatious. When one Hebrew comes in late to a show, marches down the aisle and on the front row deliberately obstructs the view of people in the audience as he stands slowly removing and folding his coat and gloves, he seems to cause more annoyance than if half a dozen Gentiles did the same thing. When a Jew stands aside and waits patiently at a ticket window, gives his seat to a lady on a street car or behaves in a refined manner in any walk of life, he immediately makes friends for our people.

Most of our people, I have found, have aggressive personalities: it is the aggressiveness which has enabled many immigrants to pass through Ellis Island to ownership of fine apartment houses all within a couple of years—but sometimes this aggressiveness becomes absolutely cruel, crushing from the very soul all the tender elements which go to make up a happy life.

Recently I thought with much bitterness of my father's last words to me: "If you need sympathy, love or help, go to your own race." Ill-health overcame me and I became involved in debt for a trifling amount. Each stage of my embarrassment and consequent suffering was contributed to by a brother Jew. First, the shyster lawyer, without principle or mercy, then his brutal clerks, sly and grafting. Next, a collector, absolutely callous, then the process server, and, at last, the "bouncer," sans heart, sans soul, sans everything. If all these agents of misfortune were Gentiles I could have borne it, but the greatest heartbreak of all was the fact that one and all of them were brother Jews. Why must a Jew always be in at the death, as it were?

There came a time soon after this when I walked the streets almost penniless. Seeking work, I applied at the store of a wealthy Hebrew. I explained to the well-groomed proprietor that I was an orthodox member of his race and appealed on that ground for a chance. He pooh-poohed the idea.

"My dear fellow," said he, "these are the enlightened days, when Judaism is not taken seriously, in fact, it doesn't pay. I am a Christian Cultist, I meet nice people and it helps my business."

Here was a poor fool with his head like the ostrich's—in the sand. I explained to him that being a Jew was not a question of religion but a question of blood. I told him that if a Jewish leopard ceased visiting the synagogue to go to a Christian Cultist chapel it did not necessarily get rid of its spots. I left him scratching his head, and I also lost the chance of a job in his store.

In and out of offices presided over by men with Jewish faces I trudged all day. Most of these men, I subsequently learned, belonged to New Thought, Christian Cultist and other up-to-date churches and societies—it was good for their business. They called themselves Christians, but nature's marks cannot be changed like one's clothes.

In the great theatrical districts I found thousands of my fellow Jews who had grown rich overnight by coining perhaps a popular song that had pleased the cabaret-mad crowd or by ridiculous impersonations of their race upon the music hall stages. A good many of these were young men, sons of fathers and mothers who had been driven from their own country with fire and sword.

The mothers and fathers stay at home blessing God every hour of the day and night for guiding them to such a country as this, while the sons and daughters are out at the theaters, in the halls and cabarets singing songs of Dixie. Passing by in this great throng are prominent actors, critics and playwrights, many under assumed names, simply because their own names are Jewish.

Flashing across the horizon as I write is a notorious Jewish doctor with a consumption cure. He could have been famous and honored had he but suppressed himself, instead of which he, with his commercial instinct and his press agent methods, made more enemies for the race. Many Gentiles, I will admit, have had consumption cures, but it remained for one of our people to float companies and open institutions before the "cure" was even reported upon by the government.

Tramping the city tired and weary of looking for friendly Jewish faces I found myself near the City Hall. I approached a milk station and bought a cent's worth of the most delicious milk I have ever tasted. A rough-looking fellow next to me said, as he smacked his lips:

"Pretty good stuff, that," and perhaps noting that I was a stranger, he added: "The guy who is doing this milk thing is saving the babies all right—he's some rich Jew—God bless him—I've got three babies of my own."

Hungering to hear a Jew praised I talked with this man for an hour, listening with keen enjoyment to the story of one of my race who had caused his millions to do good for the people irrespective of creed, and had kept himself suppressed. I learned of this Jew's efforts for the dying babies at home and for his starving co-religionists in Palestine and felt proud. Proud and happy for the first time, I sat in the little park watching the passing procession till I dozed off into a sound sleep. My happiness continued in my sleep, for I had a most beautiful dream.

Before me in my dream passed a grand parade; it was a series of "For the good of the race" tableaux. All the prominent professional Jews headed the procession with their real names and the name of their race emblazoned upon silk banners in letters of gold. Then came all the Hebrew gambling house keepers bearing aloft broken roulette wheels and other emblems of a discarded and disgraced "business."

Next in order was a large army of Hebrews who were professional bondsmen for arrested street walkers headed by two crooked ward politicians carrying a streamer with the words: "Henceforth we will go to work." These men looked a little sad as they marched along thinking of the easy money they were leaving behind, but the cheers of the multitude exulting over their great sacrifice somewhat atoned for their agony of mind. Next followed the amalgamated Jewish usurers, real estate and company promoters' union. This part of the parade took four hours and a half to pass a given point.

All the marchers had discarded their expensive clothing and their diamonds and were modestly attired. They had also discarded their automobiles—many of the prominent men in this section carried flags and banners upon which were inscribed the legends: "We will not lie about values." "We will not charge exorbitant interest" and "We will not water our stock." These inscriptions were received with incredulous looks of astonishment, and many of the crowd called out: "We're from Missouri," whatever that meant.

Then came a beautiful torchlight brigade called "The Hebrew Firebugs' Union." Nearly all these men had their hair close-cropped and wore prison clothes, a fact which filled the crowd with relief. Next came that part of the procession which showed the greatest following among its marchers. It was the large army of Hebrew "aggressives." Hundreds and thousands of them passed by with reformed looks upon their faces. Oh, I felt so happy as I read the buttons they wore and saw the flags they carried. Most of the streamers read: "We will suppress ourselves." "We will stand back and keep quiet." "We will be un-ostentatious." There they were, hundreds of well-known faces and types—end-seat hogs, front-seat hogs, loud talkers, inconsiderates, bargainers and the terrible army of people that go to make up the crowd which is directly responsible for the anti-Semitic feeling. The line of them was miles long.

I was awakened from my happy dream by a rude thump from a Jewish policeman who hurried me to a police station, where I was surrounded by shyster lawyers, my brethren, who wanted money with which they could square other brethren. I could not gain the services of a Hebrew bondsman because I had no pull. A Hebrew magistrate called me a "bum" and a loafer for going to sleep in a public park.

"Keep awake in the future," he said as I was roughly bundled out of the court.

Keep awake! This is the worst advice he could have given me, for I was so happy asleep and dreaming that my brethren and sisters had reformed and had become real Jews for the sake of the race.

I now look upon my police court humiliation as the best thing that could have happened to me, for a kindly old Jewish scholar, who acted as court interpreter, was attracted by my appearance. His long contact with human misery and his great experience with foreigners stranded in a strange country enabled him to understand me.

That night he took me to his poverty-stricken little room behind a delicatessen shop in the Ghetto. After supper he went to the street door and called the neighbors from their stoops. He called them by their first names and I said kaddish for my father as they stood around among the pickle barrels.

Since then I have lived among Jews, real Jews. I have learned that beneath the ragged coat of a push-cart vender there may beat a heart of gold, and that a poor seller of collar buttons or suspenders may be a student of the Talmud with a mind that is a gift of the gods.

Leaving the seething, modern, fashionable life of upper Broadway to enter the religious atmosphere of the numerous schools of Jewish literature on the East Side entails a violent contrast in conditions.

To see the deeply furrowed, time-scarred faces of the grand old men pouring over their beloved Talmud is to get a glimpse of another world—a world of resignation, peace and love. Within earshot of the thundering traffic of Broadway I stood gazing at the bowed figures engaged in study and prayer. As I gazed the sordid walls of the poverty-stricken room faded from my sight, and in their stead I saw (in my mind's eye) the wailing wall of Jerusalem or some ruin of the Holy City—a more fitting background to the rabbinical figures so strangely out of place in hustling America.

The great passion for the dead and gone past reflected in the Rembrandtesque faces of the aged students lends to their lives a religious grandeur which the uptown tourist (hastily passing on a rubber-neck wagon) would never suspect. Behind many a shabby-looking little store, or maybe, above some corner saloon, are the societies for the study of Hebrew literature, where congregate the types of Jewish scholars and philosophers that make the heart of the writer and artist glad.

Gray-haired, bewhiskered, sad old men, many of whom have tasted only the bitterness of life—yet such is their faith in the Almighty that they cling to the praying shawl and Bible to blot out the memory of a Kishineff—their lives of study and prayer amid abject poverty giving the lie to the fallacy that the Jew lives but for money.

I have often wandered among these scholars picking up the crumbs of wisdom which fall from the lips of the old men, grateful that my Jewish face and blood gave me the privilege to sit and sketch among them. Somehow or other my ramblings on the East Side are like the calm after the storm of the uptown struggle.

Many times, I have felt the heart tug—the longing to be among my people—the real Jews—and, leaving theatrical uptown, the land of make-believe and unrest, I have sought the little schools of study where the wonderful real old men who live by optimism and nourish their souls by faith teach me the lesson of patience and the love of humanity.

There is something restful and inspiring when an old man long past the biblical three score and ten—places his hand on your shoulder and murmurs in Yiddish, "It is God's will." I have envied the profound peace of many of these aged students living in the past and undisturbed by thoughts of the future. Their Jewish view of life is as beautiful as it is simple. It disregards neither earth nor heaven. I looks to earth and observes the evil prevailing among men; it thinks of heaven and ponders on the bliss of "the future state," and it urges man to strive to bring heaven on earth, to establish by justice and equity those blessed conditions on earth which so many associate with heaven.

Their Jewish view of death is equally beautiful. For those who die they feel no sorrow. Having once torn aside the veil which parts the known and the unknown, having once entered into the shadow, or rather the sunshine, of the beyond, they are better off in the other life. Whether death means eternal sleep or eternal life, those who have left our side, having passed into the arms of pitiless death, repose in a condition which should give survivors no cause for anxiety on account of their beloved dead.

In the pathetic chapter of "The Old Curiosity Shop," in which Dickens tells of the death of Little Nell, he makes the Schoolmaster utter these words of wisdom, on which all who mourn for their dead may well ponder. "If," said he, "one deliberate wish expressed in solemn terms above the bed could call her back to life, which of us would utter it?"

Dickens took this view of death from the Talmud.

The interpretation of a difficult passage from the Talmud, or the coining of an epigram, is as food and wine to the wise old students, and there is not an ill in their lives that cannot be soothed or a blessing that cannot be acknowledged in a quotation from their beloved book. To watch them at their study and devotions undisturbed by the turmoil about them is to marvel at the faith which has enabled some of them to live more than one hundred years with no other interest in life than their God and their books.

From the dingy windows of the schools the mass of sordid buildings looks to their eyes like the hills of Palestine, and the shriek of the passing elevated trains and the clanging of the car bells and the din of passing traffic disturb them not, for they live in the past.

The alleged Jew of the fashionable uptown lobster palaces—the blatant, pushing type, who is the direct cause of much anti-Semitic feeling—knows and cares nothing for the submerged student of his race. The latter is equally oblivious of the alleged Jew who is contemptuously referred to as a meshumad (apostate). But while the former stands out in the world of money and worldly success as a target for much abuse and hatred, the latter lives with books, unknown and unheeded, drawing from the Talmud a joy that riches cannot buy and solacing himself with the love of humanity.

In strong contrast to their fathers and grandfathers are the children of these old men. Modern America, with its opportunities for all, has torn them from the religious atmosphere and sent them uptown to become the lawyers, the artists and the actors.

The Jewish comedian of the vaudeville theater who nightly sets the audience shrieking at his Yiddish idioms is in nine cases out of ten the son of a scholar, and though the glamour of Broadway success claims him and he no longer lives home, in his heart of hearts he is a Jew and never forgets the old people. He will tell many stories of his parents to his Gentile friends, imitating and exaggerating their many characteristics, but he is mighty sore when he hears a Gentile do the same thing. But, after all, the comic Jew of the modern stage is but an imaginary sketch.

There is absolutely nothing humorous in these old men of Judea. Even in the sordid surroundings where you find them engaged in prayer or study, their attitude is one of quiet dignity—a dignity enhanced by their extreme old age. In a little dark den behind a poultry store I was sketching some of the old men at study. One old fellow one hundred and four years old was explaining to a young fellow of sixty a passage in the Talmud about which the latter was in doubt. Both men were without coats. The younger man had left his push-cart at the door, entirely forgetting the perishable goods thereon and quite oblivious to the fact that hundreds of dirty children were surrounding his cart and fooling with his wares. Other old men were in the school, and the background to their somber faces was the shop with its ghastly poultry suspended by the necks. One of the old Talmudic students would now and again leave his ponderous Bible to serve in the shop, returning after wrapping a fowl in a newspaper, to the verse he had been propounding. There was absolutely nothing humorous in all this, but I would love to have had some of my non-Jewish friends see how little thought of money and business the real Jew has.

Sometimes when I have felt full of shame at the behavior in public places of men and women with Jewish faces but with no Judaism in their hearts, I have wished that the simple, studious lives of the old men of the East Side could be the standard by which our race is judged, and that the Talmudic saying so aptly put into verse by Rabbi Myers was better known:

"Which is the path, both right and wise,
That for himself a man should find?
That which himself much dignifies,
And brings him honor from mankind."

The Dearborn Independent, issue of 7 May 1921

"It can hardly be an accident that antagonism directed against the Jews is to be found pretty much everywhere in the world where Jews and non-Jews are associated. And as the Jews are the common element of the situation it would seem probable, on the face of it, that the cause will be found in them rather than in the widely varying groups which feel this antagonism." —Jesse H. Holmes, in *The American Hebrew.*

79: Candid Address to Jews on the Jewish Problem

This is a candid address to the Jews of the United States. Without subterfuge, without flattery, wholly without fear of all that they may threaten or can do, this attempt is made to set before them the Jewish Question as their question, theirs to acknowledge, theirs to consider, theirs to solve.

It is not a question of *The Dearborn Independent* at all. This paper has merely become the vehicle of unwelcome facts which have finally thrust themselves up for final disposal in this country.

Damning this paper, compelling cheap city politicians to interfere with its sale, indulging in ribald humor concerning it, will not affect the facts at all.

What *The Dearborn Independent* says is true or it is untrue. If true, it ought to be considered. If untrue, it ought to be disproved. The present policy of Jewish leaders is to do neither, but to indulge in antics which go a long way toward illustrating what this paper has said.

What *The Dearborn Independent* says is true, and tens of thousands of Jews know it is true. No representative Jew has ever approached us with a denial of the truth of what has been stated in this paper. Neither has any unrepresentative Jew.

The chief objection made against the publication of the facts is always stated in this form: "What you say is true. Certain Jews are guilty of the things you charge. But why do you say 'Jew'? Why do you not say Al Wood, Morris Gest, Louis Marshall, Samuel Untermyer, 'Wolf' Lamar, Edward Lauterbach, Felix Warburg—why not let it go with these men's names, why say 'Jew'? When you say 'Jew,' it sounds as if you blamed all the Jews."

This objection has been seriously and courteously made by a number of Jews who have conferred with *The Dearborn Independent* on this series of articles, and has been as seriously and courteously considered.

What is the answer? First, that these men are Jews. Second, that being Jews these men constitute a problem for the Jews themselves. Third, it is time for some one to call attention to the necessity of cleaning up on that problem. There has been too much mincing of words. There has been too much concealment of names and relationship. The method which Jews were taking in this country with regard to concealment was heading them swiftly toward the same conditions which have menaced their race in Europe, and *The Dearborn Independent* would count no labor lost that would rouse the Jews to a sense of the responsibility which rests on them to solve the Jewish Question in this country, possibly the only country where it can be solved.

Let us be frank: if this paper had mentioned only the names of individual Jews, never mentioning their race, and had exposed them as isolated persons, it would have made no difference in the general Jewish reaction, the cry would still have been that "the Jews were being attacked"; whereas the other people of the country would have been just as much in the dark regarding the close bonds which unite all the groups of evil influences in this country. The purpose of this series of articles is to let in the light—to show the Jews generally that the stench had become too great, and to show the rest of the people where the stench arose.

The list of charges for the Jews of the United States to consider as affecting the distinguished members of their race is very serious. And the charges are true.

It is true that there is a distinct "Jewish idea" in business and professional life which has eaten away the traditional principles of honor on which Anglo-Saxon life was erected. Every Jew knows that, every non-Jew knows it. Here and there a Jew in business or professional life makes a breakaway from trickery, deception, dishonesty, and exploitation of the gullible public, and achieves success with honor, but that Jew also knows that the majority of his brethren in the same line practice different methods.

It is true that behind the amazing degeneracy of the modern stage and motion picture is a solid wall of Jewish ownership and control. This ownership and control must bear the responsibility for the rapid and dangerous deterioration which has come since such ownership and control was achieved.

It is true that behind all the shoddy and make-believe and adulteration in the staples of life is the Jewish idea of profits, "making the ephah small and the shekel great," and that the initiators of American business into these shady practices were Jewish. It is idle to retort that apt pupils have been found among non-Jews; the point is that before Jewish influence began to be felt in American business, sound quality and a fair price were the rule. It is the Jews' ceaseless boast that wherever they go they change business, but not for the better.

It is true that beneath all the network of trivializing influences in literature, art, politics, economics, fashion and sport, is Jewish influence controlled by Jewish groups. Their Orientalism has served as a subtle poison to dry up the sound serum of Anglo-Saxon morality on which this country thrived in its formative years. Is it necessary to specify? In every movement toward a lower standard, a looser relationship, especially toward the overthrow of the old Christian safeguards, do not Jewish names predominate?

These charges and many more have all been made in detail with evidence submitted, and need not be repeated here. The present purpose is simply to get the problem squarely before the Jews of the United States.

These charges are true, they cannot be disproved, Jewish leaders have not attempted to disprove them. Thousands of Jews have said that they are true.

Then where is the obstacle to a settlement?

This question is best answered by three typical replies made by Jews during the course of the present series.

1. "What you say is true, but you should not say it."

There is a principle, seldom expressed among the Jews, but always acted on, that Jews should not have public attention called to them except by themselves or their chosen spokesmen. This is unfortunate, because any establishment of the Jews as an accepted and trusted part of the general citizenry must include their being known as such. In this country the Jew should not only welcome the widest knowledge (unless he has something he fears to have known) but should himself undertake the exposure of those things which will eventually bring a shadow on the name of his race. The Jew has never done this. When exposure could no longer be suppressed, the Jewish attitude has always been one of defense, regardless of the merits of the case. "The Jew can do no wrong" is the principle acted upon. Never must a "Gentile" charge be admitted, however true it may be. Never must a "Gentile" reform be assisted, no matter how much needed.

Now, that principle may do for other countries, but not for the United States. If the Jew is wise, he ought speedily to take warning that in this country the old line of action will not succeed. If Jews continue to show a disposition to defend the malefactors of their race against the just expostulations of the rest of the people, they must not be surprised if the public begins to view them as all one crowd—an inner nation set against the outer nation.

2. "What you say is true, but your conclusion is wrong: it is not for the Jew to change to your standards, it is for you to change to the Jew's standards."

This is the fighting view. It admits that there are two ideas in conflict in the United States, what it unfairly terms the "Puritanic" idea, opposed by what it calls the Jewish Universal idea.

This view would command respect if it represented a superior morality in conflict with a lesser morality, if it represented a higher civilization against a lower civilization. Will any Jew contend that it does? Will any Jew deny that the influence of the Jewish idea in this generation is to break down such morality as we had? Will any Jew deny that the civilization of the United States before the advent of the Jews thither was superior to the highest civilization ever achieved by the Jews anywhere at any period of their history?

There are two ideas in conflict—that is certain. The Jewish idea has a tremendous infiltrating force and a serious degenerative power. It is a powerfully disintegrating influence. It eats the substance out of the civilization which it attacks, destroys its moral virility, throws down its reverence, saps its respect for authority, casts a shadow on every basic principle.

That is the way the Jewish idea works in American civilization. Moral gravitation being, like physical gravitation, downward, it is not difficult to seduce human nature to lower levels, but it is a massive task to lift it to higher levels of morality and reverence and sober justice. And this latter task, organized Jewish effort has never attempted. The campaign in the United States is a campaign for the breakdown of the ideas that now obtain, not a lifting of them to a higher degree of nobility.

If it were an attempt to substitute the austerity of the Mosaic law—the law given to Moses, not the ordinances decreed by Moses—for the half-hearted Christian idealism of the day, even that would be a task in which all right-hearted men could join. But Moses condemns the modern Jews more severely than anyone else could. They have rejected the Mosaic law. They have built their international power upon the exact opposite of the Mosaic law. Moses was given a law of human society which would have saved civilization its greatest tragedies. Moses has a social program, obedience to which for one day would completely wreck the Jewish international power. Moses is their judge, and when the Law is established Moses will be their destroyer.

Let the Jews think seriously what is this idea which they set up to follow. Let them penetrate the mists and seek out where this idea originated. Let them think forward and visualize the effect if this idea should become regnant. It will not become regnant here; there are safeguards here which the true Israelite will understand; but it is as certain as day that the idea will in the end destroy, utterly destroy, all who trust in it.

This much is gained, however, from the attitude we are now discussing: we have gained clarity of understanding as to just what it is that is in collision; it is two ideas, and one of them is the idea of disruption, fostered by the false and delusive hope that disruption will spare the disrupter.

3. "What you say is true, and we Jews could change it if we only would. The trouble is, we don't want to seem to be driven to it. But I don't see how otherwise we are to do it."

Many Jews will recognize this sentiment as their own, but they will be readier to express it to a non-Jew than to a Jew. Why? Because prophets must be prepared to suffer in Judah. "Well, if you insist on playing Christ, you must expect to be crucified," said Lilienthal to Isaac Wise. "O Jerusalem, that stonest them that are sent to thee!"

Yet there is need of prophets in Judah today, men who will rise among the people and tell them plainly. The rabbinate is utterly bankrupt of the prophetic spirit. It has fallen into the blindness of the old priesthood. Here and there a literary man attempts to speak, but Jewish "art" has so accustomed the Jews to make-believe that the writing is looked upon as a performance, nothing more.

No one with a sense for such things—and there are believers still left in Judah—will doubt that the times are ripe for a great change respecting the Jews. So strong is the feeling among the remnant of believing Jews that it is interpreted as forewarnings of the Messianic period. Among the Judaized Christian sects, other interpretations are given to the times, most of which are used to support political Zionism which represents the materialism and unbelief of present-day Judaism and which will undoubtedly fail as a national restorative and as a political program. But however misinterpretative these sectarian and Jewish conclusions may be, they indicate a sense of imminent change. A greater change is indicated than migration to Palestine would be—for that would not mean any change at all in the world, and certainly no change for the better in the fortunes of the Jews. Christians—misguided Christians, one must say—who see God's alleged will of universal Jewish dominion fulfilled by means of the Jews' defiance and despite of the Law given to Moses, ought to re-examine their ground for so strange and immoral a conclusion. The break-up of this civilization, this age of civilization, will occur because of the collapse of this system by which the Jew has obtained his hold on the nations. The system that gives him his hold is doomed, is passing, and the fallacy of Jewish tribal destiny to rule the world will pass with it.

With this change already on the threshold, prophets should be expected to arise in Judah to recall their people to the Law whose previous denial meant their overthrow. These prophets will not be of the "Reform school" which denies the God of Israel as a divine Person, nor will they be of the ultra-orthodox school which makes much of fringes and cookery—they will be of the race of the ancient prophets who spake boldly against Judah's violation of the fundamental law.

Our confidence is that a sufficient number of Jews will see the truth and act upon it.

What would be the greatest overturn the present Jewish idea, the disruptive Jewish idea, could possibly have? This: a knowledge that the way they are going is the way their own Law foredooms to failure, and that the people they hope to triumph over are the people their own Scriptures say they are not to triumph over.

The first is beyond dispute: there is no success for the Jew, no establishment of him in the world except upon the basic law given to Moses. In any other attempt he must fall when the structure collapses.

The second is in dispute, but is by no means beyond consideration, especially by Jews. In these matters the Jews are much wiser than the so-called Christians. There is among the Jews "the law of the brother" and "the law of the stranger."

The "law of the stranger" permits several important things which the "law of the brother" prohibits. The Jews have been treating the rest of the world, often intentionally, sometimes as a matter of course, according to the "law of the stranger." This is one of the influences which has helped to solidify Jewry against the rest of the world. Suppose it should be shown that the people in whose lands the Jews have never been persecuted, the people of those lands to which the Jews have never been "driven" but to which they have hopefully and joyfully come, are not "strangers" and are not to be treated as "strangers" and, so far from being "strangers," are really the leaders and rulers of that ethical stream of influence of which the Jews, but for their disloyalty to their destiny, might have been an important part!

Suppose it should be shown that Judah, the "driven" part of Israel, has been blindly attacking the "led" part of Israel. Suppose it should be shown that Judah is not the Israel upon whom great destiny is to come, but a small part of that Israel and not even a participating part, until it "returns, returns, returns."

If these things should once take hold of the intensified consciousness of Judah, as facts, there would be such a change in human society in general, such a change in the Jewish situation in particular, as would make a return to Palestine a mere summer excursion in comparison.

Jews are thinking about those very matters now. They are thinking from within. They are seeking a reason (the thoughtful among them) for the sense of unfitness which they feel when they adopt the traditional attitude of enmity toward the "others," the "others" in this case being the Anglo-Saxon peoples. The reason for this sense of impropriety is that here, in this land, the Jew will have to change his attitude of antagonism and dwell in peace as in a land prepared for him. Not as lord of it, by any means, but as a grateful wanderer at last come home. Not as a ruler, but as adding his bit to the righteousness, prosperity and peace of the people.

It is not a question of religion. Let the Jew get back his Mosaic religion—it is the most perfect social system ever devised and directly contrary to the practical modern Jew's idea of things.

It is not a question of intermarriage. Let the Jew keep as long as he pleases his idea that he is racially different. The suggestion of intermarriage is a crude one and always indicates a lack of grasp of the Jewish Question.

Let the Jew keep all his traditions. They are not objectionable in any way; the slightest regard for them can only hold them as romantic.

But let him shed his false notion of "the Jew against the world!"

Let him shed his false program of breaking down Christendom by the infiltration of Orientalism into business, art, entertainment and the professions. Let him abolish the false ideal that it is an honor to Jewry to save a guilty Jew from the common law, and a disgrace to Jewry to see a guilty Jew punished by the common law.

Let him draw up notice on all the Jews of the United States who by hook or crook are sowing vile seed in society, that the Jewish community charges itself with their misbehavior and will use methods well known to Jews to bring that misbehavior to an end.

Let the Jew end forever the disgrace of an anti-defamation committee which grows frantic over innocent remarks on the part of "Gentiles," and is absolutely indifferent to the misdeeds of thousands of Jews who do more damage to the Jewish name than all the "Gentile" critics and newspapers could do in twenty years. No one can give the Jews a bad reputation but the Jews themselves.

Most Jews who have given this matter a thought will agree. A good deal of bad temper exists among them, no doubt, and it will be hard for them to admit that anything *The Dearborn Independent* may contend for is right, but the idea here expressed, when divorced from this paper, does command respect from many Jews.

The question remains: When will they start on the program here suggested?

Human nature being what it is, they will hate to start at all if it will seem that the present agitation has compelled them. But would they have started without the agitation?

Is it possible for an additional number of Jews to catch the thought that this series of articles cannot be so easily explained away we are not referring to the contents now, but to the fact that these articles exist at all—as being the creation of prejudice, or hatred or vindictiveness or ignorance?

Suppose these articles should be truly a sign of the times for American Jewry! Suppose they offer a warning word, however unwelcome, and a light, however undesired, which it would be most unwise for Jews to ignore.

Suppose these articles were conceived in a spirit far different than the average pro-Jewish spouter is competent to understand. Suppose the ultimate benefit will be mostly Judah's. Suppose the set time has now come for the Jews to quit their attitude of attacking everyone who shows them the truth, and to profit by this report of the poor figure they cut in American life today. Suppose these people who are moved to search and report the truth about Judah are truly the shophar calling the people to a new day—is it wise to let stubborness counsel? Is it wise to let pride close the ear?

The enemies of the Jews are those who defend them for the pay of hire or praise or votes. The enemies of the Jews are those who bespeak them fair to their faces and express quite different thoughts behind their backs. The writer of this personally knows that two of the principal "Gentile" defenders of the Jews, men who have shouted and ranted through the Press on the Jews' behalf, are men who privately hold and express thoughts about the Jews which are sheer hatred and enmity and fear. Mostly fear! The enemies of the Jews are those who encourage them to take an attitude that they cannot hold in America—not as affecting their personal liberty at all, but their social attitude and the Public Right.

These are the enemies of the Jews, and yet these are the ones whom Judah counts his friends. They are hired friends, false friends, incapable of realizing for a moment what this whole Question means. Judah's friends today are those who will speak the surgical truth to him, braving his fury in the knowledge that the future will justify the word.

Judah's leaders have betrayed him in this country—they do not know they have crossed the Jordan. The Jews are as sheep without shepherds in this land. And the chief objection which the Jewish leaders have to *The Dearborn Independent* is that the Jews may read it and learn how shepherdless they are, the Jewish leaders' opposition to *The Dearborn Independent* rises mostly from the fear that the Jews may read it! The Jews have read it, and they have not found hatred, they have not found abuse and calumny, they have not found ignorance and malice; they have found statements of fact calmly set forth, not to arouse hatred among the non-Jews, but to arouse a sense of social responsibility among the Jews.

These are significant times. The emergence of the Jewish Question is a part of the culmination of destiny that has come upon us, not for harm but for good. The Jews must uncover their eyes and unstop their ears, and they will see the beginning of the end of their travail, and they will hear that to which they have been too long heedless.

The justification of a discussion of the Jewish Question is the good of the Jews, and the greatest present obstacle to that good is the Jews themselves. The time is here when they shall see it.

The Dearborn Independent, issue of 7 January 1922

Everywhere they wanted to remain Jews, and everywhere they were granted the privilege of establishing a State within a State. By virtue of these privileges and exemptions, and immunity from taxes, they would soon rise above the general condition of the citizens of the municipalities where they resided; they had better opportunities for trade and accumulation of wealth, whereby they excited jealousy and hatred." —Lazare.

80: An Address to "Gentiles" on the Jewish Problem

The heading of this article presents difficulties. The correct use of the term "Gentile" is in question. It is a name that has been given us, not by ourselves, but by Jews, and it is by no means certain that it is accurately given. A very great chance exists that it is not. That, however, is a matter which "gentiles" do not bother to understand; they think, of course, that if one is not a Jew one must be a gentile This is only another instance of the Jewish view being "put over" without the "gentile" understanding or even questioning it.

There is another difficulty: how shall one address "gentiles" collectively? When one addresses Jews he knows that the Jew is always a Jew; that every Jew acknowledges every other Jew; that Jews understand each other and are loyal to each other as against "outsiders"; that they think together and act together; that they stand together for Jewish defense, no matter how just the charge brought against them. When you address Jews you address a unit, and when you discuss Jews you get a united reaction from them.

This cannot be said of gentiles. They are of many races, many nationalities, many religions, many tongues. They never think of themselves as being united under the name "gentiles." They are not race or class conscious; certainly they do not think of themselves as a unit with reference to the Jews as an opposite unit. "Gentiles" cannot be organized into one group nationally, let alone internationally, as Jews can. Jews of every shade of opinion, of every degree of religion and of unreligion, can unite all round the world, and do unite, having their own news service, their own telegraph service, their own "foreign department" (as they themselves describe it), by which they keep themselves united and informed for mass action. There is nothing even remotely approaching that among "gentiles."

Not that this fact can be urged against the "gentiles" as a fault. There are reasons why the "gentiles" never can be united. And one reason is that among the so-called "gentiles" there is a regnant superior strain that is not "gentile" at all; no more is it Jewish. There are racial and moral strains among the non-Jewish section of the world which never can be brought into agreement. And, outside this superior strain, among the gentiles proper, the very basis for enduring union is lacking.

So that the only union that can be expected is a union of the superior strain, which physically and morally is unconquerable, and whose task it is to liberate the lesser peoples who easily fall victims to subversion and have no reactive power to rescue themselves.

It is to this human Gulf Stream that flows through the ocean of humanity, blessing it, that this address is offered. As to the identity of this section of humanity—"He that hath ears to hear, let him hear." The others will not, because they cannot. There are many genuine gentiles mixed up in our common population, but it is not to them that these words are offered.

The Jewish Question has existed for a long time, as the Jew knows and admits, and is a consequence of certain un-Jewish, or rather unIsraelitish ideas held by Jewish persons of power. The disability under which the Jew labors is that he is not a Jew, properly speaking, and does not desire to be. Just at that point is the soil and the root of the Jewish Question.

Tackling the Jewish Question is not congenial work. The Race which this article now addresses has always shrunk from tackling it. Our Race has little disposition to chastise any portion of humanity, to arouse feeling or resist it. We have little taste for this surgical work which becomes absolutely necessary when certain corrupt influences deeply dislocate and seriously injure the common life. Nothing but a clear vision of the danger, nothing but an imperative sense of duty would impel any one of us to embark on a course which is subject to misunderstanding and which must, in the nature of things, wait long for its complete justification. Our Race is too fair, and has always been too fair, to enter hastily into judgement and upon this fairness and long-suffering the offending groups have often seriously trespassed.

Regarded by itself, as a separate entity, the Jewish Power is most impressive. International Jews today occupy literally every controlling lever of power. Building up for centuries, perfecting their teamwork from generation to generation, from country to country, they have practically reached the summit. Nothing but the Christian religion remains unvanquished by them, though through false "liberalism" even that has felt the Jewish assault. So great is this power that the very knowledge of it kills hope that any movement can ever dislodge it. Earnest, honest men have walked around it, surveyed it, measured its strength, and have given up the dream of changing it. In Russia they tried to segregate it, but while segregation went on from one side, infiltration proceeded from the other, and even the "anti-Semitic" Russian Government was honey-combed with Jews, as the end showed.

In Germany they endeavored to vote the Jewish power out of politics, only to find the root deep-set in finance—and no country has yet attacked the sacred image of gold. In England the policy of absorption was adopted, and the result is that wherever a Jew was put in power the British Empire has reaped trouble, in Ireland, in India, in Palestine, the present vice-regents of all these possessions being Jews. Other little countries, exasperated beyond endurance, tried violence, and failed just as miserably as the others.

Why? Because every one of these methods is precisely the method that the Jew prefers to have people try. He knows their futility first; they find it out later. He knows how these methods positively help him; they discover that later. The knowledge thus won would be pure gain, were it not that it also seems to discourage the hope of men who know how seriously wrong the situation is.

Besides this massive array of power, immovable as it appears, there is the veil cast over the Christian mind as to the supposedly peculiar destiny of "God's chosen people." The Christian cannot read the Bible except through Jewish spectacles, and, therefore, reads it wrong. The idea of "the chosen people" is one of the two great biblical ideas, but that the Jews constitute this Chosen People is entirely opposed to the statement of the Bible—even of the Bible which the Jews acknowledge, the Old Testament of the Christians. The blessings of world possession, world rule, superior population, commercial greatness, military power, constituted governments, "a great nation and a company of nations"—all of these means by which to spread light and healing among the nations—were truly promised to one people, to Israel, not to Judah. Judah's destiny was to be quite different. Very few Bible readers ever note the distinction between the House of Israel and the House of Judah, yet this distinction was marked from the time of Jacob; the prophets absolutely insist upon it. Israel seceded from Judah, being unable to live with that people any longer. Israel's destiny took them out into the world, and if the Bible be true, then Israel's destiny of greatness is being fulfilled in Israel, and not in Judah. The two Houses are distinct to this day, although a future reunion, a spiritual reunion, is prophesied to come.

Yet the false idea that the Jews constitute All Israel has penetrated the Christian consciousness to an alarming extent, so that when the Jewish press insists, as it does every week, "We gave you your God, we gave you your Bible, we gave you your Christ," even Christian ministers cannot find an answer. The answer is that the Old Testament is nine-tenths an Israelitish book, and not a Jewish book. Abraham was not a Jew; Isaac was not a Jew; Jacob was not a Jew; Moses was not a Jew; Joshua was not a Jew; Gideon was not a Jew; Samuel was not a Jew; even Esther and Mordecai were not Jews, but Benjamites; the majority of the prophets were not Jews, but Israelites. Upon the coming of Judah into power, in the persons of David and Solomon, the misrule was so great that Israel seceded, and the secession was sanctioned by the prophets. In the New Testament, Jesus Christ found his disciples in Galilee, far out of Judea, and of them there was but one, Judas, whose name indicates that he was a Jew. St. Paul was of the tribe of Benjamin, "the light tribe," which was left with Judah "for a light."

But there is a constant patter of preaching (the Russellites make it the great theme) that "the Jews are to rule the world because it is so prophesied." The amazing blindness with which Christians have regarded the open pages of their Bible is the only explanation of this one-sided teaching which is confusing to the Christians and exceedingly dangerous to the Jews. In the Bible, Israel is the Chosen People of Blessing, and the time is announced when Judah shall walk to Israel and recognize them and become one with them. There is a chosen racial breed, a select seed, a superior strain of blood and soul in the world, but it is not Judah. One thing, therefore, that Christians can do, as a contribution to the solution of the Jewish Question, is to read their Bibles carefully.

The Jewish Question will be solved, and its solution will begin in the United States. But that does not mean that it will come as the result of a popular movement. Great changes do not occur that way. It makes little difference whether the mass of the people see this Question or not; the mass of the people are not always called into such matters. Their work is to hold the world steady while the change takes place. But a sufficient number of qualified persons have seen the Question to insure that now the era of solution has set in. The timid, the soft literary men in pulpits (with whose ilk Jeremiah had a keen acquaintance), the false preachers of "Peace, peace," the hush brothers and sisters of every name, the shallow shouters for "fairness," and all who are afraid of the truth in its surgical forms—these have no place in the healing of the hurt of these times; they are wedded to their softness. Nothing has been more shameful in the last two years than the spectacle of men bidding for the applause of bootleggers, and gamblers, and the lecherous masters of the modern stage, and the sinister Kehillah, and the anti-Christian American Jewish Committee, because, forsooth, some one has fulfilled the duty to tell the truth. However, these things must always be, and the evil influences among the Jews have learned just what kind of help they may expect and from what kind of people.

The Dearborn Independent has not been making a fight but fulfilling a duty to shed light on a matter crying for light. *The Dearborn Independent*, therefore, has never urged any individual or organization to join it in this work. Nor has it charged with cowardice those who for prudential or other reasons have kept silent. Editors especially have been absolved; not one of them was asked to lend his aid, although the files of this office hold thousands of written assurances from newspaper men all over the land, and from all parts of the world, testifying to the truth of our statements. Organizations have been proposed, for various purposes; strong organizations have offered themselves as vehicles for the carrying out of any plan *The Dearborn Independent* might propose. But all such undertakings have been avoided, our belief being that simply to state the truth, and let it work its own right will, was sufficient at this time. And to that belief and policy we have adhered.

"But what shall we do?" is the constant question; "How shall we balk this system which surrounds us and infects so much of our common life?"

Observe it, identify it, eschew it—that is more powerful than active opposition. The clear eye of the man who sees and understands is something that even the evil powers of Jewry cannot endure.

But the most potent action any awakened person can take is this: to erect again our own moral landmarks, which the Oriental Jewish invasion has broken down. This would spell sheer doom to the whole evil system sponsored by the Jews. And this is the course which has never been tried. To go back to the principles which made our race great, the principles to which we have been recreant and therefore have fallen an easy prey—this is the only invincible course. It is an opposition which evil Jews cannot understand and cannot defeat.

In place of the way of doing business which Jewish dealers have introduced, let the business men of the country adopt the old way of the white man, when a man's word was as good as his bond, and when business was service and not exploitation.

Let the men and women of the country learn how to buy, let them learn how to test quallity in fabric and food, instead of being dependent on price tags. The merchandising practices of this country, in the hands of ruthless exploiters, have all but ruined honest merchants. Let any dweller in a great city recall the last twenty years, how the Christian merchants have been growing fewer and fewer. Why? Is it because the owners of Jewish department stores are better business men? No! The Jewish merchants began the practice of filling their store windows with goods that looked like the goods in reputable merchants' windows, and sold them for a much lower price. The helpless public, no longer able to determine the quality of goods, and guided solely by price tags, flocked to the Jews' store. The result is that one hears everywhere in ordinary conversation the complaint that "everything is shoddy." Of course it is, and it will remain so, until we educate people in the art of buying. That of itself will break down three-fourths of the abuses practiced in the commercial world today.

Another contribution that can be made to the defeat of Jewish subversive influence is the examination of so-called "liberal" ideas, their source, their effect, their whole tendency. Men are thinking ideas today that poison them morally, socially and economically. These ideas are as deliberately shot into society as poison gas was shot into ranks of soldiers in France. Our mental hospitality has been grossly abused, the public mind has been made a sewer. The time has come for a custom barrier to be raised for the examination of imported ideas. Unrestricted immigration of ideas has been as bad for the American mentality as unrestricted immigration of people has been for American society.

We have taken our amusements withought thought of what was behind them in the way of deliberate intent to make us common and careless and coarse. We have read our newspapers, wholly innocent of the propaganda mixed with the news. We have even taken our religion in a Judaized form, without toubling to inquire whether it squared with the Bible, the textbook of religion. We have read our novels and have failed to see what serum the author was injecting along with his story.

And all this has been possible because we have been asleep, enjoying, as we thought, a life which was swiftly being taken from us, and dreaming that the old principles still held sway.

It is perfectly obvious that the cure for all this is to become awake, alert, to challenge the foreign influence, and to seek out again the principles that gave us our greatness.

We have been weaned away from our natural leaders. We have been taught to look to those who cannot even speak our language and who do not hold our institutions dear. A people that turns from its own leaders, or a people whose leaders have been turned from the sacred responsibilities of the high office of leading, is in a precarious position, and becomes an easy victim to confusion of soul. There is a dearth of voices in the land today, the prophets are dumb, or are reading beautiful essays to the people. Suspicion has been sowed like darnel seed between classes of the same race, the people have been broken up, and the subversive Jewish influence supports the oligarchy of unserviceable wealth at one end of the social scale, while it stimulates the baser elements of industrial unrest at the other end. And the race thus rent asunder to its own undoing, does not see this—capital does not see, and labor does not see—that the leaders of chaos are alien in blood and soul.

To keep American and Christian the school, the church, the legislature, the jury room and the Government, is the most potent resistance that can be made to the evil influences which have been upon us and which this series of articles has partly uncovered.

The strength of all subversive influence is in proportion as we cease to be what we ought to be. The evil influences surrounding this people can succeed only as they change this people into something less than it ought to be. Therefore, to go back to the old landmarks, whereby we made all the progress we ever made, is not only the part of wisdom, but the need of the hour. The school must be cleansed.

The jury box must be kept inviolate—trial by jury has almost disappeared in Jewish New York. The church must be unJudaized and Christianized. The Government must be Americanized. Let there be the utmost freedom of thought and speech, but let there be also with it a discrimination which will prevent the people being victimized by every spurious idea, every "gold brick" economic proposal which comes along. It needs only that men be awake to their better interests and to leave no place in their scheme of life for the practices which destroy the very foundations of confidence.